W9-CKJ-499

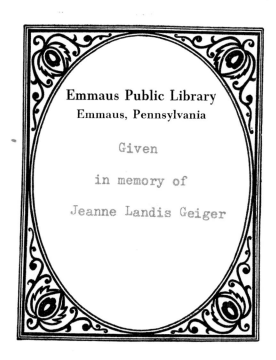

PATRICIA PHILLIPS

The Prehistory of Europe

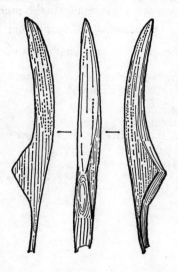

INDIANA UNIVERSITY PRESS
BLOOMINGTON AND LONDON

Manufactured in Great Britain

Library of Congress Cataloging in Publication Data

Phillips, Ann Patricia.
 The prehistory of Europe.

 Bibliography: p.
 Includes index.
 1. Man, Prehistoric–Europe. 2. Europe–Antiquities.
 1. Title.
GN803.P45   936   79-3787
ISBN 0-253-11956-1   1 2 3 4 5 84 83 82 81 80

CONTENTS

LIST OF FIGURES

The author and publishers are grateful to all those who have given permission to use illustrative material from works that have already been published. Special acknowledgement is made to the following: Harper & Row Publishers Inc. (Figs. 1, 29); the University of Chicago (Figs. 4, 6, 14, 20); Scottish Academic Press Ltd (Fig. 5); Unesco (Fig. 9); the American Association for the Advancement of Science (Figs. 12, 13); Academia Publishing House, the Czechoslovak Academy of Sciences (Fig. 23); Veröffentlichungen des Museums für Frühgeschichte Potsdam (Fig. 38); the Royal Anthropological Institute of Great Britain and Northern Ireland (Fig. 43); and Methuen & Co. Ltd (Fig. 65).

LIST OF PLATES

1. Froth flotation (courtesy G. Barker)

2. Excavation of shell midden, Oronsay, Scotland (courtesy P. Mellars)

3. Reconstruction of mammoth-bone frameworks of Upper Palaeolithic huts (a) at Mezhirich, Ukraine (MacBurney, 1976, pl. IId; courtesy C. MacBurney) and (b) at Cracow, Poland (Kozłowski and Kubiak, 1972, fig. 2; courtesy J. K. Kozłowski)

4. Carved river boulder from Lepenski Vir, Yugoslavia (Srejovic, 1967, Cat. No. 15) (photograph Bratislav Lukič)

5. Linear Pottery sites, Merzbach valley, West Germany (Farrugia *et al.*, *Bonn. Jb.*, 173, 1973, pl. 1) (photograph Reg. Präs. Düsseldorf Nr. 18/31/573)

6. Tell excavation at Argissa Magula, Greece (Milojcic, 1976, pl. A) (photograph Institut für Ur- und Frühgeschichte der Universität Heidelberg)

7. Floor plans of Neolithic and Early Bronze Age houses at Brezno, Czechoslovakia (K. Pleinerova, *Archeol. Rozhl.*, 24, 1972, pl. II. 1; courtesy K. Pleinerova)

8. Hafted flint daggers from Copper Age lakeside settlement at Charavines, eastern France (Bocquet, 1974, frontispiece) (photograph Centre de Documentation de la Préhistoire Alpine)

9. Late Neolithic figurines from Eastern Europe (courtesy M. Gimbutas) (Gimbutas, 1974*d*, p. 277, 1974*c*, pls. 38, 47 and 207) (photographs M. Djordjovic, R. Galovic, J. Czalog, Naturhistorisches Museum, Vienna)

10. Main mound and satellite burial mounds from the Neolithic cemetery at Knowth, Eire (courtesy G. Eogan) (photograph L. Swan)

11. Neolithic hurdle trackway used to cross boggy ground, Walton Heath, Somerset, England (courtesy J. Coles)

12. Lakeside rescue excavations at Twann, Switzerland (author's photographs)

13. Wooden coffin of central grave of Magdalenenberg barrow, southern Germany (Spindler, 1972*b*, pl. 10) (courtesy Römisch-Germanische Kommission des Deutschen Archäologischen Instituts)

14. Greave of silver and gold from Vratsa treasure, Bulgaria (Bulgarian Committee for Art and Culture/Trustees of the British Museum 1976, fig. 292)

15. Cave site at Verdelpino, southern Spain (courtesy M. Fernández-Miranda)

16. Underwater excavation of first-century B.C. shipwreck off Giens, southern France (courtesy J.-M. Gassend/Laboratoire Photographique, Centre Camille Julian, Université de Provence, Aix-en-Provence)

17. La Tène burial, Dietikon, Zürich, Switzerland (courtesy Schweizerisches Landesmuseum, Zürich)

18. Bronze 'warriors' and 'chieftain' from Sardinia, late first millennium B.C. (courtesy Mansell Collection)

19. Square-ditched Iron Age barrows seen from the air at Wetwang Slack, Yorkshire, England (courtesy J. Dent)

ACKNOWLEDGEMENTS

I should like to thank Professor Glyn Daniel, advisory editor on Penguin archaeological books, for offering me the opportunity of writing this book. A grant by the Foreign Travel Fund of the University of Sheffield to attend the 1976 Nice International Conference of Pre- and Protohistoric Sciences permitted an up-to-date picture of European prehistory at that point. My ideas have been stimulated by colleagues and students in the Department of Prehistory and Archaeology at the University of Sheffield, particularly by Dr Robin Dennell, who kindly read some of the early chapters. The library work involved was made much easier by the help of Miss Heather Bell, Librarian of the University of London Institute of Archaeology library, and her staff, and of Miss Ruth Wells, head of the Interlibrary Loan service at the University of Sheffield library. Janice Wilkinson has acted as a most efficient part-time secretary. Finally, my husband, Christopher Outhwaite, has helped in checking typescript at different stages of production, and in providing crucial moral support. To all the above I am most grateful. Any errors or misinterpretations, however, are solely my responsibility.

DATES

The dates quoted in this volume are given either as B.P. (Before Present) in Chapters 1 to 4, or B.C. (calibrated carbon-14 dates) in Chapters 5 to 7. From about 6500 B.P. to the present day it is possible to correct standard carbon-14 dates by matching the proportion of carbon-14 in a given sample with the proportion in tree-rings of known age. Several sets of correction (calibration) tables are available, though no single set has been generally adopted. The tables of Ralph, Michael and Han (1976) have been used to correct the standard carbon-14 dates from sites mentioned in this book. As the text indicates, however, some of the B.C. dates in Chapter 7 are derived from the historic civilizations of the Mediterranean basin.

INTRODUCTION

The prehistory of Europe has been discussed in many major syntheses, of which some of the most famous available in English are Gordon Childe's *Dawn of European Civilisation* (1925, rewritten 1955), Stuart Piggott's *Ancient Europe* (1965), and Grahame Clark's *World Prehistory* (1969, 1977).

The present book offers a personal view of what archaeologists working on European prehistory have achieved and attempted to achieve over the last ten years (1968–78). The idea is to make available to a wider public than those researching in a particular epoch or subject some of the new information and new theories that have emerged. The volume of published material has precluded reading of more than a sample of research results, but consultation of abstracts services (particularly the *Bulletin Signalétique*) and of papers delivered at the ninth International Congress of Pre- and Protohistorical Sciences (Nice, 1976) has helped provide a guide to some aspects of the present state of research.

How to define the boundaries of Europe? Geographers today use varied criteria to define its boundaries (ranging from standards of literacy to demography or even use of fertilizers, e.g. Jordan, 1973); for prehistoric periods such criteria are impossible to establish, but this book will follow the geographers and exclude Anatolia, while including part of Russia (Fig. 1). More precisely, the eastern boundary of the Ukrainian S.S.R. will be taken as an eastern limit, extended to the north along the line of 40° longitude to approximately Archangel. This will permit consideration of very important finds in European Russia, even though the vast north European plain is unfortunately bisected by the north–south boundary.

The exclusion of Anatolia would have been a serious drawback in earlier

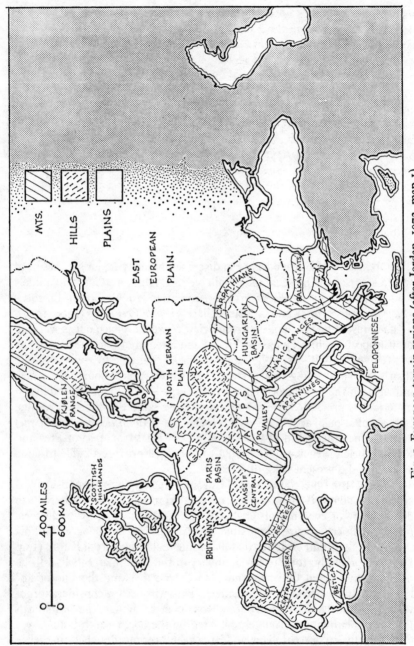

Fig. 1. European terrain regions (after Jordan, 1973, map 1)

years due to prevailing ideas of east–west cultural influences, and the dependence of Europe on the Near East for dating; Anatolia is included, for instance, in Piggott's *Ancient Europe*. It is less crucial in the late 1970s, with a range of radiometric and geomagnetic dating techniques allowing for independent dating of European events from the earliest stone-users onwards. None the less, Anatolian and Middle Eastern data are obviously important and are included, for instance, in the two crucial debates on the origin of modern man and the origin of farming.

The exclusion of north Africa is less important at the moment, since the relationships of this area with Europe are still largely ill-defined. Future developments in research might deal with African–European re-lationships in the days of the first colonization of Europe, and also with Africa's role in the beginning of farming. The circum-arctic region is also largely ignored, although modern research is struggling to produce a new outline of development in this region (Fitzhugh, 1975). None the less, information from areas outside Europe which seems to have theoreti-cal or practical bearing on a particular question is included in the relevant chapters.

The time limits are from the earliest signs of man in Europe to approxi-mately the birth of Christ.

The format adopted in this book has been the following: to present information on a chronological basis, not attempting coverage of all sub-jects or themes, but trying to incorporate new excavation data and demon-strate the application of new theories. A few areas (parts of Iberia and the west Mediterranean islands, for example) still lack detailed chronological sequences, and further excavation and data collection are urgently needed. In many parts of Europe, however, the chronological sequence was well established several decades ago, and new theories and research designs were needed to prevent the repetition of old excavation techniques deriv-ing the same types of information.

Producing new theories has involved what David Clarke has called 'the loss of innocence' in archaeology. Clarke has described the stages by which archaeologists change their outlook (1973). After a recognition that earlier theories of past behaviour are no longer tenable, archaeologists turn to data collection and interpretation on a more local scale. Later still the barriers between localized research groups are broken down by a general questioning of the new results and theories. All European archae-ologists are touched by these changes, but differences of speed in use of new theories and research designs mean that the published literature of the last decade includes examples of all three stages of outlook. Clarke (1968) usefully divides the types of conceptual model (theories) now used into four: those that reveal more about the technology; those that give more information about the social set-up of past societies; those that analyse the environmental background to the different settlements; and those that discuss the spatial distribution of sites. Many excavations are now planned to produce data relative to one or more of these models. Theorizing about Upper Palaeolithic art, for instance, has led to the research design of total recording of caves decorated in this way; theories about the social structure of past societies have led to horizontal excavation and more precise recording techniques. The environmental background to settlements is most commonly obtained by team-work involving natural scientists in the field and the laboratory, but there is also the 'site catchment' approach (see p. 119). Theories about settlement distribution, derived ultimately from geographers like Christaller, have led archaeologists to improve their total knowledge of sites in particular regions by field survey and use of data banks, particularly aerial photographs. Many aspects of prehistoric activity have been analysed mathematically. Distribution maps have been used for 'spatial analysis' (e.g. Hodder and Orton, 1976); the relationships of graves and their contents have been statistically compared, both within a single cemetery and between cemeteries. Statistical techniques and computers have been particularly valuable for sites with massive quantities of artifacts, for instance stone tools or potsherds. Some of the studies will be mentioned in the following chapters.

SOURCES AND RECOVERY RATES

Archaeologists have always been aware that they are dealing with only a partial sample of the assemblage of tools, utensils, furniture, architecture and food utilized by an ancient population. It is recognized that losses have occurred through incomplete deposition (the fact that only a fragment of the artifacts or food utilized is dropped on an activity or settlement site); through unequal preservation; and through inadequate excavation methods. In only rare cases do we find intentional 'curation', that is, deliberate storage or placing of artifacts or pieces of raw material. 'Hoards' of objects, and undisturbed grave-goods, are important as deliberate groupings of objects. Recent research has questioned how the archaeological assemblage originates (taking into account the frequency of use of an object, how long it lasts, how many of that type of object were in use, and so forth). Ammerman and Feldman (1974) have demonstrated that the number of times an activity is performed per year, the likelihood that a particular tool type will be used in an activity, and the 'dropping rate' are all likely to influence deposition rates – and thus archaeological analyses. This line of research has so far been applied mainly to objects made in stone, but it could be usefully extended to all classes of raw material.

Practical improvements in on-site conservation of fragile objects, more precise excavation and recording, and use of wet-sieving techniques can reduce the loss of information through excavation. Wet-sieving, in which soil from selected levels is agitated in water treated with a frothing agent, has revolutionized the recovery of both tiny artifacts like beads, and of remains of plants and animal bone (Pl. 1). The recovery is so impressive that a new problem has been created – an over-abundance of material to be analysed. The wet-sieving technique is particularly useful to identify the economic strategies of the group being studied, and many of the advances in the past decade in European prehistory have been in the fields of economy and subsistence.

STONE-TOOL TYPOLOGY

Another important aspect of recent research has been work on stone tools. Artifacts made of stone have survived a longer time and in greater numbers than any other raw material. Bone, antler, ivory and wood were no doubt also used from the earliest times up to the present day, but owing to their organic nature are less frequently preserved. Stone tools are thus the main source for our understanding of past differences and similarities in culture in many archaeological periods.

The questions currently asked in European prehistory are the following: how far does stone-tool morphology (the shape of the finished tool, its dimensions, areas of retouch, degree of retouch, utilization scars, etc.) reflect *cultural* choice and how far the requirements of a particular task or action? If both factors are involved, how can one separate the characteristics of one from the other? Workers in many areas and periods feel that the first task is to reveal the functional characteristics (those qualities required by a particular action); only then can stylistic or cultural differences be recognized. Studies of use marks and micro-wear using powerful microscopes are relevant to this problem (e.g. Semenov, 1964; Keeley, 1974; Tringham *et al.*, 1974). Results have shown that in favourable cases it is possible to discover the original function of tools; Semenov has shown, for instance, that pointed tools found at the Kostienki, Ukraine, Upper Palaeolithic site were used as knives. Keeley has had excellent results detecting micro-wear on Lower Palaeolithic tools, using a magnification of $\times$ 200 to photograph the micro-wear, or polish, on the implement. Characteristic polish results from using an implement on

bone, sinew, meat, wood and other materials. The researcher has first
to prepare a series of modern stone tools, and test them on likely
materials, and then compare the wear patterns with those on prehistoric
specimens. The use of this technique is, of course, rendered much more
difficult where implements are used for several different tasks. Micro-
scopic remains of plant and animal residues on ancient tools have also
been used to help identify their function (Briuer, 1976).

Another approach to understanding stone tools is that of experimental
tool manufacture. Two of the best-known practitioners are François
Bordes and Donald Crabtree. The idea is to reconstruct the motor movements necessary to produce certain shapes of flake or blade, and the
instruments and actions necessary to effect retouching or fine flaking. Ex-
perimentally made implements can be used in conjunction with micro-
scopic investigations on wear. A new lexicon of terms has been developed
from these experiments, and whole assemblages can now be analysed in
terms of the stages of production which the various chipped-stone elements
represent. One researcher claims he can recognize the chipping technique
of any individual (modern or ancient) by laser-beam study of the retouching scars on his products (Gunn, 1976). Perhaps not surprisingly,
the ancient flint-knapper in his sample was the most consistent.

An important factor which can influence stone-tool manufacture is the
raw material used. Varieties of flint, chert, radiolarite, obsidian, quartz,
rock crystal and other rocks have different hardnesses and resistance
qualities. Some are formed as nodules, others in plaque or seam form.
These physical characteristics all affect the shape or treatment of the artifact in some way, and some researchers have explained tool types made on
particular raw materials in terms of these characteristics.

One of the first uses to which prehistorians put stone tools was to mark
chronological steps. From the nineteenth century onwards, stratigraphic
levels and the tools contained in them – in cave deposits for instance –
were used to define chronological sequences. In at least some areas and
periods this can now be superseded, with the advent of independent
methods of dating. Instead, stone tools may be identified technologically
in five 'modes' of stone-tool manufacture (Grahame Clark, 1969,
p. 31):

Mode 1: Chopper-tools and flakes.
Mode 2: Bifacially flaked hand-axes.
Mode 3: Flake tools from prepared cores.
Mode 4: Punch-struck blades with steep retouch.
Mode 5: Microlithic components of composite artifacts.

The five modes are described by Clark as the *dominant* types of stone-tool technology in different periods (Modes 1 and 2, Lower Palaeolithic; Mode 3, Middle Palaeolithic; Mode 4, Upper Palaeolithic; Mode 5, Mesolithic). This does not prevent earlier technologies surfacing in some numbers as a part of a later assemblage, like the 'choppers' used in the southern French Neolithic (Courtin, 1975). The increase of detailed study of stone-tool assemblages has made it possible for researchers to show that certain types of tools persist into the period of the next prevailing mode, for instance when Modes 1 and 2 are replaced by Mode 3, or Mode 3 is replaced by Mode 4.

As explained above, the problem of stone-tool studies revolves about the questions of the relative importance of culture (learned tradition) and function in determining the shape of an implement. In an effort to see how far similar activities demand similar-shaped artifacts, researchers test groups of tools suspected of being used for a particular job against the by-products of that job. Where organic materials are concerned, this requires very good recovery techniques. For instance, Sally Binford has claimed that a major change in how food was procured accompanied the shift from flake tools to blade tools, but the food remains are insufficient to test this theory rigorously. Lewis Binford, who has been particularly involved with research into tool function, studied how tools are grouped, preserved or dropped as different jobs are carried out in present-day Eskimo societies (1973). At present there is a strong feedback relationship between horizontal excavation, with careful three-dimensional recording of finds and recovery of environmental information, and progress in the analysis of stone tools and their functions.

CULTURES

In 1925 Gordon Childe provided a new method of ordering archaeological discoveries by dividing them into cultures. As he emphasized in a later work, 'In archaeology, societies are represented by the durable results of their behaviour. Such remains archaeologists classify into *types*, and when the same types are repeatedly found together at different sites in a limited region, they are grouped together to represent what we call *cultures*' (1958). This proved a valuable concept, enabling finds from different excavations to be grouped into a series of units over space and time. However, the word 'culture' ended up covering both small localized assemblages, limited in time, and widely spaced, long-lived, associations of tools. Clarke has recently suggested that three terms be used. A 'culture' is redefined as belonging to a limited geographical area, and consisting of a polythetic (variously grouped) set of artifact types consistently recurring together in assemblages. A 'culture group', on the other hand, is made up of two or more cultures with polythetic assemblages, where specific artifact-types may vary in form. A 'technocomplex' is defined as a group of cultures with assemblages containing individually varied, but broadly the same families of artifact-types, as a 'response to common factors in environment, economy and technology' (Clarke, 1968, p. 188). The crucial factor is the degree of 'networking' within and between assemblages; one can visualize a culture as very tightly meshed whereas collateral cultures and technocomplexes would have successively looser meshes.

The link between a 'culture' and the makers of the archaeological assemblages is less clear. Lewis Binford, the first American to introduce the 'New Archaeology', regards culture as 'all those means whose forms are not under direct genetic control ("extrasomatic") which serve to adjust individuals and groups within their ecological communities' (1972a, p. 431). This, while laying emphasis on the important ecological environment of any population, as also stressed by Clarke, gives importance to the group as a unit and as individuals.

Both Binford and Clarke have suggested that systems theory is of value to the archaeologist. Put simply, the culture or the society making the assemblage is regarded as a system made up of subsystems – religious, social, technological, and so on. The idea has been widely used, and archaeologists, linking together a number of artifacts and features from their sites, find it convenient to speak of the social or other subsystem which they seem to represent. There have been particularly interesting attempts to explain the economic and environmental subsystems. The relationship *between* the different subsystems and their relationship to the total system, or culture, is much harder to establish, especially in the later periods of prehistory, and is only beginning to be attempted, on the basis of the best and most detailed excavations.

In the following chapters, Clarke's usage of cultures, culture groups and technocomplexes will be followed, with the proviso that, however useful they may be for grouping archaeological remains, their actual reality in terms of individuals and groups is completely unknown.

DATING

Dating of the earlier phases of human evolution presents a considerable problem at the moment, since the familiar sequence of Pleistocene glacial episodes (originally called after the Swiss rivers Günz, Mindel, Riss and Würm) is now understood to be a gross simplification. However, most archaeological literature still attempts to position sites and skeletal material in this framework (or in its more recent and detailed Dutch variant). The recovery of deep-sea cores (vertical samples of sediments accumulated on the ocean bottom) has provided a much more complete record of climatic change than was previously available, and shown the inadequacy of the four glacial epochs chronology. This is because deep-sea sediments record events both at water surface and on distant continents. When ice accumulated in the northern hemisphere the oceans shrank and became slightly more salty, enriching the surface in the oxygen isotope 18. Studies

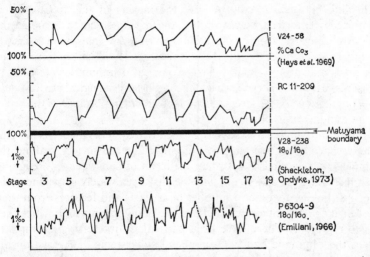

Fig. 2. Calcium carbonate and oxygen-isotope records of deep-sea cores (after Shackleton, 1975, fig. 4)

of the changes in oxygen-isotope composition can be used as a stratigraphic tool not only for correlating sediments from different cores, but also for Pleistocene developments on land. The oxygen-isotope and calcium carbonate records of four cores recently illustrated by Shackleton (1975) demonstrate that at least eight glacials and eight interglacials occurred since c. 700,000 years Before Present (B.P.) (Fig. 2). It is possible that parts of the sequence may even be missing from the deep-sea sediments, but they are certainly much more complete than the land records. Careful work on the development of loesses (wind-borne soils formed during periglacial conditions) in Czechoslovakia and Austria still only suggests seven glaciations (Kukla, 1975); no more than seven cycles of glacials and interglacials can be seen in the Rhine terraces (Brunnacker, 1975); and six in pollen evidence

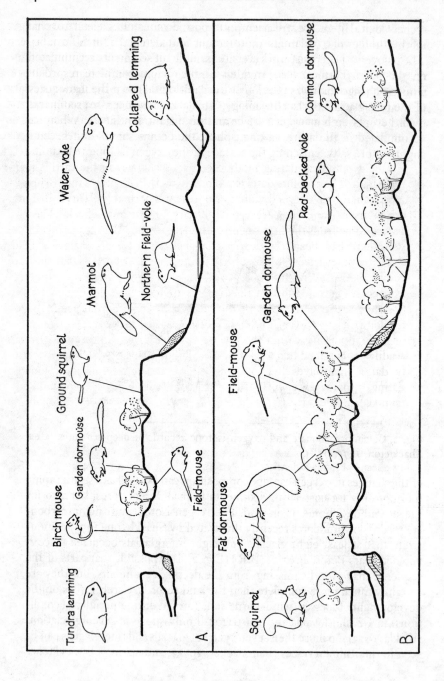

(Turner, 1975). Study of microfauna also demonstrates a series of changes useful for relative dating in continental Europe (e.g. Fig. 3). It can be seen that even this recent work on land is difficult to correlate with the more complete oceanic record. In studying the early period of man's existence, encompassing much of the Pleistocene geological epoch, it is now necessary to demonstrate the relative or absolute date of any skeleton or archaeological site by pollen analysis, by biostratigraphic analysis (of microfauna), or by geophysical dating, or by a combination of two or all of these methods (Isaac, 1975).

One geophysical-dating method concerns changes in the earth's magnetic field. The absolute date of 700,000 years B.P. identifies the 'Brunhes-Matuyama boundary' dividing the recent 'normal polarity' Brunhes epoch from the earlier 'reversed polarity' Matuyama epoch. The two names come from the first scientists to demonstrate that at periods in the past there had been 180-degree changes in the earth's magnetic field. Recent studies have confirmed that these changes occurred, that they are completed in several thousand years (represented by several centimetres in deep-sea cores), and that they can be divided into (long) epochs and (shorter) events. Examples of the latter are the Jaramillo event c. 0·91 million years ago (Myr), and the Olduvai event c. 1·96 Myr, both episodes of normal polarity within the reversed-polarity Matuyama epoch. It can readily be imagined that these changes in the earth's magnetism (absolutely dated themselves by potassium–argon and uranium–disequilibrium dating) provide excellent dating yardsticks within marine or land sediments. However, away from the moments of change there are obviously long periods that are difficult to date by this means.

Fig. 3 (*opposite*). Reconstruction of glacial (A) and interglacial (B) environments by means of fossil rodents (after Chaline, 1975, p. 79)

A. *Glacial landscape*. The plateaux are the domain of the cold steppe, with the tundra lemming, the birch mouse and the ground squirrel. Here and there in the shallow basins and at lower levels, clumps of trees exist as 'oases' or refuge zones for field-mice and garden dormice. Marmots are to be found on the scree slopes. In the valleys, which become marshes in spring after the ice melts, live the northern field-vole, the water vole and the collared lemming

B. *Interglacial landscape*. Forest covers most of the landscape. There are a number of open spaces, both dry (stubble) and damp (meadows). In the forest there are squirrels, fat dormice, field-mice, garden dormice, red-backed voles and common dormice. Water voles and pine voles live in the meadows, common field-voles are common in the dry open spaces.

The date of *c.* 700,000 years B.P. has recently been adopted as the boundary between the Early and Middle Pleistocene; the Middle Pleistocene then continues to the 'beginning of the last interglacial transgression', *c.* 125,000 years B.P. (Isaac, 1975). For the Early and Middle Pleistocene, and for the Upper Pleistocene until about 30,000 years B.P., absolute (geophysical) dating methods consist of potassium–argon dating, the uranium–disequilibrium series, and fission-track dating.

Potassium–argon dating has been used for about fifteen years to obtain dates on rocks of volcanic origin, and was responsible for the shock elongation of man's past when tuffs surrounding hominid fossils at Olduvai Gorge, Tanzania, were dated 1·786 million years old. There are three types of measurement that can be taken: the relative quantities of potassium 40 and argon 40 in the sample (radioactive K-40 decays to the gas Ar-40); the proportion of argon 40 to argon 39 (both these measurements by the 'total degassing' technique); and the proportion of argon 40 to argon 39 by age spectra (the most time-consuming but ultimately most accurate method). The technique can date volcanic events and formation of some sedimentary rocks from the beginning of the earth to *c.* 5000 years B.P. (Bishop and Miller, 1972, p. 472). Another technique used to date early-man sites is fission track: 'tracks' or marks 5 to 20 microns long appear on the surface of uranium-rich minerals and rocks which have undergone heating as a result of the spontaneous fission of the uranium isotope uranium 238. These tracks can be counted and compared with the tracks produced by exposing a sample to a known dose of radioactivity, and a date for the original heating can be deduced. This technique can be used both on ancient artifacts, made of suitable raw materials, and on man-made glass.

Uranium-series dating covers a number of decay relationships, of which the most useful are the decay of uranium 234 to protoactinium 231 to thorium 230, the half-life for protoactinium 231 being 32,400 years, while that for thorium 230 is 75,200 years. Uranium-decay dating can be used both on layers in deep-sea cores and on land sites, where it can date not only volcanic rocks containing uranium, but also unaltered tufas and travertines. Since travertines are commonly found sealing ancient archaeological deposits, uranium-decay dating has recently been applied to a number of cave and open sites. It has also been used to 'calibrate' another dating method, amino-acid racemization of fossil bone. This is a technique applicable on all sites from the earliest hominid camps up to settlements of a few thousand years ago. Fossil sediments, shells and organic material are all datable by amino-acid racemization: its half-life depends on the general temperature of the sample's environment.

The 'absolute' dating methods described above are liable to various contaminations, and are of course subject to an error factor.

Another technique, thermoluminescence dating, has recently been used on early-man sites, to date burnt artifacts such as flint and obsidian, and rocks heated by camp-fires. However, the initial applications of thermoluminescence (TL) were to kilns, recent hearths, pottery and the detection of fakes. Most results have thus been confined to the last seven or eight millennia. The technique depends on an object being heated sufficiently in an archaeological context to drive off its 'geological' thermoluminescence, and 'set its TL clock back to zero', in Aitken's evocative phrase. Measurement in the laboratory of the TL acquired since the object was burned can give a date for the original burning or firing (with up to a 10 per cent error). The method is particularly useful on sites where there are no remains suitable for carbon-14 dating, but where potsherds or clay figurines, for instance, are numerous.

The recent phases of European prehistory, from 50,000 years ago to the present day, fall into the time-span measurable by carbon-14 dating, which gives statistically likely ages for ancient materials. (A new method which will take the limits of radiocarbon dating back to 100,000 years using measurement of the carbon-14 itself, rather than its radioactivity, is still in the development stage.) Because of the difficulty of measuring the radioactivity of the small amount of carbon-14 remaining in a sample about 30,000 years old, let alone the tiny quantity remaining in a 50,000 years old sample, datings for the first half of this time span should be regarded as minimum ages (Bishop and Miller, 1972). Since the development of carbon-14 dating in the 1950s, it has been shown that there is a difference between carbon-14 ages estimated using a half-life for the carbon-14 isotope of 5568 (or even 5730) years, and the actual ages when tree-rings of known years are tested. At present it has only been possible to 'correct' dates up to the earliest tree-ring known. Although the bristle-cone pine tree used in the work is phenomenally long-lived, dendrochronologists have only been able to match tree-rings of standing and fallen trees back for about 6500 years. In this volume dates in Chapters 1 to 4 are given as Before Present (B.P.). From about 6500 B.P. it is possible to correct standard carbon-14 dates by matching the proportion of carbon-14 in a given sample with the proportion in tree-rings of known date ('calibration'). A number of laboratories and statisticians have published calibration tables, and those of Ralph, Michael and Han are followed here. The dates so derived are written as B.C., with their appropriate error limits, in Chapters 5 to 7. (Some B.C. dates in Chapter 7 derive directly from the historic civilizations of the Mediterranean.)

Carbon-14 dating is applicable to a wide range of materials including bone (widely used for the Upper Palaeolithic dates), non-marine molluscs, and iron. There are areas where very precise correlations have been established between pollen samples and carbon-14 dates, so that sites lacking samples datable by carbon-14 can still be linked into a local chronology by pollen samples (e.g. Mesolithic and Neolithic Scandinavia – Welinder and Larsen, personal communication). The time-span least well dated in European prehistory remains the Bronze Age, where typological dating remained in force for so long that the importance of obtaining samples for carbon-14 dating has only recently been recognized (yet the skeletal material of the predominantly burial finds would be quite suitable for dating).

From the subjects discussed above, it can be seen that European prehistory has benefited by advances in many other disciplines. Scientists have provided many dating methods, which locate objects in time, and analytical methods, which suggest their source. Technological improvements like earth-moving equipment, photographic towers, infra-red photography and computers, to name but a few, have revolutionized site location, excavation and analysis of finds. A further crucial development has been in the field of theorizing; theories borrowed from the disciplines of geography, mathematics and biology, to name three, have affected research work, and have involved archaeologists, in some cases, in the formulation of general 'laws' of human behaviour (Watson *et al.*, 1971). The general public is being made aware of the new data and new theories; publicity on television has increased greatly over the last decade, and television has had considerable impact in giving up-to-date accounts of particular fields of study (early hominid evolution in Africa, for example) of interest to the lay public and archaeologists alike. In addition, greater government involvement in archaeology has increased both public knowledge and public accountability of excavators.

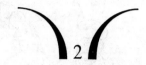

THE LOWER AND MIDDLE
PALAEOLITHIC

HUMAN ORIGINS

Skeletons of early primates known as dryopithecines and ramapithecines are known from Miocene primate fossil sources in Africa, India, the Far East, Turkey, Greece and Hungary. Dryopithecines are considered to have evolved into present-day apes (chimpanzee, orang-utan and gorilla) and the ramapithecines into early hominids, some of which, at least, are the ancestors of today's human beings. Dryopithecines were present from 23 to 10 million years ago, and ramapithecines from 13 to 7 million years ago. Early habitats were in forests, but later (ramapithecine) fossils are found in what were more open environments (Pilbeam, 1975). Many of the fossil remains have been obtained from north-west India and Pakistan where early hominids are so far unknown, and there is a gap in the African fossil record from 13 to approximately 3 or 4 million years ago, when the first hominids are found. Ramapithecines recognized as such are only known from skull fragments; their link to hominids is in the palate shape and dentition (Fig. 4). It can be seen how similar the shape and dentition are to australopithecine (first hominid) jaws, and even to the jaws of modern man, and how different from the parallel-sided jaws and large canines and incisors of modern chimpanzees. Kretzoi has recently discussed the European finds, *Rudapithecus hungaricus* (a ramapithecine) and *Bodvapithecus altipalatus* (a dryopithecine), and concluded that 'hominization did not originate in certain isolated and more or less small tropical–subtropical gene pools, but was an evolutionary trend covering the whole Afro-Eurasian faunal radiation with its pongo-hominids' (1975, p. 581). To

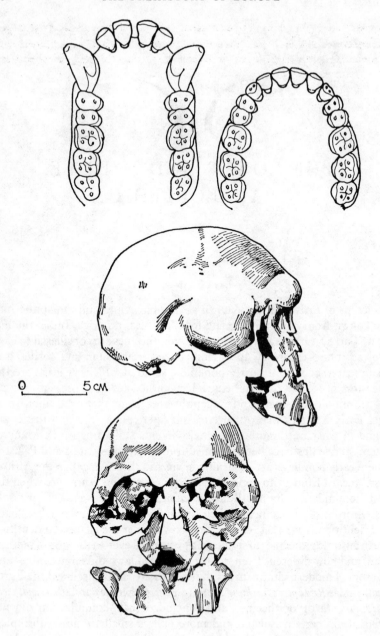

0   5 CM

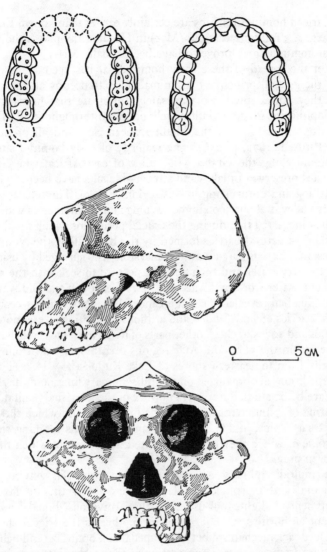

Fig. 4. Upper jaws of chimpanzee, *Australopithecus*, *Ramapithecus* and modern man (after Birdsell, 1972, figs. 6 and 7) and *Homo* and *Australopithecus* skulls from Lake Rudolf, Kenya (after Coppens *et al.*, 1976, pls. 1 and 5)

date, African hominid remains are certainly earlier than known European finds (e.g. *c.* 3 million years old (Myr) in Hadar, Ethiopia), although Far Eastern hominids may prove to have been equally early.

As for the spread of these early hominids, it has been suggested that given 'the general principle that animals tend to occupy all the space to which they are adapted, we may safely anticipate that humans of the australopithecine grade will ultimately be found throughout all of Africa, the European margins of the Mediterranean Sea, and all of Southern Asia' (Birdsell, 1972, p. 256). The majority of early hominid sites have been found along the Grand Rift Valley of east Africa, where ancient camp-sites preserved in lake- and stream-side silts have been exposed by earth tilting and upthrusting in this region (Fig. 5). The relevant part of the Rift Valley is about 500 kilometres long and 70 kilometres wide. Kortlandt has suggested that during the crucial period for which fossil records are lacking, a natural barrier formed by the Rift Valley, the Nile and the Zambesi may have isolated hominid ancestors who survived by using their hands to carry water and their upright posture to seek it in the arid environment. After work by Louis and Mary Leakey in the Olduvai Gorge of Tanzania had revealed the significance of the Rift Valley to early-man studies, a series of well-funded and arduous expeditions were mounted in the 1960s and 1970s to check other parts of it. Significant results have been obtained from the Omo and Afar regions of Ethiopia, and from Kenya, especially from the eastern shores of Lake Rudolf (now Lake Turkana). The expeditions are organized on multidisciplinary lines, and the hominid fossils are being studied in the framework of their original habitat, that is, the setting of water channels and shade bushes around which they established their camps, and the various types of animals roaming the same area, some of which they probably hunted, for others of which they may have been prey.

The multidisciplinary approach indicates how far environmental, behavioural and morphological factors were interacting to favour the development of slight, tool-using, partly carnivorous, bipedal hominids. Different authorities see one factor or another as the trigger, but agree on the feedback mechanism between bipedalism, brain size and behaviour; Isaac, for instance, favours meat-eating as the mechanism permitting the expansion and spread of the hominids.

What is a hominid? The description covers primates morphologically similar to modern man except in their brain capacities, which are only $\frac{1}{3}$ to $\frac{1}{2}$ modern size. Up to a decade ago, it was assumed that these earliest men belonged to a single genus, the australopithecines, and that they were probably the ancestors of modern man. *Australopithecus* ('southern ape')

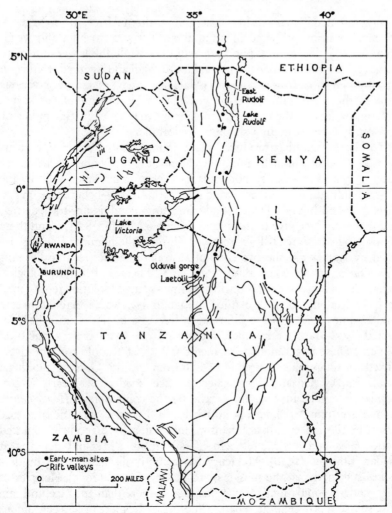

Fig. 5. East African early-man sites (after Howell, 1972, fig. 1)

was represented in deposits in eastern and southern Africa, in two 'sizes' – the smaller form estimated to stand about 4 ft (1·2 m) high and weigh from 61 to 95 lb (27·6 to 43·0 kg maximum), while the larger and more massively built form stood about 5 ft (1·5 m) high and weighed from 79 to 116 lb (35·8 to 52·6 kg maximum) (McHenry, 1975, p. 429). For various reasons these size differences proved not to be attributable to sexual differences, leaving the puzzling problem of two types of australopithecine apparently co-existing in a single ecological niche.

The last decade has produced many more hominid remains, and increased the problem of hominid development. Fragmentary remains belonging to as many as 120 hominids have been found since 1968 by the East Rudolf research project, which Richard Leakey believes belong to three hominid lineages (1974). Potassium–argon and fission-track dating, and faunal studies, give dates ranging from 2·6 Myr to 1·8 Myr, and these contrasting dates are still not resolved. Two of the hominid lineages defined by Leakey are the two sizes of australopithecine (technically *Australopithecus africanus* and *A. robustus/boisei*). There is little morphological variability in these hominids during the time-span of evolution represented at Lake Rudolf, unlike the third lineage *Homo*, which extends over a similar time-span. *Homo* is different in having a larger brain – the celebrated 1470 Man, for instance, found in 1972, has a brain capacity of 780 c.c. These larger cranial fragments from East Rudolf are tentatively linked with hominids OH 7 and OH 16 from Olduvai Gorge. At Olduvai Louis Leakey had already revealed the likelihood of very early larger-brained hominids in 1964 by excavating the controversial *Homo habilis* from a stratum 18 inches (45 cm) below a 'living floor' with large-size australopithecine remains. Johanson and Taieb have recently reported both *Homo* and australopithecine fossils from 3-Myr-old deposits at Hadar, Ethiopia (1976). McHenry has recently discussed what he describes succinctly as 'the mosaic of human evolution' (1975). He stresses that modern populations range from 1000 to more than 2000 c.c. in brain size, so that it is difficult to separate lineages in the more or less continuous series of brain sizes reported from east African sites (506, 510, 530, 590, 650, 687 and 775 c.c.). However, by estimating body weight and comparing it with brain sizes McHenry has revealed that the specimens classified as *Homo*, despite their larger body weights, have *relatively* larger brain capacities than those classified as australopithecine. After multivariate analyses of the lower limb bones he suggests there may be a link between the relatively larger head of the femur in East Rudolf *Homo* specimens, and the larger birth canal which would be required for bigger-brained babies.

McHenry's model for human evolution visualizes an adaption to bi-pedalism (upright walking) before 3 Myr ago (the immediately earlier stages not being known, at present). By 2 Myr ago hominid brains begin to vary in size, becoming larger *on average*. This is also seen as the approximate date for the beginning of tool manufacture, meat-eating and shelter-building, and food sharing. A few implements are known from Hadar, however, in a level dated older than 2·6 Myr.

In the lower floor of Bed I at Olduvai Gorge (dated 2·1 to 1·7 Myr), tool-making and shelter-building have been elegantly demonstrated. This 'living floor' is spread with stone tools in the shape of choppers and flakes, and with the remains of antelope, wild cattle, short-necked giraffes, large pigs, and an early type of elephant. A skeleton of a large-size australopi-thecine (*Zinjanthropus*, or Nutcracker Man) was found at the same level. A semicircular construction of several hundred rocks represents the earliest known shelter or wind-break.

In South Africa, where australopithecines were first identified by Professor Dart's famous recognition of a hominid child's skull, the 'Taung baby', in 1925, the two types of australopithecine and *Homo* are also present in the breccia of fossil-bearing limestone caves (Leakey and Lewin 1977).

It is assumed here, following a number of African archaeologists and physical anthropologists, that the small and large australopithecines were eventually supplanted in Africa, while the *Homo* type of man continued to increase in brain size through a complex feedback of the use of hands, tools and brain, to evolve into the *Homo erectus* grade. *Homo erectus* is present in Beds II to IV at Olduvai Gorge, in the nearby Laetolil beds (Leakey, M., 1976: dates 1·4 to 0·30 Myr), and at Lake Omo, while a new skeleton from Ndutu, Tanzania, is claimed to show an evolution towards modern man (R. J. Clark, 1976). Skeletally *Homo erectus* is reconstructed to stand about the same height as a large australopithecine, but to stride more like modern man. The skull is long and low, with rather emphasized brow ridges at the front, and a bony spur at the back to support the neck muscles. The Olduvai Gorge specimen is *c.* 1000 c.c. in brain capacity. These early men evolved more complex stone tools, including bifaces or hand-axes (stone tools with flakes chipped from either side so that the edges are thinned down). Isaac and Curtis have dated such industries from Peninj sediments, Tanzania, to at least 1·0 Myr ago (1974). Presumably the same warm, tectonically unstable environment prevailed as before, and the range of animal quarries remained wide. Mary Leakey states that sites in the upper part of Bed II and in III/IV lay in or near former river or stream channels. Hunting techniques and slightly more complex social behaviour may have evolved, and it would also have been possible, as in earlier millennia, to eat a variety of plant foods and tubers.

Very different conditions prevailed in Asia, where the majority of *Homo erectus* finds have been made. Skeletal remains with brains of 750 to 975 c.c. are found in the Djetis and Trinil beds of Java, recently dated by K–Ar to between 1·9 and 0·7 Myr. It is generally assumed that this area was a separate area of origin for hominids, and it is significant that the australopithecines are not found here. Local archaeologists believe that at least two types of *Homo erectus* are present in Java and that a third species, *Meganthropus palaeojavanicus*, may have been ancestral or contemporary to *Homo erectus* (Sartono, 1976; von Koenigswald, 1976). Casino has emphasized that Asian hominids should be viewed as if the South China sea were a vast water-hole, which filled or dried up as the glaciers retreated and advanced. When much water was locked up in the form of ice, occupation would have been possible on the 'Sunda shelf' (now a high part of the sea-bed between Indonesia and China), making the resemblances between *Homo erectus* in Java, the Philippines and China more easy to comprehend (Casino, 1976).

The biggest sample of *Homo erectus* skeletal material came from the Choukoutien caves near Peking; there are earlier skeletal fragments from mainland China (e.g. Lantian Man or Woman, with a cranial capacity of 780 c.c.) but the forty Middle Pleistocene skeletons from Choukoutien still represent the biggest sample. All the skulls had been broken at the base, as if to extract the brain, and many of the limb-bones smashed to obtain marrow. Weidenreich, the original excavator of Choukoutien, claimed that the bones were treated in the same way as the animal bones, which is interesting in view of a similar comment made for a French Neanderthal site. Certainly the inhabitants of the giant Chinese cave, in an environment shown by pollen and charcoal analysis to be extremely cold, hunted a wide variety of animals (deer, boar, bison, horse, gazelle, rhinoceros). and survived the chilly temperatures by eating a high protein diet, stoking their fires and possibly wearing fur clothing.

Although Africa and Asia are important for australopithecine and *Homo erectus* remains, there are fewer signs of the Neanderthal stage of human evolution so important in Europe. Aigner has argued that China was effectively isolated in the latter part of the Pleistocene, and that there was local development towards *Homo sapiens* status (based on similarities in skull, jaw and teeth morphology between 'Peking Man' and later Mongoloid populations) (1976). Other writers have suggested a rather long persistence of *Homo erectus*, perhaps side by side with modern forms of men, in Malaysia (Harrison, 1976). It can thus be seen that modern research tends to regard human evolution as polymorphic, with different developments in different parts of the world. The picture changes constantly, as new results appear and are evaluated.

THE FIRST OCCUPANTS OF EUROPE

Where did the first occupants of Europe come from and what type of men were they? It is usually assumed that north Africa would be the place of origin, with three routes being possible, via the Bosphorus, the ex-Tunisian gulf, and the Gibraltar straits. Each seems equally feasible, since early Palaeolithic sites are known, for instance, in Romania, Sicily, and at Cádiz in Spain, even though none of them is securely dated (Džambazov, 1969; Radmilli, 1976; Thibault, 1975). The low sea levels necessary to provide suitable land bridges might feasibly have occurred during periods of ice formation in the northern hemisphere, perhaps combined with isostatic and eustatic movements (rise of the land and sea relative to each other). The geological history of the Mediterranean basin at this time period needs to be better understood before definite hypotheses can be made and tested.

The mechanism for the spread of men into Europe has already been mentioned – Birdsell's claim that animals, including types of man, expand into all the niches to which they are adapted. The varied characteristics of early human skeletons from Europe suggest a number of movements, with immigrations by men of different type.

In Europe there are no claims for human occupation before 1·8 Myr. Until recently many authors regarded all known skeletal remains as those of a form of *Homo sapiens*. Birdsell, writing in 1972, says that 'Europe provides us with unexpected evidence that the grade *Homo sapiens* was present there (in the Middle Pleistocene) and there is no evidence of pithecanthropine (*Homo erectus*) occupancy'.

Given the problems with glacial-linked dating mentioned in Chapter 1, only tentative dates can be given for the earliest signs of human penetration into Europe. The animal populations associated with the earliest evidence are of Villefranchian type, an assemblage of species first established in geologically dated strata in Italy. Kurten has published a table indicating which species were present in five phases of the Villefranchian (1968, table 15). Using this type of relative dating by animal species, the oldest known European site may be that of Chilhac I (Haute Loire, France), which has produced mainly middle Villefranchian fauna, and four tools including one chopping tool and a primitive biface. Its excavator, Professor Guth, suggested that extrapolation from K-Ar dates for other such faunal assemblages would indicate a date of 1·8 Myr for the site (Guth, 1974).

Much further east, in Yugoslavia, the site of Šandalja 1, discovered during limestone quarrying, is estimated to be 1·5 million years old on the basis of its middle and late Villefranchian fauna and the typology of the chopper found there (Valoch, 1976b, p. 182). Cavities in the limestone contained ancient sediments and bones of warm steppe animals and forest-loving animals such as extinct species of horse, rhinoceros, pig, deer and cattle. Most of the bones came from young animals, and many of them were burnt. A chopper (Fig. 6) and a bashed stone were found, and the excavator believes that the bones, teeth and antler were used as tools (Dart first suggested the name of 'osteodontokeratic' for such industries, in examining material from the bone caves of southern Africa). At Šandalja 1 the most important find was of a human tooth, a left upper incisor, described as 'advanced australopithecine' in character (Malez, 1976, p. 116). This slender piece of evidence is the only one for the australopithecine grade in Europe – and it is disputed. Another molar was found in Czecho-slovakia at Přezletice, but it is too fragmentary to allow identification. The earliest bones of any size are the jaw-bone from Mauer, Germany, the skull fragment from Petralona, Greece, and the skull fragment and teeth found at Vértesszöllös in Hungary. Physical anthropologists regard these specimens as belonging to types of *Homo sapiens*. The Mauer jaw-bone was discovered in 1907 during sand digging, and has been assigned, on the basis of animal species found in the same sands, to the interglacial between the now-obsolete Günz and Mindel glaciations. Neither for it nor for the Petralona skull are there definite associations with artifacts or food remains.

However, both the Přezletice and Vértesszöllös specimens were found in such a context. At Přezletice quarrying revealed old lake sediments which, when excavated, proved to contain four levels of redeposited occu-pation material such as burnt bone and stones and charcoal, indicating the presence of hearths. Stone tools included choppers and polyhedrons and 'proto-bifaces' (rough hand-axes). Animal long bones had been made into bone knives. Ancient forms of mammoth, horse, ass, bison and deer suggested that these successive camps had been located in open terrain near river flood plains, with some forested areas in the vicinity (Fejfar, 1969). The site has been dated palaeomagnetically by Buchato between 750,000 and 890,000 years ago (Valoch, 1976b). This means it is the oldest directly dated European site.

In large animal species changes in response to climatic and environ-mental variation are likely to be slow; relative dating dependent upon such changes is necessarily hazardous. In central Europe, however, much finer

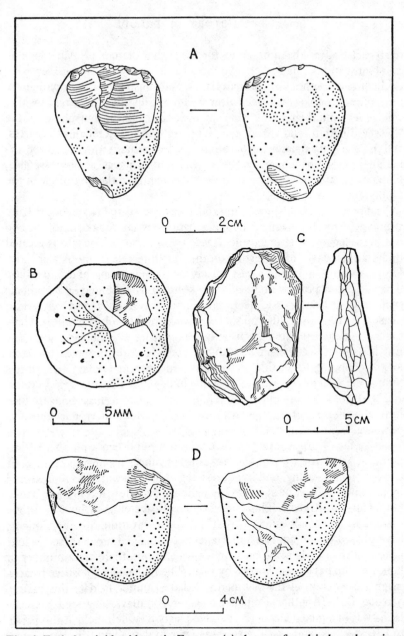

Fig. 6. Early hominid evidence in Europe: (A) chopper found in bone breccia at
Šandalja I, Yugoslavia; (B) fragment of a *Homo* molar from Přezletice, Yugoslavia; (C) stone implement (front and side views) from Přezletice; (D) quartzite-
pebble chopping tools from Vértesszöllös, Hungary (after Malez, 1976, fig. 3;
Fejfar, 1969, figs. 4 and 5; and Kretzoi and Vértes, 1965, fig. 6:1)

relative dating has been obtained for the earlier periods of man's habitation by use of microfaunal change. Small animals are much more sensitive
to climatic and other change than larger, and subspecies alter rapidly over
time. The chronology is named after the former district of Bihar, Hungary;
vole genera and their subdivisions provide the basis for four phases of the
'Lower Biharian' and two of the 'Upper Biharian' (Kretzoi and Vértes,
1965). The palaeomagnetic date for Přezletice fits with the Lower Biharian microfauna characteristic of the site, whereas at Vértesszöllös,
Hungary, a later microfauna is present, belonging to the first phase of the
Upper Biharian.

The bone material from Vértesszöllös has been dated to 370,000 B.P. by
amino-acid racemization, although a date between 700,000 and 400,000
has been suggested (Butzer and Isaac, 1975, p. 893). The site is located
under a thick layer of travertine on the fourth terrace of the Ataler river.
Hearths were found, and a vast variety of chopping tools and flint flakes.
The early Europeans who lived there seem to have hunted large animals
such as cave bear, horse, deer, cattle and beaver, in a relatively warm
phase between two colder episodes. From a tool-typology point of view,
the East European sites are usually classified as 'Clactonian', after the
English site of Clacton-on-Sea which produced cores of biconical shape,
lots of chopping tools, thick flakes and some notched flakes. In Clarke's
terms, the Clactonian would be a 'technocomplex'. Although Vértesszöllös fits into this broad framework, the excavators of Přezletice are firm
in their belief that it belongs to a much older, Oldowan-type technocomplex (e.g. Fridrich, 1972).

In western Europe, Henri de Lumley has published a number of important early-man sites in south-western France, placing them in their
environmental setting, and hypothesizing about the activities represented
by the finds. The earliest is the Le Vallonet cave near the Franco-Italian
border on the Riviera. This is a very small cave entered by a 5-m long
passage from a small valley. It is still under excavation. So far sediments
have proved to contain late Villefranchian fauna and nine artifacts – four
flakes and five tools made on pebbles; in addition there are a number of
bones said to have been worked by man. The fauna, and a positive palaeomagnetic reading on the sediments, led de Lumley to date this cave c.
900,000 B.P. (Another French excavator, Bonifay, suggested that the
fauna was of a mixed character, datable partly to Villefranchian and partly
to later periods, and that the site was later in date. The Brunhes normal
polarity (positive palaeomagnetic) epoch began c. 700,000 B.P., a date
which de Lumley admits is also a possible one for the Vallonet assemblage.)
Le Vallonet has not produced any human skeletal material, but in south-

west France another cave, Cauna de l'Arago, also excavated by de Lumley, produced two jaws, a fragment of skull and other smaller remains. One jaw and the skull fragment seemed to belong to men of about twenty years of age, while the other jaw was that of a forty-year-old woman. They are of particular interest because de Lumley and Mme de Lumley, a physical anthropologist, regard them as lying somewhere between *Homo erectus* and Neanderthal man, and originally dated them *c.* 200,000 years old (1971). Other dating methods, including microfaunal study and amino-acid racemization, have since been used at Arago, suggesting that the bones date somewhere between 220,000 and 320,000 years ago. De Lumley visualizes repeated visits to the cave, by hunters who made flint and quartz tools there and butchered their animal quarries. The majority of bones belonged to Merck's rhinoceros and large horses, suggesting steppe-like conditions beyond the cave.

The Arago human remains, and a skull found in East Germany at the site of Bilzingsleben, are the only ones to have been classified as *Homo erectus* by their excavators. Bilzingsleben has not been dated, but the skull is generally regarded as dating from the same interglacial as the early *Homo sapiens* remains from Swanscombe, England, and Steinheim, Germany (Holstein interglacial, between Mindel and Riss glaciations – e.g. Valoch, 1976*b*). At Swanscombe, the camp-site on a former terrace of the Thames was used first by people with a Clactonian industry, and later by others with pointed hand-axes. The skull fragments were associated with the second occupation, and fossil bones from *near* the skull location (i.e. not positively associated with it) have been recently dated by uranium-decay dating to more than 272,000 years B.P. (Roe, 1976*a*). The possibility is therefore strong that between, say, 300,000 and 200,000 years ago at least two grades of hominid were present in Europe. Thoma, in a recent review of the evidence, has suggested that early, pre-Neanderthal Europeans could best be described as polymorphic, the issue of several immigration movements, possibly of different grades of hominid, and with further variation taking place, perhaps, as a result of isolation or migration due to glacial movements (1976).

A further point of interest is that the Swanscombe skull fragments, as has already been mentioned, were associated with a hand-axe industry, of the type usually named Acheulian, after the type-site of Saint-Acheul in northern France. By contrast, the Arago and Bilzingsleben sites have 'Clactonian' assemblages. The north German site produced side-scrapers, borers and points, most of them chipped out of quartz pebbles. Bilzings-leben men had camped near where a stream entered a lake, and travertine deposited over the remains sealed the site. Plant imprints found in the travertine suggested there had been a deciduous mixed-woodland environment, with species like the box tree, which is no longer found in this area; molluscan remains from the travertine and the archaeological level also suggested much warmer conditions. The animals represented were mainly forest species of elephant, rhinoceros, hippopotamus, giant cattle, horse, and red deer; other mammals and mice, fish and birds were also identified (Mania, 1976).

The Clactonian technocomplex is broadly known from northern and eastern Europe (e.g. Collins, 1976, maps 1, 2), and comes to an end before the close of the Acheulian, which is most widely represented in Iberia and France. Some authorities regard the two technocomplexes as representing cultural and traditional differences, with environmental preferences being reflected in their geographical distribution, despite the very long time periods involved. Others, such as Binford, would put down most of the variability to task differentiation (1972b). In his view, different groupings of tools might be expected to distinguish a gathering or butchering site, a base camp, or bivouac, or an exploitation site; the whole tool-kit must be analysed and compared, which is difficult given the relative rarity of new sites. Isaac also emphasizes the factor of 'drift' in tool forms and associations which would account for further variation beyond task differences (1972a). The importance of raw materials in determining tool shape has to be considered – the northern Europe Clactonian sites are north of the line where flint occurs, for instance. An interesting study of the raw materials used in an Acheulian context along the Tarn valley in south-western France showed that the use of quartzites varied, depending on the distance of each camp from the Garonne river, which brought down such quartzites from the Pyrenees. In addition this raw material was the only one used to make certain tools, for instance cleavers (Tavoso, 1976). The environment may also have affected tool appearance. A German archaeologist, Müller-Beck, believes the size of hand-axes related quite closely to the environment, with larger ones being more frequently manufactured during cold steppe conditions (1976).

Acheulian tools consist of flakes, scrapers and a varying number of hand-axes in ovate, pointed or cleaver forms; the cleavers are relatively rare, as compared with the Acheulian industries of Africa. In 1974 Isaac and Curtis discussed the anomaly that East African Acheulian assemblages had been dated by K–Ar or palaeomagnetism to over 1 Myr old, whereas the European Acheulian (e.g. at the Italian site of Torre in Pietra) was dated over 500,000 years later. Some European archaeologists now hypothesize that the European Acheulian began nearly as early as the African, and persisted a very long time. In one scheme the Abbevillian (the supposed prototype of the Acheulian) lasts from 900,000 to 600,000 B.P., the Early Acheulian from 600,000 to 350,000 B.P., and the Middle and Upper Acheulian from 350,000 to 170,000 B.P. A final Acheulian persists longer in some areas (Combier, 1976). Combier outlined in the same article the still unresolved questions which arise about the Acheulian: Did it develop as a unit, or did a number of regional forms develop independently? How far do environmental differences, or task differences, account for the differing proportions of hand-axes and other tools in the industries? How far can finds from the river terraces of north-west Europe be correlated with the open-air sites recently discovered?

One of the open-air sites, only partially published to date, is Terra Amata on the southern French coast. Remains of eleven successive camp-sites were found in ancient dunes in what is now the town of Nice; a reconstruction of one of the camps has just been created in a museum not far distant from the original excavation spot. Oval settings of stones are assumed to have held the bases of branches bent over to form a central ridge. Inside the supposed shelter were hearths, and places where flint tools had been made. The pollen analysis of fossilized human faeces found near the huts shows that most of the plants represented were species which would be shedding at the end of spring or near the beginning of summer, so this gives a probable season for the visits of the hunters to Terra Amata. Remains of red deer, wild boar, ibex and extinct forms of elephant, rhinoceros and cattle suggest they were good hunters. They also collected fish, shellfish (oyster, limpet) and turtle, and hunted birds. There is no direct skeletal evidence from Terra Amata, but the imprint of a right foot was found preserved in the sand of the dunes (Fig. 7). This area was a very popular temporary camp, because in addition to the dune deposits there are four more occupation levels on a sand-bar, and another six on the beach seaward of the bar.

The tools were made mostly on local pebbles, and even toothed and scraping implements were often made on the whole pebble. There were a very few hand-axes. The industry has been described as Early or Middle Acheulian in character. The complexity of analysis which is going to be necessary to explain the differences and similarities in Acheulian assemblages is shown by the fact that at Terra Amata the sites below the sand-bar contained a lot of choppers, whereas in the dunes there were more side-scrapers, denticulate scrapers, and points. The presence of a few tools in non-local materials like quartz or rhyolite suggested that the visitors to Terra Amata brought some of their flint tools with them.

De Lumley has estimated that a particular level (C1a) at Terra Amata dates from between 380,000 and 450,000 years ago, on the basis of com-

Fig. 7. Foot imprint from Terra Amata, Nice, France (contours every 0.5 mm) (after de Lumley, 1976*b*, fig. 4)

parisons of animal remains and tools. There is only one absolute date for this site, obtained by the thermoluminescent dating of two burnt flints from level Cla. Wintle and Aitken obtained a date of 230,000 + 40,000 years B.P. The result represents the earliest obtained so far by the Oxford Laboratory, and needs to be backed up by a series of experiments on samples of the same period (Wintle and Aitken, 1977). It means, however, that level Cla might be later than de Lumley estimates.

Widely differing ages have also been suggested for two Spanish sites excavated by Clark Howell; in terms of the old glacial chronology they have been variously assigned to the Mindel or Riss glaciations, or the inter-glacial between them! Butzer and Isaac place them somewhere in the time range 600,000 to 300,000 B.P. (1975, p. 894). The sites when fully re-ported should reveal much detail about the organization of activities and behaviour. The first, Torralba, lies at 1115 metres above sea level (the Iberian sites generally are located higher than elsewhere), in the valley of the Ambrona. Pollen analysis of the archaeological sediments indicated a pine parkland environment. A total of 300 m² were excavated, and ten archaeological levels discovered. In one area the left side of an elephant minus its pelvis and skull was revealed; another area to the south-east re-vealed humerus, vertebrae and rib bones. The excavator, Howell, suggested that there was a primary kill or dismemberment area, and a secondary butchering and meat-processing area (1966, p. 130). The elephant may have been chased into a boggy area by use of fire, killed by wooden spears while sinking, and stripped of the right side of its carcass by the hunters. The stone tools associated with the bones included hand-axes and cleavers, in equal quantity.

The second site, Ambrona, lay at the bottom of a steep-sided valley, and had two stratigraphically distinguishable levels, the lower of which was probably contemporary with Torralba. Of this lower level 1200 m² were excavated, revealing localized groups of bone and stone representing some thirty to thirty-five elephants. Either there were relatively few stone implements and the elephant skeletons were more or less intact, or there were concentrations of broken bone and tools (hand-axes, cleavers, side-scrapers, toothed flakes, and a few borers and cores). In the upper level, there were fewer hand-axes, but many cores and waste flakes, and bones of horses, red deer, cattle and rhinoceros. Altogether the sites present an unusual picture, in the context of the Early Palaeolithic, of concentration on one animal species. It has been suggested that the elephants used the valley as a seasonal migration route, and that the Torralba and Ambrona (level 1) sites were the activity areas of their hunters in that season. Freeman has recently emphasized the similarity of the Torralba and

Ambrona, and other Iberian industries, to those in north Africa (1975).

Incidences of Early Palaeolithic living floors have recently been gathered together and analysed (Villa, 1976), and the point made that the only recently excavated one to be fully published is the Grotte du Lazaret, Nice, France (de Lumley, 1969*b*). The Le Lazaret cave contains a sequence of deposits, but the presumed living floor lies in the upper levels. It dates

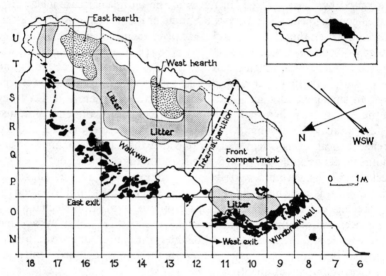

Fig. 8. Ground plan of Le Lazaret 'tent', southern France (inset shows protected area of cave) (after de Lumley, 1969*b*, fig. 54)

to the third stage of the Riss glaciation in conventional terms, while amino-acid tests have produced dates *c.* 150,000 B.P. De Lumley has published detailed distribution maps of the position of stones, flint tools and debris, bone, charcoal and shell, and suggested that the Acheulian hunters created a shelter about 11 m × 3·50 m at one side of the cave (Fig. 8). The bottom of the shelter wall is defined by rows of stones, including possible post-supports. A skin curtain and roof may have been draped over the posts. The distribution of finds suggested entrances and internal compartments, with two hearths in the larger compartment and none in the smaller. The presence of tiny sea shells, which would have been attached to seaweed, and of the foot bones of fur-bearing animals like wolf, fox, lynx and panther, around the hearth and in the smaller compartment, may indicate bedding. The tools include hand-axes and choppers, and lots of tools made of pebbles, of Upper Acheulian type.

Study of the pollen contained in coprolites suggested that the climate had been colder than today, with stands of pine trees in the vicinity of the cave. The shelter would have provided protection from wind and cold, and represents an attempt to achieve a 'home'.

While the organization of the Le Lazaret cave is the only one fully published for the first long period of man's occupation of Europe, it can be seen that in fact Europeans seem to have organized their camp-sites from the beginning. They created structures in wood and stone; used fire, often in prepared hearths; and slept and worked flint and other materials in defined areas. As has been shown above, regional differences showing possible territories of hunting groups, seem to be present from the Middle Acheulian onwards.

Butzer and Isaac, who have edited a recent volume on the Middle Pleistocene, suggest that some European Late Acheulian industries persist till c. 100,000 B.P. At Orgnac 3 cave, Ardèche, a long succession of Acheulian deposits demonstrates slow changes in tool typology, including techniques like Levallois flaking. The Levallois technique, whereby the core is prepared before flakes are struck, off it, in such a way as to produce a 'tortoise' outline, although first employed in the Lower Palaeolithic came into more widespread use in the Middle Palaeolithic. There are many differing estimates for the beginnings of both Middle Palaeolithic stone-tool types, and of a new skeletal variant, 'Neanderthal man'. These are generally dated in the traditional framework to the Riss–Würm interglacial and the early part of the Würm glacial, possibly from c. 125/100,000 B.P. to c. 30,000 B.P., although there is a unique date of 220,000 B.P. for the Middle Palaeolithic cave deposit at Ehringsdorf, East Germany. Gabori has suggested that the Mousterian developed in two main zones, western Europe and Caucasia, and spread from there into the rest of Europe (1976a). The majority of dates obtained by both radiocarbon and uranium decay fall into the time-span 50,000 to 30,000 B.P.

Middle Palaeolithic artifacts, many falling into Clark's Mode 2, seem thus to have been taken up relatively slowly. Suggestions accounting for the change in tool-kits include alterations in activities, linked to environmental change, especially reduction in the forest cover. The artifacts of the Middle Palaeolithic are generally called Mousterian, after the type-site of Le Moustier cave in the Dordogne. Professor Bordes has identified sixty-three types of Mousterian implement, and believes that these are combined in different proportions in five different types of assemblage (1968a) (Fig. 9).

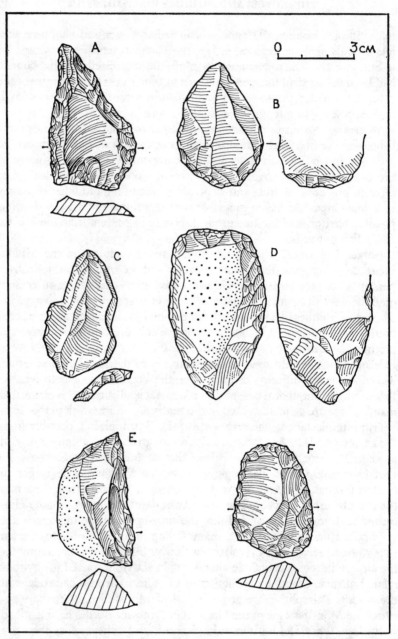

Fig. 9. Mousterian tool types (after Valoch, 1972, fig. 2, and Freund, 1975, figs. 9 and 10)

In Bordes' system, the 'typical Mousterian' assemblage has from 25 to 55 per cent side-scrapers, which are the most frequently represented implement type. The 'Mousterian of Acheulian tradition' assemblage has 20 to 40 per cent side-scrapers, plus 10 to 15 per cent hand-axes and some Upper Palaeolithic implement types. Much larger proportions of side-scrapers, 50 to 80 per cent, are found in 'Quina' and 'Ferrassie' types of Mousterian. Ferrassie is further specialized by the fact that most of the tools are made by the Levallois flaking technique. Fewer side-scrapers, 5 to 25 per cent, are found in the 'denticulate Mousterian' assemblage, in which, as its name suggests, many of the tools have denticulate or toothed edges. These five types of assemblage produce 'cumulative frequency graphs' of different outlines; such graphs have been produced for many sites, and levels of sites, over the Dordogne and Charente regions of south-western France. Bordes sees the five different assemblages as representing five separate cultures. These would persist through the many thousands of years of the Mousterian, without noticeably influencing each other. Laville has recently used pollen analysis to cross-date levels of different Dordogne caves, concluding that three of the assemblage types (Mousterian of Acheulian tradition, Quina, and Ferrassie) definitely coexisted in the first two stages of the Würm glaciation (1973). Bordes' cultural explanation of assemblage variability is followed by de Lumley, who regards the assemblages as representing the rest stops of different bands of hunters within their territories. The hunting territories are more clearly separated in southern France than in the Dordogne, and de Lumley visualizes that the sites in the Dordogne where different Mousterian industries lie on top of one another would have been on the edge of several hunting territories (1972).

Other authors consider such explanations unlikely in view of the vast time period involved. Mellars has suggested that there is an element of chronological difference in the assemblages in that Quina and Ferrassie assemblages are frequently followed in the stratigraphies by Mousterian of Acheulian tradition (1969). He further suggests an evolutionary trend within the Quina–Ferrassie type-site itself; this trend has been supported by multivariate analysis by Hodson (1969).

A contrasting explanation of the assemblages was provided by the Binfords, who separated out *groups* of tools using multivariate factor analysis (1968). These groups of tools were supposedly used for food procurement, food preparation, plant or bone preparation, or maintenance activities. The location of one or several factors in a site or part of a site could indicate the purpose of that site – perhaps as a base camp, where the children and women would form the permanent core of the occupation, or as a specific task or work camp (kill-site, quarry, etc.). Thus the explanation for the various types of stone-tool groupings through the long Mousterian period would be that there had been variability in tasks and uses of these tools and not that different cultural groups had coexisted through nearly 100,000 years in genetic isolation from each other. Freeman, excavator of a cave in Santander province, northern Spain, has demonstrated 'activity-specific' areas in the Mousterian levels, and strongly supports the functional explanation (1973).

In evaluating the different explanations of variation in Mousterian assemblages in south-western France, the dating of deposits and the fine correlation of stone-tool kits with contemporary faunal remains, sediments, pollen and microfauna are essential. Sedimentological work at the Bordeaux laboratory by Laville has produced a detailed sequence of the climatic changes in the Riss and Würm glaciations, and this is supplemented by work of colleagues on pollen and fauna. Bordes has published an outline of this work on two caves, Combe Grenal and Pech de l'Azé (1970a), demonstrating in the form of a chart the succession of industries, environmental changes and the main animal quarries pursued. Although one or two quarries were predominant (e.g. red deer, wild cattle, reindeer), the faunal remains covered a wide variety of animals hunted for both meat and skins. Very detailed work is necessary to detect the subtle differences in treatment of bone and other remains which support the theory of task differentiation.

The five types of Mousterian present in the south-west of France are not found together elsewhere. De Lumley has compared Combe Grenal with an approximately contemporary site, the Hortus cave, in Languedoc, showing differences in both micro-environments and assemblages. Even relatively close to the Dordogne region, therefore, Mousterian industries do not show identical groupings of tools.

Bordes has claimed that the types of assemblages detected in the Dordogne can be found over much of Europe. Mousterian of Acheulian tradition is found in the Low Countries and Germany and possibly also in southern England, Romania and Poland. In Italy industries of the Quina, Ferrassie, Typical and possibly Denticulate types are present. In Spain Quina, Typical and Denticulate types of Mousterian can be found (Bordes, 1968a). It is much harder to link the German leaf-point (*Blattspitzen*) industries or the industries of central and eastern Europe to the sequence found in south-west France.

Italian archaeologists have found Mousterian deposits containing a variety of industries from the Ligurian coast, through the Po valley region to the Euganean hills near Padua (Carraro et al., 1976), and as far south as Sicily. There are also small-tool Mousterian industries in central Italy (Pesce *et al.*, 1975).

Further east at the Greek rock-shelter site of Asprochaliko, Epirus, excavations by the late Eric Higgs of Cambridge discovered levels with large, well-retouched Mousterian tools. Large blades with thick platforms, finely retouched side-scrapers, thick broad points and tortoise and disc cores are represented (Higgs, 1966, fig. 14). This large-tool Mousterian was dated by radiocarbon to 39,900 years B.P. Beginning at level 14 is a micro-Mousterian industry: the tools are smaller and there are thousands of waste flakes. This is dated to 35,000 years B.P. (Higgs, 1970).

Different types of flake industries occur in central and eastern Europe.

A recent publication concerning the site of Königsaue, to the north-west of Halle, West Germany, revealed three types of industry, A and C described as 'Central European Micoquian with bifaces' and B described as 'Mousterian without bifacial working'. The authors feel that the Königsaue A and C industries may be directly antecedent to the leaf-point Mousterian of central Europe (Mania and Toepfer, 1973, p. 135).

Another very different tradition is found at the site of Érd, Hungary; here tools are made on pebbles of quartzite, chalcedony and opal found in Helvetian gravels some 500 metres away from the site. The proportion of 808 tools to 2155 flakes indicates considerable economy in the use of raw materials. Forty-eight implement types are recognized in the larger of the two gulleys which form the site, twenty-five in the smaller (Gabori-Csank, 1968). There are few links with the west European industries. Further east, in European Russia, Klein has analysed industries from eight Mousterian occupations; here fifty-five of Bordes' implement types are present, in varying proportions at each of the sites and levels (Klein, 1969a, fig. 4), but they are not combined as in the French types of assemblage. The bulk of flint materials at Molodova consisted of unretouched flakes and the disc-shaped cores from which the flakes were struck, together with side-scrapers and low numbers of notched and denticulated tools (Klein, 1973, p. 61).

Mousterian industries from the Alps to the Urals have recently been reviewed by Gabori (1976a, ch. 4). He has studied the industries in relation to the topography of sites, the climate and vegetation and the animals hunted (the fauna). Gabori concludes that neither faunal nor other environmental differences can be correlated with industrial differences, although topography may play a part in preventing contacts, or isolating groups; however, very few faunal samples are quantified, so that cross-comparisons are difficult to make. Both better chronology and much better faunal and pollen analyses are necessary to establish the range of variability in stone-tool types at any given point, and to offer explanations taking possible task variations into account.

It is generally assumed that raw materials were obtained during seasonal movements. Bosinski has divided west–central European Middle Palaeolithic sites on the basis of raw materials into: those using several types of flint (frequent or long occupation sites); those using a single type of flint (ephemeral camps); and working or extraction sites (1976a). Schmid has identified a flint extraction site at Pleigne (Bern, Switzerland); her dating is based on the characteristics of the loessic loam overlying the limestone containing the flint, and two Mousterian tools (1972). At Pleigne men had dug vertical pits into the limestone to a depth of 60 cm and used antler to prise out the nodules and boulder hammers to smash them. Lots of flakes with cortex indicated preliminary working on the site.

The majority of Mousterian assemblages have been found in caves or rock shelters, of which González and Freeman's excavation of the Morín cave in north Spain is one of the most recently published (González Echegeray et al., 1971, 1973). The cave is part of a system of limestone galleries, and the area investigated measures approximately 12 × 12 m². The cave has a sequence of Middle and Upper Palaeolithic deposits, with both typical and less typical industries of the Denticulate Mousterian (upper levels) and Mousterian of Acheulian tradition (lower levels). Fifty per cent of the bone remains were of large cattle, with red deer and horse making up the other half.

Some oyster- and top-shell also came from these levels. Freeman has outlined the general picture of subsistence activities in northern Spain, concluding that there was no deliberate specialization, and that base camps centrally located between, for instance, sea resources and mountains with chamois and deer, were regularly reoccupied (1973).

The Hortus cave site has already been mentioned briefly. In the rather narrow confines of this cave were a succession of Mousterian deposits, excavated and analysed on a multidisciplinary basis (de Lumley, 1972). The faunal and microfaunal remains suggested that levels 3 and 4A would have been produced by winter occupation, and levels 4B, 5A, 5B and 5C by summer occupation. The main quarry of the Hortus hunters was ibex, but they also killed cave bear and red deer and many smaller mammals and birds. This site is also interesting in that Boulinier has tested for possible correlations between the flint types and principal elements of the animal fauna and the skeletal remains of approximately twenty Neanderthalers. His studies indicate that the principal elements of the fauna correlate well together and, surprisingly, that the human remains correlate with them, but that the flint is separate. One interpretation of this might be that human remains were being used in the same way as animal remains, i.e. as food sources. Apparently there were no internal structures built in the narrow galleries of the Hortus cave but structural remains are known from other west European Mousterian sites (a post-hole at Combe Grenal, level 14, possibly for supporting a screen of skins, and remains of a wall at Cueva Morín) (Bordes, 1970a; Freeman, 1976).

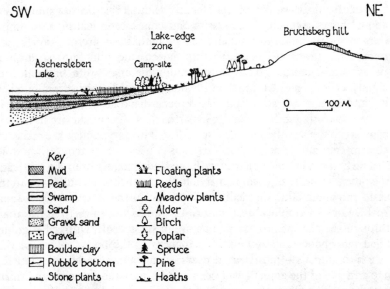

Fig. 10. Ecological profile of Lake Aschersleben, Königsaue, East Germany with Middle Palaeolithic camp-site (after Mania and Toepfer, 1973, fig. 39)

In northern and eastern Europe, open sites are relatively frequent, and particularly interesting results have been obtained at Königsaue, near the Harz mountains. Here brown-coal quarrying revealed twenty-five metres of sediments dated by geologists and palaeontologists to the last interglacial and the early phases of the Würm on the basis of analyses of molluscs, ostracods, plant remains, vertebrate bones and pollen. The Groningen laboratory dated the lake-shore sediments containing the archaeological levels to >55,800 and >49,000 B.P. Three levels with archaeological material indicated that camps had been set up beside the lake in a fairly open environment of reed swamps and light woodland (alder, birch, poplar and spruce) (Fig. 10). Animal bones were poorly preserved, so although they were studied for signs of use and reworking, no whittling marks were found, although some might have been used as retouchers (at the German site of Lebenstedt-Salzgitter mammoth bone and red-deer antler seem to have been worked). Analysis of the Königsaue bone (58 per cent mammoth, plus rhinoceros, wild horse and cattle) suggested that a group of thirty persons averaging 2000 calories daily could have been supported for 253 days during the Königsaue A occupation. The reindeer teeth and antler suggest a possible season for their camp, from April to October. Whether the camp-site was used once or repeatedly is not known. The excavators (Mania and Toepfer, 1973) think that the low numbers of animal bones recovered (3000 teeth and bones, representing a minimum number of thirty-seven animals) reflect both poor preservation conditions and, probably, contemporary butchering and rubbish-disposal behaviour. They suggest that mammoth carcasses were brought back mainly as flesh, and that much of the bone and other debris from butchering and meal preparation could have been disposed of in the lake itself. The 3000 teeth and bones and 5800 artifacts at Königsaue are in marked contrast to the situation at the site of Erd, Hungary, where the ratios are 50,000 teeth and bones to 3000 artifacts.

The Erd site lies on a plateau with the Buda mountains to the north and the much lower Transdanubian area to the south; the Danube runs to the east, and mountains of medium height lie to the west (Gabori-Csank, 1968). For topographical reasons animal movements in the past had to go through the Erd plateau area. The site consisted of two parallel gullies filled with bones and stone tools. Analysis of the bones suggested that over 500 animals – mostly cave bears – had been slaughtered. Between 350 and 450 of the animals had been adults, with 100 juveniles and thirty new-born. The former occupants of the Erd plateau seem to have visited the site in the spring to kill the bears, and in the summer to catch the horses and rhinoceros browsing along the Danube flood-plain. Total meat-weight from the bears was about 40–50,000 kg, and from the large herbivores and other animals 32–38,000 kg. The bones and stone tools were distributed in five archaeological levels, E, D, C, B and A, and charcoal and sediments indicate a gradual deterioration of climate from level E to level A. There are relatively few tools in the earliest occupation, and the excavators wonder if at least some of the animals were scavenged rather than hunted. At each level the bones were arranged in approximately oval accumulations in the two parallel gullies. The position of these ovals shifted very little in the small gulley in successive levels, but shifted sideways a little in the large gulley (Fig. 11). The excavators suggest that the small gulley was used for meat stocking, while more occupation took place in the large gulley, where flint tools are more numerous, and hearths larger. Close associations between stone implements and bone remains

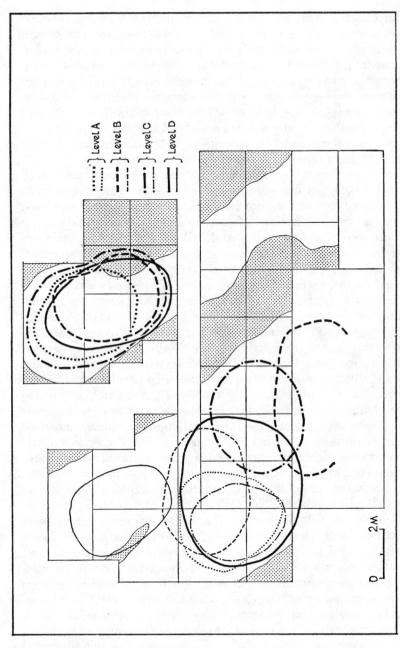

Fig. 11. Shifts in accumulation of bones in two gullies at Erd, Hungary (the heavy lines indicate accumulations of cave-bear bones, the light lines accumulations of horse bones) (after Gábori-Czánk, 1968, figs. 6 and 43)

are impossible to establish, because artifacts were collected and recorded in 2 × 2 m squares, not three-dimensionally. However, some differences can be seen. In level B, for instance, flint tools were found near to, but separate from the bone piles to the north and north-east, whereas in level C, Sector 8, stone tools were found in among the bones. The massive quantity of bone suggests something like sixteen times as many days' food as estimated for Königsaue A. If the site was used over sufficient centuries to permit the climatic deterioration visible from levels E to A to take place, however, the apparently vast quantity of bone could indicate nothing more than seasonal hunting to catch one or two animals.

Other open sites are found in Russia. During the Mousterian, nearly all the major valleys of European Russia were occupied, and twenty-three cave sites and ten open sites are known (Klein 1969a, 1973). Two sites at Molodova in the Ukraine have Mousterian industries, and are assumed to have been occupied in the Early to Middle Würm (Klein 1969a). Molodova lies midway along the Dniester river, and the ancient occupations are contained in colluvium resulting from gravity and hill-wash. The valley would have been wooded, but cold-loving snail species and soil-frost phenomena suggest very cold conditions (Fig. 12). Molodova V has minimum carbon-14 dates for the Mousterian levels of > 45,600, > 40,300 and > 35,500 B.P. Horizon 11 of Molodova V (dated > 45,600 B.P.) shows a distribution of cultural remains within an arc of mammoth bones measuring roughly 9 × 7 m. The arc encloses five hearths, and bone and flint are scattered within it. An even clearer ring of mammoth bones in Horizon 4 at Molodova I has an internal measurement of 8 × 5 m, and contains fifteen hearths and more than 20,000 pieces of flint, plus hundreds of animal bones (Fig. 13). In the same level, sandstone, slate and limestone pebbles were used as grinders and hammer-stones. The excavator suggested that the mammoth bones held down skins stretched over a wooden framework. The season of occupation, and length of time spent, is not certain in either case, but Klein suggests the occupations were shorter than in the Upper Palaeolithic (1969a).

Klein believes with the Russians that artifact differences between sites reflect cultural differences, even though some variation may be due to activities carried out at the different sites. Only a few Russian sites have quantified bone reports – Klein's chart for Molodova V mainly indicates the presence of mammoth, for instance, while at Molodova I horse, bison and reindeer also appear (1969a, fig. 3). Klein suggests that large herbivores are more common than mammoth in the Dniester river sites, while mammoth are relatively commoner than reindeer and horse on the Dnieper and Desna river terraces. However, only one site in each region has

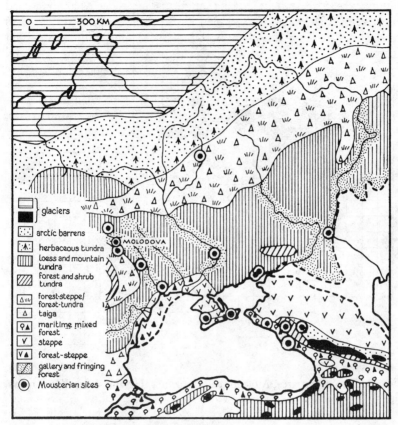

Fig. 12. Vegetation zones of European Russia at the height of the last glacial, indicating Mousterian sites (after Klein, 1969a, fig. 1)

minimum numbers of individuals of the different animal species worked out (Vykhvatintsy and Kodak respectively). Given the limited faunal data, it is unclear how far Mousterian groups concentrated on single species or a few species, although the data from Erd and a few other central European sites seem to indicate specialization on cave bear, while reindeer are preponderant at Salzgitter-Lebenstedt in Germany, and mammoth at the Prut valley site of Ripiceni-Izvor (Gabori, 1976).

Earlier in this chapter the wide variation in human skeletal types of the Lower Palaeolithic was discussed. The majority of the skeletons associated with Mousterian artifacts are described as 'Neanderthal', after the first specimen found in the Neander valley in Germany, or technically

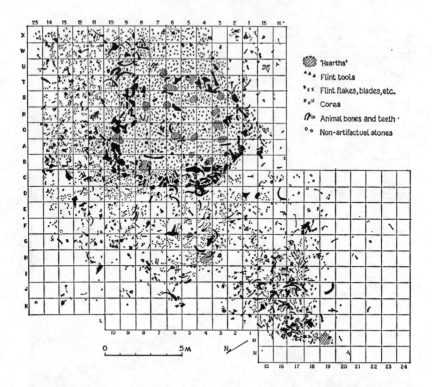

'Hearths'
Flint tools
Flint flakes, blades, etc.
Cores
Animal bones and teeth ·
Non-artifactual stones

Fig. 13. Plan of hut area, Molodova I, Horizon 4, Ukraine (after Klein 1969*a*, fig. 5)

as *Homo sapiens neanderthalensis*. Birdsell has recently described classic Neanderthalers of Europe as 'characteristically a very short, heavily built, and big headed people' (1972). Brain capacities of Neanderthal skulls are as great as or greater than those of modern man, but the skull shape is long and has a bun-shaped protrusion or occiput at the rear. It has been suggested that there is very little variation in Neanderthal skeletons but this conclusion is at odds with the very wide range of variability in specimens from single sites in central Europe described in a recent article by Jelinek (1969) (Fig. 14). At the site of Ehringsdorf, East Germany, for instance, the anthropologists report great morphological variability in the four skull- and two jaw-bones; for instance, the four parietals of the skull varied in thickness and degree of curvature. Similarly, at the Krapina rock shelter in Yugoslavia, teeth, skull fragments, and post-cranial (i.e.

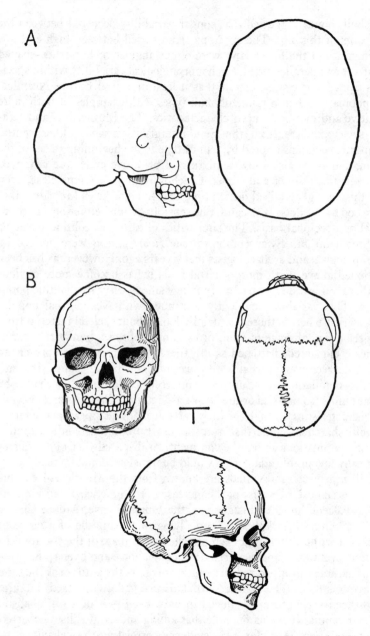

Fig. 14. Central and east European Neanderthal skulls: A from Dolní Věstonice;
B from Kostienki (after Jelinek, 1969, figs. 9 and 12)

non-skull) bones suggested that similar variability occurred between the occupants of this site. The six upper jaws varied between high and low specimens, and the lower jaws were either angular or horseshoe-shaped or narrow and parallel-sided. Such morphological variability within specimens from a single site suggests that at least in central Europe Neanderthal populations had a range of skull types with examples of both more primitive and more advanced characteristics. The Ehringsdorf and Krapina skeletons date from the Eem interglacial period. Other central European specimens quoted by Jelinek date to the beginning stages of the. Würm, and these also show a mixture of primitive and more advanced characteristics (Kulna and Sipka, Czechoslovakia). It seems clear, even from this very generalized description, that human skeletal remains from *c.* 125,000 to *c.* 35,000 B.P. cannot be sensibly divided either on a chronological or a regional basis. The similarities of early Palaeolithic skeletons like Steinheim and Swanscombe to true *Homo sapiens* were noticed by anthropologists and archaeologists many years ago. However, as has been mentioned above, with more skeletal finds it has become more obvious that there was a wide range of morphology among early Palaeolithic populations. This variability evidently continued with Neanderthal populations, so that whereas there is a 'family look' about skeletal material from this period (i.e. absence of chin, protruding eyebrows, bun at the rear of the head, elongated, flattened skull), these characteristics are present to varying degrees even in what were apparently cohabiting groups. It seems that the populations of Europe, reinforced periodically, perhaps, by migrant units from Africa or the Near East, retained plasticity and generalized characteristics through the early Palaeolithic. The appearance of rather generally shared 'Neanderthal' traits across Europe must indicate interbreeding populations across the continent, so disposed that mutations or genetically favourable adaptation would be transferred and increase.

In all nearly 200 individuals are known from the Middle Palaeolithic sites. This is mostly because of the increase in the practice of burial in the Middle Palaeolithic. For instance, at the Guattari cave, Monte Circeo, Italy, a Neanderthal skull was found lying in the middle of a circle of stones. An artificial hole had been punched at the base of the cranium. In the same level were remains of red deer, cattle, horse and hyena; the presence of naturally dropped red-deer antler suggests the autumn as the time the cave was used. The Ehringsdorf skull also had a depressed fracture, and thirteen skeletons are believed to have been part of a cannibalistic feast at Krapina. It seems possible that killing and cannibalism occurred (Roper, 1969), and the statistical evidence correlating the behaviour towards human skeletal remains with that towards animal fauna at the

Hortus cave is relevant in this connection. Sally Binford (1968) has compared Mousterian burials in western Europe and the Middle East in the
Middle and Upper Palaeolithic periods, and concludes that western European Mousterian burial practices are more distinct from Upper Palaeolithic than are the Middle Eastern. This is one element of several suggesting
an ultimately Middle Eastern origin for modern man. For a long time
western European Neanderthals in particular have been regarded as on an
evolutionary 'branch line' and totally unlikely to have evolved into *Homo
sapiens sapiens*. Support for this model comes from the interesting theory of
Lieberman and Crelin (1971) that Neanderthal man as represented by the
La Chapelle skeleton could not have used language as we do today, and
that this may have accounted for his lack of success (i.e. survival). Basing
their tests on the belief that the vocal apparatus of Neanderthal man above
the larynx was similar to that of a new-born human infant, the investigators reconstructed Neanderthal air passages (1971; Fig. 15), and by using
a computer simulation programme indicated that Neanderthal man would
have had difficulty with American-English vowels and the letters G and K,
although he could have managed a few vowels and the consonants pro-
nounced with the teeth and lips like D, B, S, Z, V, and F. These conclusions for La Chapelle man contrast with Crelin's work on the Steinheim
skull where the computer indicated that the Steinheim vocal tract would
have been capable of producing all the sounds of present-day articulate
speech (1973, p. 14).

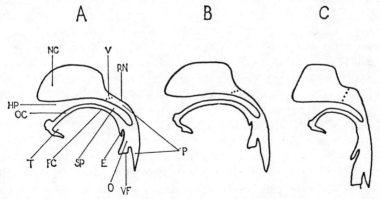

Fig. 15. Reconstructed larynx of La Chapelle man (B) compared with modern
new-born (A) and adult (C) larynx (after Lieberman and Crelin, 1971, fig. 9)

NC Nasal cavity, V Vomer bone, RN Roof of nasopharynx, P Pharynx, HP Hard
palate, SP Soft palate, OC Oral cavity, T Tip of tongue, FC Foramen caecum of
tongue, E Epiglottis, O Opening of larynx into pharynx, VF Level of vocal folds

Although such research is fascinating in adding unexpected new dimensions to the study of early man, the conclusions have been criticized (e.g. Carlisle and Siegel, 1974) and can only be regarded as hypothetical.

CONCLUSION

We now know something about the environment, activities, and behaviour of Neanderthal man. A strong chronological outline is still lacking, as is information about the response of these populations to extremes of climate and environmental change. More research is needed to clarify the distinctions between this grade of man, and ourselves. The question of the persistence of Neanderthalers into later periods will be dealt with in the next chapter.

THE UPPER PALAEOLITHIC

The Upper Palaeolithic marks one of the great leaps forward of European prehistory. Changes occurred in the subspecies of man living in Europe, and in the possibly correlated fields of improved and more complex tools, and art forms. But first we must consider the time and the environment that the Upper Palaeolithic occupied. All of the period is within the range of the carbon-14 dating method, and the Groningen laboratory in particular has obtained a wide range of dates associated with a series of colder and warmer phases of the Würm glacial period. These dates enable the succession of climatic events to be more accurately pinpointed than in the earlier periods.

The Groningen results are illustrated in Figure 16 (after Waterbolk 1972, fig. 2). They indicate that the earliest Upper Palaeolithic dates from western Europe fall in the slightly cooler gap between the warm interstadials of Hengelo and Denekamp (*c.* 39,000 to 37,000 and *c.* 32,000 to 29,000 B.P. respectively). In eastern Europe there are two earlier dates, from the Istallöskö cave in Hungary. There is thus some overlap with dated Mousterian sites (Chapter 2). Waterbolk's table also suggests that for much of the Upper Palaeolithic period the occupants of Europe were living in something like a tundra environment veering to polar-desert conditions in the colder epochs and only reaching coniferous forest conditions at the very end of the Würm. These conclusions are based on palynological and other data from the Netherlands, but Waterbolk believes that they may be correlated with certain levels in sites in the Paris basin, south-western France, Belgium and Germany. A more ambitious attempt at correlation of the environment in different areas of Europe,

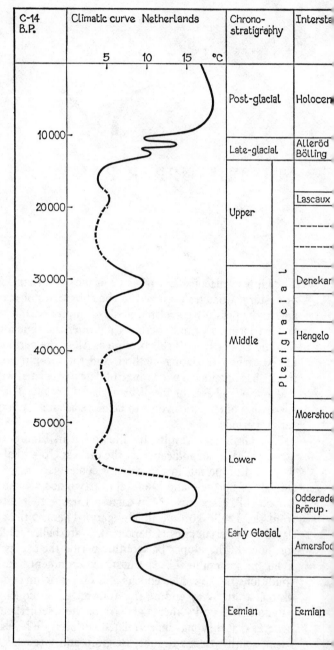

C-14 B.P.	Climatic curve Netherlands	Chrono-stratigraphy		Intersta
	5 10 15 °C			
		Post-glacial		Holocen
10 000		Late-glacial		Alleröd Bölling
20 000		Upper		Lascaux
30 000			P l e n i g l a c i a l	Denekar
40 000		Middle		Hengelo
50 000				Moershoc
		Lower		
		Early Glacial		Odderade Brörup.
				Amersfoc
		Eemian		Eemian

Fig. 16. Radiocarbon dates from Palaeolithic sites in western Europe com)

ogne		Germany	Belgium			Paris basin
Regourdou	La Micoque	Balve	Coversand zone	Transition zone	Loess zone	
						Würm III b Würm III a
			Zelzate soil		Kesselt soil	Würm II/III
			Hoboken soil			
2		IV sterile layer			Loess Loam Loess	Würm II
Soil 3		III		Poperinge soil	Soil	Würm I/II
8·4	6	II I			Loam	Würm I b Würm I a
		Erosion		Warneton soil		
	Soil				Rocourt soil	
			Rocourt	soil		

the climatic curve of the Netherlands (after Waterbolk, 1972, fig. 2) from the north-west to the south-east, has been attempted by Mania (1970, fig. 2). This was a pioneering attempt to provide a cross-European dating framework, but in time multiple carbon-14 dates will provide a more secure basis for such comparisons, while the influence of deep-sea core chronology (see Chapter 1) has still to be felt.

Carbon-14 dating will in time establish the contemporaneity or otherwise of different Upper Palaeolithic industries in Europe. Meanwhile many other traditional relative dating methods are still being used and are very valuable on a regional basis. The most important relative dating methods used in Upper Palaeolithic sites are those of sedimentology, pollen analysis and the study of microfaunas. For instance, a number of occupations in south German caves are considered to be of roughly the same period because similar yellow clay with lots of sharp limestone fragments is the matrix in which the artifacts are found (Hahn, 1976). Microfauna are useful on a local scale to indicate micro-environmental change; for instance, lemmings of different types have been located in successive levels at the Brillenhöhle (Brillen cave) in Germany. Pollen analysis is widely used, even more than in the Middle Palaeolithic: sequences established for small regions are particularly important (e.g. Romania, the Dordogne). Beetles, molluscs and larger animals are used both to reconstruct the environmental situation and for relative dating. Sometimes the results of these studies do not coincide. For instance, at the Flageolet II cave, Dordogne, the faunal remains (of saiga antelope) and the carbon-14 date clash with the artifact typology, so that a 'typical Magdalenian' industry was probably being used at a date earlier than generally expected.

Settlement sites of Upper Palaeolithic date are being investigated at present in the framework of the length of stay at the site, the activities undertaken while at the site, and the size of the group occupying the site. Research workers in the French area in particular have been concentrating on ultra-careful excavation and recording, complex laboratory analysis, and the production of a theoretical framework for the reconstruction of past activities.

The theoretical framework includes the necessity for working out all the possible options and variations suggested by the basic data. Leroi-Gourhan has been particularly active in this regard and has provided frameworks for description of all types of structure and artifact distributions (hearths, working areas, etc.). Sackett has written about the necessity for open-mindedness when faced with new types of site, and different organization of remains on the site. He has stressed the necessity to look beyond individual sites and regions to neighbouring areas where different qualities of information may be available (Sackett and Gaussen, 1976).

Many sites are now excavated by locating all artifacts and debris in three dimensions and by plotting all fugitive signs of ochre, ash, etc. on site plans as they appear. Overhead photography has also been used as a recording tool. Such methods allow archaeologists to obtain information about relationships between artifacts which would be impossible by less exact methods of recording.

Laboratory analysis involves the study of flint, rock and bone tools and of the by-products of their manufacture, and the identification of the activities involved in their manufacture, use and discard. Edge-wear and micro-wear studies are also important in determining the possible function of the artifacts. On a more analytical level the formal variation between artifacts has to be measured and statistical analyses made of how they vary in relation to each other over space (e.g. Sackett, 1966; Sackett and Gaussen, 1976).

UPPER PALAEOLITHIC TECHNOCOMPLEXES

The most important technocomplexes of Late Würm Europe were the Aurignacian, the Gravettian, the Solutrean and the Magdalenian. Aurignacian industries have mostly been dated from c. 37,000 to c. 30,000 years B.P. in different areas of Europe. The Gravettian apparently dated from c. 29,000 B.P. until the end of the Würm (c. 10,000 B.P.) in eastern Europe, while being replaced in western Europe by the Solutrean and Magdalenian industries at approximately 20,000 B.P. There is a strong regional cast to the development of Upper Palaeolithic industries.

The reasons for change in stone-tool industries at the time of transition to the Upper Palaeolithic are a matter of controversy. The change to industries based mainly on blades (parallel-sided thin flakes) was originally regarded as due to the (unexplained) demise of Neanderthal populations and their replacement by *Homo sapiens sapiens*. Louis Leakey believed that Neanderthal man was a parallel development to true *Homo* stock, and that he was replaced by populations of *Homo sapiens sapiens* individuals, early examples of which he quotes from Kenya to Germany towards the end of the Middle Pleistocene (1972). The explanation for this replacement can be expressed in terms of 'territorial imperative', or expansionism of the new *Homo sapiens sapiens* populations. Archaeologists have looked at the industries in their regions recently to see if there are in fact clear-cut differences between the flake industries attributed to the Middle Palaeolithic and the blade-based industries attributable to the Upper Palaeolithic. Where assemblages seem to contain a mixture of tool types, it is suggested that there was some continuity between the two periods (e.g. in

Slovakia, Bosnia, Romania, Hungary, France, and possibly also in Italy, Moravia, and Spain). Chmielewski has claimed clear typological links between Crimean Kiik-Koba and the later Kostienki-Sugit cultures among others (1971). Mellars has outlined the similarities between French Middle and Upper Palaeolithic industries (1973). A typologically mixed industry is known from the lower level of the Busag site in north-eastern Romania, where older discoid and globular nuclei are found together with newer prismatic nuclei, muzzled scrapers and blades, but no burins or other Upper Palaeolithic implements (Bitiri, 1976). The changeover to blade-tool industries varied both regionally and chronologically, and some blade industries were made by Neanderthal men (Valoch, 1972). What explanations have been provided for the differences and similarities between most Mousterian and Upper Palaeolithic tool types? At the Unesco symposium on the origins of modern man in 1969 there were a number of interesting hypotheses. S. Binford suggested that the adoption of a different hunting pattern played a crucial role; Chmielewski suggested that extreme climatic and environmental change affected certain areas and groups producing a change in hunting methods and an improvement of weapons. Environmental change, producing tundra conditions on which huge herds of browsing animals could feed, may have been largely responsible for the change in hunting techniques.

Chmielewski adds a further dimension in discussing continuity in central and eastern Europe between about 55,000 and 25,000 years B.P. by suggesting that the increasing cold, which may have forced some migration southwards, led to the development of new social systems including marriage out of the community (exogamy), thus reducing what he sees as former regional isolation.

In discussing the change in skeletal type which occurs at the beginning of the Upper Palaeolithic the Unesco conference concluded that 'the principal agent of human evolution can only be a culture "cerebralization" feedback under the pressure of the environment' (1972). This formula combined the opposing viewpoints of experts on the relative importance of cultural and environmental selection, and is not particularly explanatory! The differences in shape between Neanderthal and Upper Palaeolithic (Cro-Magnon) skulls include greater height and reduced brow ridges in the latter. The range of cranial capacity was similar in both subspecies, but Cro-Magnon man is assumed to have been able to think and speak exactly like modern man. Cro-Magnon body shape was taller but less robust than Neanderthal. In the light of the assumption made above about coexistence of several types of man in early hominid populations, the question is how to account for these differences and

similarities, since few authorities now believe that there was total replacement of Neanderthal types of men, and consider that at least some of their
genes are still present in modern populations.

An opposing explanation would be that which sees some sort of
evolution of the Neanderthal populations. In the previous chapter, the
very wide ranges in morphology among Neanderthal populations of
eastern and central Europe were mentioned, and similar mixed characteristics have long been known from the burials in the Skhul cave, Mount
Carmel, Israel, dated approximately 36,000 B.P. Ferembach has expressed clearly the mechanism which might have brought about the
bodily changes. She visualizes the Neanderthals in terms of local races,
and believes that modern men probably appeared at different times and
places because of a dominant mutation of the brain involving the remodel-
ling of the brain case (1972). The rapid spread of the mutation might have
been due to the sort of intermarriage between previously isolated populations suggested by Chmielewski. Mutation is a frequent cause of change in
populations in the animal kingdom. A Russian expert, Velitchko, agrees
that by the end of the Mousterian very cold conditions had given an
advantage to 'mutants' contemporary with normal Neanderthals, and it
was this mutant stock which developed into modern man (1972). An
argument often quoted against the hypothesis that some Neanderthal
populations developed into Upper Palaeolithic types of men has been the
relatively short time gap between known classic Neanderthal specimens
and early Cro-Magnon ones. Change can occur relatively rapidly, however. For instance Billy has studied height and face size in populations
dating from the early to the final Upper Palaeolithic (Aurignacian to
Magdalenian) (1972, p. 10). During this time period a definite reduction
in height and face size took place. Billy accounts for the changes
by 'profound genetic transformations conditioned by environmental
influence'. It is possible that, at an earlier period, mutations in genes of
Neanderthal populations might have developed and become dominant.
There are several areas where this might have taken place, such as central
and eastern Europe, and the Near East, and possibly south-western
France.

The continuity of settlement seen in different parts of Europe in itself
suggests a certain continuity in populations. Cave sites like La Ferrassie
in the Dordogne were used by successive populations, while open-air
sites in similar situations to earlier ones occurred in places as far apart as
Romania and north Spain. Hahn has suggested that the small huts of the
early Upper Palaeolithic reflect small groups similar in size to the Mousterian.

THE AURIGNACIAN

Industries described as Aurignacian are reported from the Near East to western Europe. In the Near East such blade industries have been dated to 40,000 B.P. (Camps, 1976, p. 177). In Europe, apart from the dates of 44,300 and 39,800 for the Hungarian cave of Istallöskö the majority of dates are between 37,000 and 30,000 B.P., with a few as late as 20,000, for instance in lower Austria. This means that Aurignacian industries are found in environments which indicate both colder and more temperate phases.

Given a technocomplex over such a vast space/time continuum, archaeologists have worked hard to divide Aurignacian industries into chronologically or regionally differentiated groups. In general, Aurignacian industries have a rather limited range of tool types (Fig. 17), including carinated and end-scrapers, muzzle- or nose-scrapers, and a range of burins or gravers, and borers. Proportions of blades and bladelets to flakes vary in different industries, as does the amount of retouch on the blades. Some have semi-invasive retouch, some just marginal retouch and others are backed or blunted along one or both margins. The rather low numbers of tools in most collections make it difficult to produce valid comparisons between the sites. For this reason changes in the morphology of bone projectile points have been used as chronological markers; in France these points have a split base in Aurignacian I, a forked base in Aurignacian III, and a simple bevelled base in Aurignacian V (de Sonneville-Bordes, 1973, p. 46). Assemblages with little or no bonework can still be distinguished by numerical methods, however. For instance, principal components analysis and seriation of twenty-nine assemblages carried out by Hahn (1972) have defined: some changes over time (broadly early and late Aurignacian technocomplexes); some regionally specific groupings of tools; and some groupings which are suspected of being linked to specific activities.

Hahn visualizes the makers of these (mostly) central European flint industries as living in smallish groups mixing only occasionally and without very strong contacts. He visualizes these groups as having hunting territories of fewer than 200 km². The chronological seriation found by Hahn in the Upper Danube valley caves is that end-scrapers and muzzle-scrapers are more often found with the earlier industries, and burins or gravers of carinated and busked form in the later Aurignacian industries. While later Aurignacian industries still flourish in the Lone valley a new industrial style, early Gravettian, appears at the same time in the Ach valley fifty kilometres away. Hahn suggested that the Ach hunting territory may have been taken over by a new group (1976a, p. 21).

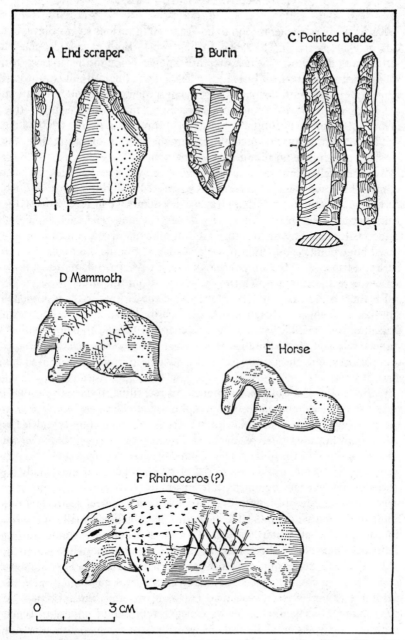

Fig. 17. Aurignacian tool types and animal figurines from Vogelherd IV and V, West Germany (after Hahn, 1972, fig. 5 and pl. 8)

Aurignacian settlements tend to be clustered in various river valleys, but this may be partly due to a bias in field-work. Both cave and open-air settlements are known. Cave sites are known from southern Belgium, south-western France, and in side valleys off the line of the Danube and Rhine rivers. In south Poland, Aurignacian settlements are often found on the loess, and repeated occupations are found in the same spots. Other favourite spots seem to be situations of middle altitude overlooking streams or gaps through which animals might pass on migrations (e.g. the Košice basin in the north-western Carpathians).

The Ach valley cave mentioned above is the Geissenklosterle cave near Ulm. This cave has been recently excavated by Hahn and Wagner, revealing a stratigraphy with a Gravettian assemblage in level 1 overlying Aurignacian assemblages in levels 2a, 2b, 2c and 3. Level 2a, dated 31,000 B.P., contains an Aurignacian flint industry accompanied by split-based bone points (possibly projectile heads). Preliminary reports indicate hare and fish among the animal remains, while ivory pendants and animal statuettes with scratched designs are known from this site.

Further to the east, on the terrace above the Hornad river in Czecho-slovakia, a string of Aurignacian sites is broadly dated to earlier warm stages and later colder stages by the charcoal of oak and pine-willow, respectively, found in habitation pits. (The excavators assume the Barca II occupation was in the Würm 1–2 interstadial, and Barca I in the Würm 2 cold phase.)

Unfortunately lack of three-dimensional recording in the excavation of the sites reduces their palaeo-ethnographic value. They were excavated in the 1950s by Prosek, and publication after his death merely revealed the plans of the various pits. At Barca II fifteen pits were exposed over an area of 1300 m², with finds dating from the early Aurignacian. The pits were dug in vaguely oval, trapezoidal or pear-shaped outline, usually $2\frac{1}{2}$ to $3\frac{1}{2}$ m wide, but varying in length from 5 m to 15 or 18 m long. The latter structures consisted of long pits joined by shallower sills between them. Some of the individual pits have been grouped together by the excavators into assumed 'habitation complexes', and post-holes distributed along their middle lines have been used to suggest possible roofing designs.

A rather later series of occupations on the same terrace, at Barca I, were in much more complex pit structures. As can be seen from Figure 18, Barca I:2 (Pit 2) was cross-shaped (14 × 14 m) and Barca I:3 (Pit 3) (24 × 14 m) H-shaped. Hearths were clearly represented, including seven in Pit 3, mostly disposed around the periphery of the pits, and stones in groups were also found in this structure, again largely around the peri-phery and sometimes in conjunction with the hearths. It is suggested that the hunters came in directly from the nearby Zemplen mountains, since the flint found at the base of the pits in finished or blank form comes from this area. About the same number of tools are made of local radiolarite. Other tools were made on much smaller quantities of obsidian, quartz, quartzite and porphyry, the sources of which are not known. The excavators of the Barca sites assumed that these pits represented winter occupation both because finds were made inside the pits only (Banesz,

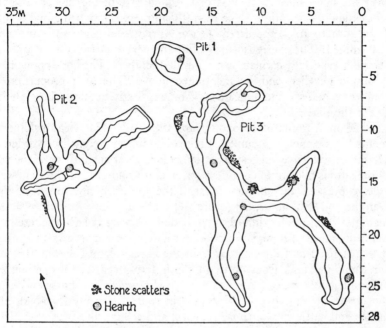

Fig. 18. Plans of dwelling pits, Barca I:2 and I:3, Czechoslovakia (after Banesz, 1968, fig. 8)

1968, p. 59), and because the flint industry was generalized, i.e. not specialized towards hunting. The flint was analysed in what was described as a functional statistical study: twenty-eight artifact types were discussed, including scrapers, borers, knives and hammer-stones. Analysis of the flint material in terms of find zones within the pits suggested that various activities were carried out in different parts of the pits, such as flint-working, hide-working, and bone- and wood-working.

Using ethnographic analogy the excavators have suggested that about five people occupied each pit, so that there would be twenty to twenty-five people in the extended habitations of Barca I (Banesz, 1968, p. 95).

The number of twenty-five correlates with Wobst's suggestion of the minimum band size for Palaeolithic social groups (1974).

The Laugerie-Haute rock-shelter in Les Eyzies, south-west France, was for a long time the only place where the final Aurignacian phase, Aurignacian V, was known. Laugerie-Haute lies on the right bank of the Vézère river, facing south, and the shelter is 180 m long by 35 m wide. There are up to 6 m of Upper Palaeolithic occupation, spread irregularly over the huge shelter. Because of the huge size of the shelter, and the succession of excavations since 1892 (the most extensive being by Peyrony from 1921 to 1935) the extent of the Aurignacian camp-site cannot be determined. The Aurignacian V flint industry consists very largely of scrapers, especially carinated and muzzled scrapers. The bone points have a simple bevelled end, as mentioned above. The high proportion of scrapers would seem to indicate very different activities from those carried out at the Barca sites.

Data on Aurignacian economy are still inadequate. Seasonal movements after game are assumed. Estimates of meat weight from different German caves have suggested a tremendous meat surplus when the size of the sites is taken into consideration. Hahn wonders if the hunters were able to preserve the surplus. Most of the species hunted in the Upper Danube and in Württemberg were those of the steppe – reindeer, horse, mammoth and woolly rhinoceros. Wooded valleys may have sheltered the red deer and ibex. Remains of cave bear and hyena may represent animals that just lived and died naturally in the caves. Hahn suggests that the variations in fauna from north to south across central Europe suggest different faunal zones (1972, p. 83). Thus reindeer and horses occur in the north, mammoth and rhinoceros in south Germany (Swabia), and horses and cattle in Romania, Bulgaria and around the Black Sea. In a similar way Klein reproduces maps of vegetation zones in European Russia during the Würm glaciation (1969a, 1973), suggesting differential availability of animal species. Even further south, at Los Mallaetes and Parpallo in northern Spain, goat was a common feature of the faunal remains (Freeman, 1973). Precise details about animal quarries are urgently needed to test S. Binford's suggestion that much more intensive large-mammal hunting was taking place in the early Upper Palaeolithic than in the Middle Palaeolithic.

Art begins to assume importance in the Aurignacian. Worked bone is much more widespread than in the preceding Mousterian, and decorated bone is known from Spain and south-western France. In the Dordogne blocks of stone were covered in vulvae designs associated with rough animal outlines, cupulae or alignments of little marks. The French caves also produced a few antler objects covered with incised lines or signs. Hahn has also detected a large number of signs at twenty-one of the 100 Aurignacian sites in central and eastern Europe. These consist mainly of different arrangements of little lines, in chevrons, crosses, parallel lines etc. (One interpretation of them is as hunters' tally marks.) An alternative interpretation of Aurignacian and later Palaeolithic art in terms of the symbolic systems will be described later. The Vogelherd site in Germany mentioned above has produced animal figurines showing all the big game types found in the animal fauna (two mammoths, one horse, one cervid, one felid or rhinoceros and one bear). The felid or, more likely, rhinoceros design is covered with red ochre and has a criss-cross design on the belly (see Fig. 17). Three vaguely human figurines are also known from Germany, one of them from Vogelherd itself. They seem to be male, and the 'Venus figurines' do not seem to be associated with the Aurignacian.

Hahn has also discussed the distribution of marine shells found in continental sites in central and eastern Europe. They came from the Mediterranean or the Black Sea. This long-distance transmission of mollusc shells for pendants fits well with the data on stone raw materials in the Carpathian area discussed by J. K. Kozlowski (1972–3). Kozlowski's study covered sites in Poland, Czechoslovakia, Hungary and the western Ukraine. He suggested that the use of imported raw materials occurred occasionally in the Middle Palaeolithic but that each Upper Palaeolithic group had a different pattern of exploitation, production and distribution of the artifacts. In the Aurignacian, local raw materials predominate but they are selected more carefully than in the Middle Palaeolithic: for instance, eastern Slovakian hornstone predominated up to 80 or 90 per cent on sites near the Hornad river, while in south Poland local Jurassic flint accounted for over 93 per cent of assemblages, although radiolarite and obsidian were imported. These exotic materials were imported in the form of unworked blocks, cores, half-made products, and tools. Other materials that travelled considerable distances included felsitic porphyry from the Bükk mountains, and special southern Polish flints. Kozlowski explains this in terms of 200 to 500 km seasonal migrations for quantities represented by under 1 per cent at the distant site (these migrations being basically north–south or east–west), and special expeditions for quantities of over 10 per cent of the assemblage to sites up to 150 to 200 km away, bringing back blocks of the raw material. One possibility is that the sources would be controlled by several groups.

What is claimed to be an early Upper Palaeolithic mine has been located at Balaton-Lovas, Hungary (Meszaros and Vértes, 1955). Here quarrying revealed pits for red clay (limonite) assumed to have been used for body decoration. The limonite would have been visible on the surface, and the miners dug pits down following it. Pit 2 began 1·20 m wide, then widened out to 2·30 m. Most of the clay-scraping bones were of giant deer (*megaloceros*). Bone chisels and red-deer antler were also used to extract the 'paint'.

Ochre and molluscs are often found associated with Aurignacian burials (e.g. at the Combe-Capelle shelter in the Dordogne). Other grave offerings seem to have consisted of flint tools and probably food. A series of three burials from Cueva Morín, Spain, excavated in laboratory conditions, produced unusually detailed information (González Echegaray *et al.*, 1973). The Aurignacian occupation at this Santander cave included a semi-subterranean foundation and a post-hole alignment, slightly east of which were two graves with low mounds over them. The tombs were dug into the earlier Middle Palaeolithic strata by digging-sticks (striations from the sticks showed at the base of the graves). Pseudomorphs of the bodies were revealed by careful excavation: there must have been a delay in decomposition to allow soil-colour differences to give the outline of the vanished bodies. The Morín I body lay extended with the hands near the chest and was probably over 185 cm tall. The head had been removed, and the feet probably mutilated. A quartzite knife, perhaps used in decapitation, was found near the head. A complete ungulate seemed to have been deposited over the chest, and part of a large animal over the legs. The body of Morín I had been covered with a mound of soil from earlier occupations, heaped over a clay-clod wall, with ochre scattered in it. The mound also covered an offering pit with burnt meat and ochre dug near to the legs (González Echegaray *et al.*, 1973) (Fig. 19).

The Morín I grave cut into an earlier grave, numbered Morín III; the older body was partly disturbed by the second interment, but seemed to have suffered amputation of the legs, at least one of which had been burnt. No pseudomorph was obtainable from the second mound burial, Morín II, but it is suggested that a woman or child may have been interred there. A hafted scraper may have formed a funerary offering.

González Echegeray *et al.* feel that the sacred character of the burial area must have persisted through later occupations of the cave, since the mounds were not flattened or reduced to facilitate movement.

CULTURES CONTEMPORARY TO THE AURIGNACIAN

In Hungary, western Slovakia and Transdanubia the first Upper Palaeolithic technocomplex, known as the Szeletian, is considered to have derived directly from the local Middle Palaeolithic. It is best known for

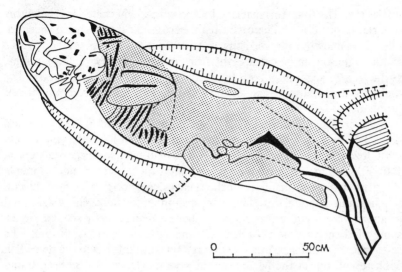

Fig. 19. Pseudomorph of Morín I body and animal offerings, Morín cave, Spain (after Gonzáles and Freeman, 1973, fig. 84)

the prevalence of leaf-points and flat retouch; otherwise the lithic industry is very similar to that of the Aurignacian. The Balaton-Lovas 'mine' is assigned to the Szeletian on the basis of a leaf-point found in the pit. Workshops have been found in the Bükk mountains where typical Szeletian leaf-shaped projectile points have been worked from felsitic porphyry. This group imported spotted Turonian flint from Świechie-chów, south Poland, possibly in distant hunting expeditions. This would have involved them in territorial groupings of about 1000 km² (J. Kozlow-ski, 1972–3).

In south-western France another industry, the Perigordian or Chatel-perronian, is regarded as having emanated from the Mousterian of Acheulian tradition. Perigordian levels often occur above Mousterian levels at the same site. At Creysse, in the Dordogne, where there are six-teen open-air sites in less than 2 km², a Perigordian living floor lies above a Mousterian level (Bordes, 1970a, 1970b). Perigordian industries are characterized by curved-backed knives and the same sort of side-scrapers and denticulates as are found in Mousterian industries. Mousterian-type tools become reduced in subsequent levels of the Perigordian and there is a proportional increase in burins, borers and end-scrapers (de Sonneville-Bordes, 1973, p. 45). Perigordian industries may be as early as approxi-mately 36,000 to 32,000 B.P. and the earliest Perigordian is stratigraphically

earlier than the first Aurignacian. Just as with the Mousterian, sequences
at certain southern French cave sites seem to indicate alternating occupation by people with Perigordian- or Aurignacian-type tools. Whether this
is due to the incoming culture, the Aurignacian, influencing local groups,
as has been suggested both here and for the Szeletian, or whether
again we are seeing the reflection of different activities, is a difficult
problem.

Another type of industry is represented in Italy, with its middle phase
dated before 31,000 B.P. This is the Uluzzian, first located at the Grotta
del Uluzzo (Apulia) and said to be widespread over southern and central
Italy. This is mainly a flake-based industry, including a majority of side
scrapers with marginally retouched flakes, abruptly retouched pieces,
notches and denticulates. There are a number of muzzled or carinated
scrapers, very few burins, and a number of geometrically shaped pieces,
some of them very small indeed (Palma di Cesnola, 1976, p. 71). The
researchers are not sure exactly what relationship this has to the preceding
Mousterian, but at the M. Bernadini cave the Uluzzian has been found
directly above the Mousterian and they both seem to have belonged to the
same climatic phase. The animals hunted change through Uluzzian levels
in the Grotta del Cavallo. From horse, red deer, boar and particularly
cattle, the inhabitants of the cave went over to hunting horse and ass, only
to return again to red deer, boar and cattle in later phases; these changes
may well be linked to climatic oscillations. Barker (1975b) has suggested
continuity of hunting activities from the Mousterian to the Uluzzian,
which might support the hypothesis of general continuity. Above the
Uluzzian levels in Italian caves are the Gravettian levels.

Another series of sites which must be mentioned, and which are certainly partly contemporary with Aurignacian in the rest of Europe, are
those of European Russia. Upper Palaeolithic sites are found in particularly large numbers in the Ukraine, nearly all the known sites being found
in the valleys of the major rivers, from west to east, the Dniester, Dnieper
and the Don. The sites are located on river terraces, and a particularly
good stratigraphic sequence was found on the middle Dniester at the
Molodova V site. Here Mousterian levels were dated older than 44,000
years B.P., and level 11 of the Mousterian occupation included an arc of
mammoth bones, possibly indicating a dwelling. Above this Mousterian
occupation, and divided from it by a sterile loam which probably represents
a longish interstadial, are a series of Upper Palaeolithic levels. The
carbon-14 dates are confusing, as Molodova V level 10 is dated 23,100 and
the lower level 9 has two dates, of 28,000 and 29,000 B.P. Charcoal of
conifers is found in the early Upper Palaeolithic levels, and the presence of

THE UPPER PALAEOLITHIC 79

many soils, none of them well developed, suggests occupation during brief, coolish interstadials. On the basis of pollen diagrams from the Don area, a forest steppe environment is suggested. The presence, together with lots of mammoth bones, of snow lemming and jerboa, whose territories do not overlap today, suggests a climate rather different from any now known. The flint industry was made on prismatic cores and consisted of blades, end-scrapers and burins. Some of the blades were backed and there were rather unusual shouldered bifacial points; tools were also made on bone, antler and ivory (Klein, 1973).

At another site, Kostienki I, carbon-14 dates have been rerun to indicate occupation around 28–29,000 B.P. The pollen diagram suggests forest steppe with a few tree species. Horizon 5 is particularly interesting in that the area where the finds are concentrated is assumed by the excavators to be a habitation structure (Klein, 1969*b*, fig. 18). The finds are concentrated in an oval area some 5 metres in maximum length, and consist of over 1200 flakes, cores and tools. The tools include fifteen points with concave base, forty-one borers, and a number of end- and side-scrapers and burins. There were relatively few blades, and all the cores are for flakes. The industry was mainly made on local flint and quartzite. Also in the oval 'occupation area' were areas of ash, charcoal and spots of ochre. Bones of woolly mammoth, saiga antelope, horse and cattle were found. Data from the Russian sites show a great variety of supposed dwellings, as will be indicated by the examples from late Ukrainian sites given below.

In 1969 a Soviet publication discussed the geology, environment, prehistoric sites and cultural setting of prehistoric society in European Russia (for a review see Perlès, 1971). The Soviet archaeologists concluded that social influence was paramount over environmental pressure during the Palaeolithic. This encouraged them to divide the material from the Ukrainian sites into a series of cultures, based on what Perles describes as 'ill-defined lithic industries, bone, art and habitation types'. The cultures are supposed to have existed in parallel over a very long period of time; for instance, the Molodova culture is supposed to persist on the middle Dniester river from the Mousterian to the end of the Palaeolithic. The assumption of cultural persistence over long periods of time suggests settled conditions, and rather small territories. Similar settled conditions have been suggested, for instance, for south-western France. However, workers like Wobst, operating from a theoretical viewpoint, and J. K. Kozlowski, working on central European assemblages, would see much wider territories (1,250 km² – Wobst, 1974). There are interesting opportunities here for designing research to check on the possible variability of territorial size in the Upper Palaeolithic, and of the possibility for reasonably settled life in environmentally favoured areas.

THE GRAVETTIAN

As indicated in the introduction, Gravettian and Aurignacian industries overlap to some degree in time, according to both geological and carbon-14 dating (see e.g. J. K. Kozlowski, 1965). Hodson made a pioneering statistical evaluation of fifty Upper Palaeolithic assemblages of stone tools,

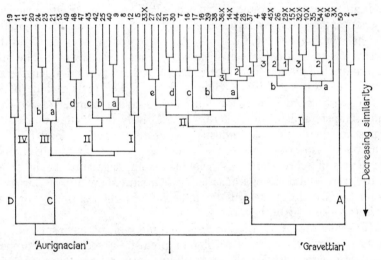

Fig. 20. Average-link cluster analysis of fifty Aurignacian and Gravettian assemblages (after Hodson, 1969, fig. 22)

mostly from the Dordogne, using the de Sonneville-Bordes typology and average-link cluster analysis (see Figure 20) and principal components analysis (1968). Hodson describes the latter as 'a sort of scatter diagram locating the subjects of the analysis on axes which are defined by significant combinations of the variables'.

The first component of the analysis contrasted generalized Aurignacian industries, containing carinated and nosed scrapers, end-scrapers, and blades with Aurignacian retouch, with generalized Gravettian industries containing gravette and related blades, and other backed and truncated blades and burins (see Fig. 21). The second component seemed to be comparing early 'Mousterian-derived' tool types from more 'progressive' types like dihedral and angle burins. The third component

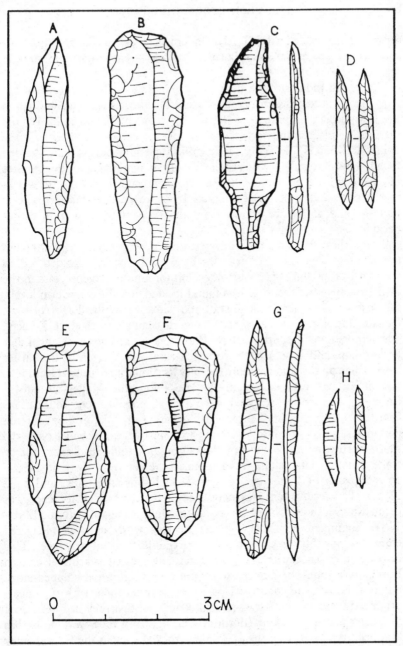

Fig. 21. Gravettian tool types (after Palma di Cesnola 1976, fig. 5, nos. 1, 3, 5, 10–14)

separated out specialized tools found at only a few sites. The results of this analysis help to explain some of the difficulties encountered in straight one-to-one assemblage comparisons.

Gravettian industries are defined by more varied tool types than the Aurignacian; there is a greater emphasis on blades, usually smaller than in the Aurignacian, and much 90° ('backed') retouch. This is applied to the margins of blades, and to the broken apex of blades, in order to make points and borers, etc. There are a great variety of burins (chisel-ended tools). This flint industry was economic of raw material, and the presence of so many little points and burins would presumably make the working of bone and antler easier. Certainly, more artifacts and art objects in bone and antler are known from the Gravettian than from earlier periods.

The earliest dates for the Gravettian are about 29,000 B.P., although the date may have been earlier in the Ukraine. It lasts to c. 20,000 B.P. in western Europe but continues to develop for another 10,000 years in the east. In many stratified sites it is found located above Aurignacian levels, for instance in such widely scattered sites as Willendorf (Austria), Geissenklosterle (Germany) and Laugerie-Haute (south-west France). The Gravettian in south-western France is often known as the Later Perigordian, and is sometimes regarded as a continuation of the earlier Perigordian phases, though more recently its similarity to central European Gravettian has been accepted. A 'late Perigordian' open-air site at Corbiac has recently revealed a couple of possible tent foundations (Bordes, 1968b). The first tent was defined as an irregular oval by fourteen post-holes, and was approximately 3 m long by 1·40 m wide. Near the south-western entrance was a pit containing flakes and blades and a large stone. Another large stone was located in the centre of the tent. Nearly 10,000 pieces of flint were recovered, including 481 tools, and 1482 blades. The second tent was only excavated over 2 m of its length, as defined by seven post-holes. It lay north–south, as opposed to the ENE–WSW alignment of Tent 1. Three hearths with 'tails' or elongated entrances, possibly flues, are located between the two tent structures. This provides a contrast with the often internally located hearths of eastern Europe. An interesting micro-wear study of twenty-five chipped-stone points from the site contrasted marks of wear on them with the effects produced by working on leather, and concluded that they had been used in leather-garment making (Bordes, 1974, fig. 6). A hide-working kit has also been reported from the Le Malpas rock shelter in the Couze valley to the south of the Dordogne valley (Montet-White, 1973). This shelter was used as a summer camp in the Early Perigordian and as an autumn or winter camp in the Late Perigordian, suggesting some change in activities, possibly associated with changing climate and animal behaviour.

In central Europe, J. K. Kozlowski considers that the first phase of Gravettian industries commenced in the second half of the cold Würm 2. The second phase of Gravettian industries developed during the more temperate period, of Würm 2 to 3a, and continued into 3a; it is represented by groups in Moravia, the valley of the Waag, Lower Austria and western Slovakia. These groups would be active in the years 25,000 to 17,000 B.P. Although all the Gravettian cultures used the various flint tool types described above, regional differences could be seen in the predominance of scrapers or burins in the assemblages. During the subsequent development of the Würm 3 glaciation, the Waag valley and lower Austria Gravettian groups continued to flourish, while other groups as defined by Kozlowski are found in the Dniester valley and the eastern Carpathians. The fourth phase – post 15,000 B.P. – described in the literature as the Late Gravettian and Epigravettian, is contemporary with the introduction of Magdalenian elements from western into central Europe.

One of the most famous Moravian sites is Dolní Věstonice, situated on the hill of Pollau, commanding good views, and with nearby springs. It was excavated in the 1920s, when the famous 'Venus' figurine was found, and again in 1947–52 (Klima, 1963) (there was a total of six levels of occupation). A fairly cold climate is suggested by the molluscs, the charcoal and the pollen from the site. Spruce and pine were used to make fires, suggesting a forest tundra environment. Two possible structures (see Fig. 22) are described by Klima, the first roughly oval in shape, 15 m long × 9 m wide. This very large structure contained five hearths, most of them with large blocks of limestone nearby. The hearths seemed to have been the focus for most activity, judging by the number of finds made near them. The excavators wonder if small ash-filled pits near the hearths represent storage places. More than 35,000 pieces of flint were found in the habitation area, and it appeared that flint working was carried out in the centre and north of the structure. Chipped-stone tools were made on local chalk flint and hornstone and on Carpathian radiolarite. Mammoth-bone artifacts, shells and ochre were also found in the structure, particularly near the southern two hearths. The walls of the structure are presumed to have been of limestone blocks, perhaps surmounted in some way by shoulder-blades and pelves of mammoths; the excavators feel this may have been a summer structure, open to the sky. Klima's plan of the hut excavation and surrounding trenches (Klima, 1963, fig. 40) reveals that a relatively clear space existed to the south-east of the hut, followed by

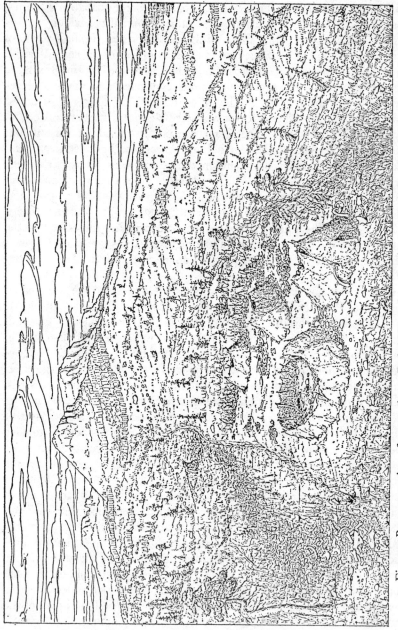

Fig. 22. Reconstruction of camp-site at Dolní Věstonice, Czechoslovakia (after Klíma, 1963, fig. 69)

enormous piles of mammoth bones. These were excavated in 1952 and revealed the remains of approximately one hundred, mostly young, individuals, with rarer bones of horse, reindeer, hare, wolf and fox. A series of hearths lay below the bone accumulations. No projectile points were found, and the excavators suggest that the mammoths could have been hunted by using ivory projectile points or wooden lances (Klima, 1963).

The second hut was about 6 m in diameter, with a central hearth and five of the original post-holes remaining. The most important artifacts were some 2000 lumps of burnt clay found near the central hearth, some of them bearing finger-prints, others modelled in the shape of animal heads (bear, wolf and fox). The excavators wondered if this 'special activity' hut belonged to a shaman. A child buried at Dolní Věstonice III had a necklace of twenty-seven pierced fox teeth; the skull area was covered with red ochre, and the whole burial lay beneath mammoth shoulder-blades. The elaborate treatment suggests that the child had some importance in the community.

Klima believes that Dolní Věstonice was occupied specifically for mammoth hunting, and that with as many as twenty to twenty-five people per hut, and a postulated five or six huts being occupied at a time on the site, the occupants may have been 100–120 strong. The length of stay each season, and the possible length of use of the site, have not been estimated.

Banesz has recently reviewed the evidence for habitation structures in central Europe, and remarked on the fact that one third of those known lie in Czechoslovakia. Extensive sites are known from Pavlov. Here eleven 'habitation units' are known, and the site is still being excavated. The structures are circular, oval and 'pinched in at the centre', all contain hearths, and there is evidence for the re-use of post-holes. This led the excavators to suggest long occupation at the site (Klima, 1976). Klima regards the Pavlovian as a specialized mammoth-hunting industrial complex, on the cold loess country of central and eastern Europe. Other authors have suggested that the mammoth bones could have been scavenged rather than hunted (Klein, 1973). The more remarkable aspects of the assemblage at Pavlovian sites are the mammoth-bone and ivory industries (Fig. 23) which include possible earth-working tools – shovels, hoes, pickaxes – and spear-points. Klima has suggested that the mammoth-hunters of Pavlov had complex and specialized hunting methods, including verbal signalling on bone pipes (found in the assemblage), and collective large-group organization. Emphasis on mammoth is overwhelming, but other animal remains are found on the sites. For instance, at Predmost, apart from a large quantity of mammoth, remains of reindeer, horse, wolf,

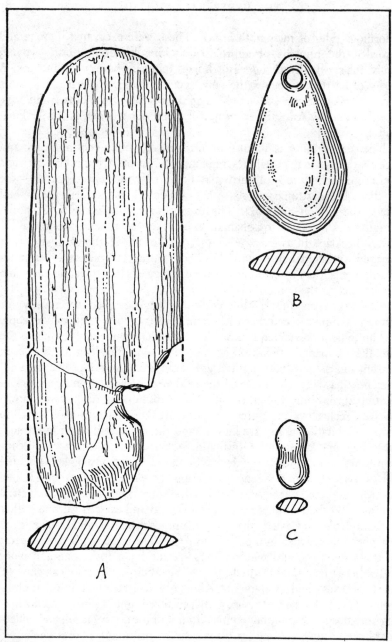

Fig. 23. Mammoth-rib mattock (A) and mammoth-ivory pendants (B and C) (after Klíma, 1968, fig. 4)

fox, glutton and hare were identified (Klima, 1963, p. 22). Very recently, habitation structures have been discovered at Cracow in Poland (Kozlowski and Kubiak, 1972). Three dwellings have been found, more than 90 per cent of the bones making up their structure being of *Mammuthus primigenius*, especially mammoth lower jaws, tusks, scapulae and pelvic bones. The dwellings are about 2 m in diameter; they lie 1 m apart, and hearths are found between them. Flint artifacts are found at the southern side of the dwellings. The excavators consider that on a foundation of lower jaws, scapulae and long bones, the inhabitants of the Cracow site built up a structure of tusks, ribs and vertebrae, which, possibly, they covered with animal skins (Pl. 3b). Other animals represented in the finds are woolly rhinoceros, bear, horse, reindeer and arctic fox. Of the approximately sixty mammoths represented at this site, the majority were young or semi-adult. It is suggested that the site represented a long-stay occupation. Among the finds was a tanged point located in a mammoth rib, where it had presumably been used for cutting and hollowing.

It can be assumed from the sites discussed above that the meat available from the vast amount of mammoth and other animals slaughtered would provide sufficient nutriment for long stays by their inhabitants. More precise work along these lines has been done on two south German caves. In the Weinberg cave overlooking a wide valley, the majority of meat weight was provided by animals from the tundra and cold steppe zones (e.g. 19,000 lb (8600 kg) out of 21,200 lb (9600 kg)). However, at the Brillen cave in the narrower, milder Ach valley quite a good proportion was represented by animals living on the forest edge (Hahn, 1976*b*). The tundra animals are the mammoth and reindeer, the forest-edge species cave bear and cave wolf, while chamois and cattle could exist in either environment.

In a very different area, Camerota, south-west Italy, Barker has indicated that after an interstadial *c*. 40,000 B.P., the environment became comparatively colder and drier, though warmer, of course, than continental Europe. Although red deer provided the mainstay of the (meat) diet during both the Middle and Upper Palaeolithic, Barker suggests that there was a change in the pattern of exploitation from animals mainly three to eight years old (Grotta del Poggio, Mousterian levels) to animals of the same ages, but also in their first year (Grotta della Cala, Gravettian levels dated 27,000 ± 1700 B.P.) (Barker 1975*b*). If grazing conditions had been good, the deer might have attained adult size by the time they were twelve months old, otherwise, the change in exploitation or management is difficult to understand.

THE SOLUTREAN

The Solutrean technocomplex seems to have originated in south-western and south-central France, and spread from there to the Pyrenees and into Catalonia and the Asturias (de Sonneville-Bordes, 1973). There are carbon-14 dates from about 21,000 B.P. to c. 16,000 B.P. (21,700 to 16,300 B.P. at Los Mallaetes, Spain, 20,898 at Laugerie-Haute, Dordogne). It seems to be confined to the Franco-Iberian area, though the importance of laurel-leaf points in Solutrean assemblages has provoked suggestions of an ultimate derivation from the Szeletian. Generally, however, Solutrean levels are situated above Upper Perigordian (= Gravettian) in France and northern Spain, and below Magdalenian levels. De Sonneville-Bordes and others have indicated the importance of unifacial points in the Lower Solutrean, laurel-leaf points in the Middle Solutrean, and willow-leaf and notched points in the Late Solutrean. Other components of Solutrean assemblages are side-scrapers and points, end-scrapers and borers, and the eyed needle in bone.

Collins has recently analysed the industries of Level 12C (Lower Solutrean, c. 20,000 B.P.) and Level 10 (Middle Solutrean, c. 19,000 B.P.) at Laugerie-Haute West, by dividing them into different product groups. Group I is the product of acquisition of raw material, and the succeeding groups reflect different stages of manufacture and refinement (Collins, 1975). Variation can be seen between the two industries in that Level 12C contains no imported materials in Group I, whereas Level 10 contains a few pieces of jasper; and in that Level 12C contains no products of secondary trimming – Group IV – whereas nearly 6000 flakes and thirty-three broken bifacial tools fall into this category in Level 10. Collins explains this discrepancy by the fact that bifacial trimming creates a lot of flakes per implement, and that forty bifaces and laurel leaves were recognized in Level 10.

A different Solutrean industry has been excavated at the Le Malpas rock-shelter, mentioned above for its Perigordian occupation. Le Malpas is a south-facing rock-shelter 50 m long by 10 m wide, but with only sufficient overhang to form a proper roof at the eastern end. Excavation carried out in the shelter and around a flint outcrop in front of it produced a workshop assemblage, with lots of chunks and split nodules, cortex flakes and small debris (the early groups of Collins's terminology). The excavator considered that nodules, flakes and blades and processing tools (possibly for wood, bone and antler working) were being manufactured at Le Malpas, in contrast to the production of hunting and butchering kits at Laugerie-Haute (Montet-White, 1973). The Le Malpas industry was classified on the basis of a polar grid (Fig. 24), where a set of measurements could be taken for data storage and retrieval. Using the measurements, a principal components analysis will extract factors relating to the size of tool blanks, shape of working area, orientation of the blank or handle, and other features. In addition to the local flint, some Dordogne-valley flint was present on the site, presumably the tool-kit of each occupant at the

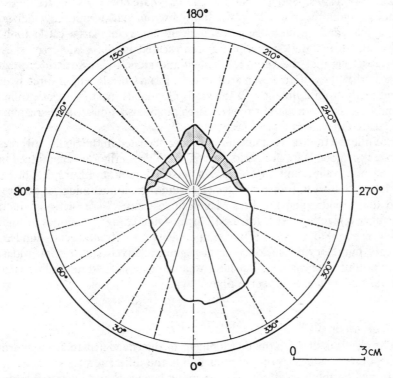

Fig. 24. Measuring an artifact from Le Malpas, France, on a polar grid (after Montet-White, 1973, fig. 25)

beginning of the seasonal occupation. Montet-White considers that spring or autumn was the most likely time for occupation of the site, as in the relatively warm humid summers of warm oscillations in Würm III–IV the reindeer would be at much higher altitudes than the rock-shelter, and in winter probably lower down.

The Cantabrian and Basque Solutrean has recently been reviewed by Straus, who has studied the artifacts, faunal remains and location of thirty-six sites. Two interesting patterns emerge, which are confirmed by principal components analysis. In the rugged Basque country, which lacks wide valleys or a coastal plain, the main animals represented were ibex and chamois, plus smaller fur-bearing animals such as fox. The main artifacts were burins, truncated pieces and backed blades, with relatively few typical Solutrean points. By contrast, many Solutrean points, plus many end- and side-scrapers and notched pieces, are found on the Cantabrian sites. Here the countryside was more open, with wider valleys and a larger area of coastal plain. This environment permitted woodland and grassland species like the red deer, horse and large cattle to be dominant, and they are regularly represented in the Cantabrian sites. Straus feels that the very clear faunal and stone-tool associations must mean that the differences in artifact assemblages result 'either directly or indirectly from differences in the kinds of animals most frequently killed and processed', though further research might also indicate some regional stylistic differences as well (1976).

While the traditions of fine flint-making persisted in the Solutrean areas to c. 17–16,000 B.P., industries derived from the Perigordian continued in the Rhône valley, and the Gravettian persisted in most of Europe. The Le Malpas Solutrean industry dates (according to sedimentological studies) to the period when the first Magdalenian camps were being made at Laugerie-Haute West (Guichard, 1976). Our dating techniques are not fine enough to be sure of contemporaneity to within several hundred years, but the evidence does seem to suggest relatively sparse populations, with limited exchange of males, at least, to enable flint traditions to persist side by side for some time.

MAGDALENIAN

The classical sites for the development of the Magdalenian are found in the Vézère valley. In the limestone cliffs the different stages are distinguished on the basis of the accompanying bonework in the stratigraphies of caves such as La Madeleine, the type-site, and the shelter of Laugerie-Haute. To the north of the Vézère valley much harder problems are faced by excavators in the Isle valley. Here more than twenty open-air sites are known in a 15-km area; at ten or more of them, rock pavements have been found. Sackett and Gaussen (1976) have indicated that most sites contain just one pavement, but the Solvieux site, one hectare of which has been investigated, has produced many. The rock pavements are very variable in size, from 4 m² to 27 m². They also vary as regards associations with tools and flint debris at the different sites. For instance, no tools or debris are found inside the pavement area at Plateau Parrain, while the pavement itself and the outside area is covered with flint at Le Mas. At Le Cerisier artifacts and debris were found on the outer margins of the rock platform. The difficulties in estimating what these different distributions mean in terms of activities is particularly great because of the lack of bone and charcoal in the Isle Valley sites. At Solvieux there are fourteen archaeological levels, each of them with one or more distinct occupations or lenses, and one rock pavement per archaeological level (Fig. 25). These vary between very large pavements and possible stone-boiling pits in lenses I and II, and limestone-block structures, one with a possible hearth, in lens IV. Other hut floors may have been excavated from the contemporary ground surface. The industries found in the archaeological levels are made of rocks and flint. There are chipping areas for the flint, but there is not a clearly patterned distribution of tools. Publication of a series of monographs on the site is obviously going to be of outstanding importance for Palaeolithic studies.

Sackett and Gaussen have to look back to the Vézère valley assemblages to find data on economy. Magdalenian economy in the Dordogne seems to have been based mainly on the reindeer, except for the warmer phases towards its end, when more red deer are represented. However, it must be recalled that when animal bones are being analysed they do not necessarily represent the proportions in which the species roamed in the area, or even all the species that were available. Delpech has produced a diagram based on one of every hundred fragments attributed to each species throughout the Würm epoch (Delpech and Prat, 1976), which demonstrates the presence of reindeer, red deer, cattle, horse, and fur-bearing animals in the Dordogne area. It also indicates a certain amount of geographic variability, as where for instance, in the high valleys of the French Pyrenees, the goat is the major species hunted at the end of Würm IV.

On the other side of the Pyrenees, Freeman has analysed the patterns of settlement and economy in Cantabria during the Magdalenian (1973). There are thirteen sites belonging to this period, and they mostly lie further inland or further seaward than in previous periods. Freeman does not regard these as 'central bases'. He suggests that there was a consistent increase in the number of mammal species exploited from the Aurignacian onwards, and also of the species of molluscs exploited. Some animals were more dangerous to catch, e.g. boar and lynx. In fact, there was 'regional specialization'. Some groups systematically went in for a single wild resource, for instance red deer, as represented in level 4, El Juyo. Freeman hypothesizes about the use of game surrounds or drives with 'previously unprecedented numbers of hunters'. He sees an increase in specialization during the different seasons, and perhaps special extractive practices, for

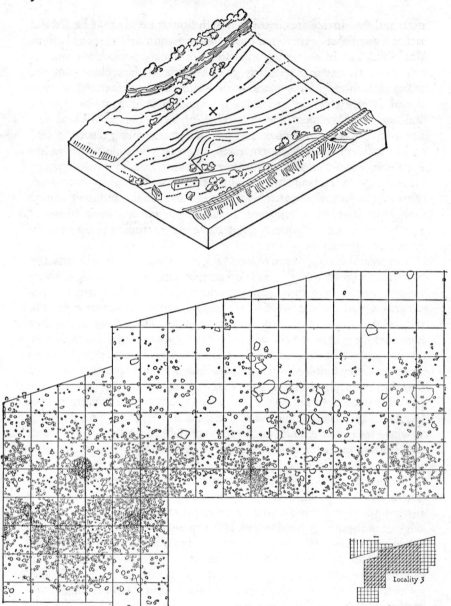

Fig. 25. Solvieux, France, Late Palaeolithic site with enlargement of Magdalenian rock-scatter at Locality 3 (after Sackett and Gaussen, 1976, figs. 5 and 6) (x on site plan indicates Locality 3)

instance to obtain molluscs. However, he suggests that this system changed back to the more generalized earlier system towards the end of the Magdalenian and the beginning of the Azilian.

In central Europe a number of Magdalenian sites have been described. Along the middle terrace of the Rhine, 50 m above the present-day level of the river, and facing another Magdalenian site on the opposite bank, lies the Magdalenian settlement of Feldkirchen-Gönnersdorf The excavation report, which included plans in colour, suggested that a circular structure approximately 6 m in diameter with an entrance to the south-east, a red-stained hearth, and several small pits had probably been a tent covered with fox pelts; it was accompanied by a smaller structure, $2\frac{1}{2}$ m in diameter, without a hearth (Bosinski, 1969). Groups of stones around the perimeter of the first 'tent' may indicate now-vanished post-holes. It was suggested that the little pits might have been used as caches, or for depositing rubbish. The external line of the second tent was marked by a rim of large stones, but there were no groups of stones as around structure I. A rough pavement of stones covered the 3-m area between the first and second tents. The chipped-stone tools were found generally scattered across the site, with most nuclei being found between the two tents The industry consisted of 60 per cent quartzite tools and waste, and 40 per cent Nordic flint, the nearest source of which was the Lower Rhine, 150 km away. Backed knives and burins were the most prominent elements in the industry, with scrapers and borers also being represented. The majority of the fauna consisted of wild horse, followed by fox (these may have been hunted for their skins), with rare representatives of reindeer, red deer, mammoth, rhinoceros and bovids. There were also mollusc remains. Several fragments of wood were analysed and proved to be 95 per cent conifers, with occasional oak, holly and ash. The opal phytoliths of plants indicated sparse vegetation.

The occupants of this tented encampment spent a great deal of their time manufacturing schist plaques decorated with engravings. Over 500 of these have been found. They are carved on plaques 10 to 30 cm in length, made of schist from beds approximately 500 m away and quartzite obtainable from the Rhine. The art works have been dated to Magdalenian VI by Bordes and Narr (in Bosinski, 1969, p. 34). There is a carbon-14 date from the site of approximately 13,000 B.P.

Further south in Thuringia a cave excavated in the 1930s has recently been re-analysed and the results published (Feustel, 1974). This is the Magdalenian VI site of the Kniegrotte near Dobritz. The carbon-14 date of 10,230 ± 90 B.P. was made on a very small sample of charcoal from a hearth possibly later than the main occupation. From the evidence of molluscs and vertebrates (Dryas II to Alleröd climatic periods) the site should be at least 10,000 years old. Feustel claims that the cave was occupied during the winter months, and that a tent was erected in front of it during the summer. It was reoccupied every few years. Structures included hearths and slabs of sandstone shale brought to the site and arranged in a rough pavement. Most of the charcoal remains are of pine and birch, and the fauna consisted of wild horses plus reindeer, especially the forest form, and a wide range of other mammals including the Saiga antelope, the arctic fox and the red deer. These are estimated to have produced about 10,000 kg in meat weight, which, given 0·6 of a kilogram minimum per man-day might have lasted between one and four generations. The small body size and shortened facial bones of the wolf found on the site, it is suggested, indicate that these animals may already have been 'domesticated' for the hunt (1974, p. 212). Evidence of long-distance movements by the inhabitants of the Kniegrotte are the presence of tertiary molluscs which may have come from the Rhine-Main region or the Paris or the Belgian basins. In addition, flint was obtained from the glacial moraines on the southern edge of the north German plain. Other materials used for the chipped-stone industry included cherts obtainable from near the cave and quartzite possibly deriving from north-western Bohemia. These materials were made into microlithic triangles, backed blades, burins, long awls, saws and spear-points. Over 100 of them were found to have wear marks in the shape of edge rounding, scratches and grooves.

Even further south, in Switzerland, excavations in the canton of Bern at the site of Moosbühl I revealed another Magdalenian camp-site. An excavation trench 84 m in length along the top of a sand-hill contained zones full of bones and flint separated by sterile areas. A couple of possible tent floors were found. Tent 2 consisted of a large number of post-holes surrounding two hearths (Schwab, 1969–70, plan 5). The hearths were nearly 1 m in diameter, and contained charcoal of spruce, birch and hazel. The tent appears to have been about 8 m². Tent 1 lay 30 m away from Tent 2 and was not fully excavated; it was estimated to be about 9 m in diameter. The hearth here was less clearly defined, and there were no post-holes. The presence of nuclei and waste flakes indicated that flint was worked on the site. Over 13,000 flakes were found near Tent 1 and over 17,000 near Tent 2. This site produced carbon-14 dates of 10,300 ± 180 B.P. for the bottom of the hearth and 8,440 ± 120 B.P. for the top of the hearth. It is suggested that these are rather late by comparison with the artifact industries. The remains of bones and teeth are all from ungulates except for two fragments from reindeer.

In discussing the faunal remains from the Kniegrotte, Feustel indicated that in Thuringia there were two hunting practices in the Magdalenian period, one based on horses and one based on reindeer. A recent study by Sturdy (1975) on north German and Swiss reindeer hunting has suggested that hunters followed the reindeer and set up their camps near the reindeer migration termini. This study was part of the British Academy Origin of Agriculture project, which is looking into man–animal relationships over the whole of the Palaeolithic and later periods, and emphasizes the study of areas around archaeological sites and their potential in terms of food value of the floral and faunal populations ('site catchment analysis'). Sturdy suggests that the hunters occupied the north German plain during the winter months, then during the summer followed the reindeer in their migration towards higher ground in southern Germany and Switzerland or south Scandinavia. One of the camp sites was the Brillenhöhle, a south German cave, where the age structure of reindeer remains in level 7 has indicated that men only occupied it in summer. In winter, cave bears used it as their lair. The occupants of the Brillenhöhle built hearths with lumps of limestone and a series of stone structures including a wall 95 cm high. It is suggested that this cave would have sheltered between five and ten people. Sturdy's suggestions about reindeer migrations and the movements of their hunters follow similar suggestions by Bouchud about reindeer migrations from lowland Aquitaine to the west of the Massif Central (1966). Leroi-Gourhan and Brezillon have also suggested reindeer migration between the Paris basin and the north of the Massif Central (1972). The latter were concerned about the relationships between men and reindeer at the site of Pincevent in the Paris basin.

The site report on Pincevent is a model of what careful recording and subsequent laboratory research can obtain from very fragmentary remains. The site of Pincevent is a complex one where Magdalenian occupation covers $1\frac{1}{2}$ ha in finely stratified flood clays. At least four late Magdalenian levels are represented. The 1972 publication covered section 36 (Fig. 26), a 600 m² exposure of one Magdalenian occupation. The 1:10 plans provide an imaginative reconstruction of the most important parts of the site. In all, twenty-three hearths were discovered in section 36 and they have been distinguished into: larger elaborate ones; those consisting of pits and stones; and flat hearths. The larger elaborate ones may represent habitation units, and the flat hearths may have been associated with some flint working. The activities carried out around the pit hearths are not clear. The main habitation units are centred in squares T112, V105 and L115. Of these, T112 and V105 are regarded as broadly contemporary, and L115 as rather later. The size of the habitation units is broadly similar, between 60 and 70 m². Structurally the habitation units are divided by the

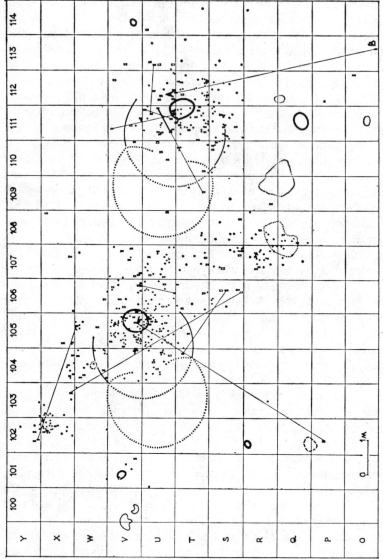

Fig. 26. Plan of distribution of burins and their spalls, Pincevent Magdalenian site, France (after Leroi-Gourhan and Brezillon, 1972, fig. 27)

excavators into a central area and evacuation areas (rubbish disposal); area A consists of the hearth itself, area B the zone of domestic activities, area C the interior of the supposed hut, and areas D to G the evacuation units. These conclusions are obtained on the basis of thirty-nine plans of the distributions of fragments of the various raw materials found on the site: worked stone, bone, antler, heated rocks, etc. The links between fragments of original pieces of flint or bone are shown by straight lines.

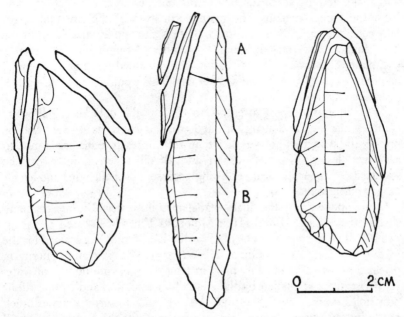

Fig. 27. Burins and spalls from Pincevent (the location of the two fragments, A and B, of the middle burin is marked on Figure 26) (after Leroi-Gourhan and Brezillon, 1972, fig. 28)

The excavators are trying to establish the relationship between the manu-facture, use and discard of the tools (Fig. 27). Bone working and flint working seem to have taken place mostly to the west of the hearths; ochre is widespread all around the hearth area but is most strongly represented to the west. The scatter of heated stones, on the other hand, tails away from the hearth in a broadly south-easterly direction.

Analysis of the flint revealed that finished objects in non-local flint seemed to have been brought in by the hunters. By far the majority of the over 16,000 pieces of flint present, however, came from the chalk with flint of the local Seine cliffs. Leroi-Gourhan and Brezillon have shown clearly how the cores and the flakes taken from them can be reconstituted, and how secondary flaking to make burins (chisel-edge tools) can be reconstructed by the location of the burin cores far from the finished tools. An example of curation or deliberate deposit is the tidy arrangement of piles of blades and bladelets to the west of a subsidiary hearth, number 1101. Similar curation is probably represented by the 'hoard' of cores and blades found at the Sesselfels cave, Bavaria (Freund, 1974/5).

A major activity at Pincevent was the butchering of reindeer. Judging from the faunal remains, the main occupation of the site took place between June and August, although there is a possibility that it may have been longer, between May and September. Assuming a five months occupation, however, each habitation unit, assumed to be of five people, could have eaten 850 g per person per day. This would mean that reindeer meat was the most important item of the diet.

The Pincevent report attempts to explain the data revealed by its complex planning and analyses, but Leroi-Gourhan has stressed that he prefers to 'sketch a ghost' rather than to 'impress the materials into an arbitrary design' (Leroi-Gourhan and Brezillon, 1972, p. 260). The standards of reporting and recording represent a challenging model for other archaeologists.

Contemporary with the final Magdalenian in western Europe are many sites in the Ukraine. Level III at Molodova V has been dated 11,740 ± 540 B.P. The site contains one of the many bone 'ruins', described for the Middle and Late Palaeolithic by Klein (1973). The excavator, Chernysh, revealed an irregular shallow pit 5 m long by a maximum of 4 m wide. Its perimeter was defined by the edge of a depression and by sixty-four post-holes running along the edge. A large central hearth occupies much of the internal space. Four of the five internal pits are closely associated with it, and it is suggested that these may have been used as caches. The site produced unretouched flint, retouched flint and animal bones. Most of the unretouched flint is found in zones along the western side. The excavators speculate that the post-holes upheld wooden posts arranged in a vaguely conical structure, which could be covered by skins. The structure and reconstruction are illustrated by Klein (1973, fig. 25).

A very different structure described by Klein comes from the loess-like loams overlying the upper humic bed in the Kostienki-Borshevo terraces. Kostienki I, Horizon I, was excavated in the 1930s, and reconstructed as a 'long house' 35 m long by approximately 16 m wide (Fig. 28). This colossal area encompassed nine hearth pits, mostly down the centre line of the structure, and sixteen large pits around the periphery, four of them interpreted as sleeping areas and twelve as caches, full of mammoth bone.

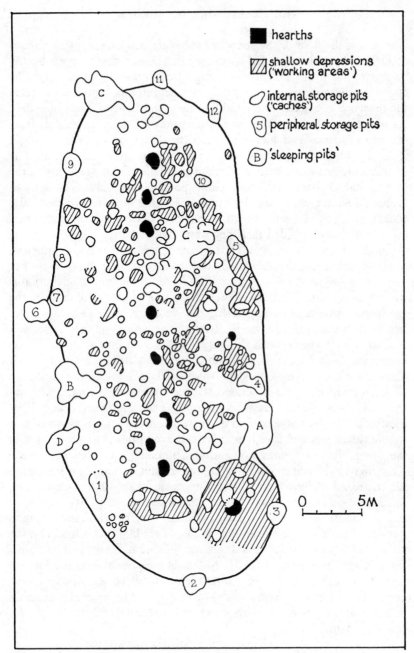

Fig. 28. Plan of Horizon I house, Kostienki I, Ukraine (after Klein, 1973, fig. 24)

The rest of the floor of the supposed structure was covered with a series of little pits, again regarded as caches. Klein is not convinced by the interpretation of the structure as a single long house (1969*b*, p. 121). The agglomeration of features is certainly of great interest, however, as is also the presence of a series of animal figurines, and bone artifacts including possible 'head' bands with incised decoration. Six female figurines from the site were made of local limestone (marl) and ivory (Klein, 1969*b*) (Fig. 29). Many fragmentary remains of figurines were also found. The figurines are decorated with bands incised around the waist and above the breast. Larger bone artifacts include possible mattocks. The famous Kostienki points, which are elongated flint points with an asymmetrically placed tang, have been examined by Semenov for evidence of microwear (1964). He has concluded that they were used as knives.

Another Kostienki site, No. IV, Horizon I, consisted of two depressions 6 m apart and approximately 6 m in diameter, considered to represent hut floors. The original huts may have been larger as the finds distribution is wider than that of the actual depressions and extends particularly to the south-west where, it is suggested, the doorway was. The excavators believe that points with burin facets on the proximal end may have been used as whittle knives, with the burin end inserted into a handle. Other interesting finds from this site include ground slate discs 3 to 6 cm in diameter which, it is suggested, were used to retouch the flints. In addition there were dot-decorated stylized figurines in ivory, and ivory rods and bone 'clothes fasteners'. Bones from Horizons I and II at Kostienki IV were not separated during excavation, but it is assumed that woolly rhinoceros and cave lion at least derived from Horizon I. As with the other Ukrainian sites previously mentioned, pits occurred in the Kostienki IV-I habitation units, the western hut containing eight pits in the centre, all under a layer of heavy grey ash. In the eastern depression, there were six ash-filled pits and others which seemed to have served as caches. Sandstone slabs around the periphery may have had something to do with the original wall structure, and two cave lion crania found on the top of the deposit are suggested to have been used to crown the original tents. Klein has suggested that from the calories available in the form of animals the different sites in the Kostienki-Borshevo region could have been occupied from as long as forty-three days to four years. He suggests that the sites represent longish occupation, probably during the winter (1969*b*, p. 219).

East European archaeologists are particularly interested in the origin of raw materials used in Palaeolithic sites, and in the wear marks visible on the retouched tools; for instance, at the Kostienki sites, brown and

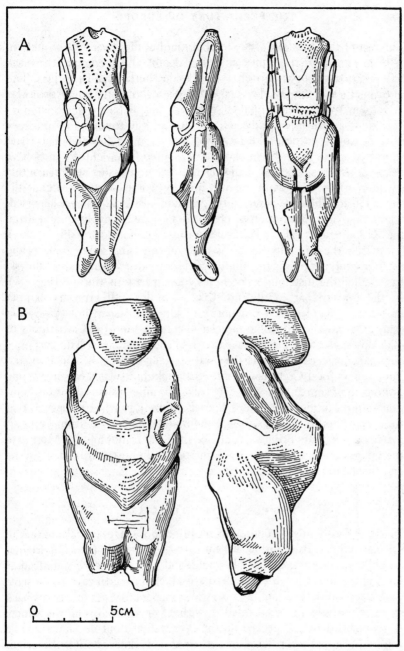

Fig. 29. Female figurines from Kostienki I, Horizon I, Ukraine (after Klein 1969*b*, figs. 43 and 44)

yellow flint and quartzite are of local origin, but the black flint brought in as blanks is not. Petrographic analysis has proved that some of the black flint comes from approximately 150 km to the south-west, from the valleys of the Valuj and the Oskol rivers. Other black flint may come from as far as 300 km away (Klein, 1969*b*, p. 227).

Kozlowski has recently discussed flint mines in southern Poland, one near Cracow, one near Częstochowa, and one near Radom. The latter source produces magnificent chocolate-coloured flint. All these sites have deep extraction shafts and shallower pits. In the Polish Late Palaeolithic (Swiderian) the flint extracted was initially worked near by, e.g. at the site of Gojac. Then pre-cores, initial cores and blank blades were exported. There is a vast distribution of chocolate flint, presumably coming from the Radom mines, along the River Vistula (J. K. Kozlowski, 1972-3). Away from the source sites there is a greater concentration of artifacts and less flint-working debris than in the workshops near the mines. Kozlowski has studied the distribution of flint types in eastern Europe (Fig. 30). In the western part of Poland, Czechoslovakia and Hungary, Upper Palaeolithic peoples used a majority of Upper Silesian flint (76–87 per cent in Moravia), with some radiolarite coming from the Carpathians or the Alps in second place. In eastern Slovakia and east Hungary, the dominant material used was the local obsidian and in the Dneister and Punt valleys local Cretaceous flint. Kozlowski has suggested inter-group ownership of source areas, or early barter, as an explanation for distribution patterns of flint and other materials (1972–3, p. 17). He suggests that these trade routes began in the Paudorf interstadial, i.e. from approximately 30,000 years B.P. One route led from the Danube to the Morava to the Oder, and another from the Dniester to the east Carpathian passes, and thence to the Carpathian basins.

UPPER PALAEOLITHIC ART

There is hardly any recognizable art prior to the Upper Palaeolithic in Europe. Upper Palaeolithic art consists of mobiliary (small, portable) art objects, sculpture in the half-round, and parietal or cave-wall decoration. There is a wide variety of decorative techniques. In cave art, designs were traced in the mud on the cave walls; engraved or pecked with a hard stone or possibly antler; painted in outline; or painted in blown colour. A mammoth figure is pecked on the cave wall at Font-de-Gaume while another mammoth is painted in outline at Rouffignac, both of the caves being in south-west France. Half-relief sculpture is known from rare clay designs modelled on rocks, like the famous bisons from Tuc d'Audoubert,

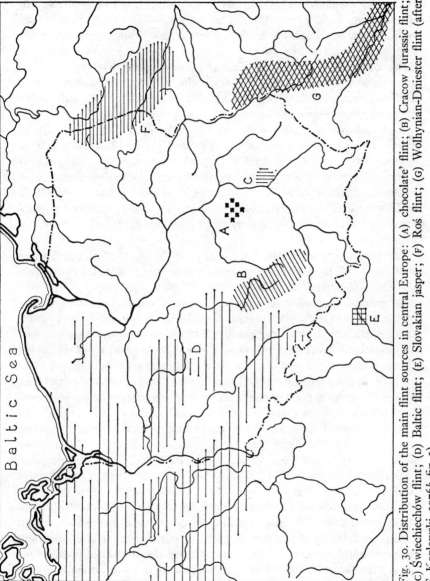

Fig. 30. Distribution of the main flint sources in central Europe: (A) chocolate' flint; (B) Cracow Jurassic flint; (C) Świechiechów flint; (D) Baltic flint; (E) Slovakian jasper; (F) Roś flint; (G) Wolhynian–Dniester flint (after S. Kozlowski, 1976b, fig. 1)

Ariège. There are also relief sculptures in stone, the most famous being the Venus of Laussel. Mobiliary art has recently been discussed by Delporte (1976), who divides it into organic and non-organic materials, and examines the possible constraints and influences on design caused by the composition itself and by the size and shape of the raw materials (reindeer antler, quartzite cobbles, etc.). Even the raw materials need not confine a determined craftsman, however (witness the bison with turned head from La Madeleine cave); Delporte believes that local preferences were at work in the choice of raw material.

Stone plaques are engraved with a variety of designs, such as the mammoth from Les Combarelles cave and the herd of horses from Limeuil cave. Three hundred of the plaques from the Feldkirchen-Gönnersdorf site in West Germany mentioned above are engraved with a series of female figures, half-bent girls or women, arranged singly or in groups (Fig. 31). It has been suggested that they may be dancing. The other schist and quartzite plaques are engraved with animal figures.

Of the organic materials, bone was used for many of the perforated staffs, ivory for the Brassempouy head, and reindeer antler for small-scale sculpture (e.g. Bandi and Mariner, 1955, figs. 23, 40, 42).

Based on a study of approximately 100 caves and rock-shelters, mainly in the Franco-Cantabrian region, but also in European Russia, south Italy and Sicily, Leroi-Gourhan has established a certain chronological development of artistic styles (1968) (Fig. 32). Style I consists of the period with representations of vulvae and poorly designed animals in France. The art is all on plaques or blocks of stone. Style II, corresponding to the later Upper Perigordian (Gravettian) sees the beginning of art in the great cave 'sanctuaries', but the majority are still on slabs or rock-shelter walls. The animals depicted have a sinuous curve to the back, as do the female statuettes. The first hand-prints belong to this period. Style III is the peak period of use of the great cave sanctuaries, with movement depicted as in the galloping horses of Lascaux. Artistically, the Solutrean and Early Magdalenian peoples were very active. Late Magdalenian Style IV gradually improves the lifelike proportions of animals, and adds a three-dimensional effect by cross-hatching or colour shading (e.g. Font-de-Gaume and Altamira cave paintings). Some of the finest art is in caves and galleries unlit by natural light. Over 80 per cent of all known designs belong to this period, which often includes the pairing of bison and horse, regarded as sexually significant by Leroi-Gourhan. This is the period of fine small sculptures, such as animal heads on perforated staffs, and the low-relief clay bisons mentioned above. It is particularly interesting that

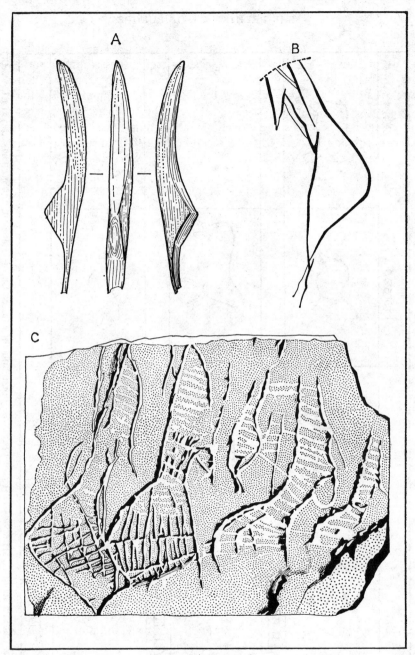

Fig. 31. Stylized figures carved in antler (A) and engraved on stone plaques (B and C), Feldkirchen-Gönnersdorf, West Germany (after Bosinski, 1969, pls. 2 and 4 and fig. 17)

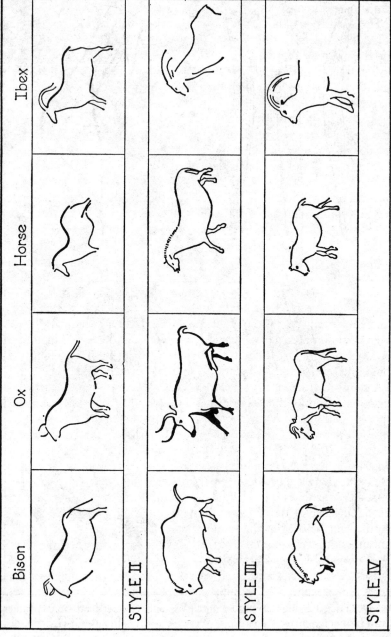

Fig. 32. Late Palaeolithic art styles II–IV of bison, ox, horse and ibex (after Leroi-Gourhan, 1968, charts XLI, XLIII, XXXIX)

the art develops smoothly across 'cultural' changes marked by different flint and bone tool styles.

The opposition of horse and bison, mentioned above, is a central thesis of Leroi-Gourhan's interpretation. The horses represent the male element, and the bison the female. The 'male' figures are generally found near the cave entrance, and at the very back. Here they are accompanied by the dangerous lion, bear and rhinoceros. Both male and female are depicted in the middle zones of caves. Leroi-Gourhan also regards the ibex, horse and deer as 'male', especially since they are frequently found on 'male' artifacts like harpoons and staffs, and at cave entrances, and oxen as female. He also divides up the abstract signs painted or pecked on the cave walls into male and female signs, based on their positioning at the front and rear, or the centre of the cave respectively. This interpretation has not been widely accepted, however.

In a book which appeared just before Leroi-Gourhan's *magnum opus*, Ucko and Rosenfeld discussed the different hypotheses offered for Palaeolithic art, including those about sexual significance and hunting magic. They concluded that none were completely correct or gave a total explanation. They felt that the placing of the designs might be important – whether they had been made, for instance, in the cave mouth, in the galleries leading into the interior, or in the innermost part of the cave or gallery system (1967). To gain more clarification, they instituted a programme on a cave in north-west Spain, investigating *all* its designs, however meagre or difficult their placing, feeling that a completely comprehensive picture of one cave's art was necessary.

A number of other approaches to Palaeolithic art have been tried or suggested. Lorblanchet reported on Australian art (1976), comparing elements of its use with the Upper Palaeolithic. He stressed the incomplete, fossil-like nature of Upper Palaeolithic art. Its interpretation is therefore made very difficult. The Australian art studied by Lorblanchet was remarkable for the continuity of use of particular rock walls, and the renewal of figures. These were not always repeated along exactly the same lines, and sometimes features of the earlier drawing were eliminated. Also, the significance of the different elements constantly changed; the same motif might be used at the same time by the same artist with two significances. A recent example of redrawing not following the same lines in the European Upper Palaeolithic was reported from the Grotte des Églises, Ussat, Ariège (Clottes, 1973). However, infra-red and ultra-violet photography have recently confirmed that all the art in this cave was carried out with the same materials – ochre and manganese (Collison and Hooper, 1976).

Bandi has suggested that progress in understanding Palaeolithic art could be obtained by closer links between archaeologists and zoologists and ethologists, or students of animal behaviour. This could lead to more accurate determination of species, for instance of tundra or forest elephants, and of sexes. Are all animals depicted with heavy bellies necessarily pregnant? A zoologist may also be able to recognize the age of an animal. Ethologists may be able to clarify some of the animal behaviours depicted, such as the fact that the reindeer on a perforated rod from Thangyen, Switzerland, is not grazing, but behaving like a male in the rut period; and that the bull from Altamira, Spain, is marking his territory with urine (Bandi, 1976).

A controversial but imaginative approach to Palaeolithic art has been used over the past decade by Alexander Marshack. This worker believes he has detected notation and symbolism in Upper Palaeolithic art. He investigates artifacts by means of a high-powered microscope, and is also working on the development of spectroscopic techniques for analysis of compositions in the painted caves (1972, 1975). The majority of his published results concern mobiliary art; a more recent publication of his draws together evidence for symbolism in the Mousterian, which he regards as the background to the sophistication evident in the early Upper Palaeolithic (for instance on the anthropomorphic figure and the 'reindeer' decorated with multiple strokes from Vogelherd) (Marshack, 1976a).

One of Marshack's early reports concerned the lines of pits, strokes or notches cut into six bone or stone plaques of the Aurignacian period, housed at the Musée des Antiquités Nationales at St-Germain-en-Laye (1970). He concluded that the pits occurred in multiples of thirty to thirty-one, and were produced by a series of techniques, for instance stabbing, curving to the left or to the right. In a bone plaque from the Abri Blanchard, Sergeac, Dordogne, in sixty-nine marks there were twenty-four changes in the type of pitting (Fig. 33). According to Marshack the type of technique changes with the different phases of the moon, when the moon becomes crescent-shaped, full or dark. The Abri Blanchard plaque bore eighty-one marginal marks which, in addition to the original sixty-nine, would comprise a record of about six months. Similar analysis suggested that the marks on both sides of a schist pebble from Barma Grande on the Riviera amounted to a total tally of fifteen months. A decorated bone bearing the design of a horse and rows of pits from La Marche, central France, bore a lunar notation of seven and a half months; the horse had been 're-used' several times (1972). These markings could possibly have been used to represent the seasonal sequence of regional phenomena or economic activities, or ceremonies (hunting, migration,

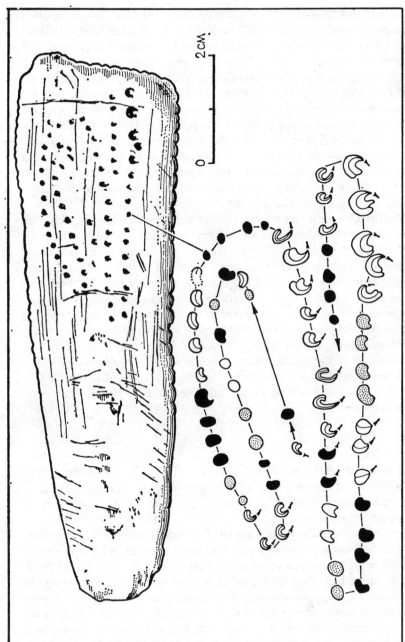

Fig. 33. Bone plaque from the Abri Blanchard, Sergeac, France, with enlargement of the series of pits, suggested to indicate phases of the moon (after Marshack, 1970, figs. 5 and 6b)

education and 'life crises'). Marshack believes that the use of notation increased throughout the Upper Palaeolithic to a maximum in Magdalenian V to VI (1970). Another study has involved the possible interpretation of 'macaronis' (bands of curving lines) in terms of water symbolism (1976b).

A composition of seals, fish and various plants is found on the perforated baton from Montgaudier, Charente (Marshack, 1975). The sequence was unravelled by Marshack as follows: probably the seals and the serpents were engraved first, as the tendency was to start realistically and then get more schematized. Tiny details of the design showed up properly under the microscope – for instance, a tiny flower with stem, leaves, septs and petals lying between the seals and the serpentine figures. The conclusion was that the baton represents a sequence of events or notations from mid-spring to the beginning of summer.

Marshack's interpretations have been received with some scepticism by other students of Palaeolithic art, but they seem to be significant both for the interpretation of Palaeolithic art and for the much more general question of the development of symbolling and notation in man; Marshack has recently questioned the twin roles of what he calls 'hand–eye cognitive' and 'vocal–auditory marking' in human development (1976a). His work is of relevance in the search for the origins of language. It is hoped that similar approaches will be used in more recent time periods; Gimbutas has already suggested that design elements in the Neolithic and Chalcolithic of the Balkans may indicate religious symbolism (1974c). Presumably more intensive study of individual series of designs might reveal complex symbolling of several different kinds in all prehistoric time periods.

CONCLUSIONS

The evidence which has been presented, albeit summarily, for Upper Palaeolithic settlement, economy and activities, has revealed a number of repeated patterns. One of the first things to note is the frequency of structural arrangements at occupation sites. This seems to be the case whether the occupation was long-term or short-term. Most occupations seem to have been well over a month in length, and anything up to half a year. The presence of cache-pits, reported from many sites, is an indication of at least partly settled conditions, and of the need for storage of particular items. However, the specialization of at least some Upper Palaeolithic economies on one or more animal food sources, which might well be migratory, suggests that there was at least an element of movement and seasonal change of camp-sites. Of particular interest in this connection is the evidence of flint 'brought in' to sites as the basic early tool-kit of the hunters, who would have left their other flint materials elsewhere (perhaps abandoned, dropped or deliberately curated somewhere). Whatever happened, they complemented the basic tool stock with locally made products. There is clear documentation of the movement of flint and other fine cutting materials from mines and sources, and for territorial interaction here.

Within the social subsystem, the presence of large quantities of possible status items, and of others that may be regarded as of symbolic value, plus specialized burial treatment of certain individuals, suggests an increasing complexity of society. The evidence of such items is heightened by the other evidence from animal remains, suggesting organization of groups for hunting on a large scale. Opportunities for leadership, outwardly recognizable by some special status items, perhaps, could surely have arisen both in the context of hunting and in the context of raw materials procurement. To have valuable flint or other raw material within one's territory could certainly give prestige, and might go as far as producing wealth in the form of goods channelled inwards in exchange for the raw material. Such items would have to be reasonably portable, in view of the likelihood of seasonal movements. Cache-pits within dwellings speak for personal or at least family ownership of the pit contents. An element of specialization may have developed, for instance in flint-mining and working, or in the field of art – the modelling of animal and human figurines in clay, the engraving of designs on schist plaques, the painting of designs on cave walls. The picture is of a mobile society, efficient in artifact manufacture, curating a basic set of tools during its moves, but abandoning less portable items when the settlement shifted. Return to particular camp-sites over several generations is suggested giving an impression of marked territorial integrity.

4

THE EPIPALAEOLITHIC AND MESOLITHIC

The post-glacial period, or Holocene, marks a watershed in European prehistory. This is mostly because we are able to recognize many of the environmental and cultural changes that occurred in it, since no subsequent ice layers have deformed the area. A major change from the earlier interglacials is that many of the huge herbivores were made extinct; current thought is that efficient human predation may have represented the last blow where these animals were in vegetation or climatic zones only marginally suitable for them (J. G. Evans, 1975; Klein, 1973). Klein has indicated that in the Ukraine, the woolly mammoth survived until Horizon III at Molodova V (c. 13,000 B.P.) while the woolly rhinoceros and the steppe bison appear to have survived into levels 1A and 1 respectively (11–10,000 B.P.) (Klein, 1973, p. 59). The musk-ox and giant deer, lion and hyena, also vanish from the scene, while the reindeer and arctic fox are displaced northwards. Similarly, after 10,250 B.P. the giant Irish deer becomes extinct in Britain, while the horse is much reduced in numbers (J. G. Evans, 1975, p. 86); in Denmark these two species are hunted a little longer, to vanish in the first half of the Pre-Boreal (Brinch Petersen, 1973).

The extinction of giant fauna is thus linked with both environmental and human factors. A series of climatic changes after the main cold of the Würm 4 has been revealed over the last thirty or forty years, mostly based on pollen analysis of bog and lake sediments and soils, but also utilizing complementary studies of charcoal, and mollusc and beetle identifications. As has already been explained, deep-sea cores indicate complex climatic change; in the post-glacial period the sea temperature and sea level varied repeatedly, and these variations are of great importance for the dating of the different stages.

Pollen analysis providing relative dating of stages of climatic change in the post-glacial has been particularly fruitful in Scandinavia and Britain. The Scandinavian sequence is now very precisely linked to the carbon-14 dating scale. The British sequence is also well dated. There are slight variations in dating the boundaries between the different climatic zones (see table below). The first warmer climatic phase of the post-glacial is termed the Pre-Boreal. Next comes the more arid Boreal, followed by the wetter and warmer Atlantic, which includes the Climatic Optimum, a period when high rainfall and warmer temperatures than today predominated. Taylor has emphasized that although such changes can be demonstrated on a 'macro-scale', locally there would be differences in the timing of changes in heat, humidity and other climatic factors, due to altitude, aspect and the ground conditions. She believes that post-glacial climatic and vegetational changes can only be viewed comprehensively on a local and regional scale, and in 'ecosystematic' terms (1975). The dates Before Present for the timing of climatic changes in different areas of Europe are as follows (after S. K. Kozlowski, 1973*b* and Jalut, 1975):

Pollen analyst	Area	Pre-Boreal	Boreal	Atlantic
Godwin	West Europe	9950–8550	8550–5950	5950–4950
Firbas	Central Europe	10,250–8750	8750–7450	7450–4650
Nilsson	North Europe	10,250–9850	9850–7950	7950–5250
Neistat	East Europe	10,150–8950	8950–7550	7550–4550
Jalut	Pyrenees	9250–8450	8450–7450	7450–4750

Kozlowski has further suggested reserving the term 'Mesolithic' for cultures to the north of the Alps, Carpathians and the Black Sea steppes, where the tundra to forest change occurred, omitting the tundra zone in the far north where reindeer hunting and other Palaeolithic-type economies survived, and also omitting the zone to the south of the Carpathians, Alps and Black Sea steppes, where changes were not so drastic. These would be described as Epipalaeolithic. Although it is hard to draw demarcation lines, this is a useful suggestion. D. Clarke makes a similar distinction, in a 'plant-usage' model seeking to contrast Mediterranean seed-based economies with more northerly root, nut and fruit economies (1976*a*).

The changes initiated *c.* 10,250 B.P. were complex, in that they involved temperature, humidity, levels of sea and land, flora and fauna. The majority of Mesolithic communities lived in much warmer conditions than those to which their immediate forebears had been accustomed. The shift northwards of the temperature zones meant that areas of Europe further to the north could be colonized (Scotland, northern Scandinavia), also higher zones of mountainous areas such as the Swiss Alps (Sauter, 1976). Shelters were not as necessary for warm-weather camps, and the evidence for constructions is poorer than in the Upper Palaeolithic. Another reason for this could be the trend, to be discussed below, of more generalized economies, perhaps resulting in shorter-term camps. Clothing may also have become less necessary over time, with reduced need for bone tools to bore holes in skins, and scrapers to clean them up.

The variations in humidity must have been much harder to cope with. Throughout the Boreal there was increasing aridity, to the extent that Gramsch has calculated that inland bodies of water in Central Europe were 1 to 3 m lower than during the Atlantic (1976). This can be shown where the rising waters have covered Early Mesolithic lake-edge camp-sites, as in Scandinavia (Brinch Petersen, 1973) and Switzerland (Wyss, 1976). However, increased rainfall in the Atlantic raised the levels of in-land waters. Combined with sea-level rises, to be discussed below, this must have forced groups to change their territories or devise some strategy to overcome the change in hydrology (Gramsch, 1976).

Evans has defined the Mesolithic populations as 'people of post-glacial age who had been forced to give up the specialized herd-hunting practices of the Upper Palaeolithic but who had not yet discovered or adopted the use of agriculture' (1975, p. 80). Specialized herd-hunting was no longer possible in all but the northernmost parts of Europe, both because of the increased temperatures unfavourable to large cold-loving mammals, and also because open ground on which herds would have grazed was in-creasingly being covered by forest. Evans has shown that the change from tundra conditions, with a few well-separated trees, to forest, meant that the leaves were higher up, in the unbroken forest canopy, and that there was little browse at ground level. This reduced grazing areas to broken ground between forest edges, and separated these grazing areas from each other. Both the quarries and the hunting methods had to change.

In Britain, after an initial birch–pine forest phase, mixed oak forest gradually gained predominance, although there was still a good proportion of pine and hazel, depending on the soil base. It is claimed that much of the British Isles was forested, including some of the offshore islands, such as the Orkneys, which in historic times have not been wooded. The extensive forest cover must have been similar in most of northern Europe (the specialized Mediterranean area will be discussed below). A certain amount of change occurred with the increase in humidity and rainfall at the beginning of the Atlantic; there is an increase of alder in Britain, and Gramsch reports very different proportions of tree species on different soils in central Europe (1976).

In and around these forests lived red and roe deer, elk, boar and aurochs (wild cattle). There was also a wide variety of smaller mammals such as marten, polecat and squirrel, while water stretches were inhabited by beaver, otter, fish and aquatic birds. Red and roe deer have a liking for forest-edge conditions while pig and elk were also at home in forests. Wild cattle are said to have been adaptable to woodland or parkland conditions. None of these animals is as naturally gregarious as reindeer, and they do not associate in large herds. Red deer form small herds of females and young males, or mature males, for most of the year, and roe deer and elk are basically solitary animals, which do not form large social groups. Pig only associate in small groups, but wild cattle usually form larger groups. The behaviour of these warmth-loving mammals inevitably affected the hunting techniques and economic strategies of the human groups preying upon them.

In the Mediterranean area, climatic changes and changes in animal quarries were less marked. Pollen analysis has advanced considerably in the last ten to fifteen years in the Mediterranean area, and there are now numerous analyses. Recent comparison of post-glacial pollen sequences from the coast, plains and low hills and from the central mountain zones of southern France demonstrated broadly similar patterns of slow increase of both temperature and humidity from the late glacial onwards. Renault-Miskovsky has suggested (1972) that although the Mediterranean climate was probably established over much of west Mediterranean Europe by the beginning of the Boreal, humidity favoured mixed oak formations and retarded the appearance of the present-day distinctive association of southern oak, pistachio, and juniper, etc. High values for mixed oak-forest species in the pollen spectra from sites in Italy and Greece suggest that this pattern was also present in the central Mediterranean. Raikes, who has studied post-glacial environmental variations from the Mediterranean to the Middle East and compared them with recent temperature variations, regards the post-glacial variations in this area as ecologically insignificant. He considers that the changes that did take place were linked to a variety of factors – sea-level changes, deforestation, drainage and human interference (1976, p. 81).

A number of factors emerge from the southern French work (Planchais et al., 1975; Jalut, 1975). One is the relatively high humidity in the Boreal, in apparent contrast to more northerly areas. Another is the importance of refuge areas for plant and tree species, from which they can spread rapidly following favourable shifts in climate (Jalut regards this as an important phenomenon in the mountain valleys of the Pyrenees, for instance). If plants and trees can be demonstrated to have survived in these refuges, it is perhaps not surprising that sheep, once regarded as extinct in southern France after the late glacial, are present in faunal assemblages of the Epipalaeolithic. A third factor of importance is the effect of man on the landscape. In northern Europe suggestions have been made that man interfered with the forest cover in the Late Mesolithic. On the Mediterranean coast, however, fluctuations in the pollen record at two sites have suggested the possibility of human interference as early as the Pre-Boreal (Renault-Miskovsky, 1972).

SEA-LEVEL FLUCTUATIONS

The major effect of sea-level rise for the north of Europe was to reduce drastically the living area of Mesolithic man. Since the retreat of the glaciers, the southern part of the North Sea had been largely dry land, so that continuous territory existed from Wales (perhaps even Ireland, if an Irish land-bridge existed) to Jutland, and south to the Netherlands and North Germany. The North Sea was separated from what is now the Baltic, then the Ancylus lake, by the solid land mass of Jutland, the Danish islands, and South Sweden. As will be seen below, the distribution of 'Maglemosian' cultural finds shows this geographical unity quite well. Progressively, during the much wetter conditions of the Atlantic, and also influenced by tectonic subsidence and compaction in adjacent territories, the North Sea flooded to the limits known today (Evans, 1976; Kooijmans, 1974). This involved breaching the straits of Dover, where there had been a land passage. Ters (1975) has demonstrated numerous changes in sea level from Calais to La Rochelle between 8150 B.P. and the present day, including a change from a low of 21 m at Le Havre *c.* 7950 B.P. to only 7–8 m below present levels in 7450 B.P. During regression (lower sea level) stages, up to 10 km of sandy or muddy coastline would have been added to the North French coastline, and possibly the Breton Mesolithic sites on Téviec and Hoedic islands were then attached to the coast by promontories. During transgression phases, sites on earlier coastlines were covered. Working from heights above sea level of dated archaeological sites in the southern Netherlands, Kooijmans has been able to reconstruct the mean high-water level from *c.* 6950 B.P. onwards (Fig. 34). Geologists have established that the rise in sea level was uniform over much of the northern hemisphere, and archaeological data certainly indicates similarities between northern and Mediterranean European

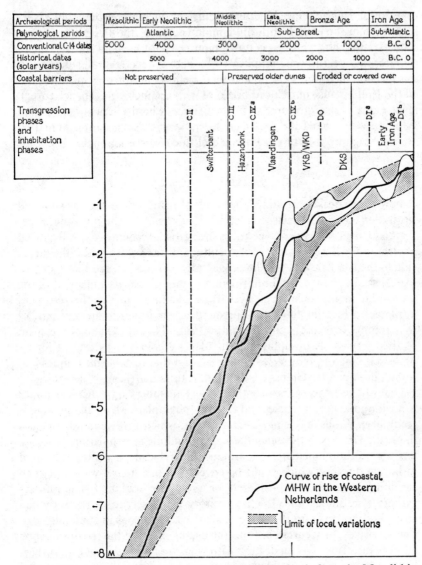

Fig. 34. Mean high-water level in the western Netherlands from the Mesolithic to the Iron Age (after Kooijmanns, 1974, fig. 14)

coastlines. In the west Mediterranean, for instance, where pottery is known from the early eighth millennium B.P., an Early Neolithic site at Leucate, French Pyrenees, is now under several meters of water.

The sea-level rise was complicated by both the tectonic subsidence and compaction mentioned above, and by the effects of isostatic uplift (raising of the land because of reduced pressure with the melting of the ice cover). This effect is clearly visible in north Britain, where a series of new open habitats were created at the sea edge by isostasy; these situations were used to advantage by men of the Late Mesolithic (Morrison, 1976).

PALAEOECONOMY

A new theoretical approach to the study of man in prehistory is summed up under the word 'palaeoeconomy'. The theory is the outcome of research by members and associates of the British Academy Major Research Project in the Early History of Agriculture at Cambridge under the direction of the late Eric Higgs. The project members considered that archaeological studies had lost sight of the importance of man as a member of the animal kingdom, constrained by natural pressures such as the resources available to him for food, the surrounding environment in the form of topography, vegetation, climate and so forth. They felt that consideration of theory in other disciplines, particularly ethology, was crucial for an understanding of prehistoric economies, and that suitable techniques had to be developed to obtain relevant data (Higgs and Jarman, 1975).

One of the concepts which the project members have made familiar to a wide audience in articles and three monographs (two of which have already been published) is *territorial analysis*, which involves study of both the *site territory* and the *annual territory* of a human population. The site territory is the immediate area around the archaeological site, calculated to be the distance which could be covered in one hour's walking (when agriculturists are being considered) or two hours' walking (when hunter-gatherers are under study). This territory is unlikely to be perfectly circular, as topography in the shape of acute rises or drops in land height, or rivers or lakes, may curtail or limit the useful extent of the territory in one or more directions. When dealing with what are now seaside sites, workers have to consider the possible sea level when the sites were occupied, and the relevance of sea resources in the diet. The majority of sites studied by the project are assumed to have been semi-nomadic ('transhumant'), that is, the prehistoric groups did not occupy a permanent home base, but moved on a seasonal basis in search of resources. The term *annual territory* relates to this assumption, covering the complex of sites inhabited by the group in a yearly cycle. It is assumed that the group will obtain the majority of its needs from the site territory, but the more global term *site catchment* covers the whole area from which the group obtains its livelihood in terms of food, raw materials and finished products.

The site territory is examined on the ground to discover what its potential was in the past, in the form of soils, vegetation cover, animal populations and so on. Pollen analyses and soil profiles are important additions to understanding for the earlier periods (most of the sites studied have dated from the Middle Palaeolithic onwards, with an em-

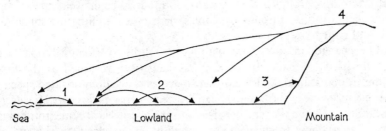

Fig. 35. Model of simplified resource areas (after Higgs and Jarman, 1975, fig. 1)

phasis on the Upper Paleolithic by Sturdy, Mesolithic by Jarman, Neolithic and Bronze Ages by Barker and Dennell). The faunal collections are often no longer available for checking, but publication at least indicates rough numbers of species found, which can be used to correlate with the site territory information. As stated above, the general assumption of the researchers is that sites are short-term. Higgs and Jarman have published a simplified model of resource areas (Fig. 35) in an ideal landscape running from the mountains to the sea. They state that the resource areas near the sea can be integrated by short-distance transhumant economies, while the mountain area would be integrated by longer-distance transhumance.

From a technical point of view, the project members have tried to obtain better recovery of floral and faunal information by wet-sieving archaeological levels and by intensive analysis of the finds (H. N. Jarman, 1972; M. Jarman, 1972). This has led to some unexpected results, in particular the identification by Dennell of what seems to be domesticated wheat in an Upper Palaeolithic level in Israel (at Nahal Oren – Dennell and Legge, 1973). The general trend, however, has been to show two things; to reveal the presence of plant foods in the diet in many periods; and to question the criteria for the 'domestic' status of many plants and animals.

The domestication of plants will be discussed more fully in the next chapter; genetic changes take place which are irreversible, and domesticated grains are recognizable from their morphology, but plants may have been encouraged for generations without specific replanting, and without genetical changes taking place. Mellars, faced with the abundance of hazel shells on Mesolithic sites in Britain, has suggested that a policy of deliberate fire-setting by Mesolithic inhabitants of Britain would have served a dual purpose – increasing deer populations on the rich new growth after the fires, and increasing stands of hazel (1975). Clarke has suggested that Mesolithic groups in the mixed oak forest areas could well have gained their main livelihood from root staples, or from controlling the spread of nut and fruit trees (1976*a*).

The changes in animal populations that lead to 'domestication' are equally hard to quantify; the dog has long been regarded as the first domesticated animal, and the presence of a possible domesticated species in the Kniegrotte in the Magdalenian has been mentioned above. However, research has shown that smaller size (one of the criteria at Kniegrotte) was a general response to changed conditions by many species at the end of the Würm. The criteria on which animal domestication is now accepted will be mentioned in the next chapter, but meanwhile the question of how far human groups in the Upper Palaeolithic and Mesolithic can be considered to have managed plant and animal populations is an important one. Sturdy is convinced that the archaeological record reflects very considerable dependence on and perhaps management of reindeer populations from north Germany to Switzerland in the Upper Palaeolithic (1975). There may well be a case for visualizing widespread 'management' of reindeer and other gregarious mammals, at least during the latter part of the Würm. In the Mesolithic, the evidence at first is less striking, except for the continuing activity of the reindeer hunters on the north German plain, but by the later Mesolithic Jarman has demonstrated that there was wide dependence on red deer and boar in particular (1972).

Jarman starts from the explicit assumptions that 'there is a close relationship between faunal remains on archaeological sites and the animal economies of the human groups concerned, and secondly that the published data can be accepted as a basis for analysing this relationship as a whole . . .' (1972, p. 125). He lists the twenty-seven main species represented at 165 Mesolithic sites, demonstrating that red deer and boar are present in nearly all of them, with roe deer and cattle being represented at 60 per cent, and equids (horse and ass) and caprines (ibex) at between 35 and 41 per cent of the sites. This is shown diagramatically in Figure 36. Red deer and boar commonly account for a high proportion of the meat

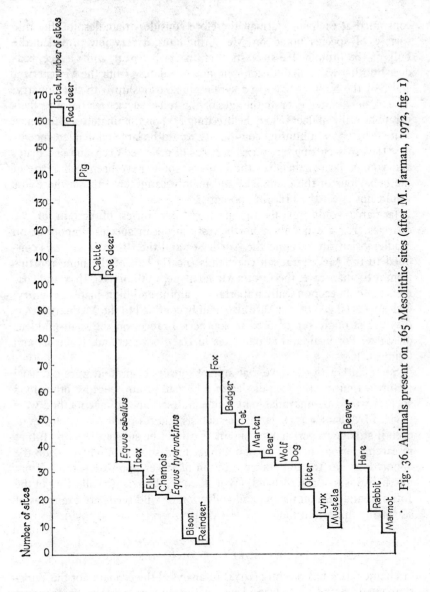

Fig. 36. Animals present on 165 Mesolithic sites (after M. Jarman, 1972, fig. 1)

consumed at each site. Jarman therefore considers that, despite the wide variety of species noted on Mesolithic sites, a very few provided the bulk of the protein. He suggests that, in Italy, Spain, and Greece, red-deer hunting was a major economic practice dating from the Mousterian, and that the hunters lived in a symbiotic relationship with their quarry. The rather limited data on the ages of the red-deer victims point to deliberate hunting of deer below the breeding age, predominately males. Since a site territory of a hunting community would be large enough to encompass the cross-cutting territories of herds of male red deer, and of females and young, Jarman believes the hunters would have been well aware of the behaviour of these animals, and mainly slaughtered those whose loss would not affect the breeding potential.

Jarman's study reveals the principal territories of certain of the quarries. Elk are mainly a north-west European species, important on Maglemosian sites around the North Sea and the Baltic. The ass is confined to the Mediterranean coastlands (nearly half of the bone remains from a Sicilian cave, the Grotta Mangiapane, were of ass). Ibex and chamois are only economically important in alpine and high-plateau country. Ovicaprids (sheep or goat) are also mainly confined to the Mediterranean; they are strongly represented in southern France, on the shell-middens of Muge, Portugal, and at odd sites in Italy, Switzerland, Romania and Crimean Russia.

Some authorities believe that animal sources of protein were a crucial factor in limiting the overall size of a human group, because other food sources would be unavailable in winter unless some storage method were devised (Mellars, 1975). Jarman's analysis ignores plant foods. However, even if storage in perishable containers cannot be substantiated by future research, periods of glut of non-animal food sources might provide the opportunity for the temporary creation of larger population units (from micro-bands to a macro-band) (Wobst, 1974). Hazel-nut collecting in the autumn, and salmon fishing and collection of wild seeds are examples of seasonally important food sources (Mellars, 1975; Harris, 1976).

PRE-BOREAL ECONOMIES

Grahame Clark has recently (1974) re-analysed the economy of the Yorkshire site of Star Carr, a lakeside site with structural remains, in the form of a birch-wood platform, on which a report was first published in 1954. Both the pollen analysis of the site, and the carbon-14 date (average of two samples) of 9488 ± 350 B.P. place the site in the late Pre-Boreal. The re-analysis has stressed that this was but one of several possible camp locations on the northern, sun-exposed shore of a former lake; none the less, at least two occupations are suggested by the change in typology from bone projectile points with big wide barbs to those with fine barbs. The site territory has been estimated as being between about 30 and 100 km² depending on how far the territory stretched in distance and uphill (Fig. 37). Red deer provided three fifths of the animal protein, so Clark esti-

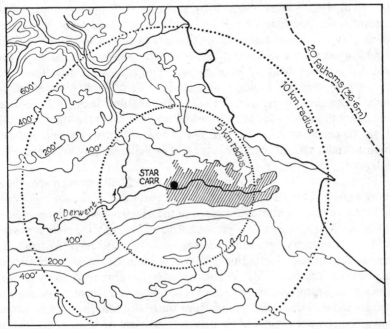

Fig. 37. Site territory of Star Carr, Yorkshire, originally situated on lake-side, now peat beds (after Clark, 1974, fig. 6)

mated the possible deer populations in the four putative site territories, based on the known densities of red-deer populations. On the basis of a culling rate of one animal in five, the possible daily supply available was from 7·4 to 27·2 kg. Since two family units (each of two adults and three children) would require 10·9 kg per day, it seems likely that no more than four family units could have been present at the site. To support such a group, it would have been necessary to exploit a territory of 6 miles (10 km) radius, and up to 61 m above sea level. The activities of the Star Carr people seem to have involved replenishing their hunting equipment. Apart from flint microliths, probably used as projectile points, they left behind

191 barbed points, the majority of red-deer antler. Most of the antler found on the site had had splinters removed to make these barbed points.

Almost all the raw materials used at the site could have been obtained within one hour's walk – the glacial stones and clay found among the birch-bark platform, the animals exploited, and the flint. Amber could been obtained from the shore, then only just over 10 km away, while iron pyrites might have come from the Yorkshire Coal Measures. Although the latter could have been obtained by exchange with other groups, Clark estimates that the Star Carr group might have moved many kilometres during their seasonal migrations. All signs of seasonality (shed antlers, etc.) suggest winter occupation of the site; the non-random culling of the red deer, represented by a large proportion of adult stags over hinds and young deer, may well indicate the sort of red-deer 'herding' or 'management' suggested by Jarman. To follow the red deer it might have been necessary to move as far as the North Yorkshire Moors or the Cleveland Hills, representing an annual territory of 60 km². Scatters of microliths at high altitudes suggest that this pattern of exploitation may well have been followed.

Flint industries of the early post-glacial in the Mediterranean area show clear signs of Late Palaeolithic origins, in particular in the use of microlithic backed points already favoured in the Magdalenian. A famous early site is the Mas d'Azil in the Pyrenees, where Magdalenian levels are overlaid by an industry first recognized at this site, and called 'Azilian'. Its characteristics are microlithic tools, and stones painted with simple geometrical designs. This Azilian industry is recognized elsewhere in France, in Spain, and in central Europe. Wyss has recently discussed a similar industry from the site of Balm unter der Fluh in the Canton of Solothurn, Switzerland. The cave lies 690 m above sea level, at the foot of the Weissenstein massif, itself 1294 m high. It is oriented towards the Swiss plateau. From the 'typical post-glacial woodland fauna', the hunters who occupied it were probably exploiting the high ground up to the top of the Weissenstein (Wyss, 1976). Apart from the standard red and roe deer, boar and wild cattle, the alpine species represented are ibex, chamois, marmot, bear, badger, marten, hare and squirrel. Fourteen species of birds are represented, including the white perdrix, which would have nested on the top of the Jura. There were many backed points in the assemblage, described as an 'Aziloid backed blade' industry and these points may well have been used as arrowheads.

Bietti and Mussi have recently (1976) listed the six Pre-Boreal sites of Italy which have carbon-14 dates and faunal samples. Although there is a wide variety of animal species, hunting of large mammal species is the main activity represented. The Italian authors indicate that internal, fairly high sites give more indications of hunting and collecting activities, while the coastal and lakeside sites are sometimes more specialist. An example of the first type is at the Grotta la Punta, Fucine basin, central Italy, where there is a series of hearths in levels 21 to 27, and a carbon-14 date for level 26 of 10,581 ± 100 B.P. The food remains are of large mammals and birds, with associated flint-scrapers, burins and a few backed tools. Such 'Epigravettian' industries persist throughout the Epipalaeolithic in central Italy. Barker has recently discussed Epipalaeolithic economies in central Italy, suggesting that there was a change from the late glacial red deer–horse economy to one based on a combination of lowland and upland resources. 'Particular sites seem to have been selected for the exploitation of specific resources, only one of which now was red deer' (Barker, 1975b, p. 128).

The famous site of Arene Candide on the Italian Ligurian coast also had a Pre-Boreal occupation; the lowest levels, III–I, are dated 10,300 ± 195 B.P. (Cardini, 1946). The flint industry contained many denticulated and notched blades, with short round scrapers, and only a few burins and backed pieces. The main food sources were large mammals – red deer, boar and bear – though some shellfish were also found in the level. The interest of the occupation is that there were plenty of hearths, suggesting occupation during fairly cold conditions, and study of the charcoal reveals cool-adopted tree species (holly, pine and a little oak). The site was obviously an important one, as half a dozen burials were found, the dead lying extended, and decorated with necklaces of animal teeth and pierced shells and ochre. Even children have ochre-coloured pebbles placed in their graves, and apparently squirrel-tail capes (Barfield, 1971).

The cave of Los Mallaetes in eastern Spain, one of a group on a limestone massif 10 kilometres from the coast, has also been studied from the point of view of the Cambridge school (Davidson, 1976). The microblade industry here is dated 10,370 ± 105 B.P. (Fortea, 1976), and Davidson's analysis of the aspect and altitude of the cave, and of the animal bone remains, suggest that it was a winter camp-site, exploiting ibex and goat, used from the Late Palaeolithic onwards. A minimum of six goat/ibex, two red deer, one horse and six rabbits are represented in the Epipalaeolithic fauna (Davidson 1976).

BOREAL ECONOMIES

Not all sites preserve the remains of bones and plants, which enable accurate estimates of the economic strategies to be made. This is particularly the problem, for instance, in the Netherlands, where no faunal remains survive on the majority of sites. However, it is known that many species of animals were available as sources of protein, and Price has constructed a most interesting model of the seasonal round of Boreal man in the Netherlands (1976). Like the British Academy History of Agriculture project workers, he has based the model on the behaviour and characteristics of the available animal species, estimating from modern populations of the animals with adjustments for their likely weight during the Boreal. Aurochs, elk, red and roe deer and boar are the main sources of protein in the model, while smaller mammals such as beaver, pine marten, otter, badger, etc. are classed as 'contingency resources'. He guesses that 5 per cent of the yearly diet in weight consists of fowl, and 15 per cent of plants. On this basis a five-season pattern of exploitation is modelled:

January to March	April to May	June to August	September to October	November to December
Red deer	Fish	Plants	Plants	Small Game
Small game	Plants	Small game	Aurochs	Wild Boar
Wild boar	Aurochs	Fish	Red deer	Aurochs
Aurochs	Red deer	Aurochs	Wild boar	Red deer

The seasonal size of groups would vary, with probably smaller groups from June to August, and potentially larger ones in March/April when fish was plentiful, or in November when hazel-nuts were ripe in vast quantities (Price, 1976).

Further to the north, in Scandinavia, an Upper Palaeolithic pattern of big-game hunting may have continued into the first half of the Pre-Boreal, with the wild horse, bison, giant deer, aurochs and elk as quarries. With the gradual increase in sea level many new rich ecological zones were created (Brinch Petersen, 1973). In the fjords, bays and lagoons the beginnings of marine exploitation took place; for instance, at the Kongemose site, fish remains include those of the spur-dog, cod, coalfish, and flounder, and there are also bones of seal. In the forests, the Maglemosian hunters pursued, in particular, aurochs and elk, followed by red and roe deer and boar. Lakeside settlement was also favoured, and the dryness of the Boreal shows up in the presence of low-water sites on the lake marl, for instance Svaerdborg I (Brinch Petersen, 1973).

The Svaerdborg bog in Zealand presented an irregular outline. Three archaeological sites were found on its original surface, of which Svaerdborg I is dated by pollen analysis to the end of the Boreal, and Svaerdborg II to the early Atlantic. Towards the end of the Boreal period, the bog began to dry up, and a peninsula developed on its south-east side, on an old moraine. Herbs and trees were established here, and it provided a useful settlement for summer fishing and hunting. The excavation of Svaerdborg I apparently uncovered a complex of about ten hut sites, but unfortunately no plan survives (Brinch Petersen, 1971). Svaerdborg II is farther out than site I, suggesting increased humidity in the Atlantic period. Pollen from the occupation layer shows that the mixed oak forest was beginning to spread at the expense of pioneer birch, hazel and pine in the surrounding woodland. This site was much smaller, and Brinch Petersen's analysis of the distribution of flint waste and tools suggests a single family hut of c. 25 m². Dog was present in the Svaerdborg I fauna, but not at Svaerdborg II, where red deer, roe deer, boar and beaver are the dominant species hunted, followed by elk, aurochs and small game. Remains of pike and duck (mallard, goosander, red-breasted merganser) show the use made of the water resources. The varied types of flint and bone tools show there was no specialized economic activity. Their weapons included obliquely blunted points in local Senonian flint, and barbed points made out of bone resembling the Star Carr ones. Brinch Petersen reports four other similar cases of single hut sites, some still with a central hearth preserved. Some of these were situated on small islands or peninsulas in shallow lakes on the lake marl. Remains of hazel-nuts indicate that they were occupied into the autumn, but the humidity prevented winter settlement. Brinch Petersen has suggested that winter sites were those like Holmegaard V and Star Carr. Holmegaard V, a report on which has yet to be published, lies on solid ground. There is a thick occupation layer, and the fauna lacks the summer pike.

ATLANTIC ECONOMIES

A particular feature of Atlantic economies is the creation of shell-middens, piles of opened shells of marine molluscs suggesting repeated occupation of the same location. Shellfish collecting has been a world-wide phenomenon over a long period of time, and this activity, also known as strand-looping was practised up to this century in northern Europe, southern Africa and Australasia. For a short period of time along the North Sea and Atlantic coasts of Europe it represented an important economic practice. The shell-middens also contain bones of animals, especially red deer, and bones of fish, and in some cases the overwhelming piles of shells hide the fact that more protein was obtained from these other resources than from the shellfish. Shell-midden exploitation seems linked with the phenomena of raised sea levels, isostatic uplift and the spread of mixed oak forest.

Brinch Petersen has published the site of Ølby Lyng, a Late Atlantic shell-midden in eastern Sjaelland, 32 km south of Copenhagen. Møhl, in analysing the faunal remains, has shown that the rising seas had disturbed communications with central Europe for animal populations; the South Jutland peninsula remained an important connection. Despite the presence of shellfish (on which dates of 5210 and 5320 B.P. were obtained) and remains of cod, sea birds and seals, the principal occupation was hunting of land mammals. Forty-eight per cent of the bone fragments were of red deer, 25 per cent of roe deer, and 10 per cent of boar. The land mammals thus provided the majority of the protein, plus vital raw materials. The seals were intensively exploited, and there are remains of many Greenland seals, which are important for skin and blubber, and of grey seals and porpoises. The porpoises and Greenland seals must have been hunted by boat. Møhl suggests a possible production of dried fish on the basis of the relationship between the number of fish vertebrae and skull fragments (1970, p. 77). Although the flint implements were all of Mesolithic type, pottery was in use, and could have been used for activities like fish storage.

An earlier shell-midden has been excavated at Culver Well, Isle of Portland, in southern England, where two carbon-14 dates average out at 7150 B.P. (Palmer, 1977). The main shellfish species represented are winkles and limpets, but the large number of picks, perhaps used to grub up roots, suggest some use at least of plant foods. Two interesting features are a densely packed stone floor, perhaps used as the base for shelters, and a deep stone-lined cooking pit. Molluscs were assumed to have been the main food resource at the Breton sites of Téviec and Hoedic, both islands now, but possibly joined by a causeway to the mainland during their occupation. The midden component was not quantified in the site report, but mussel, winkle, limpet, oyster and scallop were reported, plus bone of a number of fish including cuttlefish, and bone fishing gouges; incised decoration was found on one fish jawbone. Other food remains included bones of birds, including wild duck and penguin, and of a few animals such as red and roe deer, boar, fox, dog and wildcat. The presence of ten burials, containing a total of twenty-three skeletons at Teviec and of nine graves containing thirteen skeletons at Hoedic, suggests that these sites were prime resource locations, where several bands might join together to exploit the various food sources. It is interesting in view of the evidence for animal and fish foods, that the physical anthropologist studying the skeletons regarded their teeth-wear patterns as due to a plant rather than a meat diet (Pequart and Pequart 1937). Whether such wear was acquired while occupying these coastal sites, or on other parts of the seasonal cycle, it is a pointer to the otherwise unproven importance of plant foods.

In the Mediterranean, a group of shell-middens was originally noted in the bay of Marseilles in the nineteenth century. Today they are nearly all destroyed, but Courtin has dated one of them, the Île Riou, to the eighth millennium B.P. by carbon-14 dating of shells. The molluscs were mainly *patella* (limpet). Fish-bones had also been found there in the nineteenth century. There are reasons for thinking that Île Riou was originally attached to the mainland; the hearth found by Courtin was associated with pottery and querns of the earliest Neolithic facies, but it has been argued from similarities in lithic industry and site locations that economic patterns continued without much alteration in the early phases of pottery usage in this area (Phillips, 1975).

Another group of middens was located at the mouth of the River Tagus in Portugal. The middens of Muge have dates from the mid eighth to the late sixth millennium B.P. (base of Moita do Sebastião 7350 ± 350 B.P. and level 3 of Cabeço da Arruda 5150 ± 300 B.P. – Roche, 1976). Only three middens are preserved, though more were present originally. No development of activities, as revealed in differing proportions of species fished or hunted, or of flint-tool changes, has been found, and Roche puts this down to the very isolated nature of the area. The large size of each midden points to repeated occupation in a favourable environment at the confluence of sea and river waters, with the availability of fish, fowl and animals in addition to shellfish. The flint used at the sites was obtained from Jurassic outcrops in Estremadura (Roche, 1972); this limestone area neighbouring Muge contains many caves definitely occupied in the Palaeolithic and probably also in the Mesolithic. There are also flint-surface scatters which may represent locations of other camps in the yearly round of the peoples which occupied Muge.

Recent work by Mellars on the shell-middens of the island of Oronsay off the west coast of Scotland has concentrated on the economic aspects of the occupation, by means of careful sampling of the midden and sorting and analysis of all the components – shellfish, fish and animal bone. Oronsay lies in the Hebrides, joined to the larger island of Colonsay today by a causeway passable on foot at low tide. Mellars has established that six shell-middens exist on the island, all on or above the 8-m contour above sea level (Pl. 2). Dates from three of the sites cluster around the mid sixth millennium. The proportion of fish to shellfish varies in the different levels, averaging about 50 per cent. Of the shellfish, the greatest calorific value comes from limpet, while winkle and crab are also present, plus some bird bones and rare remains of red deer and boar. A study of fish ear-bones, otoliths, which change in size with age (Wilkinson, quoted in Mellars, in press), suggests a certain seasonality of occupation (two sites occupied in the early summer; one in the autumn; and one in the winter). Boats would have been needed to catch some of the fish, so seasonal travel to other areas is quite feasible. In speaking of the nearby island of Jura, Mercer has quoted stalking of red deer and wild pig and collecting of hazelnuts and acorns and perhaps also chickweed, bramble, strawberry and wild pear as possible economic activities (1976). The Oronsay studies are important, however, as they indicate some occupation in seasons of greatest scarcity, suggesting that fishing and shellfish collecting were crucial resources on which the maximum size of a seasonal band would be based.

On the basis of excavations at the Newferry site in the Bann valley, which was occupied from about 8000 to 4000 B.P., Woodman has produced a model for exploitation in this area which can be compared for detail with that of Price for the Boreal of the Netherlands (1976). The model provides for movement between the estuary, coast and islands in the spring, and the inland rivers and lakes in the summer into the autumn. The exploitation of salmon, eels and sea birds (auks) is proposed. The Bann valley has a precocious Neolithic development, and it is suggested that the successful Mesolithic economy was still practised during at least part of the first pottery-using phase.

SOUTH-EAST AND EASTERN EUROPE

While the northern zones of eastern Europe were markedly affected by the post-glacial climatic changes, the alterations of lake and sea margins and the changes in tree cover and animal species were not so extreme further to the south. Sulimirski has suggested that the central and northern parts of European Russia and neighbouring eastern Europe provided rich resources for game, fish and plants throughout the Pre-Boreal, Boreal and Atlantic climatic periods, while further south the increasing warmth created more arid conditions. Here forests were confined to the river valleys, and Mesolithic sites occur on the lowest terraces of rivers or on islands in the rivers (Sulimirski, 1970). Previously important areas like Kostienki-Borshevo are largely abandoned, the last occupied site, Borshevo II, being significantly located on the lowest terrace.

In the Middle Dniester valley two important sites have been excavated at Soroki, located on a bank between the river and the lower terrace, and dated by carbon-14 to c. 7450 B.P. (Tringham, 1973). There are oval pits assumed to represent former winter huts, with hearths inside, and other hearths containing molluscs and roach bones, which may indicate summer camps. Most of the animal bones are of forest species like red and roe deer and boar. In a later occupation, pottery and domesticated animal species are present, but there is continuity from the Late Mesolithic in the flint-tool industry (the flint was obtained from nearby chalk cliffs and made into large blades and a few microlithic blades). Among the activities carried out at Soroki, according to wear analysis on the flint tools, were the cutting of both soft and hard organic materials, and the scraping of meat or hides.

The Epipalaeolithic sites at the Iron Gates, at either side of the Danube in Yugoslavia and Romania respectively, are particularly interesting in that data on both the fauna and pollen are recently available (Bolomey, 1973; Carciumaru, 1973). Bolomey has traced the site territories used by the two groups of Romanian sites, which overlap very considerably. He therefore suggests that probably the bulk of the community lived at one site, possibly Icoana cave, while a few people were sent 'for strategic reasons' to the other end of the territory. The data reveal that between about 12,000 and 10,000 B.P. there was a rather diversified animal economy, with the ibex and chamois becoming more important; around 8000 B.C., however, the economy seems to have been firmly based on the exploitation of red deer and pig. It is not certain whether the pigs were 'managed' in any way by human populations, although Bolomey thinks this is likely. He divides the economy up into the 'large scale permanent (?) exploitation of red and roe deer for meat and artifactual raw material'; the selective killing of pig; and three other exploitative activities. These are fishing, the gathering of land snails, etc., and the gathering of furred animals, plus chamois, cattle and birds. Carciumaru has examined human coprolites from two of the sites, Icoana and Vlasac. Among the pollen in these coprolites is a cereal grain. The analyst says that it would be difficult to determine how far man used cereals in his diet, even more to know how he 'cultivated' them. Pending further pollen analyses in the area, this remains an interesting and tantalizing suggestion of pre-Neolithic cultivation.

In a discussion of the Mesolithic of south-east Europe, Tringham has indicated that the Dniester valley, the Danube gorges and north Greece are the only areas with good evidence for Mesolithic economies prior to the use of farming. The principal Greek evidence comes from the cave of Franchthi, opening on to the Gulf of Argos.

The Franchthi excavation has revealed Upper Palaeolithic, Epipalaeolithic and Neolithic levels (Jacobsen, 1973). The Epipalaeolithic chipped-stone industry, in levels dating from the eleventh to the ninth millennia B.P., shows considerable continuity from the preceding Upper Palaeolithic. The majority of the tools are notched flakes, denticulate tools and marginally retouched blades, struck in rather irregular shapes with a soft hammer technique. Towards the end of the period microlithic lunates, triangles and trapezes appear. The majority of the industry is on local flint or chert, as in the Upper Palaeolithic, but from the tenth millennium B.P. onwards obsidian is represented in the form of small unretouched blades, and later as retouched tools. The obsidian has been identified as coming from the island of Melos in the Cyclades. The use of boats implied by this acquisition suggests that the inhabitants of Franchthi could also have used boats for fishing. In some of the deposits fish bones form 20 to 40 per cent of the total quantity of bone. However, red-deer bones are the most frequent, followed by pig, with a few remains of large cattle, fox, hare and birds. The relative importance to the diet of the fish and land resources awaits detailed analysis. Other food resources are indicated by the find of over 450 almonds and 200 pistachio nuts (plus a few wild pear and vetch) in the Epipalaeolithic levels.

POPULATION SIZES AND SETTLEMENT

Meiklejohn has recently suggested that although populations were organized in smaller units in the Mesolithic than in the Upper Palaeolithic, none the less quite large populations could be kept going by a diversification of activities, because the resources on the whole were more stable and dependable than in the Upper Palaeolithic (1976). The evidence from the *numbers* of sites is that there was an increase in population throughout the Boreal, and that by Atlantic times there was a considerable body of population in Europe (e.g. Newell, 1973). Using ethnographic data based on present-day groups living on the east Canadian taiga, with annual territories of 12 – 75,000 km², Price has suggested that Mesolithic groups might have been able to agglomerate into larger subsistence units at favourable times of the year, which would mean that the breeding population was quite sizeable. During the less ecologically favourable seasons the primary subsistence unit would be larger than one family, but not so great as to use up the firewood in the area surrounding the camp, which is a crucial factor in the taiga forest environment.

A number of illustrations will be given regarding the distribution and organization of sites in Mesolithic Europe, and whether they can be regarded as representing the camp-sites of large or small subsistence units. In Lithuania, for instance, Burow has excavated a series of Mesolithic sites along the river Wytschegda. Two types of site are known, those which appear to be 'permanent', situated near a lake edge, usually near a river inlet, and about 600 m² in size; and those regarded as temporary, and located by large rivers. The 'permanent' site of Wis I is located by its pollen diagram in the Boreal, and C-14 dates for two areas of the excavation are a millennium apart (8080 ± 90, 7090 ± 70 B.P.). The interest of the site, which has produced only about 1,000 flints, lies in two factors. In the first place, a large group of ground-stone axes is present; in the second, over 200 finds of wood, bark and woven material were made. These include bows, arrowshafts, throwing sticks, sledge-runners, skis, and a decorated bow-shaped artifact. There were three types of bow, the biggest type being 3½ m long, made of spruce or pine wood. It is suggested that these huge bows might have been put on animal paths as traps. Some of the smaller bows are decorated on the upper parts with geometrical motifs (zigzag, net, parallel vertical lines, curved lines). One of the skis is decorated with an elk-head design. Birch bark was used to make little boxes, whose folded edges were sewn together with a wooden needle, and bark was also used for net-swimmers. The net-swimmers held up woven nets of double-thread sedge twine. A twined mat was also found, made of plant threads and bits of pine. Burow mentions the similarity of the stone axes to tools of the Suomosjärvi culture of Finland, and feels that the decorated woodwork shows links with both the Finnish Kunda and the Danish-south Swedish Maglemosian sites (1973).

Other authors are less convinced about the permanent nature of sites, and in dealing with the north German plain between the Elbe and the Oder Gramsch suggests that the majority of excavated sites and flint scatters represent short-term occupation. Larger sites are rare, but include the Late Mesolithic site of Jühnsdorf-Autobahn in East Germany, where the motorway destroyed a number of features interpreted as hut-pits, leaving twenty-seven to be excavated (Gramsch, 1973). The pits were roughly oval (varying from about 8 m² to 3·5 m²). Hearths were found in all of them, established in deep fire-pits usually towards one side of the dwelling pit. The presence of charcoal high up the pits indicated that the dwelling levels were not at the base of the pits. Gramsch calculates that, if between eight and fifteen pits were in occupation simultaneously, from forty to 100 people might have occupied the site, representing a 'local group' (1973, p. 76).

Gramsch suggests that the majority of Mesolithic sites between the Elbe and the Oder are situated near water, on the Baltic sea-coast or the edges of lakes, rivers or pools, and nearly all on light sandy soils. The proximity of water means that animals can be captured as they come to drink, and that there are plenty of fish and waterfowl. In fact, faunal results from the site of Hohen Viecheln, situated beside Lake Schwerin, revealed that many types of divers, duck, geese and lakeside birds had been consumed, plus thirty-two pike and other fish totalling 150 kg edible weight. By contrast, large animals such as red deer, aurochs, boar, reindeer and elk represented over 4,000 kg meat weight. Good preservation conditions revealed that the

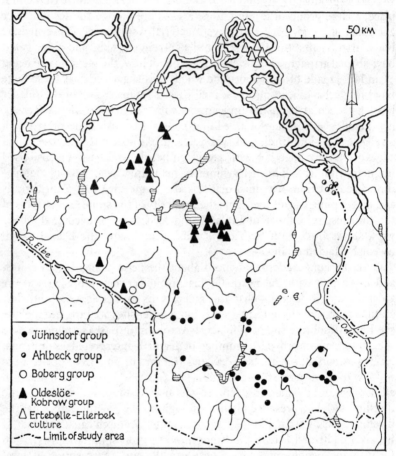

Fig. 38. Polish Mesolithic 'territories' (after Gramsch, 1973, map 6)

inhabitants of Hohen Viecheln had used blunt-ended wooden arrowheads and a wooden spear, possibly mounted with a bone point, as well as microlithic points.

Figure 38 (after Gramsch, 1973, fig. 5) can be interpreted as showing the limits of contemporary territories. Gramsch calculates that fifteen territories are represented: if each held a local group (of the 40–100-people size estimated for Jühnsdorf), then a population of between 600 and 1500 people might have been distributed over more than 47,000 km², i.e. 1·3 to 3·2 people per 100 km² (Gramsch, 1973, p. 76).

The variability in site location within Europe can be seen by the fact that to the south of the area discussed by Gramsch a review of the Mesolithic sites of Bohemia has produced very different conclusions. Here Vencl suggests that Mesolithic groups had much more circumscribed territories than Upper Palaeolithic groups in the same area (1970, 1971). Vencl has located forty-two Mesolithic sites in Bohemia, and strongly disputes the idea that these were always on sandy ground, or located close to water. The majority of the sites in fact are on relatively high ground, and relatively far from water. They are located on dry pervious weathered soils, about half of them on sand or gravel, and some even on clay (Fig. 39). The real reason behind the location of particular sites seems to have been that they were hunting camps, although this is not capable of proof in the absence of bone remains. Only one clear case of fishing has been found. It is also interesting that one quarter of the sites were previously occupied in the Palaeolithic. Vencl concludes that a whole range of reasons, geological, topographical, to do with climate and biological richness, and also cultural reasons, would lead to the location of settlements. Flint tools found on the sites were made on micro-cores, most of them in a poor-quality local flint of Silurian origin. Other sites use local schists as a raw material. Vencl contrasts this use of local resources with the situation in the late and final Palaeolithic (1970).

The problem of establishing activities at the Dutch sites, which, like the Bohemian ones, lack bone and other organic remains, has already been mentioned. Newell found great difficulty in seriating the stone-tool assemblages from the various sites before dividing them up on the basis of size. He regarded the actual settlement area as that of the maximum distribution of *retouched* tools. This gave the following four divisions: (a) small round sites c. 6 – 8 m², with a mean of eighteen retouched tools; (b) small oval sites c. 32 m² with a mean of thirty-seven retouched tools; (c) trapezoidal-shaped sites c. 480 m² with a mean of 243 retouched tools; and (d) large elliptical sites c. 2800 m² with over 5,000 retouched tools. Only the last two types of site had the full range of tool types amenable to seriation, and Newell regards these as home-base or maintenance camps. The small round and small oval types are interpreted as subordinate extraction camps, where only a few activities were carried out, resulting in a biased sample of tools. Types (a), (b) and (c) are known from the early phases of the Mesolithic in the Netherlands, but type (d) only appears towards the beginning of the Atlantic, contemporary with the rise in sea

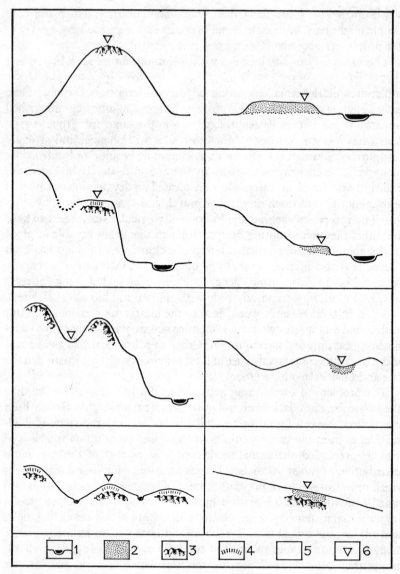

Fig. 39. Topographic location of Mesolithic sites in Czechoslovakia (after Vencl, 1971, fig. 8)

1 River, stream	3 Rock	5 Unexcavated
2 Sand, gravel	4 Disintegrated layer	6 Location of site

level (Fig. 40). It is associated with a culture known as the De Leien-Wartena, assumed to derive from the tool-kits of Maglemosian-type peoples moving inland from the lost North Sea plains. Some plant remains are recorded on some of their sites (remains of waternuts, acorns and cherry pips).

A number of sites with recognizable structures are beginning to be reported not only in the Netherlands (e.g. Bergumeer; Newell, 1973), but also in the Paris basin. Hinout has published a partial plan of the site of Sonchamp S3 (1976, fig. 3), revealing the plan of a hut with a central stone-packed hearth; Rozoy has estimated that it could have housed from five to twenty people (1976). The flint-working area at Sonchamp lies to the south of the hut, associated with small hearths in the sand near by, and one might question if these were not used to heat the flint, to make it easier to work. The presence of carbonized hazel-nuts suggests an autumn occupation. Sonchamp is one of a number of open and cave sites in the Paris basin which contain evidence of the materials used for art in the round and on cave walls at this period.

CULTURES AND TECHNOCOMPLEXES IN THE EUROPEAN MESOLITHIC

In the above section a number of cultures and technocomplexes were alluded to: these are defined on the basis of the chipped-stone industries (and ground stone in north-east Europe), on artifacts in organic materials, art, and features of settlement and activities. On a small scale, in favourable areas, an extremely detailed picture of variability over time and space can be built up (e.g. southern France or Denmark). However, since the Meso-lithic period covers aproximately 5000 years of changing environments and economic practices, assumed to involve seasonal differences in activi-ty (and thereby material culture), it is very difficult to define clear-cut cultural blocks at any point in time. Workers like S. K. Kozlowski have tried to define three or four great zones ('culture cycles') of Europe on the basis of their flint industries. The first is the northern zone, which developed from the Late Palaeolithic of north-west and central Europe, and reaches from Poland to Britain. North-east Poland and the forest zone of Europe and Russia comprise the north-eastern zone, derived from Palaeolithic 'Siberian' cultures. In western Europe another cycle derives from local Palaeolithic cultures. These divisions are broadly useful, but the central Mediterranean and south-east Europe remain to be incor-porated. In these areas there is no sharp change at the beginning of the post-glacial either in environment or industries: in Italy the Epigravettian persists until the eleventh millennium B.P. in north Italy and the mid

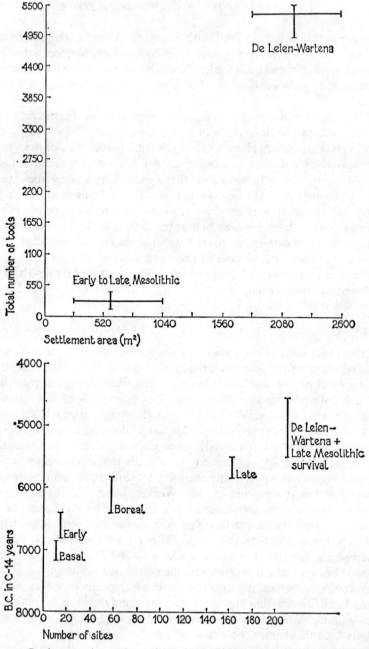

Fig. 40. Settlement size and number of Dutch Mesolithic sites (after Newell, 1973, graphs 6 and 7)

ninth millennium B.P. in the Italian peninsula. Despite the lack of good dating evidence in much of south-east Europe, Epigravettian industries *seem* to continue during the post-glacial. Four large zones can thus be recognized.

Mesolithic industries are usually distinguished by the presence of very small flint blades, either struck from small cores, or consisting of snapped-off segments of blades struck from larger cores. These small blades may be vertically retouched on one margin or on both. In the Mesolithic period the bow came into prominence (a number of wooden bow-shafts have been preserved, such as the Lithuanian examples mentioned above). Not only recognizable arrowheads, like those of the Polish Swiderian culture of the Early Mesolithic, but also some of the sharp-edged blade fragments and carefully retouched microliths represent elements of multi-tooth hunting arrows. Others may have been incorporated in tools for plant-food preparation, like graters, according to David Clarke (1976a).

At a late stage in the Mesolithic there is Europe-wide distribution of small triangular points (called Sauveterrian after the type-site of Sauve-terre-la-Lemance) and chisel-edged blade segments (called Tardenoisian after the type-site of Fère-en-Tardenois; both type-sites are in south-west France), in the ninth and eighth millennia B.P. respectively. S. K. Kozlowski visualizes these points and trapezes as parts of stone industries, or components. The 'S' (Sauveterrian) component, according to Kozlow-ski, consists of two types of triangles, Sauveterrian points, small lunate flints and backed blades, and narrow blades. In Kozlowski's view this component spreads from a southern French homeland to much of western and central Europe, and to England and Wales (1976a, fig. 2). In its area of origin it comprised the most important part of the tool-kit, but as it spread it occupied a smaller and smaller place in the tool-kits of those with whom it came into contact. Component 'K' (Tardenoisian) consists of trapezes, mainly asymmetrical, and long 'Montbani-type' blades (Fig. 41). The 'K' component spreads from southern France, fails to penetrate Britain, but otherwise extends from the Iberian peninsula to southern Sweden. It is not found east of the Danube (S. K. Kozlowski, 1976a, fig. 3). The 'K' components vanish most quickly in their area of origin. Kozlowski does not regard migration as the major explanation of this phenomenon, but suggests that certain groups of individuals could have moved northwards. Whether these changes were important in the techno-logical, economic or artistic subsystems is still open to question, as is the articulation of the populations adopting them. The speed of spread is reminiscent of similar diffusions of art or dance styles among the Australian aborigines in the recent past (Mulvaney, personal communication), and

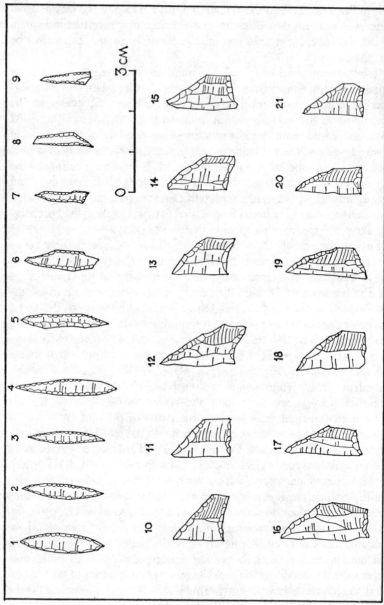

Fig. 41. Mesolithic microliths: 's' and 'κ' components ('s' components in top row) (after S. Kozlowski, 1764, fig. 1)

gives the impression that the seasonal agglomerations of Late Mesolithic populations were ideal vehicles for the exchange of artifacts or ideas.

ART AND BURIAL

Some intesting new information is available about art and burial practices in the European Epipalaeolithic-Mesolithic, which must reflect aspects both of the technological and – to a much greater extent – the belief subsystems. More cemeteries have come to light, and three in particular will be discussed below – from the north-east, northern and south-east zones of Europe respectively.

The north-east zone cemetery is at Zvejnieki, Lithuania (Zagorski, 1973). The cemetery lies to the west of a settlement located on a sandy hill at the junction of a river and a lake. The settlement was occupied in both the Late Mesolithic and the Neolithic, and only sixty of the 304 graves can be definitely assigned (by their grave-goods) to the Late Mesolithic. Others which lack grave-goods may belong to either period. Typologically the graves have been dated from the second half of the eighth millennium to about the end of the sixth millennium B.P. Several graves are multiple. For instance, in grave-pit 16, a sixteen-year-old girl lay extended, with a bone spear-point over her hip, and five elk-teeth pendants near her head. The body had been covered with red ochre, and above it were two other graves, Nos. 14 and 15, both containing skeletons of adults lying on their backs. Another multiple grave was 2 m long by 90 cm wide, and contained the bodies of two adults and three children. The first adult lay supine, accompanied by twenty-three grooved teeth pendants and ochre. Near the head on the right side, lay one child accompanied by twenty-three grooved teeth pendants and ochre, and near the feet, still on the right side, a child accompanied by a decorated bone dagger, a curved bone dagger, forty-six unbored teeth, one bored tooth, and again ochre. A third child lay to the left of the adult's legs, with four grooved boar-tusk pendants over the head, thirty-seven grooved elk molars in the hip region, and a covering of ochre. Single burials also occurred, like grave 57, which was full of ochre, and contained the body of a woman lying on her back; her arms and legs had been tied tightly together. A stone axe lay below her head, and a small scraper on her chest. Between her knees was a bone dagger with the handle in the shape of an elk, and a couple of flint knives. Below the left tibia lay a bone spear-point, and teeth pendants lay near the left hip (Zagorski, 1973) (Fig. 42A).

There are obviously differences in treatment of the various adults and children buried in these graves, and the presence of richly endowed child

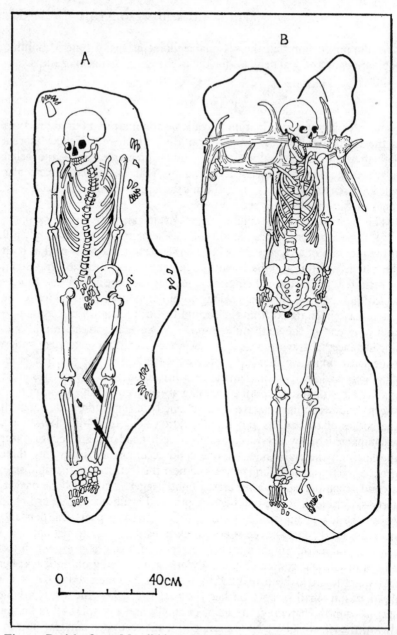

Fig. 42. Burials from Mesolithic cemeteries: (A) Zvejnieki, Lithuania; and (B) Vedbæk, Denmark (after Zagorski, 1973, fig. 1, and Albrethsen and Brinch Petersen 1975, end-plate)

graves suggests some degree of status acquired at birth. The occurrence of multiple graves gives the impression that a definite memory of the earlier event existed, and that perhaps families were grouped in particular areas of the cemetery. The skeletal remains are described as belonging to two different types, an Europoid with a fairly massive, long skull, and very wide and high-profiled, protruding nose, and a round-headed type with a wide, low, flat face and flattish nose. Perhaps this site was on the boundary of territories of people who had previously been genetically more isolated, accounting for the diversity in the skeletal remains. The flattish-faced skeletal type is also represented further to the north-east, in the Olen'i Ostrove cemetery, and to the south in cemeteries on the middle Dnieper.

Mesolithic cemeteries are normally rare, but a recent find at Vedbæk in Denmark provides a good contrast to the Lithuanian site (Albrethsen and Brinch Petersen, 1975). Here the date, according to archaeological typology, is c. 6000 B.P. The site is in an area well-known for Mesolithic settlement, but was found accidentally. So far, seventeen graves are known. All of them are contained in a ½-m-deep pit, of rectangular or approximately oval outline. Most graves only contain one body (e.g. Fig 42B), though multiple burials do occur. As with the Lithuanian site most of the bodies are buried in extended form, on the back. Among the most remarkable finds was that of a multiple burial of man, woman and new-born foetus; the man was aged twenty to twenty-five, and the woman somewhat older. She had a necklace of pierced teeth, and there was ochre around the skull and pelvic areas of both. Otherwise there were no grave-goods, and the presence of a bone dagger, apparently in the man's chest, and the fact that their arms seem to have been staked together suggest that they came to an untimely end.

The grave-goods vary in richness, as at Zvejnieki. No. 4, which was a male grave, contained a long flint knife and a slotted bone dagger near the waist, and six wild-boar teeth in the hip region. Grave No. 8 contained the bodies of a woman and new-born baby. The woman was about twenty years old, and around her head lay about 190 teeth of red deer and wild boar, and a little heap of perforated snail shells. Around the hip lay another fifty tooth pendants of red deer, and one of elk, and several rows of perforated snail shells of the same species (*Neritina fluviatalis*). The child's skeleton had a flint blade at the waist, and lay on a swan's wing. This special treatment of a very young child seems to indicate that a certain amount of status was already obtained by heredity, rather than achievement.

The use of ochre, continuing from the Upper Palaeolithic, marks most Mesolithic burials, including the cemeteries off the Breton coast and at the mouth of the Tagus in Portugal. At a new site on Kythnos in the Cyclades, the same feature has been noted. The site is called Maroula, and consists of a seaside camp and a burial ground. The site has a carbon-14 date of 7875 ± 500 B.P., which the excavator regards as too recent, since the chipped-stone industry – containing denticulates and a few geometric microliths and bladelets – is not unlike the Franchthi industry (Honea, 1976). Obsidian from Melos and chert from Paros bear witness to the trade and exchange taking place within the Cycladic islands. There are about a dozen burials, some of which are complete and lying in a flexed position, others only partial burials. All of them were sprinkled with red ochre.

Detailed palaeoanthropological information is available for burials at the Iron Gates gorge on the Danube; burials have been found at Lepenski Vir, Padina and Vlasac in Yugoslavia, and at six sites on the left bank in Romania (Nemeskeri, 1976). A brief report on the Padina skeletons by Zvinanovic indicates that these consisted of Cro-Magnon type people, with long skulls and low vaults, large eyebrow ridges and large jaws. Both the skull and limb-bones bear the imprints of heavy muscles. Nemeskeri has worked on the principle that the nine sites on either side of the Danube were occupied by a single population (1976). A total of approximately 350 bodies have been found at the sites, but the series from Vlasac level I (dated 7950–7650 B.P.), consisting of fifty-seven bodies, was an important sample. Despite the favourable palaeoecological situation, providing fish and meat protein, as discussed above, Nemeskeri found evidence of malnutrition among some of the younger subjects. However, when the twelve skeletons from Vlasac II and nine from Vlasac III (extending in time from 7650 to 7350 B.P.) are added to those from Vlasac I the number of child burials is remarkably low. Nemeskeri considers that the majority of very young children would not be buried at all, and might in fact be thrown into the Danube, where scattered bones from young children have occasionally been found. Nemeskeri estimates that average life expectancy for people in the Vlasac I settlement would have been just over twenty-six years, and for the Vlasac II people about twenty-nine years. Once past juvenile status, however, the average age of death seemed to be between thirty and thirty-nine years for women, and fifty to fifty-nine years for men. Eight men and two women survived to between sixty-four and sixty-nine years old. Interestingly enough, there were signs that some people had had severe illnesses which produced pathological deformations of their bones, and had none the less lived to what was a good age. Nemeskeri regards this as indicating the evolved nature of social organization. Taking the Yugoslavian and Romanian sites of the Iron Gates as a whole, Nemes-keri calculates that one generation could vary between sixty-six and 115 people in all, distributed in eight or ten subpopulations on the two banks of the Danube. The population only increased very slowly, by 0.005 per cent, as the number of births and deaths seems to have remained more or less steady.

Reflections of a society's beliefs can be found not only in the way people bury their dead, but in the art forms they create. At Lepenski Vir, boulders from the river were sculpted to form massive heads (Pl. 4). In the Iberian peninsula the walls of rock-shelters were covered with paintings, including compositions of hunting and food-collecting and warfare. Spanish archae-ologists have been divided in their attitude towards the dating of this art; once it was all regarded as of Epipalaeolithic date, but Fortea has recently suggested that, while the lineal geometric art *is* Epipalaeolithic, the natur-alistic art is later (beginning *c*. 7000 B.P.). At three caves the Levantine or naturalistic art is superimposed on the lineal art styles (Fortea, 1975, p. 254). Fortea feels there is also a geographical dimension to the diversity of art, in that the Upper Aragon area has more of the Epipalaeolithic art, while Lower Aragon has more of the 'naturalistic' art. He links this with new economic activities. Cerda also considers that the naturalistic art is to be dated to the Neolithic. Other workers, including Savory, have proposed that the naturalistic art began, at least, in the Epipalaeolithic (1968). Perhaps it will prove possible to date the paints used in these paintings to obtain independent evidence for dating. The question is an important one because of the compositions, including the warfare scenes; do these reflect Epipalaeolithic men defending their territories? Aggression and defence on a group scale can often be suggested in Neolithic contexts, but there is no such data as yet from the Epipalaeolithic, if these paintings be excluded. Certainly some of the scenes reflect events that could well have occurred in the Mesolithic: for instance, the red painting of a hunter shooting an ibex (Cueva Maringer, Castellón), the painting of another hunter shooting an enormous red deer (Mas d'en Josep, Castellón), and the honey-gathering scene from Cueva de la Araña, Valencia. Other areas with rock-shelter art are near Trieste, where animals are again depicted, and the Paris basin. Here Hinout has recently published what appear to be outlines of huts, schematic people and animals, and geometric designs (1975).

The Paris-basin sites also produced engravings on schist and sandstone blocks, and other decorated stones are known from Sicily and eastern Spain. Recently an engraving of a woman in bas relief, on a piece of deer antler, was found in a Mesolithic level at the Gaban rock-shelter in north

Italy (Graziosi, 1975). Further north 175 examples of bone, antler or amber artifacts decorated with naturalistic or more often impressionistic designs are known from Maglemosian contexts in Denmark, with similar designs on soapstone in south-west Norway. Brinch Petersen has indicated that, of the small percentage of art found on habitation sites, half comes from summer and half from winter camps (1976).

Mesolithic art has increased considerably in quantity in the last decade, and its study will further our understanding of some of the aspects of this very dynamic and varied period.

THE NEOLITHIC
(*c.* 8000–4000 B.P./*c.* 6800–2550 B.C.)

The Neolithic or New Stone Age has been the subject of many debates and discussions during the last decade. The Neolithic as conceived by early archaeologists was a period in which particular artifacts were associated with farming and pastoral economies. Both the artifacts and the economy represented a change from earlier periods. The artifactual changes included the first use of pottery, and the widespread manufacture and use of querns and axes in ground stone. The economic changes involved the transfer from hunting and gathering as the main modes of subsistence to either arable or pastoral farming. More precise methods of both excavation and dating have made it obvious that the artifactual and economic changes did not occur simultaneously – for instance, domesticated crops were apparently used *before* pottery in Greece and well *after* pottery in the west Mediterranean and Scandinavia. In addition, studies have shown that there was a difference in speed of take-up of the new techniques in different areas of Europe and this forms a fascinating area of research.

NEOLITHIC ECONOMIES

From the examples given in the last chapter, it will have been obvious that post-glacial economies were often closely tied to a series of plant or animal resources, and that knowledge of the behaviour of both plants and animals was very considerable. There are numerous stages between completely random acquisition of natural products and complete domestication of crops and animals. Many of these must have occurred during the

Epipalaeolithic and Mesolithic in Europe. Members of the Cambridge Early History of Agriculture Project see domestication as the 'end product of a series of gradually intensifying man–animal (and man–plant) relationships' (Jarman and Wilkinson, 1972). For archaeologists the interest lies in the changing relationships of man, animals and plants, whereas the morphological changes used by natural scientists to determine whether an animal or plant is domesticated appear long after changes in man–animal or man–plant behaviour have occurred. As Jarman and Wilkinson indicate, 'evidence from modern experiments suggests that rapid and striking phenotypic changes do not characterize most newly domesticated animals' (1972, p. 96). These authors have pointed out the drawbacks in nearly all the criteria formerly used to identify domesticated animals, finding the population structure the most hopeful of them. A thorough knowledge of the behaviour of each species at different times of the year is necessary to establish what the natural structure in the wild would have been. Bender (1975) also feels that the age/sex structure of the bone remains on an archaeological site is the best criterion to indicate potential domestication, and suggests that in the Near East this sort of change occurs well before any morphological change (for instance the foreshortening of the face in the pig and dog in contrast to their wild prototypes). Bender defines domestication as 'manipulation that resulted in genetic change', so that only animals which show some differences in facial characteristics, reduction in size of joint facets, horn or hair changes, would be regarded as truly domesticated.

Terms like 'herding' or 'husbandry' have been used for stages of animal manipulation prior to the obvious signs of morphological change.

Genetical changes in plants could apparently have occurred quite rapidly, much more rapidly than in animal populations, but there are no generally accepted methods for measuring the amount of human control being exerted over plant populations prior to their botanical determination as domesticates. In general, the botanical criteria for domesticated grasses are the toughening of the rachis, which holds the ear on to the stem, and the loss of the husk from around the seed. However, one frequently cultivated prehistoric wheat, spelt, has a brittle rachis, and tough rachis specimens occur even amid wild populations. Bender suggests that grain samples should only be regarded as domesticated when most of the grains have a tough rachis (1975). The modern distribution of the wild ancestors of wheats and barleys was supposed to indicate the probable area of their original domestication (e.g. Piggott, 1965) but both Heather Jarman and Bender throw doubt on this interpretation, Jarman suggesting that changes in plant cover can take place rapidly as a result of either human or natural changes, and pointing out that in any case the present-day wild species may differ from those which gave rise to domesticated crops. The genetical relationship between the various wheats (diploid, tetraploid and hexaploid) is still under discussion (J. M. Renfrew, 1973; H. N. Jarman, 1972). The stages of domestication of pulse crops and fruits are also only partially understood (J. M. Renfrew, 1973).

In the next chapter animal and plant samples will be accepted as domesticated when they have been subjected to recent analysis, but the problems mentioned above, still in the course of discussion and only partially resolved, must be kept in mind by the reader. Other evidence can also be useful in estimating the likely status of the plants and animals consumed on any particular site. Pollen analysis can indicate a decline in tree pollen and an increase in crop weeds or cereals, suggesting farming activities carried out near the site. A study of the site territory from the point of view of soil type and vegetation is also useful. Higgs and H. Jarman have contrasted the general economies possible in lowland and upland territories (Higgs, 1975b; Jarman, 1975), while on a more regional scale research workers have analysed the site territories of many Neolithic sites. Many European archaeologists have provided distribution maps for Neolithic settlements at different periods, obtained by site survey and excavation, and linked them to the soils and geomorphology.

A crucial element in the understanding of the spread of both farming and potting techniques is radiocarbon dating. A decade ago Grahame Clark's map of radiocarbon dates for sites of domesticated animals and plants illustrated the primacy of the east over the west of Europe (1965). This seemed to confirm the traditional hypothesis that the knowledge of animal and plant domestication had spread from the Near East into Europe. In the past decade refinements of radiocarbon dating methods, and comparison of carbon-14 dates derived from wood with their true tree-ring dates Before Present, have made the chronology of much of the Neolithic period more precise. Calibration to more accurate dates not only elongates the period allotted in this chapter to the development of farming systems by nearly 350 years, but also alters the relationships between some of the sites. For instance, radiocarbon dating of animal bones by Protsch and Berger has indicated that cattle and pig were domesticated earlier in Greece than in the Near East (1973). These authors conclude, however, that sheep and goat were probably first domesticated in the Near East (assuming that sheep became extinct in western Europe after the end of the Pleistocene). Of the other domesticated animals, the domesticated dog is known in the Mesolithic in western Europe, as already indicated in the last chapter. Even earlier dogs are reported from north America and Late Palaeolithic Mezin, Ukraine. The earliest domestication of the horse seems to have been in the Russian Ukraine.

The dates reported by Protsch and Berger were run on actual bones taken from carefully excavated sites. The site which provided most of the early dates was Argissa Magula in north Greece, where domesticated animal bones and cereal remains, but no pottery, are found in the lowest levels (Milojcic *et al.*, 1962).

Although wild cattle and boar and perhaps sheep in some areas were native to Europe, the assumed progenitors of domesticated grain like wheat and barley are not known today from the European area. No large-scale study has used seeds as the test material for carbon-14 dates. It has been generally assumed by workers in palaeoethnobotany that cereal crops were first domesticated somewhere in the Anatolia–Iran area, and that the idea of their domestication, and very likely bags of grain, were taken from east to west. According to J. Renfrew much the same crops appear in Greece as in the Near East, with emmer as the main wheat type plus einkorn wheat, hulled and naked two-row barley, and hulled six-row barley, millet and oats. Other plant foods consist of peas, lentils, vetch, acorns and pistachio nutlets. As was noted in the last chapter, vetch was widely collected in the Mediterranean lands prior to the Neolithic. Pulses such as vetch, lentils, peas and beans can replace some of the soil fertility lost in growing cereals, and provide a valuable added source of protein. The crops mentioned above, with the addition of bread and spelt wheat, flax and other fruits are represented on European sites in the central European area from Holland to Poland, along the Mediterranean coasts, and as far as southern Britain. Chronologically, these areas all seem to post-date the Near East and the Aegean in their use of cereals and pulses.

Apart from an increasing number of well-excavated sites, where the soil deposits have been water-sieved to provide the most accurate samples of grain and seed and nut remains, there is inadequate information over Europe as a whole for the type of economy practised at each Neolithic site. For this reason, there has been some criticism of an otherwise interesting study on measuring the rate of spread of early farming in Europe carried out by Ammerman and Cavalli-Sforza (1971). This study took fifty-three European Early Neolithic sites with carbon-14 dates, and plotted their distance from a number of supposed centres of domestication, such as Jericho and Jarmo in the Near East (Fig. 43). The distances between the European sites and the Near Eastern centres were computed as great-circle routes. There were very high correlations when the data were tested to see if a constant rate of spread had been achieved over time and space. The authors interpreted their results as a wave-of-advance model, with populations on the frontier increasing dramatically and pushing forward some 18 km every generation (twenty-five years). Given this rate of advance, from the Near East, Europe would have been covered by farming populations by approximately 3800 B.C. However, the validity of the Ammerman and Cavalli-Sforza study is slightly reduced by the fact that

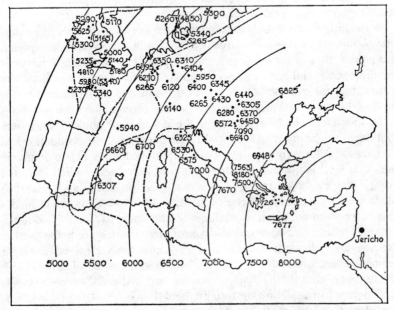

Fig. 43. The spread of early farming in Europe (B.P. dates) (after Ammerman and Cavalli-Sforza, 1971, fig. 6)

not all their sites actually contained cereals. It could be argued that they were measuring the spread of pottery rather than the spread of cereals, and further that the small number of sites was not truly representative. Their conclusion that differences of soil and vegetation type and climatic variability were of no importance in this spread can also be criticized in the light of studies quoted below. A further study by these authors, using only sites with proven cereal economies, would be very useful.

TECHNOLOGY AND SOCIETY

Apart from studies relevant to the economic subsystem, the last decade has increased our knowledge and provided new interpretations in many other subsystems. Investigators have studied the working of bone, wood, stone and pottery. Handles of Swiss Neolithic axes have been proved by study of their tree rings to have been manufactured from part of the tree trunk and part of the root (Müller-Beck, 1965), while other experiments have proved that the resistance of these handles is equal or superior to those manufactured by craftsmen today. The work of Mme Camps-Fabrer and her collaborators has suggested new refinements in our methods of studying bone and antler artifacts (1974).

With chipped-stone tools in particular, the use of computers and quantitative methods has enabled large bodies of information to be interpreted more precisely and for cultures to be compared, for instance, in terms of the dimensions and edge angles of scrapers and flake tools, which usually form a high proportion of any Neolithic industry. Much more work is needed, however. A Polish archaeologist has listed among the questions to be answered, the 'elucidation of the question of holding sway over flint deposits, the problem of specialization in exploitation, production and exchange' (Balcer, 1971a). The types of chipped-stone debris found in mines, at workshops and on settlement sites have been studied from the points of view of morphology, technological processes and quantity; blade scars on cores have been counted, to show the numbers of blades that were exported from workshops at the source (S. K. Kozlowski, 1976b). Physical and chemical analyses of raw materials are being used to provide an independent indication of connections between different regions. The study of thin-sections of hard stone or pottery has indicated, for instance, that in the Early Neolithic fine red-polished pottery was traded from Cornwall into western England (Peacock 1969). Thin-sectioning of axes, adzes, mace-heads and other implements with shaftholes, especially in areas well studied geologically, such as Britain and France, can provide a definite attribution of at least 50 per cent of these tools to known sources of material (Cummins, 1974; Le Roux, 1975). Optical-emission spectroscopy and neutron-activation analyses of flint and obsidian are well advanced in western Europe. It has proved possible to distinguish British and Continental flint-mine products from each other (Sieveking et al., 1970), and preliminary studies of flint axes and other artifacts suggest the likelihood that some at least can be assigned to probable source sites.

Obsidian is easier than flint to 'fingerprint', and the pattern of distribution from obsidian sources in the Mediterranean – mostly islands – to other islands and the mainland has been demonstrated in a number of articles (e.g. Dixon et al., 1968; Hallam et al., 1976). These studies have demonstrated that the east Mediterranean and the west Mediterranean were two separate trading areas in obsidian, and also that their exchange spheres hardly overlapped with those of the Hungarian source in the Bükk mountains (Fig. 44).

Studies of sources of raw materials, of the pattern of working of the material near to the source, and of its final distribution, are important not only in the economic, but also in the social subsystem (Sherratt, 1976). Although each Neolithic settlement is assumed to have been self-sufficient in subsistence terms, the scientifically documented spread of stone and other materials clearly shows that exchanges of useful materials occurred, based on social relationships between different populations. Interpretations of the distributions of, for instance, particular raw materials for axes in Britain, or obsidian types in the Mediterranean, mostly show what Renfrew has called an 'exponential fall-off' from the source site to the far point of distribution. However, in a number of cases there are indications of different mechanisms: for instance, the axes made from volcanic tuff originating in north-west England are mainly found around the Humber estuary in east England, from where they may have been redistributed. Similarly, there are several hundred pieces of obsidian in Pescale, north Italy, which may also have been a redistribution point: the pieces tested came from Sardinia (Hallam et al., 1976). Such anomalies, demanding more sophisticated explanations, are frequent throughout this period.

The social subsystems of Neolithic Europe are also being studied via analysis of whole settlements and the location of different activities within them, and on a smaller scale by using details of manufacture and design to identify, for instance, family-tradition or specialist potters. Another area of study is the actual skeletal remains of Neolithic men and women.

Ammerman and Cavalli-Sforza's wave-of-advance model for the adoption of farming in Europe visualized a series of frontier situations where farmers were face to face with hunter-gatherers. On these frontiers the rate of population increase would be very high, while further back among settled farmers it would steady. The hunter-gatherer populations would be pushed back by force of numbers. One test for this model is to look at the skeletal remains of European Epipalaeolithic-Mesolithic and Neolithic populations. This has been done in Volume VIII of an important series of publications edited by Schwabedissen, *Die Anfänge des Neolithikums vom Orient bis Europa* (The Beginnings of the Neolithic from the Orient to Europe). It is a difficult problem, owing to the low numbers of Epipalaeolithic-Mesolithic skeletons, most of them in fact contemporary with the beginnings of farming populations in other parts of Europe (Asmus, 1973), and to the varied criteria used to study them. Asmus visualizes rather variable post-glacial populations, going from tall people with

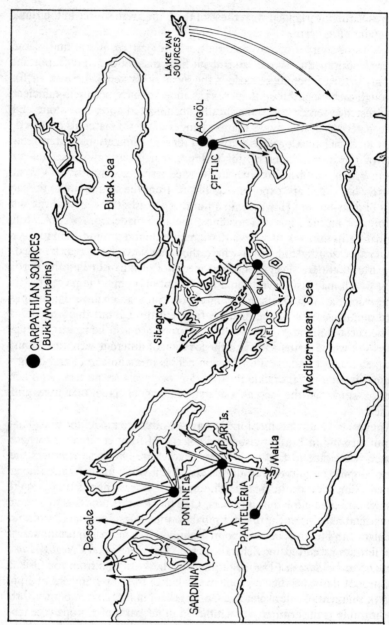

Fig. 44. Distribution zones of obsidian in Europe and the Mediterranean basin (after S. Warren, unpublished, with additions)

elongated narrow heads in the Ukraine to more robust individuals of average or sub-average height in Brittany. However, there is variability within populations; for instance, the occupants of the Muge middens in Portugal are mostly gracile individuals while a few skulls tend towards brachycephaly. This shortening and widening of the cranium coincides with the beginning of the Neolithic. Since present-day studies of changes in stature, robustness and facial characteristics emphasize the importance that environment and diet can play, it is difficult without very clear evidence to claim immigration as a mechanism for change. Most European physical anthropologists contributing to the Schwabedissen volume reported little obvious physical change at the beginning of the Neolithic; for instance, Czech populations described as Mediterranean types, with very long heads, were regarded as having persisted broadly unchanged since the Palaeolithic, and similar findings were reported from Austria, Romania, the Balkans and the west Mediterranean. In a few areas such as northern France change was indicated. The greatest changes in the European Neolithic populations take place in fact in the Late Neolithic, when for instance skulls of a different, flat-backed and steep-sided shape are reported in Bell Beaker graves in central Europe and in ochre graves in east Europe, and much taller individuals are buried in Scandinavian stone cists. Anthropologically speaking, the advance of farming techniques seems to depend more on the transmission of ideas than people, and the constant 'frontier population explosion' of Ammerman and Cavalli-Sforza is not visible on present evidence. However, the gradual increase of European populations over time to much higher levels by the beginning of the Bronze Age is undisputed.

The practice of collective burial in tombs, or of burial in cemeteries, is important in that once the age and sex of those buried has been determined, these results can be analysed to see if the whole local population was buried, or only a sample. Children under five, for instance, were rarely buried. The state of the bones can suggest pre-burial rites, such as exposure until the flesh rotted off, or partial burning. By dint of blood groupings or the presence of certain bone anomalies it has proved possible to detect the presence of genetically linked individuals in specific tombs. The fertility rate of women has been estimated; for instance at the Greek site of Nea Nikomedia, the physical anthropologist Angel suggested that the population would only have reproduced itself, not grown in size (1973). Ailments such as malaria in Greece and arthritis in Britain are recognizable from bone remains, and the Late Neolithic practice of trepanation (cutting a circlet of bone from the skull) suggests both considerable skill, since the victims often lived afterwards, and an interest in the cause of death indicated by post-mortem trepanation (Dastugue, 1973). Modern genetically based physical anthropology still has a long way to go in understanding the Neolithic, but this is an important growth area in research.

Details of the architecture and contents of Neolithic collective tombs, both stone-built and rock-cut, have been extensively published in the last decade (e.g. by the CNRS in France, Sprockhoff in Germany, Henshall in Britain), providing an essential basis for up-to-date theorizing and interpretation. The decade has been fruitful in providing ideas about the possible position of these tombs in the social and religious subsystems of their builders. The work of Thom, Hawkins and others on the tombs, the circles of standing stones, and the alignments of stones in Brittany and Britain has suggested the likelihood of considerable mathematical and astronomical capacity in Neolithic and Early Bronze Age societies, a point of view which has received some support from professional archaeologists (Hawkins, 1966; Thom, 1967; Atkinson, 1975).

In general, the increase in population which took place over this 4500-year span was of great importance for the social structure of the people involved. The social environment of most Early Neolithic groups would have been rather similar; however, by the Late Neolithic there is no doubt that in certain areas population increase had caused considerable revision in the social structures while in others the social environment remained relatively unchanged. In this chapter we shall follow the developments of the Neolithic in certain areas, and see some of this variability.

THE EARLY NEOLITHIC
(c. 8000 – 6000 B.P./6800 – 4900 B.C.)

This time period covers a large span of Neolithic development in some areas (Mediterranean, Balkans and Central Europe) while in others the Neolithic has hardly begun (Scandinavia, Switzerland, Britain). About 8000 B.P. there are two different sorts of 'neolithic' societies in the lands bordering the Mediterranean, some with domesticated animals and cereals but no pottery, others with pottery but less evidence for domesticated crops or animals. In the west Mediterranean, the Coppa Nevigata seacoast site in south-east Italy, with a single radiocarbon date of 8150 B.P., provides an illustration of a site with cockle-shell impressed pottery and subsistence based mainly on shellfish. In the south of France, at Cap Ragnon, a cave opening on to the Bay of Marseilles, two carbon-14 dates of 7970 and 7650 B.P. date an Early Neolithic occupation with cockle (= *Cardium*) impressed pottery. The inhabitants had caught fish (tunny, grouper, wrasse, and a number of other species), collected shellfish and land snails, and hunted a few land animals including red deer, rabbit, sheep and wild cattle. A number of the fish could have been caught by nets, as they are today, but tunny would have had to have been caught by boat (Courtin et al., 1970–72). There are no signs of cereal cultivation at this carefully excavated site, nor do cereals appear on other early sites in the west Mediterranean. For instance, at the rock-shelter site of Verdelpino near Cuenca in Spain (Pl. 15), Fernández-Miranda has excavated a level with a radiocarbon date of 7950 B.P. containing smooth-faced pottery and sheep bones, but with no sign of cereals (1974). Sheep bones were also found in south-west Corsica, at the pottery-using site of Basi, dated 7700 ± 150 B.P. (Bailloud, 1972). Sheep seem to have persisted from the post-Pleistocene in several parts of the west Mediterranean, and are represented on a number of eighth-millennium-B.P. sites, some of them pottery-using, others not. The presence of obsidian flakes at Basi, emanating from central Sardinia, is a further indicator of maritime activity in the west Mediterranean at this time.

The activities of fishermen or people sailing to trade or exchange obsidian could easily have diffused the idea of pottery within the west Mediterranean once it had been developed in one area. In the west Mediterranean, on Corsica and Sardinia, and from Italy to Spain, societies using cereals and domesticated animals continued to develop in the succeeding millennium, having been influenced by this time by the domestication techniques ultimately derived from the Near East. Tree-ring calibration can be used to give an accurate date (5320 B.C.) for the presence of emmer, einkorn, club wheat and naked six-row barley in eastern Spain, and at this same time period there is evidence of cereal cultivation in southern France. However, the regional quality of these developments has been emphasized recently (Phillips, 1975; Guilaine, 1976). There is slow evolution locally in the flint-tool industries from the Epipalaeolithic into the early Cardial period. Crouched burials with ochre and shell offerings continue. Regional differences are very evident in the way the cockle impression is organized on the surface of the pots. Diversification intensifies c. 4900 B.C. with some areas continuing to use the cockle-shell as the main item of decoration, for instance in the Provence area, while others go in for dot impressions, soft channelling or other decorative devices. Variety in economic practice can also be suggested because of the locations of the sites, many of them still the cave sites used by hunter-gatherer forebears or predecessors, others open sites containing one or several hut floors. Rather more complex settlements are located in south-eastern Italy, on the Tavolieri plain, where from c. 7000 B.P. plant and animal

domestication seems to have been practised. These settlements are surrounded by deep ditches, and consist of varied numbers of mostly round
huts, up to several hundred visible in some cases on aerial photographs.
The good agricultural potential of this region in the favourable Atlantic
climate has recently been emphasized by Jarman and Webley (1975).
These researchers have looked at the 1-km territories around the ditched
settlements and concluded that two thirds of the surrounding area
consisted of arable soils, which would have supported on average approximately fifty-five people annually at each site. In addition to cereals,
all domesticated animals are known from these sites and would also have
been a source of food. Jarman and Webley mention that other Early
Neolithic settlements exist on similar light, lowland soils, for instance in
the Matera area and on the coastal lowlands of Sicily (1975, p. 198). In
southern Italy pottery is decorated with red paint and scratched decoration in addition to shell impression. The three wares are found together
on many sites, and the question of whether one was earlier than the others
is still not satisfactorily answered.

Barker has recently discussed settlement and economy in central Italy
from a similar viewpoint (1975b). Using faunal evidence from both Epipalaeolithic sites and the earliest Neolithic sites, the latter dated about 5300
B.C., he has suggested that the changes probably resulted from a movement of people with knowledge of farming into the area. At the Leopardi
(Abruzzi) settlement, four new features appear simultaneously, pottery,
obsidian, cereals and sheep. The site territory was suitable for agriculture,
but in the summer the sheep would have had to have been taken to pastures several hours' travel away. However, elsewhere in the Abruzzi and
in the neighbouring Marche regions, Barker tentatively suggests that local
Epipalaeolithic groups persisted. Although pottery and domesticated
sheep are found on these sites, the stone-tool industries are very similar
to those of the preceding Epipalaeolithic in the area, and there are no
signs of cereal production. The sites are located in similar zones to those
of the previous hunting and gathering economies, at the junction of high
and low land. In northern Italy at this time the earliest Neolithic site is
the cave of Arene Candide on the Ligurian coast with a date of c. 5380 ±
135 B.C. for level 25. Here the main animal herded was sheep, followed
by pig, goat, cattle and red deer. The pottery is cockle impressed, and
obsidian is present, and in the absence of local Late Mesolithic occupation
this may represent an intrusive population. On the other side of the Ligurian Alps, hunter-gatherer societies continued until about 4900 B.C. or
slightly before, when the first pottery-using culture of the Po valley
began. On these Fiorano-culture pottery sites, the lithic industry suggests

continuity from the earlier hunter-gatherer culture; the development of farming economy in northern Italy was slow (M. Jarman, 1976).

In the Aegean area, careful new test excavations at the site of Knossos have revealed a sequence of occupation from about 8000 B.P. onwards (J. D. Evans, 1971a). Three radiocarbon dates date a pre-pottery occupation on the knoll of Knossos which extended over approximately half an acre (0·25 ha). Mud-brick walls were found, but no complete house plans; the occupants of the site cultivated bread wheat, emmer and einkorn, as well as barley and lentils. They had sheep, goats, pigs, and cattle, and imported obsidian from the Cycladic island of Melos. Although no potsherds were found during excavation, two baked clay figurines are known from this period. This site must have proved a promising one, for in the succeeding 1500 years about five acres (2 ha) of the natural promontory overlooking the Kairatos river were occupied. Pottery, spindle whorls and loom-weights were now in use, and several rooms of a house have been excavated (Evans, 1971a, fig. 5). The carbon-14 dates for this Early Neolithic I phase suggest that it was long and slow to change. The Early Neolithic II occupation of the early fifth millennium B.C. was over an even wider area than Early Neolithic I and included a number of houses with long rectangular rooms.

Evans and Renfrew have cooperated in the excavation of a pottery-using site on the small island of Saliagos, Cyclades, contemporary with Early Neolithic II at Knossos (carbon-14 dates 5130 to 4580 B.C.). Here Melos obsidian was used, and the greatest meat weight derived from bone remains was of tunny fish (possibly killed with obsidian arrowheads?). Goat, pig and cattle were kept, but provided a smaller percentage of the occupants' nourishment (Evans and Renfrew, 1968).

Milojcic's excavations at Argissa Magula in north Thessaly (Pl. 6) in the 1950s revealed levels without pottery (or with only a very few potsherds), yet with domesticated crops, below the level with the first Greek pottery (proto-Sesklo and Sesklo), the latter usually dated c. 8000 B.P. There is no carbon-14 date for the pre-pottery level, but obsidian from Melos was present, together with a few ornaments such as bone ear-plugs and perforated slate discs. The occupants of the riverside site, which was to develop into a tell, lived in a rectangular house with a clay floor and post-built walls and grew emmer, spelt, einkorn, barley, millet and lentils.

An American expedition recently tried to find the same pre-pottery level at the site of Achilleion, Thessaly; however, pottery was present from the earliest occupation, which dated from the mid eighth millennium B.P. (Ferguson et al., 1976). The site lay on a hillside in an area favourable for arable farming or pastoralism and with a perennial source of water

(Gimbutas, 1974a). It is suggested that the climate was wetter and cooler than at present, with areas of forest around. The inhabitants of the site depended mainly on domesticated animals and plants for their subsistence (93 per cent domesticated fauna, with a majority of sheep and goat). The cereals cultivated were emmer, einkorn, club wheat, millet and six-row barley. It is suggested that antler hoes were used for tilling the earth, and querns for grinding the grain; obsidian blades with sickle sheen from harvesting had come originally from Melos. Rectangular houses were found, 12 m² and 21 m² in different levels. The richness of Aegean inventories at this period is shown by the quantity of seals, stone vessels, pendants and figurines. Two hundred and twenty-seven figurines were found in dwellings and around the circular hearth of the courtyard (Gimbutas regards this as possibly a sacrificial hearth). She also concludes that a number of important ritual associations are represented by the finding together of figurines, cult vessels (for instance triangular-shaped pots) and fragments of vases with a face or mask modelled on them. The inhabitants of Achilleion had a busy range of activities, indicated by the presence of spindle whorls and bone needles (it is not known whether they spun flax or wool); they also manufactured reed mats, the impressions of which are found on the bases of some of the pots. The pots included plain rough wares, with painted pottery beginning in Phase Ib. By Phase III there were many footed vessels and rich painted designs in red on white.

Evidence from the Franchthi cave in the Argolid, mentioned in the last chapter, suggests that obsidian was being traded from Melos by the tenth millennium B.P. This evidence for early communications by sea in the Aegean makes it likely that a number of Mesolithic sites are still awaiting discovery. There are no confirmed Mesolithic sites on Crete, for instance, although Hutchinson mentions an old find of a site with obsidian but no pottery 3 km west of Heraklion (1962). Although many Early Neolithic sites in the Aegean are not located in the same spots as those of hunter-gatherer predecessors, the Franchthi cave itself does demonstrate a continuity of occupation in the same spot (Jacobsen, 1973). Technologically there are changes in the Neolithic levels, with an increase in the working of shell and polishing of stone and the presence of stone amulets and pottery, 75 per cent of it monochrome, the rest red-patterned. New crops include emmer, six-row barley and lentils. Although erosion has removed some of the levels immediately prior to Early Neolithic I, the site might represent acculturated hunter-gatherers rather than incoming colonists. Angel, in discussing the skeletal remains (in Jacobsen, 1973), claims that they could either derive from the local Mesolithic or be of ultimately eastern origin; there are no clear signs either way.

1 (top). Froth flotation (wet sieving) used to obtain seeds, plant remains, small bones and artifacts

2. Excavation of shell midden, Oronsay, Scotland

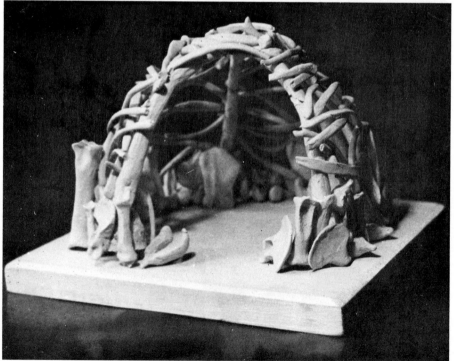

3 *(opposite)*. Reconstruction
framework of mammoth-bone
of Upper Palaeolithic huts
(a) at Mezhirich, Ukraine,
and (b) at Cracow, Poland

4 *(left)*. Carved river boulder (36 cm high)
from Epipalaeolithic site
at Lepenski Vir, Yugoslavia

5 *(below)*. Linear Pottery sites
menaced by lignite exploitation,
Merzbach valley, West Germany

6 (*opposite*). Tell excavation
at Argissa Magula, Greece

7 (*right*). Floor plans of
Neolithic (background)
and Early Bronze Age (foreground)
houses at Brezno, Czechoslovakia

8 (*below*). Hafted flint daggers
from Copper Age lakeside settlement
at Charavines, Isère, France

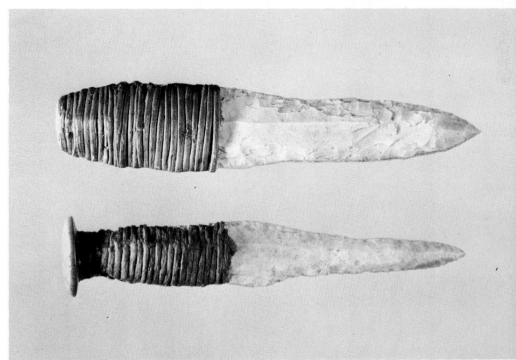

9. Late Neolithic figurines
from Eastern Europe:
(a, opposite) 16 cm high
and *(b, left)* 10 cm high,
from Predionica, Yugoslavia;
(c, below left) 25.6 cm high,
from Szegvar-Tüzköves, Hungary,
and *(d, below right)* 15 cm high,
from Pazardzik, Bulgaria

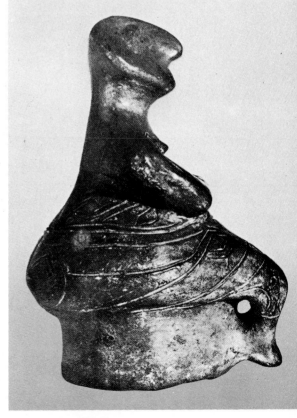

10. Main mound and satellite burial mounds from the Neolithic cemetery at Knowth, Eire

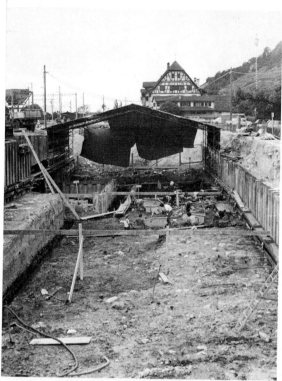

11 *(opposite)*. Neolithic hurdle trackway used to cross boggy ground, Walton Heath, Somerset, England

12 a and b. Lakeside rescue excavations of Neolithic settlement at Twann, Switzerland

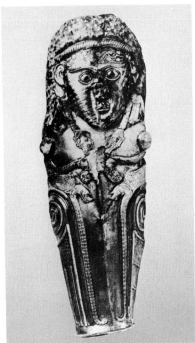

13 *(left)*. Wooden coffin of central grave of Early Iron Age Magdalenenberg barrow, southern Germany

14. Greave of silver and gold from the third century B.C. Vratsa treasure, Bulgaria (46 cm high)

15 (*opposite*). Cave site at Verdelpino, southern Spain

16 (*above*). Underwater excavation of first century B.C. shipwreck off Giens, southern France

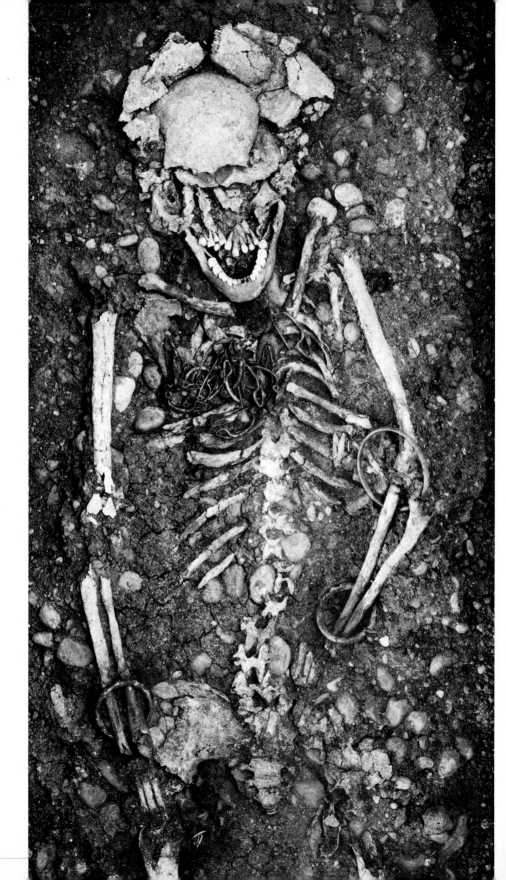

17 *(opposite)*. La Tène burial, Dietikon, Zürich, Switzerland

18 *(above)*. Bronze 'warriors' and 'chieftain' from Sardinia, late first millennium B.C.

19. Square-ditched Iron Age barrows seen from the air at Wetwang Slack, Yorkshire, England

Many cultural items are intrusive in the early Aegean Neolithic including things like stone and baked-clay lip plugs and seals, but Nandris has emphasized that local differentiation took place after the inception of cereal growing and animal herding. Nandris and other writers have also emphasized the importance of local environmental differences as the domestication processes spread northwards into the Balkans (1970). The transition was essentially from a Mediterranean to a temperate climate, with the Macedonia–Bulgaria area lying between the two extremes. In this area Gimbutas has recently excavated the site of Anzabegovo (1974b). Early levels of the site, which was settled about 7150 B.P., were occupied by people of the Starčevo culture, part of a broadly similar cultural block of the Early Neolithic in the Balkans (Karanovo I–Kremikovice–Starčevo–Körös–Criş). Anzabegovo is located in a shallow basin called Ovce Polje, drained by the Nikolska river whose waters eventually run into the Vardar. The site was settled when the climate was wetter than at present, and oak, pine, juniper and elm are well represented. The houses were of the same type of clay-plastered posts as in north Greece at Argissa Magula (Gimbutas, 1974b, fig. 11). The presence of spondylus beads and bracelets and figurines also showed links with the Aegean. However, studies of the stone materials used indicated that the majority could have been found locally, for instance the quartz and jasper and opalites used in the chipped-stone industry, and the dense metamorphic rocks used for grindstones. Axes were made of a serpentine-jadeite found in the nearby Bogoslav mountains. Wear-pattern analysis suggested that they had been used as both axes and adzes. Three varieties of wheat – emmer, einkorn and club – were grown together with hulled six-row barley and peas and lentils. Ninety per cent of the bones recovered were of domesticated animals, the majority caprines, the others being cattle, pig and dog. Anzabegovo is one of the few sites with such good economic evidence in the area and was used by Barker in his consideration of Early Neolithic settlement in Yugoslavia–Macedonia (1975a). Barker has suggested that the coarse alluviums covering the Ovce Polje basin would have been used for over-wintering of sheep, while the cereals and lentils could have been grown on a narrow strip alongside the river. He hypothesized that Anzabegovo and Vrsnik in the same area may have been slightly more pastoral in economic bias than the more southerly sites in Macedonia proper. On the other hand they may have been slightly more cereal-oriented than the sites to the north in the Morava valley. These suggestions are based on the site territories of the settlements involved, and are particularly related to the suitability of the local soils for the kind of agriculture practised. Lack of excavation prevented knowing whether chronological differences might be involved in the location of different sites, but on the whole it seemed likely that during the first millennium of cereal and pastoral economy in Yugoslavia settlers had chosen a variety of different habitats, and practised varying strategies.

Tringham has emphasized the great variability in environment, temperature and other regimes in the areas settled by the first Neolithic peoples of the Balkans (1971). She has also distinguished those areas where Neolithic settlers occupied sites different from those of Mesolithic inhabitants of the area, and those where they settled on the same or adjacent sites. For instance, in much of Bulgaria, where tell settlements were founded at this period, the middle of fertile plains or the area of spring lines were preferred to the riverside locations of hunters. Sherratt has explained that these areas had permanently moist soils, similar to the areas used for cereal growing in the Near East and Anatolia. The importance of the groundwater level on farming sites is one that is emphasized by a number of writers.

Dennell and Webley have looked at settlements and land use in southern Bulgaria using site location analysis (1975). Early Neolithic settlements in Bulgaria have produced emmer, einkorn and pulse crops (Karanovo I) and barley (Chevdar and Kazanluk). At the latter two sites the commonest animals were caprines, although cattle, deer and pig were also exploited. In the Nova Zagora region studied, the majority of sites were located on or near good arable soils although it seemed likely that the sheep would have had to have been moved into nearby hill areas during spring and early summer. There was an interesting relationship between the heights of tells and the amount of potential arable land within the site territory; the biggest tells such as Karanovo had the largest amounts of such land (i.e. the agricultural potential seems to have permitted more people to live there for longer), while the smallest tells had much less arable land in their territories. Tringham emphasizes two patterns in the Balkan Neolithic. The first is of the gradual loss of some of the more exotic products, such as painted pottery, in the move from south to north in the Balkans. The second is the difference between the high numbers of domesticated animals on sites not previously occupied by hunter-gatherers, and lower numbers on sites where hunter-gatherers had been previously located. At the Lepenski Vir fishing site on the banks of the Danube, the third settlement by Körös culture people had different architecture and flint tools from the earlier settlements, but they did some hunting and fishing, and only three quarters of the animal bone was from domesticated species. In the Prut river basin of north-east Romania, from about 7000 B.P. the Bug–Dniester culture shows considerable similarity to the preceding

Mesolithic, the majority of the faunal remains being of red deer and wild cattle, while only a few domesticated cattle bones, einkorn-wheat grains, axes, querns or sickle blades are identified from these sites. Further to the west, in coastal Yugoslavia, the first impressed pottery is found overlying non-pottery levels in caves, with the same type of stone tools in both levels. Here, as in the western Mediterranean, it is suggested that plant domestication, at least, was acquired later than pottery.

The Starçevo-Körös culture group continues in the Balkans until approximately 5280 or 5080 B.C. At that period the Vinča-Tordos culture group gradually develops with black burnished pottery, decorated by channelling and incising, replacing the painted and plain wares, and with a great deal more emphasis on trade or exchange, as evidenced by the presence of lots of obsidian and shell in these inland settlements. There is also an increase in figurines and 'face lids'. In a recent book, Gimbutas has claimed that over 30,000 miniature sculptures in clay and other raw materials are known from the Neolithic and Chalcolithic periods in southeast Europe (1974c). Gimbutas believes that the figurines represent a pantheon of gods later assimilated into Greek mythology, and that the various designs found on pottery and sculpture, for instance parallel lines, zigzags, chevrons, meanders, spirals etc. have symbolic meaning in the religion of the time. She has identified various figurines as representing the Pregnant Vegetation Goddess, the Great Goddess, the Bird and Snake Goddesses, and the Year God. The vast numbers of these figurines, and their association in some cases with apparent shrines, does seem to argue for an important religious subsystem within the cultures. In the Vinča period the figurines have strange flat faces, slightly tilted back, and Gimbutas has suggested that these represent masks (e.g. Pl. 9c); seventy figurines were found at the Anzabegovo mound, most in the later (Vinča) period of occupation. The last phase of the site is dated c. 5170 B.C.

The Linear Pottery cultures, dated from approximately 5320 to 4590 B.C., are distributed across central and northern Europe from Poland to Holland. It is generally accepted that they are an offshoot of Balkan farming cultures. In transitional zones in eastern Hungary and southeast Slovakia the fine-walled painted pottery of the Balkans is still found, but only the thicker organic-tempered wares penetrate further north. In the Linear Pottery sites stamp seals are lacking and figurines, spindle whorls and clay-loom weights are rare. The pottery is decorated with incised lines, in curvilinear or rectilinear designs (Fig. 45A). Later regional variation develops with dots or strokes inside the lines, and on the Pannonian plain a decoration like musical notes is added. Within the Linear Pottery populations a certain amount of exchange takes place, most clearly

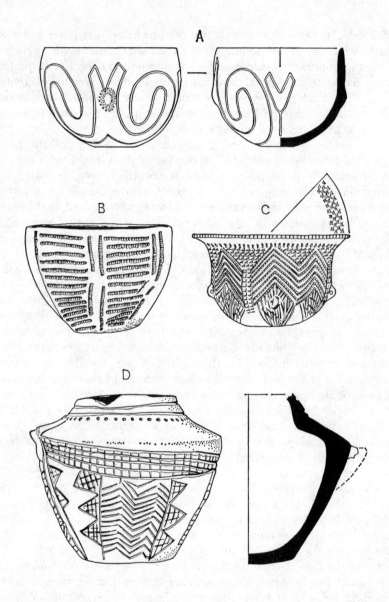

Fig. 45. Neolithic pottery styles: (A) Linear pottery, (B) Cardial ware, (C) Rossen pottery and (D) Incised ware (after Schwabedissen 1972, Va, pls. 5 and 5a; and VII, pls. 67, and 70)

shown by finds of spondylus shell from the Mediterranean and obsidian from Hungary. A number of Neolithic cave and open-air sites are known from the Bükk mountains of Hungary and they represent either trans-humant sites or settlements of people exploiting the obsidian.

Nearly 200 pieces of obsidian were found at the Polish site of Olszanica near Cracow, most probably deriving from Hungary or Slovakia (Milisaus-kas, 1976). Olszanica, which spreads over approximately 50 ha, 1½ ha of which have been excavated, is dated 5320 to 4590 B.C. The site lies on a loess plateau above a flood plain, and unfortunately the occupation levels have largely vanished, only leaving the outline of post-holes (this is a feature of the majority of Linear Pottery sites). However, the excavator has been able to establish that approximately seven or eight long-houses were occupied at any one time, accommodating some sixteen or seventeen fami-lies perhaps. The houses vary in size from 7 to 41·5 m long by 4·75 to 7 m wide. The majority are under 20 m long. One very long house was occupied with a number of shorter ones at any one time, for instance long-house 6 is the giant house in the second of the occupation periods (Fig. 46). Because most of the polished-stone tools were found in its vicinity, the excavator hypothesizes that this may have been a men's house, or the house of the leading person in the community where the other men would forgather. Correlation tests have been tried on much of the material, indi-cating that the flint end scrapers (possibly used for both hide and wood-working) correlate with the obsidian strongly, and that cores correlate with hammer-stones, a not unlikely situation. A settlement of similar size was excavated a little to the north-west at Bylany in Czechoslovakia by Soudsky (1973) and in this case 10 ha were cleared, revealing house plans and pits relating to twenty-five phases of occupation (the number of phases is based on studies of the shapes and technological characteristics of the pottery). Soudsky estimated that perhaps five to six houses – ten at most – had been occupied in each phase. Bones were preserved on this site in contrast to the Polish site, and 80 per cent of the fauna was of domesti-cated cattle. Grain cultivation was revealed by grain imprints, by ovens for grain drying (also at Olszanica), and the presence of saddle querns and of sickle blades. Soudsky suggested that the occupation of Bylany was cyclic, with other sites being occupied from time to time so as to allow the fields to recover fertility. However, other authorities believe that it would have been perfectly possible to remain permanently at a single settlement and exploit fields around its periphery.

For instance, in southern Poland, Kruk has made an interesting study of a small zone to the north-east of the city of Cracow (1973). The distribution map (Fig. 47) shows the Linear Pottery sites in this area,

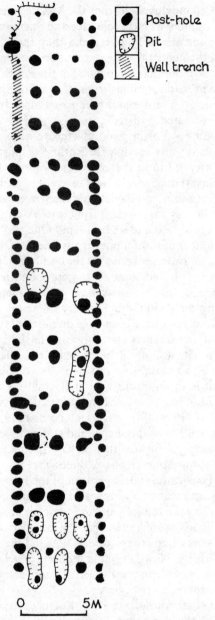

Fig. 46. Linear Pottery long-house 6 at Olszanica, Poland (after Milisauskas, 1976, p. 35)

concentrated on the lowest parts of the valley slopes, just above the flood soils. The sites were located in a few micro-regions, and consisted of large permanent settlements on rather exposed sites, with a number of small accessory settlements or camp sites associated with them. Kruk regards this settlement pattern as being due to the technique of farming a large area from a central permanent village, with the satellite camps being occupied seasonally. Settled conditions were possible because of the natural

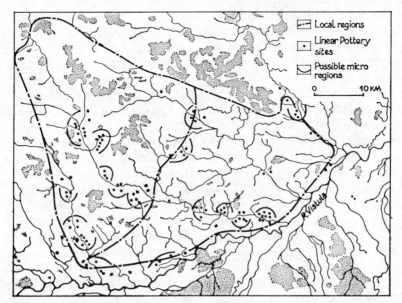

Fig. 47. Distribution of Linear Pottery settlements in south-western Niecka Nidziańska, southern Poland (after Kruk, 1973, map 4)

regeneration of the valley soils by flooding. He considers that stock-breeding was probably limited, by being contained in the zone of valley forest (Kruk, 1973, p. 257).

At the far end of the Linear Pottery culture area, sites in southern Holland at Elsloo, Sittard, Geleen and Stein have revealed nearly 200 Linear Pottery structures to date (Modderman, 1972). Sixty-two of these belong to the earlier Linear Pottery culture and seventy-six to the later. Modderman suggests that at any time ten to fifteen houses would be standing. The types of houses vary from the large buildings with three sections to buildings with a north-west section and a central section, and small buildings with only one (central) section. This author and several other authorities regard the central section as the living quarters, the south-east section as the store-room and the north-west section as an animal stall. Other authorities are not convinced that animals were housed in part of the building, while nitrate tests (to see if traces of manure remain) have not been conclusive in this connection. Modderman has recently calculated that some ninety house plans are known in all from the earlier Linear Pottery sites, including five at Bylany and seventy in the south Netherlands, and 225 from the later Linear Pottery sites, including eighty at Bylany and ninety in the Netherlands. The elongated Linear Pottery houses of the Netherlands vary from those which have a continuous bedding trench all the way around their peripheries, and those that have it merely at the north-west end, to smaller houses which are merely structures of separate posts with wattle and daub in between.

In very considerable contrast to these large settlements are the results recently obtained near Cologne during the archaeological investigation of the lignite exploitation area on the Aldenhoven plateau. Here, researchers from the Prehistoric Institute and the Museum at Cologne have revealed the pattern of Early Neolithic settlement up an entire valley, the Merzbach valley (Pl. 5). Five large habitations and two smaller have been revealed (Farrugia et al., 1973). A recent interpretation of one of the sites, Langweiler IX, suggests that four small houses were constantly replaced in the same area, 'as though by a transmitted right' and that these separate structures were occupied contemporaneously with other isolated farmsteads up the valley (Lüning, 1976). The houses were on average 136 m apart at Langweiler IX. Lüning feels that the Merzbach site is highly significant in terms of the generally accepted model of village life in this period, and of the cyclical suggestion put forward by Soudsky. Lüning's model for this area would be of permanent habitation by family groups in very small units (1976).

A number of interesting pieces of research have recently taken place on the location of Linear Pottery settlements in central Europe. An analysis by Sielmann (1971) has suggested that there were two modes of settlement, mode A and mode B. Mode A was in areas with moderate rainfall, temperature and aridity, in central Germany and the north Rhineland, settled by people originating from the Starčevo-Körös cultures of central Europe. Sixty to 80 per cent of these settlements were on loess lands (easily worked soils derived from periglacial wind-borne material), whereas nearly all were on loess in the mode B area (Bavaria, and around Heidelberg). In mode B, settlers were opting for higher rainfall, favourable temperatures and lower aridity. Sielmann suggests that the people who practised this type of settlement pattern emanated from west of Budapest and came to

Bavaria and the Neckar basin following the sort of climatic regime to which they had been accustomed. Sielmann believes that these settlers would have looked at the prevalent plant cover and been able to see that they were in a suitable zone for settlement. As has already been mentioned, damp sites were favoured in the early agricultural phases, and were also suitable for cattle. Settlements on the drier, non-loess lands in the Middle Neolithic should theoretically have been less favourable for cattle: Sielmann reports with pleasure that in fact in certain areas of central Germany sheep and goat proportions of the fauna increased to as much as 80 per cent while cattle occasionally dropped down as far as 10 per cent (1971).

A series of other regional studies has shown the importance of soils and other environmental factors in settlement. In the Magdeburg area on the Elbe river early farmers preferred the west Elbe high plateau with few trees to the east Elbe totally wooded sandy areas (Lies, 1974). To the west of the Elbe in central Saxony, a survey following the route of a gas pipeline revealed Early Neolithic settlements predominantly in damp areas of the Lommatzscher Pflege, including some on non-loess soils (Baumann and Quietzsch, 1969). In the Leipzig area, along the Elster and Pleiss rivers, a large number of Linear Pottery settlements can be found on loess and fine sandy clays overlying loess soils. In general the distribution runs parallel to the river valleys, but avoids the very clayey areas (Quitta, 1970). These studies just reveal a part of the complexity of the settlement situation, and demonstrate the vast amount of research work that remains to be carried out.

NEOLITHIC EUROPE, 4900 – 3200 B.C.

In the fifth millennium B.C. farming cultures spread to nearly all remaining areas of Europe. In the central and northern Netherlands, both actual archaeological sites and the isolated finds of perforated axes (some of them the so-called shoe-last type) seem to indicate a wide distribution of farming and pottery-using groups. The axes are made of amphibolite, and a search for the origins of amphibolite and basalt axes from both Linear Pottery and Rössen sites is being conducted at Leiden University; the earlier hypothesis of an origin in Poland is probably going to be replaced by that of an origin in central Germany (Bakels and Arps, 1977). Since the Neolithic axes are found on the edge of the loess and along watercourses, also favoured sites for Mesolithic peoples, a certain amount of feedback can be presumed, and at the Swifterbant site on the East Flevoland polder, dated 4200 B.C., half the fauna are of wild species and half of domesticated, suggesting a partial continuance of the earlier economy (Kooijmans, 1974). Kooijmans visualizes this movement into less favourable agricultural areas as linked to population pressure (1976a).

The Linear Pottery groups are succeeded by the Rössen in central and southern Germany, east France and the Netherlands. Rössen pottery is angular, with carinated bowls and footed pots, decorated by incision and white-filled decoration (Fig. 45c). Spondylus bracelets are still found. In areas like Magdeburg the post-Linear Pottery settlements are found not only on the west bank of the Elbe as were the earlier sites but also on the originally forested east Elbe sands. In the Cologne region, settlements move away from the river courses, into the more mountainous regions, and consist of long-term villages (Kuper, 1976). A continuity in house type from the Linear Pottery period can be seen here at Inden, a site dated between 4700 and 4500 B.C., where ten long houses of trapezoid design, built of split trunk walls, were found, together with some smaller houses. The settlement was surrounded by a double palisade (Kuper and Piepers, 1966). A similar site was found recently in the Aisne valley to the north-east of Paris, where aerial photography during gravel-digging revealed the presence of a large village dating from c. 4600 to 3350 B.C. In an excavation of 15,000 m² at the site, Cuiry-les-Chaudardes, five trapezoid and three rectangular houses were revealed, outlined by post-holes 50 to 70 cm apart. Unfortunately erosion had removed the floor areas, but the artifacts included late Linear Pottery (CRPUP, 1974).

In southern France settled communities with a strong dependence on agriculture and animal-herding (both sheep and cattle) restructured their societies at the beginning of the fourth millennium. Completely new areas were opened up to agriculture. One of these was the Verdon valley of Upper Provence, systematically explored over the last decade (Courtin, 1974). The pioneer nature of the settlements in and around the caves of this limestone gorge can be seen by the fact that lots of piercing arrowheads are used, and that in some cases there is a reasonably large wild element to the fauna, although contemporary larger sites nearer the coast were much more dependent on domesticated stock. Remains of cereals and pulse crops, including vetches and beans from sites in the Verdon gorges and elsewhere, indicate the main plant foods of their diet. The social readjustments of the fifth millennium B.C. created widespread cultural uniformity, and a single cultural group, the Chasseen, named after a central French type-site, extended from the Pyrenees to Liguria. The uniformity, which may ultimately be shown to depend on complex exchange systems, is demonstrated by the standard shapes and sizes of pottery (low bowls, globular-necked jars), by a blade industry often made on honey-coloured flint, and by the presence of (mainly Sardinian) obsidian on many of the sites.

Analyses of obsidian artifacts found on west Mediterranean islands and coastlands have revealed an interesting pattern of distribution (Hallam et al., 1976). All the major islands (Sicily, Sardinia, Corsica, Majorca, Minorca and Malta) were occupied during the Neolithic; all except the Balearic islands participated in the obsidian 'trade'. In the sixth millennium B.C. obsidian from Sardinia reached Corsica and north Italy, and obsidian from Lipari reached central and southern Italy. In the next thousand years the use of obsidian spread thinly but widely along the west Mediterranean coastlands, from Italy via Provence and Languedoc to Catalonia. Most of the French samples tested come from Sardinia, and Hallam et al. (1976) describe the area to the north and west of the island of Elba as the 'Sardinian obsidian interaction zone', while the majority of the Italian peninsula forms part of the 'Lipari interaction zone'. The obsidian trade crosses 'cultural' boundaries such as that between the square-mouthed pottery culture of Liguria and the southern Chasseen. Obsidian is also traded into the island of Malta (sixty miles south of Sicily) where Trump's excavations at Skorba have demonstrated the presence of Liparian and Pantellerian obsidian from the early fifth millennium B.C. to the early fourth millennium B.C. (Ghar Darlam to Tarxian phases, with Liparian obsidian always in the majority). Here also the obsidian does not seem to have affected the independent evolution of the island's Neolithic phase, although the links established with Lipari or Sicily may account for the start of the practice of burial in rock-cut tombs by c. 4000 B.C. (the first tombs of this type occurred on the southern Italian mainland – Whitehouse, 1972). By the same time Chasseen pottery styles had spread up the Rhône valley as far as Switzerland, and up the Saône into central France. In both areas they had moved from a Mediterranean to a temperate climate. In a recent article on colonization, Diamond suggested that nearly all colonization was carried out by coastal peoples, who altered their original culture considerably once they got into a new environment (1977). Some of this can be seen in the Chasseen expansion, in the fact that certain pottery types expanded at the expense of others in the new habitat, and also in that a different range of flint tools was used in the more northerly area. There was also a change of settlement location, from the caves or open sites of the Mediterranean region to defended spurs in eastern and western France. In parts of eastern France where good flint was lacking, aphanite was widely exploited during the fifth and fourth millennia B.C. Some of the workshop areas were in defended camps, others were on open sites up to 10 km away from the source area (Piningre,

1974). Chasseen 'colonization', possibly more by exchange of goods and ideas than population, passed up the Loire to Brittany, where pottery manufacture had been taking place since the early fifth millennium B.C., the period of the earliest stone tombs in Brittany.

Renfrew has suggested that it is quite possible that the building of megalithic tombs was an independent invention in at least five areas, and has linked their creation in Brittany in particular with the presence of rich Mesolithic communities established in the previous millennium, communities which might have wished to assert their independence and territoriality against any incoming group (1973b). The establishment of many megalithic tombs and other large-scale enterprises such as stone circles and lines of standing stones (Er Lannic, Carnac) suggests a thriving population in the Breton area by the fourth millennium B.C. at least. Excavations at Plussulien, a source of dolerite used for stone axes, have revealed three different phases of exploitation: about 3740 B.C., shallow pits were dug to obtain blocks of dolerite contained in the clay; in the next 250 years, the parent rock was exploited with large hammers; and after a period of abandonment, c. 2650 B.C., fire was used to split the parent rock (Delibrias and Le Roux, 1975). Axes made of this dolerite have been traced over much of France and into south-west Britain (Fig. 48).

The expansion of farming into the British Isles probably took place over a broad front from Brittany to the Low Countries (Case, 1969). The earliest carbon-14 dates for farming in Ireland are approximately 4600 B.C., but areas of Ireland such as the Bann valley had had large Mesolithic populations, and it is not inconceivable that pottery manufacture and megalithic building were independently invented by them. However, the full complement of Neolithic cereals and domesticated animals had to come from elsewhere. The majority of carbon-14 dates for the British Neolithic are from 4300 B.C. onwards. Case suggests that the earliest farmers were visitors on a seasonal scale, perhaps coming over to pasture animals for a short period or to harvest crops planted earlier in the spring. For either seasonal or communal movement, suitable boats would have been necessary and he has suggested that skin boats would have been the lightest and most manoeuvrable in the prevalent currents. A 32-ft (10 m) boat rowed by eight paddlers and a steersman could have carried an additional eight tons weight, either in animals or in grain. Early dates for sites in south-west England, Sussex, East Anglia and Yorkshire suggest the possibility of a series of voyages and explorations. Successful agricultural systems seem to have been set up in all these areas, with occupation either limited to single huts or farms, or in the form of a number of huts on a single site.

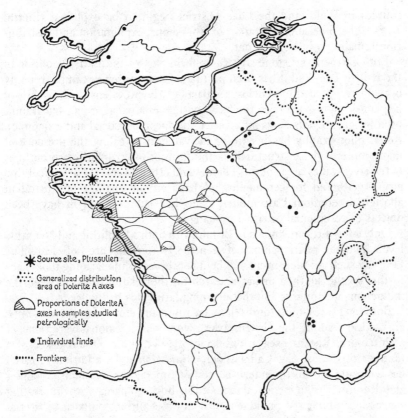

Fig. 48. Distribution of axes in Breton dolerite A (after Leroux, 1975, p. 46)

Carbon-14 dates have indicated that mining for flint commenced about 4000 B.C. in southern Britain, the main source for flint axes and other artifacts being the Easton Down mine. The same technology was used as on the continent: digging a shaft to reach the seam, using fire to loosen the flint, antler picks to prise it out of the seam, and cattle shoulder-blades as shovels. The flint would have been excavated in containers, probably baskets either hauled up by ropes or carried up ladders resting against a platform midway up the shaft (Mercer, 1976). The find of an untouched flint axe and a pristine jade axe lying beside one of the timber trackways excavated in the Somerset Levels (Pl. 11) suggests that such implements at times acted not only in the economic, but also in the ritual subsystem (Coles *et al.*, 1974). Several of the hard stones used for axes were also being traded in southern Britain before 3750 B.C., and after that date sources in Wales and the Lake District begin to be exploited (Smith, 1977). The precise organization of workshops, exploitation and distribution remains to be worked out.

Both earthen and stone structures form part of the Early Neolithic of the British Isles and it has been postulated that causeway camps (roughly oval, interrupted-ditch enclosures particularly prevalent in the south of England) might have been the headquarters of a tribal or pan-tribal unit, used for group gatherings for a variety of purposes (social and economic). Aerial photography has been of great value in revealing the presence of many more of these structures, in the form of interrupted-ditch outlines in the river-valley areas of the Thames and other rivers. If Early Neolithic groups gathered for ceremonies, perhaps on the analogy of Australian aboriginal ceremonial assemblies, items like jade axes might have been objects of ceremonial or ritual exchange.

Only a few sites are known in Britain with both Mesolithic and Neolithic levels, and the relationships between the two groups are not clear. The Oronsay shell-middens were still being occupied while farming took place further to the south. Further research on the relationships between the indigenous inhabitants and the incoming farmers is badly needed.

Both long earth-built tombs (long barrows) and stone-chambered tombs are widespread in the British Isles, with many regional variations of architecture. Recent excavations have revealed multi-period usage of a number of tombs, e.g. Callis Wold, Humberside. In addition research has concentrated on the interpretation of funerary monuments. Fleming and Renfrew have made valuable contributions here, with interesting suggestions about the possible position of megalithic tombs as territorial markers, as locations for ceremonies, and as the central point of territories from which their builders farmed (Fleming, 1972, 1973; Renfrew, 1973b). Major excavations such as those at Knowth in Ireland are revealing a complex of main and satellite burials (Pl. 10) and putting into question the social subsystem of the group which built the grave (Eogan, 1969).

Rather more is known in north Poland about the interrelationships of hunter-gatherer and farming populations. Gramsch's study of the plains between the Elbe and Oder has revealed that a few pots and ground-stone tools of Linear Pottery culture type occur in Late Mesolithic contexts (1973, map 5). Gramsch suggests that these items were obtained by exchange or theft from the Neolithic settlers of the lower Oder and Elbe–Saal areas. Other workers have suggested that pottery was probably used in north Poland before any change in the subsistence pattern occurred, whereas in south Poland the adoption of pottery and agriculture had happened simultaneously (Kowalezyk, 1969). The first farmers in the north of Poland seem to have belonged to the Funnel Beaker culture, which is typified by pointed, heavily impressed pots, battle-axes and cult vessels, and is said to originate from a mixture of Linear Pottery and Final Mesolithic elements, presumably by the descendants of those who acquired the first pots and axes (Wislanski, 1975). The Funnel Beaker people were mixed farmers, with cattle as their main stock animal, in common with many other Late Neolithic populations of central and north-west Europe (Clason, 1971). Kruk, in his study area of the loess uplands of Little Poland, demonstrates that Funnel Beaker settlement was distinctly different from that of earlier Neolithic periods, moving into drier, higher regions, and using fire to clear areas for agriculture to such an extent that the upper loess areas became largely deforested (1973). The settlement pattern is randomly distributed in the main, although density varies depending on the position of the rivers (Hodder and Orton, 1976).

A Funnel Beaker settlement has recently been excavated at Niedzwiedz, Miechow, south Poland (Burchard, 1973). The site is on the upland loess, on a ridge above a river, and excavation revealed two long post-built structures, and 100 pits, described as 'habitation pits', although two of them had been used for burials. One of the buildings was 16 m long (with eleven posts along the side) by 3 m wide (with three posts along the ends). This would create a building 48 m² in area, sufficient for a family of eight or nine people. Since settlement debris is found over nearly 2 ha, the occupation at Niedzwiedz seems to represent a small farming community.

Although at Niedzwiedz burials were found in odd pits, cemetery burial is more usual among Funnel Beaker populations, and the presence of seventeen separate Funnel Beaker cemeteries in the parish of Klementowice, Pulawy district, in eastern Poland, suggests that this was a fairly densely settled region.

In one of the cemeteries the dead lay on their backs in pits, and out of the sixteen graves, seven were of children, mostly below the age of seven. Grave-goods included bone and stone artifacts, and pots. The majority of women died between the ages of twenty and forty-five; some men survived to the age of sixty. Three hearths may have been connected with the ritual of burial.

Funnel Beaker pottery was used widely over northern Europe, for instance in Schleswig and the Jutland peninsula in the fifth millennium B.C. (Tauber, 1972), but it was not the earliest pottery in the area. Seasonal exploitation of fish and shellfish had been in practice since the late Mesolithic, and on the sites of the Ertebølle culture 'kitchen middens', pottery was made from at least 4600 B.C. onwards, in the shape of conical-based vessels and rectangular lamps. Remains of cereals and domesticated animals on Ertebølle sites suggest that they had acquired domesticated products from neighbouring farming groups, or by practising local domestication (Nobis, 1978). The excellent preservation conditions of the Danish bogs has made it possible to recover a large number of wooden implements little known outside this area and Switzerland. Several spades have been found at Satrup moor, and it has been suggested that they might have been pulled by ropes as a type of ard or plough in cultivation (Steensberg, 1973).

In the Gothenburg area of Sweden rescue excavations have revealed a number of Early Neolithic sites overlying previous Mesolithic habitations, unfortunately without direct economic evidence. However, from other sites, it is obvious that both agriculture and cattle breeding were practised from at least the late fifth millennium B.C. in southern Scandinavia, and that these production systems were transported as far as 60° north in Sweden (Moberg, 1966). Moberg suggested that the moves north in Scandinavia took place in a series of impulses separated by interruptions and even withdrawals at times. Recent research has tended to confirm this hypothesis. Welinder has discussed the penetration of farming and herding systems into the Baltic, and the beginning of intensive sea hunting. The Baltic was sufficiently saline to permit the entry of seals and other mammals into it from about the beginning of the Atlantic onwards. Not until approximately 4400 B.C., however, did seal hunting play an important part in the subsistence of this area, and Welinder questions whether it was not part of a seasonal cycle.

In Denmark some of the funnel beakers are found associated with megalithic stone tombs, others with simple earth graves. The distributions are not mutually exclusive, but most of the megalithic tombs are in southern Denmark and the earth graves in the north. Randsborg, in a recent reconsideration of the early Danish Neolithic, considers that these differences can be accounted for in the main by the poorer quality of soil and therefore sparser populations in the north. However, in a few areas a study of the economic return in the form of barrels of hard corn per hectare obtainable today does not fit with the pattern of megalithic versus non-megalithic tomb structure. These richer areas have produced relatively more stone axes and mace-heads than the others (Randsborg, 1975, fig. 2), which leads Randsborg to suggest that the population ought to be estimated from the numbers of such finds. Randsborg regards the tombs as a focus for the life of particular groups, and is interested in the social situation among groups which would lead to their constructing such monuments. Early Funnel Beaker peoples seem to have built the visually impressive megalithic graves (Fig. 49), and clustered together, giving the

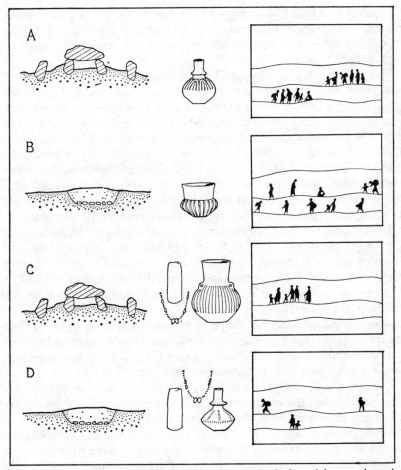

Fig. 49. Tomb types, pottery vessels and hypothetical social groupings in Neolithic Denmark (after Randsborg, 1975, fig. 7)

A Stone grave – few grave goods – high population density –
   high degree of clustering
B Earth grave – few grave goods – high population density –
   low degree of clustering
C Stone grave – many grave goods – low population density –
   high degree of clustering
D Earth grave – many grave goods – low population density –
   low degree of clustering

impression of a non-egalitarian society; however, the later Funnel Beaker peoples built more earth graves, although they still continued to use the megalithic graves, and Randsborg suggests that their pattern of settlement was more dispersed.

Apart from the penetration of Funnel-necked Beaker people (or their wares) into the Swedish area, from about 3350 B.C. onwards Pitted Ware groups were established on the Finnish coast subsisting on a mixture of seal hunting and pig breeding. In addition to the Finnish sites, over 1000 Pitted Ware sites are known from Sweden, Norway and Denmark. Their distribution along the shores of the then Litorina sea, together with the bone remains from the sites, indicates that subsistence was based on maritime (e.g. seal) and inland hunting, although domesticated animals such as pigs were also kept, and some of the pottery bears cereal impressions (Kaelas, 1976). Kivikoski has discussed the Finnish Pitted Ware groups, who had the same type of ground-stone axes as earlier Mesolithic Suomosjärvi populations. They carved elaborate animal heads on axes, sometimes made in green slate imported from Russia. They also obtained fine flint from north Finland and south Scandinavia and Russia, diabase from west Finland, and amber from the East Baltic. There are three main amber-working areas known from the Neolithic: Kourchskaia-Palanga, Lithuania; Sarnate, West Estonia; and Lubana, East Estonia. Lose has published a report on the 870 finished pieces and thousands of flakes and natural pieces of amber found at Lubana (1969, fig. 5). The finished pieces include beads, some with V-perforations; pendants; and rings.

Several teams of archaeologists and natural scientists in Scandinavia are investigating the changes in subsistence practice over time. In the Norrland project in north Sweden, and in the Varanger fjord project in Norway, the technological and subsistence systems are being followed from about 5000 B.C. onwards. One interesting result has been to demonstrate north-south trading systems in the early third millennium B.C.; c. 2970 B.C., south Scandinavian flint, red Russian flint and asbestos, used as a filler for pottery, were all being traded north (Simonsen, 1975) (Fig. 50).

Switzerland was the scene of hunter-gatherer economies until about the beginning of the fifth millennium B.C., and levels dating to this period at the Birsmatten cave in Canton Bern still contain backed blades and antler harpoons, and lack pottery. Elsewhere, however, domesticated animals and plants, Neolithic pottery and ground-stone tools are found; Stickel has recently obtained a series of carbon-14 dates which indicate near contemporaneity of the earliest east Swiss Neolithic, the Pfyn culture, with that of western Switzerland (1976). The pottery of these two groups remains distinct until about 3200 B.C., although there are signs of exchanges of

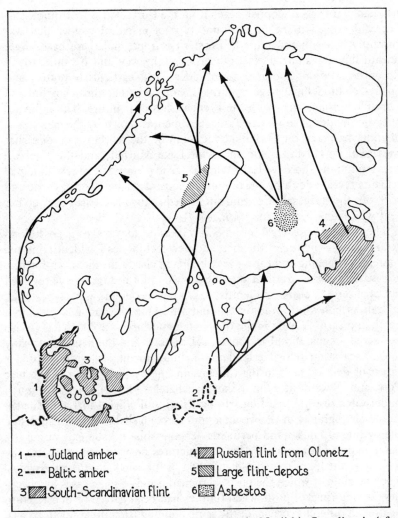

Fig. 50. Exchange of flint, amber and asbestos in Neolithic Scandinavia (after Simonsen, 1975, fig. 6)

artifacts. Two sets of copper beads from the Cortaillod site of Burgäschi-See Süd proved to be of the same type of arsenical copper that was currently being manufactured in eastern Europe, and these beads were presumably transmitted via Pfyn groups (Ottaway and Strahm, 1975). Recent excavations and analyses of older finds (particularly pottery and honey-coloured flint) have confirmed, however, that the main links of Cortaillod groups were with the French Chasseen culture. The influence of earlier modes of subsistence and settlement is shown by the persistence of antler harpoons on Cortaillod sites, and by the reoccupation of earlier sites (e.g. Portalban on the shores of Lake Murten; and the Egolzwil sites around the shores of Lake Wauwil). The majority of sites with faunal remains reveal a high proportion of domesticates (sheep, goat, cattle and pig), but the Burgäschi-See Süd site, dated *c.* 3600 B.C., had over 90 per cent wild fauna (Boessneck *et al.*, 1963).

The excellent preservation on Swiss lakeside sites makes it possible to get a balanced picture of the diet, and new techniques for identifying the contents of cooking and eating vessels should clarify the diet even further. Excavations at the stratified site of Egolzwil 4, for instance, have revealed traces of cereals, beans and lentils, flax, strawberries and water-chestnuts, as well as bones of domesticated and wild animals, and duck, salmon, perch and carp. A wide range of wooden and birch-bark artifacts is also preserved – cups, birchbark boxes, ladles, trays and the handles of many tools. Excavation in Switzerland now includes not only lakeside sites under threat of development, using caissons and heavy pumps (e.g. Auvernier Port and Twann sites on Lake Neuchâtel – Pl. 12), but also much underwater research, particularly by Ruoff and Stickel in Lake Zürich. Aerial photography of the wooden piles through shallow water can define the outline of houses and perimeter fences, while caisson excavation has made it possible to identify house structures on very complex sites, by looking at the fill of the post-holes, the type of wood (for instance white-wood or pine) of which the posts were made, and in some cases by check-ing the tree-rings of posts when timbers had been halved or quartered to be used in different corners of the same building (Boisaubert *et al.*, 1974).

Another area of farming expansion in the fifth and fourth millennia B.C. was eastern Europe. In the central and eastern Ukraine the Dnieper–Donetz culture may have been based on farming, as may the Narva culture of the Soviet Baltic states (Doluchanov, 1971). Elsewhere in eastern Europe changes took place in regions long adapted to agriculture and animal domestication. The dark pottery wares called after the type-site of Vinča developed in the early fifth millennium B.C. in areas originally occupied by Starčevo and allied cultures. At the site of Anzabegovo these occur on top of the Starčevo ones, and there is continuity in spondylus imports, and the presence of figurines from the earlier period. An expansion of population seems to be visible in the presence of larger villages, deeper depths of deposits on tells and the occupation of new sites in the western Balkans. Settlement was mainly on river terraces, high river banks and naturally protected areas, although the provision of enclosures in the Vinča and succeeding cultures may have been more a defining of territory rather than an expectation of attack. Elsewhere in central Europe and the eastern Balkans similar settlements were established by cultural groups such as the Lengyel of west Hungary, Austria and southern Poland, the Tisza of eastern Hungary, and the Boian of the east Balkans (Gimbutas, 1974*d*). The period coincides with the climatic optimum, and a series of agricultural settlements was established on the plains, exploiting mainly sheep. At the tell site of Karanovo, Bulgaria, remains of carbonized emmer, einkorn, lentils, vetch and six-row barley have been found, and there is considerable depth of deposit in levels V and VI. By level VI (4510 B.C.) there were fifty houses on the Karanovo site, and the occupants were exploiting the Madara honey-flint from east Bulgaria, improving the technique of its production in cores and blanks (Tringham, 1971). A similarly large settlement was established at Radovanu, Romania, about 4400 B.C. The first (Boian culture) occupation consisted of an open settlement, then a ditch was cut around the twelve houses of this period. Later a loom-weaver's hut was located outside the ditch although only four or five houses were being occupied inside at the time. The houses were rectangular and provided with a bench, hearths and place for a quern. They were lined up parallel to each other in two rows of six. The excavator considered that approximately sixty people lived on the site, exploiting mainly cattle, sheep, goat, pig and plant foods in an environment with forest, steppe and marshlands near by (Comsa, 1976).

Most archaeologists regard the developments in south-east and central Europe as principally due to local changes, not influenced by the Aegean nor the Near East. Spondylus shells were imported into the area from the Aegean (Shackleton and Renfrew, 1970) but, as with west Mediterranean obsidian, these imports did not necessarily involve cultural changes. The original idea of strong Aegean or Near Eastern influence was revived in the late 1960s by the discovery in Hungary at the site of Tartaria of a cache of twenty-six figurines and three baked-clay tablets. The tablets bore signs interpreted as 'Mesopotamian' by a number of archaeologists. However, in contemporary cultures there are a variety of signs which appear both on figurines and pots, and a study by Winn has shown that all the signs on the Tartaria tablets can in fact be replicated on Vinča

material (1974). Winn does not regard the signs as necessarily representing writing, but thinks they may have functioned in different subsystems
of the culture, including some in a religious role because of their presence
on figurines.

The question of the relationships between the south-east European and
the Near Eastern worlds is linked to the beginnings of copper metallurgy
in Europe. Carbon-14 dates and stratified excavations now indicate a very
early development of copper metallurgy (c. 4600 B.C.) in south-east
Europe, not linked, as far as can be seen, with earlier developments in the
Near East.

John Coles has recently argued persuasively that the sorts of knowledge
which were a prerequisite to successful metallurgy were already present
in Late Neolithic communities in Europe. He emphasizes that stone-
workers already knew the precise properties of the parent rock, quarrying
methods, flaking, smoothing, pre-treatment by heat, and drilling (1976b).
Jovanovic had suggested that in south-east Europe copper metallurgy
began in the framework of an impressive production of stone tools, using
the expertise in mining already developed to procure flint. Flint-mining
technology was exactly identical to that employed in the Yugoslav copper-
ore mines at Rudna Glava (Jovanovic, 1972). Here Copper Age miners
sank vertical pits to follow veins of magnetite, and the technology consisted of picking out the magnetite with antler picks, then smashing it with
heavy hammers made from river cobbles. Late Vinča pottery was found
on the access platforms to the vertical pits.

Copper was obviously used as an interesting sort of stone before its
smelting properties were realized. At Cernica near Bucharest (dated c.
5320 to 5210 B.C. – Cantacuzino, personal communication), grave-goods
included pottery, ground- and chipped-stone tools, bone and antler implements, shell bracelets and copper beads. The eighty copper beads were
analysed and proved to have been of malachite or a very similar ore, and to
have been hammered but not heated. In later cemeteries the metal goods
were cast. In Hungary the Tiszapolgar cemetery (c. 4000–3800 B.C.) contained 156 bodies, laid out in rows which may reflect family grouping
(Kalicz, 1970, fig. 39). Men were laid on their right sides, accompanied
by such grave-goods as stone knives, obsidian arrowheads, antler axes,
stone axes and maces, copper and gold jewellery and the jaw-bones of
pigs. Females rested on their left sides, and their grave goods included
pottery, shell or limestone beads which seem to have been worn around
the hips, and copper and gold jewels. The very uniform Tiszapolgar culture area stretched over the Carpathian basin, itself devoid of both stone
and metal ores, and Kalicz (1972) has pointed out how far this culture

reflects differences from the preceding Late Neolithic in the area, particularly the reduction in emphasis on tells and defences, and the increased imports from outside the basin. Settlements were established on the edges of the basin to obtain raw materials from nearby mountain zones, while occupation of open sites on flood-plains may indicate increased agricultural production, possibly to create an excess for barter. The presence of metal hammer-axes and of jewellery items on sites from phase B onwards reflects the success of this strategy.

In the last decade considerable advances have been made in establishing the chronology of early metallurgy in Europe. In particular, it has been demonstrated that in south-east Europe (Romania and Bulgaria in particular) metallurgy began as early as 4600 B.C. Carbon-14 dates have confirmed that in the mid fifth millennium B.C., cultures such as the Gumelnitsa, Tiszapolgar, Lengyel and Cucuteni-Petreşti in Romania all demonstrated the capacity to smelt a pure copper with natural impurities into two main artifact types, shaft-hole axes and adzes, and pins. Carbon-14 dates for Gumelnitsa phase A2 (the earliest with copper) run from *c.* 4500 to 4300 B.C. Professor Charles has investigated the method of manufacture of these shaft-hole axes, and has confirmed that the holes were not made by subsequent boring, but were developed in the casting process by means of charcoal inserts. The axes are widespread in south-east Europe, and are different from early metal types found on the Anatolian peninsula. It has recently been suggested by Cernych that the Romanian and Bulgarian industries rapidly developed high production capacity and overtook the industries of the Near East which had been established a good two millennia earlier (1976). Copper metallurgy using oxide ores is generally regarded as being widespread over Anatolia by about 3750 B.C., while by 3200 B.C. sulphide ores were also being employed there (Muhly, 1970). Renfrew has argued cogently for the primacy of the south-east European copper metallurgy over that of Anatolia, based on traditional cultural cross-comparisons, stratigraphy and on the calibrated carbon-14 chronology (1969, 1970). Excavations at the Thessaly site of Sitagroi have enabled Renfrew to demonstrate that Gumelnitsa finds pre-date those of Troy I type (the first west Anatolian bronze culture). Thus there is stratigraphic proof in the intervening area between Anatolia and the early metallurgical cultures of south-east Europe for the primacy of European metallurgy over that of west Anatolia.

Although the south-east European area is notable for both its varied metal-tool types, and its high output, the idea of independent development of metallurgy has been mooted for many other parts of Europe. This is in contrast to older ideas of a generalized diffusion of metallurgical knowledge from the Near East. In the first place, Renfrew has carried out a very detailed study of the Aegean area (1973c) detailing the development of early Bronze Age cultures from about 3200 B.C. and suggesting that the necessary technology, in particular for creating the heat necessary for smelting, would already have been present in the form of ovens to parch grain, or to fire pottery. The Aegean area is, however, lacking in the main metal ores at the present day. Branigan and Warren suggested that Crete was rich in metal ores but recent investigations have only revealed small pockets of malachite and cuprite in western Crete. The Greek sources are unlikely to have been exploitable in the Bronze Age (McDonald and Rapp, 1972). However, Crete may well have acquired metallurgy in the course of its widespread trading in the east Mediterranean, and the Cycladic islands and the Greek mainland industries may have been derived from the Cretan. The Italian and Iberian metal industries were suggested originally to have derived from the east Mediterranean, particularly the Aegean. Carbon-14 dates are rare from Italian and Iberian sites with metallurgical remains, but it seems possible both because of tool design, and of the general context in which they are located, that these industries may have developed independently. The Alps and Apennines contain suitable ores, and early copper artifacts are found in the context of local Late Neolithic assemblages. For instance, the fifteen undated cemeteries of the Fiora valley, central Italy, only contain a few copper axes, copper daggers and antimony ornaments among the battle-axes, mace-heads, flint arrowheads and flint daggers which form the bulk of the grave-goods (Rittatore Vonwiller, 1974). Similarly in Iberia, where it has been possible to establish a stratigraphy at defended sites like Los Millares, Vila Nova de São Pedro and Zambujal (Sangmeister and Schubart, 1972) (Fig. 51), pottery, stone and flint types derived from the preceding Late Neolithic cultures appear in association with the earliest metal tools and remains of metallurgical activity (kilns, and slag from copper, silver and lead working). In the upper levels at these sites Bell Beaker pottery is present and at a central Spanish site a melting crucible decorated with Bell Beaker motifs has recently been found (R. Harrison et al., 1975). The widespread associations of metal tools with both Bell Beaker pottery and Corded Ware pottery, both of which achieve very wide distribution in the late Neolithic (c. 3000–2200 B.C.), led in the past to the makers of these wares being regarded as the earliest European metallurgists, but the present evidence both from the areas already cited, and from elsewhere in northern and central Europe, in the form of mainly small objects like tubes and beads, indicates that metal was widespread prior to the spread of either of the two pottery types (e.g. Ottaway, 1973).

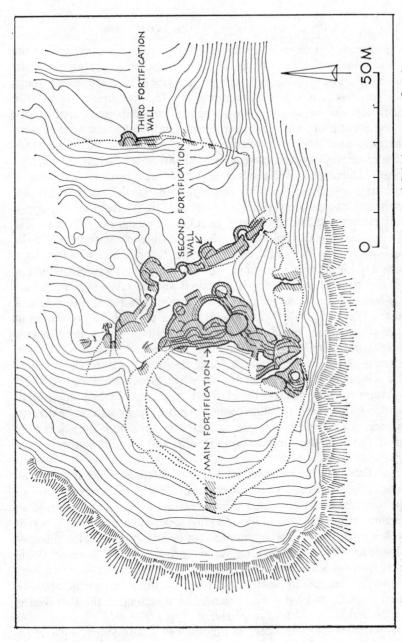

THIRD FORTIFICATION WALL

SECOND FORTIFICATION WALL

MAIN FORTIFICATION →

50M

Fig. 51. Defences of Zambujal settlement, Portugal (after Sangmeister and Schubart, 1972, fig. 1)

LATE NEOLITHIC–CHALCOLITHIC EUROPE

A number of factors seem to suggest large populations at the end of the Neolithic period in parts of Europe. In some areas, such as south-east Europe, the size of settlements and the presence of several hundred tombs in a single cemetery give this impression. In other areas, for instance north-west Europe, the presence of huge rampart and ditch constructions, or stone-built structures, suggest many man-hours spent in their construction, and thereby a relatively large population. Wainwright has recently carried out rescue excavations at three giant henges in southern Britain (Durrington Walls, Marden and Mount Pleasant). Stripping of wide areas and excavation of ditch profiles has revealed complex wooden structures internally, at a date of *c*. 2550 B.C. (Burleigh *et al.*, 1972). Renfrew has indicated that henge monuments in southern Britain could take anything up to 1 million man-hours of time to construct, while the biggest barrow, Silbury Hill, and the long cursus monuments would have taken anything up to 10 million man-hours apiece. The construction of the final stage of Stonehenge is suggested to have taken over 30 million man-hours, since the stones had to be transported to the site, dressed and erected (Renfrew, 1973*b*). Renfrew calculates that a local population of some 5000 persons could have supplied 1 million man-hours per year towards great building projects. The occurrence throughout Europe generally of massive enclosures and defences (e.g. at Zambujal, Portugal), of stone-built or rock-cut tombs, or of stone-built dwellings or ritual structures (e.g. the Maltese temples), all suggest locally high densities of population. At the Hal Saflieni three-level rock-cut tomb on Malta, for instance, some 7000 people are estimated to have been buried, mainly during the early third millennium Ggantija and Tarxien phases (Evans, 1971*b*).

Together with the evidence for larger populations, there is some evidence in the Late Neolithic for inegalitarian societies. The actual construction of massive earth or stone monuments might be an indication of an inegalitarian society. On a more individual scale, however, variety in grave-goods is often regarded as an indication of variety in the social standing of individuals. In parts of northern Europe 'prestige goods' buried in single rather than collective graves might consist of beakers and copper daggers, or fine flint daggers or battle-axes. These occur in varying numbers in different areas, and have been regarded as representing the Bell Beaker and Corded Ware cultures respectively.

In northern and north-central Europe, in the late fourth millennium B.C., a new type of pottery decorated with twisted-cord designs comes into use in much the same area as that previously occupied by the Funnel Beaker cultures. A number of studies have suggested that there are differences in the style of pottery manufacture, the skeletal types and the settlement pattern of these people. Ottaway also regards them as using new metal sources (Alpine Fahlerz – Ottaway, 1973). There seems to be more continuity in Poland than in Denmark and north-west Germany with the advent of the new pottery, battle-axe and burial types. Randsborg has accounted for the presence of Corded Ware pottery and associated arti-facts in Denmark in the framework of alterations in exchange systems which took place at this time. It seems likely that the larger populations of the Late Neolithic permitted more specialization, that their density forced more complexity of social structure, and these complexities fuelled the demand for high-value goods to indicate their status. These goods might acquire value because of their rarity, or because of the length of time they took in manufacture. Fine-walled pots like Beakers, for instance, needed to be wrapped and scraped from the inside to ensure their fine thin walls (van der Leeuw, 1976). The boring of holes through beads, pen-dants, axes and other objects was a lengthy operation, and similarly very finely chipped flint daggers (e.g. Pl. 8), made in emulation of metal types (with which there was eventually a feedback relationship–Bocquet, 1974), were time-consuming to prepare. Visualized in this way, the distribution of Bell Beaker pottery, of the perforated buttons, fine stone wrist guards perforated with two or four holes, and flat cast metal daggers have been seen as a 'status kit' (S. J. Shennan, 1976). According to this view, a group of prestige items was more likely to have been the prerogative of individuals of high status, than of a particular race or caste, individuals identifiable after death by the 'costly' goods buried with them. In fact over much of Europe, as a recent symposium about Bell Beaker finds re-vealed (Lanting and van der Waals, 1976), Bell Beaker 'status kits' were an insertion into the smooth development of Late Neolithic popu-lations, only forming a substantial part of the artifact assemblage in a couple of areas, the Netherlands and the British Isles. In eastern Europe (central and eastern Germany, Bohemia, Moravia and Hungary) there is some change in skeletal type associated with Bell Beaker graves, the dead having flat-backed, steep-sided skulls. However, the exact timing of this change within the approximately 700 years time-span in which Bell Beakers are found here is not known. In central Europe the problem is also complicated by the nearly simultaneous development of the Corded Ware complex in some areas.

Swiss archaeologists have detected a difference in distribution in their area between the users of Corded Ware and Bell Beakers. Corded Ware

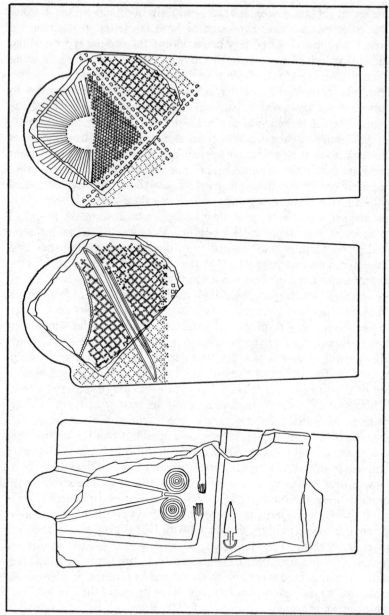

Fig. 52. Decorated stelae from Sion, Switzerland (after Gallay and Spindler 1972, pp. 80–81)

pottery is found in the northern and central part of Switzerland, occupying both sides of Lake Neuchâtel, and on the western side of Lake Geneva, i.e. in the good agricultural areas. Bell Beakers are found in three zones encircling this distribution, in southern France, the Jura mountains and the Upper Rhône valley. All these are zones of very varied topography, the sort of country that Sherratt (1976) has suggested would be excellent for inducing redistribution schemes in times of population increase, and thereby no doubt of social complexity, to be reflected in the energy spent on grave monuments and offerings. The cemetery site of Sion in the Upper Rhône valley might bear out this suggestion. Here great stone slabs minutely pecked with anthropomorphic designs and dating from at least 3200 B.C. were re-used about 2500 B.C. to make huge cist graves (Fig. 52). The dead were interred with fine flint daggers and boar's-tusk decorative plaques. These cist graves were re-used by people depositing Bell Beakers, more boar's-tusk carvings, including a miniature bow shape, and silver ear-rings with the dead (Gallay, 1972, 1976). The tendency for more elaborate burial treatment for one or more sections of the population persists into the Early Bronze Age.

THE EUROPEAN BRONZE AGE
(*c*. 2550–1250 B.C.)

This chapter covers the full development of the Bronze Age in the Aegean, but only the early and middle phases in western and northern Europe. The later phases of the Bronze Age and the pre-Roman Iron Age in these latter areas will be covered in the next chapter.

BRONZE AGE ECONOMIES

Less work has been done on Bronze Age farming and pastoralism than on the Neolithic, but sufficient results have been obtained to indicate that most groups were efficient mixed farmers, although the proportion of their diet derived from plants and animals remains to be worked out. It has been suggested, on ethnographic analogy, that many wild plants might have been incorporated in the diet (Sarnowska, 1973). In all cases, however, the actual locations and quantities of plant remains on sites need to be checked, in order to try to distinguish what plants were actually being deliberately cultivated or cropped, and which others were being accidentally incorporated in the harvest.

Wild animals were still being hunted, probably for a variety of reasons, including dietary additions, sport and to reduce damage to crops in newly opened up regions.

Various kinds of evidence, including high proportions of silt in various Bronze Age soils, seem to suggest a certain drying up of the environment in the second half of the third millennium B.C. In the early part of the second millennium, however, there is a period of increased wetness. This has been demonstrated in north-west Bohemia, where a combination of mollusc, pollen and soil evidence has suggested more oceanic weather, with high rainfall, cool summers and mild winters (Bouzek *et al.*, 1976). This wetter episode coincides with the Tumulus Middle Bronze Age culture in Czechoslovakia and the authors suggest a population of between 10,000 and 15,000 people for north-west Bohemia at this time. In the earlier, drier period they calculated that 20,000 to 30,000 people occupied the area during the period of the Unetice culture.

Present-day conditions are not always an ideal indication of the situation that pertained in the Bronze Age, especially in the hilly locations exploited by so many Bronze Age groups. Pollen analysis of soils under the Bronze Age barrows in parts of highland North Yorkshire suggests that cereals were grown there during the Bronze Age, which would be impossible today (Evans, 1975). Pollen evidence is also important in indicating that both small temporary and larger-scale forest clearings were carried out in the Bronze Age. Fleming has compared these clearings in both the British Isles and the Netherlands, but believes that in both cases the clearings were insufficiently large to permit very large-scale pastoralism in the Early or Middle Bronze Age (1973).

Studies of carbonized grain and grain impressions show the importance of emmer, bread wheat and barley among Bronze Age groups: emmer was the most frequently found grain on Polish sites (Ostoja-Zagorski, 1974*b*), and was also important in the Early Bronze Age of Slovakia (Hajnalova, 1973). It is obvious however, that domesticated animals, particularly cattle, were important both for subsistence and in the religious sphere. There is an increasing proportion of cattle in north European faunal lists over time, and sheep, goat and cattle are reported from the Mediterranean area. In Denmark, Bronze Age burial mounds are sometimes located beside wide roads which were used in the Middle Ages for cattle droving, and it is suggested that cattle droving was similarly an important feature of the Danish Early Bronze Age (Glob, 1974). These same burial mounds in some cases have preserved burials in oak coffins where an ox hide was used to wrap the dead person. In a more obviously ritual intent, burials of animals were placed beside human burials in Early and Middle Bronze Age cemeteries, with for instance, pairs of cattle being buried in graves at the site of Iwanowice in Poland. Horses may have been eaten in the Bronze Age (Mozsolics, 1974) and from about 1850 B.C. onwards they were also used for traction, pulling chariots and wagons. Jarman has emphasized the continuing decrease in size of animals like cattle and pig from the Neolithic to the Iron Age in Europe, and links this with increasing pressure on grazing space. He also considers that the more upland location of Bronze Age sites is a reflection of similar pressure due to increased populations. The evidence for Europe is admittedly piecemeal but the demographic situation indicated by studies of cemeteries and settlements seems to be that groups were of medium size, and only when complex redistribution systems were evolved was there any pressure on the environment. In these circumstances, fluctuations in temperature or rainfall might affect not only the immediate farming communities but also those dependent on exchanging other goods or services with them for foodstuffs.

Attempts have also been made recently to use the quantity and quality of artifacts to indicate agricultural activity. Harding has suggested that the Bronze Age farming kit can be seen from hoards: these contain axes which may have been used for tilling the ground (analysis of wear marks could show relevant signs of wear), spades for earth moving and sickles for harvesting (Harding, 1976). Furmánek has used graph representations of axes, knives and hammers to indicate that the majority of such finds date from about 1500 to 1400 B.C., suggesting that these tools represent farming activity at this time (1973). Actual finds of ards, particularly in Scandinavia, Switzerland and Italy, plus representations of ploughing in these areas on rock faces, also tends to confirm the impression of the Bronze Age as one of mixed farming, although obviously some groups must have emphasized agriculture over pastoralism, or vice versa, and there may well have been changes over time.

Another feature of rock art, particularly in Scandinavia, is the depiction of boats. These commonly seem to have numerous rowers, and high prows, and an attempt to re-create one in wood and hide for a BBC television programme was a comparative success (Johnstone, 1972). Sketches of boats are also scratched on the bottom of pottery used in the Aegean islands in the Early Bronze Age, and frescoes depicting boats have been found in the excavations on Santorini. Underwater archaeology has been instrumental in demonstrating the cargoes and in some cases the building techniques of such boats (Bass, 1972). Metal must have formed an important item of exchange, as is shown by the ingots and axes found in the shipwrecks off Cape Gelidonya in Anatolia and off the coast near Béziers in southern France. One authority has claimed that 'the Mediterranean copper trade was a seaborne trade' (Muhly, 1970). Recent discoveries of metal weapons and tools off the British coast may also derive from shipwrecks (Coombs, 1975). In addition to this water-borne trade, the indications of chariots and wagons in rock art and on pottery from the Aegean, the Balkans and northern Europe suggest an increase in exchange of goods, possibly increased redistribution. By the use of physical and chemical tests, other raw materials can be demonstrated to have travelled long distances; thus X-ray fluorescence testing of amber demonstrates movement of this valued yellow resin from the Baltic to north Italy, southern France and Greece (Guerreschi, 1971; Roudil and Soulier, 1976). East Mediterranean trade in Mycenaean pottery has been demonstrated by optical emission spectroscopy and neutron activation analysis. The distribution patterns of other pots and many other types of artifact, when analysed, will be important for a thorough understanding of the exchange complexities of the European Bronze Age.

TECHNOLOGY AND SOCIETY

The technological and social subsystems are closely interlinked with the economic. The Bronze Age saw the production of artifacts in a wide range of materials, pottery, stone, bone, textiles, organic materials and metal, and many of these have been re-analysed in the past decade. Textiles have been preserved in a number of contexts, particularly the oak-coffin burials in Denmark mentioned above, and studies have indicated the use of a variety of materials (flax, nettle fibre, wool, horsehair etc.) in weaving.

The greatest amount of work has concentrated on the metal products, both in order to identify distribution areas of typologically similar artifacts, and to try to establish on an independent basis whether these have been made in the same workshop. A project for studying prehistoric bronze finds ('Prähistorische Bronzefunde') has been initiated at the Institute for Prehistory, University of Frankfurt am Main, West Germany. All classes of bronze material from weapons to tools and ornaments are included in the study. The research plan is to have a particular scholar study a particular artifact type, say swords, in a geographically defined region. Then the results of these studies are published in separate monographs, with the artifacts redrawn by the Frankfurt Institute to a standard format. Hoards containing the particular artifact studied are also included in each monograph, as are moulds for the manufacture of the particular tool or weapon. (Fig. 53) Each volume contains a distribution map with each artifact located by its number on the map. When the project is completed (forty-two volumes have already been published), it will provide excellent data for the types of spatial analyses suggested by Hodder and Orton (1976).

Physical and chemical analyses of metal objects have been carried out in an attempt to achieve a non-subjective indentification of artifacts from a particular source. Such characterization or finger-printing studies have been particularly useful in Austria, where it has been possible to compare artifacts with copper ores with a surprising degrees of success (Pittioni,

1957). A more controversial project, the Studies of the Beginnings of Metallurgy Project (Studien zu den Anfängen der Metallurgie – SAM) also at Frankfurt am Main, West Germany, has produced two reports on Copper Age and Early Bronze Age finds from Europe, comprising some 12,000 analyses (1960, 1968). These researchers are not looking for ore sources, but for *workshops*, that is, the general areas in which the products were manufactured. Workshops are defined by groupings of trace-element impurities within the copper or bronze artifact. The statistical process establishing the twenty-nine metal groups published in the second report volume (Junghans *et al.*, 1968) involved using five elements to differentiate the groups: bismuth, silver, nickel, arsenic and antimony. Some groups are found in particular periods, for instance the majority of E00, E01, and E10 groups with low impurities, nearly 'pure copper', belong to the Copper Age when native copper or secondary ores were being worked. The majority of C2, B2 and A groups belong to the Early Bronze Age period, when different ore bodies (particularly Bohemian and central German grey 'fahlerz' ores) were being used, and when techniques of smelting may have changed somewhat.

Criticisms of the programme have centred on three main problems: the division of the groups on a strictly statistical basis, ignoring archaeological information; the imbalance created by the fact that the majority of samples come from central Europe; and the fact that some of the trace elements used in the analyses have been since proved to vary in quantity depending on the techniques used in smelting. The latter difficulties include the possible segregation of bismuth, lead and nickel during heating (e.g. Slater and Charles, 1970; Charles, 1973; Tylecote, 1970). Segregation means that 'clumps' of these elements can occur in particular parts of the artifact, due to the different speed of cooling in different parts of the artifact. This means that a single metal sample taken from an artifact might well not be representative of the proportions of trace elements in the rest of the artifact. The SAM authors have taken account of some of these problems, and in an article on French copper beads (1971) Sangmeister recognizes the dangers of increased nickel arising from temperature increase during smelting, and regards as a single group two sets of artifacts which only differ in their nickel content. In this way, eighty-one artifacts out of the total of 275 analysed are linked together, and regarded as emanating from a local south French workshop.

To avoid the dangers of single-sampling, a number of samples were taken from each of a number of Remedello and Rinaldone Early Bronze Age artifacts from north and central Italy. In general more arsenic was visible in the Rinaldone culture artifacts, and arsenic and antimony were present as impurities in the Remedello artifacts. In both cases the differences were put down to the use of local ores. Barker and Slater, in analysing the results (1971), admit that in this case relatively small differences existed between the results of the multi-sample analyses and the single-sample analyses (sometimes on the same artifact) made by Sangmeister and his associates.

The consensus of opinion seems to be that it is not possible to use the analyses and groups exactly as given by the SAM project, particularly because of the technological problems. However, a number of European archaeologists are finding them useful when used on a more guarded basis and with local geological knowledge. Shortly after the publication of SAM volume 1, Dutch archaeologists produced a graph-like method of studying the analyses which seemed to produce more archaeologically satisfactory groupings of the artifacts from particular hoards, i.e. the Dieskau hoard from central Germany (Butler and van der Waals, 1965). The Scottish Bronze Age results have been similarly reworked to give more archaeologically satisfactory results (Coles, 1969).

From the statistical point of view, Doran and Hodson have suggested that multi-dimensional cluster analysis of the SAM data gives more archaeologically acceptable results (1975). Ottaway has used cluster analysis on trace element compositions of flat daggers from Early Bronze Age Brittany and southern Britain, avoiding the use of bismuth and iron as discriminators. She was able to confirm predictions from typology that the earlier daggers fell into three clusters, all found on both sides of the Channel, whereas the more developed Camerton-Snowshill variety had compositions found only in Britain (Ottaway, 1974).

In the context of the difficulty of dealing with the trace-element analyses on metal artifacts, it is important to note that a new method for defining sources, lead-isotope analysis, has recently been suggested (Fleming *et al.*, 1976; Gale, 1978). The method is based on the fact that the ratios of lead isotopes 206, 207, and 208 always reflect the original ratios in the source material. Ancient artifacts of bronze, silver and gold contain smaller or larger quantities of lead because of the simple refining methods used (Gale, 1978). The method must surely be one of great potential importance in any discussion of metal workshops and sources. It is to be hoped that metallurgical analysis overcomes the present snags as it could provide a good independent indication of distribution and exchange in the different phases of the Bronze Age, and give interesting answers to questions about the technological and social subsystems.

One of the results of the analytical work being carried out in Germany and elsewhere has been the recognition of the importance of arsenical bronze in early metallurgy. This can be defined as copper with arsenic additive, whether natural because of incorporation in the copper ore, or deliberately added during smelting. As was indicated above, in the earliest south-east European metallurgy relatively pure copper was used, but in the second phase of the Copper Age a number of hoards have both the heavy axes and the hammer-axes known from previous periods, plus finely made flat and trapezoidal axes. The latter, when analysed, contain arsenic, albeit in small quantities, and it is obvious that it was possible to make these fine narrow-edged tools because of the presence of this hardening agent (Sangmeister, 1973). At the same time, or perhaps even slightly earlier, similar arsenical bronzes are present in south-west Europe. Some Italian analyses have already been mentioned, and approximately 30 per cent of the artifacts tested from the Iberian peninsula also contained a quantity of arsenic. The use of arsenical bronze continues in the Iberian peninsula into the Early Bronze Age phases while dropping off in central and eastern Europe. The quantities of arsenic in these artifacts may have been there by accident or design. Certainly in Portugal and southern Spain, where the copper ore naturally contains up to 6 per cent arsenic, the use of local ores without additives might well be assumed. However, experiments by McKerrell and others have made it clear that it is quite possible to add arsenical ores to copper ores and create an arsenic-rich copper. Concentrations of arsenical bronze may thus indicate workshops using this technique.

It has been suggested that some of the ores in eastern Europe may well have been worked out by the beginning of the Bronze Age, and it was necessary to develop new techniques for using deeper-mined ores. In the early phases of the Bronze Age a few cultures continued to use arsenical bronze, but in the main the technology changes to tin-bronze metallurgy. The alloying of up to 10 per cent tin with copper produces excellent cutting edges, and a hard weapon or implement. Both gold and tin are obtainable from alluvial sources, and both were being used in the Balkans by about 4800 B.C. Cassiterite (the ore from which tin is commonly obtained) is much less widespread than copper. There are sources of tin in east Portugal, Sardinia and Tuscany, but the major sources used in antiquity and quoted by classical authors are Cornwall and the Scilly Islands. There is no clear proof of Bronze Age requirements being met from these areas, however. Other sources in veins of granite in central and eastern Europe would have been inaccessible by contemporary technology (Muhly, 1970). Muhly concludes that alluvial and Cornish sources are the only ones likely to have been used in the Bronze Age. It seems likely, however, that other Mediterranean sources may have been investigated

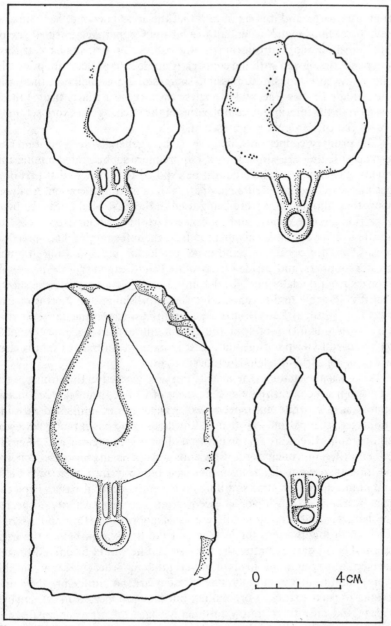

Fig. 53. Late Bronze Age razors and a razor mould from central Europe (after Jockenhövel, 1971, pl. 26, nos. 321, 322, 324, and 325)

at an early date, and it is significant that the areas known to have tin also have precocious metal-using cultures (at the Copper Age fortified site of Vila Nova de São Pedro in Portugal a number of artifacts have at least 5 per cent tin alloyed with the copper). A number of projects are presently under way to establish the possible sources of tin available in the Early and Middle Bronze Age, and to analyse the rare tin artifacts against those sources; in the interim the complexities of the exchange network set up to obtain the tin can only be guessed at.

The primary copper ores, because of their generally deep position and also because they are sulphide ores, require more sophisticated mining and smelting techniques. The ore must be exposed to the air so that part of it becomes oxidized as a preliminary part of the smelting operation. Analyses show that sulphide ores were being used in the East Mediterranean by c. 2550 B.C., in the Minoan and Mycenaean world by about 2100 B.C., and a little later in Spain. By about 1200 B.C. these techniques had spread to most of the European area, and metal products were appearing in much greater numbers, and a wide variety of tool and weapon types. Analyses of bronzes from the later periods, despite re-use of scrap metal, have shown that it is possible to differentiate between workshops, and Northover has recently identified Late Bronze Age smiths using continental scrap and very high quantities of lead ore (much more than necessary from a technological viewpoint) in south-east Britain, in contrast to smiths elsewhere in the British Isles (Northover, 1978).

What was the status of the metalsmith who worked in the Bronze Age? The two main contrasting views are those of Childe, who regarded metalsmiths as a separate and specialized group, master craftsmen possibly supported by a patron, and that of Rowlands, who has recently reviewed ethnographic literature on the position of smiths in society, and comes to rather different conclusions. Rowlands's work is mainly based on the position of present-day ironsmiths, who typically own their own fields and animals, and practise smithing on a purely seasonal basis. Typically metalworking is a kinship or a descent-group organized activity, dispersed in character and serving small centres of population (Rowlands, 1971). The smith might work, for instance, in the dry season before the agricultural cycle starts, or after the harvest, and he would be offered broken tools plus payment of food or other gifts in order to carry out his work. Smiths in the ethnographic present are not itinerant, they may belong to particular clans or families, but they are located in a particular village and only travel rarely to other villages to carry out repairs and make new tools. Rowlands concludes that given the great regional and industrial differences in metalwork, especially in the Middle and Late

Bronze Age in Europe, the idea of itinerant specialists does not fit the facts.

While Rowlands's thesis may be generally true for much of Bronze Age metallurgy, and many European archaeologists have pointed out that the total volume of Early and Middle Bronze Age metalwork could not possibly reflect full-time working of a large number of bronzesmiths, it must nevertheless be realized that these analogies are taken from the work of *iron*smiths, where the organization of supply of raw materials is very different. There are also signs of professional craftsmanship of a very high standard in some European Bronze Age metallurgy. For instance, Taylor has suggested that many of the gold objects found in the burial mounds of Wessex (south-west Britain) in the Early Bronze Age may be the work of a single craftsman. The gold objects (lozenge-shaped plates, belt-hooks, casings for amber discs, etc.) are all finely engraved in what Taylor and Coles regard as the same hand (1971). There is the intriguing possibility that this craftsman also worked on the other side of the Channel in Brittany. In a completely different setting, in the Late Bronze Age of the Aegean, readings of the clay tablets inscribed with Linear B script suggest that the smiths or armourers of the period were an organized group of craftsmen in a society of specialists (Chadwick, 1972). In Messenia, there were perhaps 400 such smiths in all, one to about every 200 or 300 men. Metal was acquired from different centres, and the smiths, grouped in small communities of about four to twenty, including some goldsmiths, smelted copper and tin and made objects with highly professional skill. The tablets indicate that rations were allotted to these men as well as to other specialist groups like the women weavers, and it is obvious that this society was organized on the basis of specialist crafts and redistribution of supplies.

Another aspect of metallurgy which can be considered as within the social subsystem is the practice of hiding both complete and fragmented artifacts and in some cases smelted ore in the ground in the form of hoards. The contents of hoards are highly variable; they consist of two to several hundred objects, and vary from single artifact types to many different varieties of artifact in one hoard. The most gigantic hoards include those from Late Bronze Age Romania, weighing up to four tons each! In Bavaria and Austria there are Early Bronze Age hoards consisting of neck rings only, usually more than ten to the hoard. These finds are taken as representing the distribution centres of such products on the pre-Alps, while other hoards containing both neck rings and other objects, and found in Czechoslovakia and Poland, may represent either private users of the rings or individual metal smelters (Bath-Bilkova, 1973). One of the reasons for Rowlands's study of the role of smiths in ethnographic situations was to try to throw some light on the reasons for the contents of a particular hoard. Classical explanations for the deposition of hoards include people burying objects of value in time of danger, communities burying their wealth for protection, and a communal 'pot latch' where for some ritual or prestige reason goods were 'destroyed' by being placed in the ground. It has been suggested that hoards of numerous copies of the same type of artifact represent a merchant's stock-in-trade, and that those with only fragmentary pieces represent a blacksmith's store for future remelting. Rowlands' analyses indicated that numerous copies of the same type of artifact might be the large-scale production at a limited time of the year of one smith, while the presence of many fragmentary pieces might indicate the material returned to a smith at a particular season for the repair or renewal of tools. Burial of objects of value is obviously a general Bronze Age phenomenon, and continuity can be seen from the Late Neolithic practice of burying hoards of stone axes.

However, the type and frequency of hoarding was much more extensive and varied in the Bronze Age. It seems likely that the many hoards that have been found can only be explained in many different frameworks, and the most valuable way of study for the present would seem to be the relationship of each particular hoard to its environment. Bergmann has investigated the ethno-sociological aspects of grave and hoard groups in Early Bronze Age north-west Germany, and indicated the relatively limited number of times that the circumstances of discovery are recorded. Finds were hidden under or near a large stone (in Brittany hoards have been found near megalithic tombs or standing stones) and sometimes the metal finds were placed inside a pot with a stone over its mouth, large objects such as swords having been broken into several pieces to get them inside the vessel (Bergmann, 1968).

The dating of hoard deposition is also something of a problem, because some of the artifact types included could have been handed down as heir-looms, and there is rarely any associated material that can be radiocarbon dated. The practice seems to have been at its height by the beginning of the second millennium B.C. – in Hungary, for instance, the main bulk of hoards dates from approximately 2100 to 1700 B.C. Much of the rich Hungarian Bronze Age material has been published by Mozsolics (1967, 1968, 1973). Unfortunately, as was noted above when discussing the analysis of bronze hoards from north-west Germany, the poor recording of the circumstances of their discovery, and even in some cases of total numbers of artifacts in the hoard, means that only a small proportion of hoards can be used for intensive study.

A common hoard location was in the neighbourhood of water, and Maringer has recently provided a descriptive analysis of goods deposited in the neighbourhood of water, which he regards as having ritual significance (1973). Deposits range from metal objects, such as pins of successive periods found near a spring in south Germany, and swords found at the salt springs at St Moritz in Switzerland, to remains of a wooden 'altar' in north Germany. One of the richest areas for water deposits is Scandinavia. Among other finds, nearly 100 pairs of bronze trumpets, lurer, have been found from bogs in Denmark and neighbouring areas of Norway and Sweden.

The re-analysis of hoards is still in its infancy, but the use of careful typological and technological re-examination, plus chemical and physical analyses of the metal composition where relevant, combined with the circumstances of discovery, may provide more hypotheses for testing with regard to the reasons for deposition, and the role that these hoards played in the lives of individuals, kin groups or village communities.

In 1970 Bergmann published a monograph about the Early Bronze Age in north-west Germany, in which he included a great number of distribution maps of the ornament, weapon and tool types found there. In each case the context of the particular artifact in a hoard, grave or as a single find was given. On the basis of these distribution maps Bergmann identified five subregions or artifact-type groupings, based mainly on the ornament types – the weapons did not differ so much (Fig. 54). These groupings were supported by a computer analysis produced by Hodder and Orton (1976). The same authors also analysed the Middle Bronze Age bronzes of the Carpathian Basin published by Hansel (1968), to indicate that, as in the north-west German case, ornament types had localized distributions, while swords and axes were much more widespread. It can thus be seen that computer methods are helping in a very real way to sort out some of the complex distributions of the European Bronze Age and to identify the different boundaries of exchange for particular artifact types, leaving archaeologists to suggest the possible social reasons behind the distributions.

THE AEGEAN AREA

The Aegean area is secondary to south-east Europe in adopting metallurgy, but rapidly acquired expertise in the medium. The earliest metallurgy is found on Crete about 3700 B.C. Renfrew has recently used metallurgy as one element in a modified form of systems theory to account for the emergence of civilization in the Aegean (1973c). He argues that two

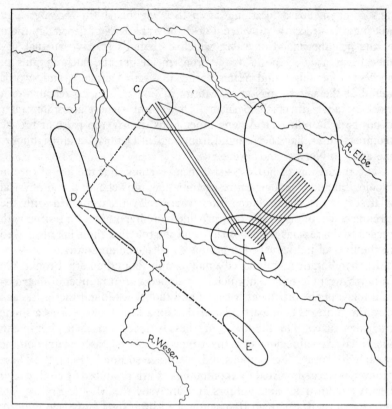

Fig. 54. Interaction as demonstrated by movement of bronzes between clusters of sites in the north German Early Bronze Age (after Hodder and Orton, 1976, fig. 5.79)

models can plausibly be presented: either changes in the subsistence and redistribution subsystems or changes in craft specialization and wealth subsystems; changes in at least two subsystems would be necessary for the development of what he calls the 'multiplier effect' in cultural change.

There are differences between Crete, the Cycladic islands and the Aegean mainland in the speed of acquisition of metallurgy. By the end of Early Minoan II, c. 2900 B.C., a number of small village communities on Crete were using ivory and stone bowls of Egyptian origin, as well as Anatolian obsidian, and it is more than likely that the copper ores for their metallurgy were acquired from Anatolia or Cyprus. Arsenic was used as a hardener, and even in the Middle Minoan samples analysed by the SAM project little tin was present. On the mainland, and in the Cyclades, metallurgy commenced rather later than on Crete. In the period *c.* 2900–2350 B.C., however, there was considerable uniformity in a number of artifacts throughout the Aegean area: shaft-hole axes, diadems and sheet metal and tweezers showed a high degree of craftsmanship in bronze, while similar vessel designs, the 'sauce-boat' and 'Depas cup' were found throughout the area produced in both pottery and metal. Folded-arm figurines in marble testify to expertise in stone-working. The widespread nature of Aegean prosperity at this time is demonstrated by the presence of eight treasures (burial goods and hoards) from Levkas off the north-western coast of Greece to Troy (Renfrew, 1973*c*). Boats would have been important for the rapid spread of wealth and more prosaic trade items, and they are illustrated both by model lead boats from the Cyclades and by scratched designs on the bottom of pottery 'frying-pans'; all have high prows, and the sketches seem to indicate lots of rowers. After *c.* 2350 B.C. the wealth horizon is lost on the mainland and in the Cyclades, until about 1850 B.C. (the period of the earlier shaft graves at Mycenae), and there are no signs of large and imposing houses such as the earlier House of the Tiles at Lerna (Dickinson, 1977). On Crete, however, it could be argued that the craft and wealth subsystems continued undisturbed, with the building of the first palaces and the continuation of contacts with the eastern Mediterranean. From there they probably acquired the potter's wheel, the tubular drill for stone-working, and writing, first the hieroglyphic script, then Linear A (Cadogan, 1976).

It could be argued that Crete also demonstrates the effective feedback between the two other subsystems mentioned by Renfrew, the subsistence economy and the redistribution of goods. Renfrew regards Mediterranean polyculture of olives, vines and cereals as fundamental to the development of Aegean civilization (1973*c*). The olive is known in large quantities from Early Minoan Myrtos and from other sites on Crete and the Cyclades, but is only evidenced shortly before the period of Mycenaean palaces on the mainland (Warren, 1977). The opportunity for exploiting this potentially rich polyculture was thus present on Crete from the beginning of the Bronze Age, and the store-rooms in the early palaces (*c.* 2400 to 2050 B.C.) – and the freeing of labour to build the palaces themselves – demonstrate that surpluses were available. It is assumed that – if they could be deciphered – the hieroglyphic and Linear A tablets would give details of the redistribution of foodstuffs, raw materials and manufactured goods, as the later Linear B ones do. On the mainland, on the other hand, a series of surveys have demonstrated that settlement was often on medium-quality land (McDonald and Rapp, 1972; Bintliff, 1977). Bintliff has pointed out that hill-slope situations were likely to

provide the best available soils, since the alluviation which enriched the
valley bottoms only occurred in the Iron Age. Sites increased in size from
the beginning of the Late Bronze Age, but only with the development of
Mycenaean palaces from *c.* 1700 B.C. onwards is it possible to see complex
redistribution taking place on the mainland.

SOUTH-EAST EUROPE

As will have been evident from the last chapter, metallurgy was by no
means a new invention in south-east Europe by about 2500 B.C. and yet
in many ways this date represents a watershed in the importance of
metallurgy in this area. There is a drop in metal production about 2500
B.C. Sherratt has indicated that this may be linked with the using up of
secondary ores, and suggests, together with other archaeologists, that
influences from the Pontic area may have been the spur to the reorganiza-
tion and redevelopment of metallurgy. After a drop in numbers of metal
goods deposited in tombs, metallurgy recommenced on a larger scale and
with different distribution patterns from the Chalcolithic. Metallurgy
also spread rapidly over central Europe, together with metal products and
probably smelted copper for remelting. In Hungary, Austria, Yugoslavia,
Bulgaria and Romania, the Baden-Cernavoda cultures mark a break with
the previous patterns of pottery design, metal artifacts, and in some cases
settlement and cemetery organization. Cernavoda channelled wares
differ markedly from earlier painted and graphite decorated pots in south
and south-east Romania, and Cernavoda riveted daggers, slender shaft-
hole axes and lightly flanged axes are of different character from earlier
Gumelnitsa metallurgy. Skeletally the populations do not differ much,
however, and the tendency towards settlement in higher areas, already
visible in late Salcuta populations, may have something to do with changes
in economic and social organization (Sherratt, 1972). By the mid third
millennium B.C. many European societies seem to have reached a
significant threshold in regard to their technology, social organization,
density of population and settlement distribution (Sherratt, 1972;
Coles, 1976*a*). These interlocking factors seem to have involved the
creation of more settlements, and settlements in different geographical
locations, than before. In particular, soils which were not used during the
earlier periods are now colonized. As mentioned above, the Cernavoda
populations in Romania favour more hilltop situations, and in a different
geomorphological situation, in the wide basin of the Maritsa river, Bronze
Age occupation levels on previously settled tell mounds increase in size.
The less relaxed social atmosphere is indicated by a stone fortification wall

at the Ezero mound. It can thus be seen that at least some present-day thinking is running along the lines of internal developments in the local societies leading to full Bronze Age cultures, although many archaeologists still visualize the initial stages of the Bronze Age as being linked to immigration from Anatolia or the Pontic region. For instance, Berciu visualized the Cernavoda culture as emanating from Anatolia and the south, and consisting of the peoples later to develop into the historic Indo-Europeans (1967). He also suggested that the importers of the 'ochre grave culture' moved from the Caucasus into eastern Romania. Physical anthropological studies, however, do not fit with this picture. A recent analysis by Dinu (1974) has suggested that tombs with lots of red and yellow ochre on the extended or flexed burials are not in fact typical of a single culture, and that those buried in cemeteries where the ochre ceremonial was used, for instance Brailita in eastern Romania, were members of local populations. The use of ochre is widespread from the Volga to the Middle Danube. Dinu suggests that such a generalized practice may be linked to large-range movements of only small numbers of people, possibly involved in pastoralism. They would have passed on the practice to populations with whom they mixed. At a site on the middle Dniester river, Vykhvatintsy, the ochre-covered skeletons were buried in pits, sometimes with a flat stone above, rather than the more usual burial mounds. The skeletons in these graves were of Mediterraneanoid type, again discounting the idea of inroads of foreign immigrants. The cemetery evidence can be taken to suggest that, although influence from outside the south-east European area during the Early Bronze Age cannot be discounted, it can no longer be taken as a single motive cause for the inception of the European Bronze Age proper.

With regard to the economic basis of Bronze Age sites in Romania and Bulgaria, we know that a full range of wheat, barley and millet was present, together with peas and lentils. Improved species of cattle, sheep or goat, pig and horse are reported. As part of the British Academy Early History of Agriculture project, Dennell and Webley have considered prehistoric settlement and land use in southern Bulgaria (1975). They record that a rotational system utilizing emmer, six-row naked barley and legumes appears to have been in practice at the tell site of Ezero, while at nearby Siganski Mogila emmer and lentils were present. From a faunal point of view, using their analysis of what soils were available to the inhabitants of Ezero, and the samples of bones obtained from sieving experiments, these researchers suggest that more emphasis was laid on sheep/goat husbandry than on cattle at the latter site. Dennell and Webley's study used the well-tried methods of soil analysis in two particular areas of southern Bulgaria, around Nova Zagora and near Celopec. Within the Nova Zagora region, already well known for its numerous archaeological sites, there is a wide range of soils available in the river valley. These include light, mainly sandy soils usable for agriculture, grazing areas suitable for permanent or seasonal occupation and browse areas. Dennell and Webley have reconstructed potential site territories for the Neolithic and Bronze Age sites in this area and emphasize that the importance of agriculture is shown in the frequent location of sites along the good arable soils (Fig. 55). However, during the Early Bronze Age river clays were deposited. Soils were less satisfactory for agriculture and the land had poorer drainage. The Early Bronze Age sites were thus sometimes located in more marginal areas for agriculture, with poorer drainage and less viable soils. Dennell and Webley suggest therefore that in addition to the main emphasis on agriculture, there would always be a mobile element in the economy

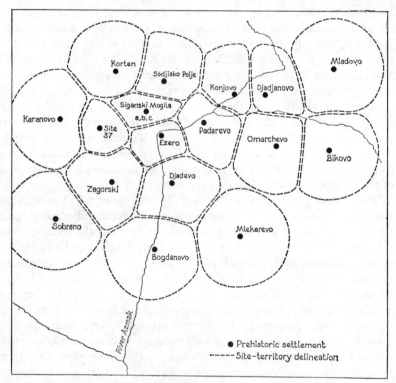

Fig. 55. Site-exploitation territories in Nova Zagora region, southern Bulgaria (after Dennell and Webley, 1975, fig. 3)

utilizing both the permanent grazing and seasonal grazing areas of the
Nova Zagora region. In contrast to the intensively settled Nova Zagora
region, the Celopec area, which is much higher and consists of steep-sided
valleys, was only able to support three widely separated settlements.

In the context of south-east European Early Bronze Age economy, it
should be emphasized that the copper sources in the Transylvanian
mountains were already of considerable importance in the Chalcolithic,
and that recent research has revealed quarry and mining areas. One of the
earlier European copper quarries, Varna in Bulgaria, dates to about 4400
B.C. (Karanovo VI). At Aibunar, Bulgaria, near the settlements of
Karanovo and Azmak, the ore may have been first quarried at a similarly
early date. At Aibunar there are eleven galleries mined over a total length
of 500 m. The longest of them is 110 m long, and nearly 20 m deep. In the
galleries the exploitation methods are revealed by the presence of antler
tools, hammer-axes and picks (Cernych, 1976). At least three other similar
mines are known in southern Bulgaria. The Varna quarry is located near
to a Copper Age cemetery, and in general the relationship between the
source areas and nearby settlements is a fruitful field of research. Sherratt
has published a number of maps illustrating the closeness of these early
quarries to settlement sites (5 to 10 km in the case of the Nova Zagora
sites) and suggested that propinquity was one of several reasons for the
development of metallurgy there.

The development of textiles in this area was also an important feature
in trade and economy. Flax may have been grown (Dennell, 1976) and
certainly the presence of sheep and goat would provide materials for
textile manufacture. The presence of many loom weights (including the
clay objects described as anchor weights, according to Sherratt, 1972)
would indicate the importance of weaving.

In Hungary the first Bronze Age cultures developed from the earlier
Vucedol and Bell Beaker populations, with the Toszeg tell beside the river
Tisza being occupied successively by the Nagyrev, Hatvan and Otomani
Bronze Age culture groups (Gimbutas, 1965). Cremation burial was
practised by both the Nagyrev group and their neighbours and contem-
poraries to the north-east, the Hatvan, whose assemblages spread later to
the Toszeg area. Kalicz has discussed Hatvan sites (1968), indicating that
all the tell sites had some form of defence, such as the double ditch at
Toszeg and the ditch between two rings of houses at Tiszaluc. In some
areas, settlement distribution was so packed that the villages were within
sight of each other. Torma has suggested that apparently undefended
Hatvan sites normally occur close to defended ones, and that the inhabitants of the first may have helped to build the second (1972). Houses on the

sites are rectangular and quite large (60 m² at the defended hilltop site of Tokod). These populations of Early Bronze Age Hungary are suggested to have practised a mixed farming economy.

To the west of Hungary, metal-using spread rather slowly in Yugoslavia (Alexander, 1972). The Mokrin settlement and cemetery, with its separate burial rites for males, females and juveniles, has recently provided an important stratigraphy for the Early Bronze Age. In Phase I there are typological resemblances with the Hungarian Nagyrev, in II with the Unetice culture.

CENTRAL AND NORTHERN EUROPE

The Unetice culture developed in Czechoslovakia in the wake of Bell Beaker and Corded Ware populations, and spread widely over north central Europe. Recent studies in this area have tried to relate settlements to geology and water sources, as in the Neolithic. In discussing the north German plain, Bergmann says that the Early Bronze Age populations commonly sought waterside locations for settlement, but that the quality of the soils was also important (1970). These settlements consisted of from one to three houses, the sort of isolated farm houses known from the Neolithic and also reported from later Middle and Late Bronze Age settlements in the Netherlands and north-west Europe generally. Elsewhere in Germany Early Bronze Age occupation is reported on good soils. Unetice settlements are not well known, but obviously involved groups of different sizes. For instance, at Brezno in Czechoslovakia nine large Unetice culture buildings were revealed, two of them with wall slots, the others with posts (Pl. 7). The seven post-built houses lay on an east–west alignment and were 20 m long by 6 m wide; the other two houses lay north-west by south-east and were longer and thinner (25 × 3 m). This suggests either inequality in the social status in the society or the provision of communal houses for meetings or ceremonies. Cemeteries were associated with these houses, and the excavator considers that each house and cemetery represents a 'sib' or patriarchal family (Pleinerova, 1972).

Much of the research in the Unetice area in recent years has concentrated upon cemeteries and possible social implications that might be gained by a study of the grave-goods and the other burial features. Between c. 2550 and 1700 B.C. the Unetice culture covered Bohemia and much of Germany and Poland. Its metal products penetrated into the Scandinavian and north-west European areas. In these areas burial was generally in single graves under mounds or barrows. The mounds could be of turf or clay. There are local differences in burial techniques, for instance timber coffins are very often used in the Early and Middle Bronze Age from Denmark to Britain. Although inhumation was the general rule among Unetice populations, some groups cremated their dead and at the Polish cemetery of Tomice both rites were used (Misz-kiewicz, 1972). At Tomice the average age of death for men was thirty-one years old, the average age for females twenty years old. These ages at death seem to make the population rather less successful than that of Early Bronze Age Lerna in Greece, where the average age at death for men was between thirty-one and thirty-seven years, and for women between twenty-nine and thirty-one years (Angel, 1969).

Recently Susan Shennan has reported on an interesting study of the cemetery at Brančr in south-western Slovakia (1975). The cemetery was used over about 200 to 400 years around 2500 B.C. It is one of several large cemeteries in the area and contains 308 inhumation burials. The organization of the cemetery was that the bodies were buried from the south to the north through time. All the skeletons were preserved, and 81 per cent of the women were buried on their left side and 69 per cent of the men on their right side. This is in line with earlier Corded Ware practice. By a series of computer studies Shennan identified the most elaborate graves, usually those of men, with grave-goods of copper daggers, metal sheet, boar tusk, bone amulets, willow-leaf knives, arrow-heads and chipped stone and pottery. Only mature or adult men seemed to get the bone amulets or arrowheads and whetstones. Females were usually provided with willow-leaf rings, which would have been worn as ear-rings from their position on the body, bone beads and bone spacer plates. Children had the willow-leaf rings on their wrists as bracelets and were also accompanied by miniature vessels. Young adults wore metal sheeting over the thigh or pelvic area. Shennan suggests that these grave-goods reflect the individual's status at death (Fig. 56).

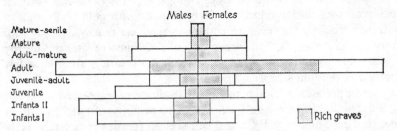

Fig. 56. Age and sex distribution and rich graves at the Brančr cemetery, Czechoslovakia (after Susan Shennan, 1975, fig. 4)

Shennan concluded that the variety, number and difficulty of acquisition of the goods defined those burials which were rich. Among these rich burials those of several children were included. Shennan hypothesizes that women, including female children, either achieved wealth on marriage or that it was ascribed at birth.

Possibly they could even have been betrothed at birth as happens in certain ethnographic instances, such as on Melville and Bathurst Islands to the north of Australia. Susan Shennan's data suggested that the living population represented by the cemetery was one consisting of thirty to forty people, half of them children. This seems a very small number for such a degree of social differentiation, but it is suggested that the Brančsettlement was only one of a number in the vicinity and that its inhabitants would marry out, so that their social organization would be part of a larger total community. This would fit with the conclusions of Pleinerova mentioned above. The other large cemeteries in this area of south-western Slovakia, for instance Nitra, include similar rich graves and seem to be part of the same system.

Inequality within the social structure in the Early Bronze Age has been suggested for a long time, because of the presence of very rich graves, for instance at Leubingen, Germany, and Łęki Małe in Poland. These date from approximately 2400–2070 B.C. At both sites funerary houses seem to have covered the extended burials, which were richly furnished with gold and bronze grave-goods. In addition at Leubingen a second adult had been killed to accompany the dead man. In other areas of Europe, richness of grave-goods has made other burials nearly as outstanding. For instance at Kernonen-en-Plouvorn in Finistère, Brittany, a 15-m diameter tumulus of clay and stones overlay a rectangular chamber in dry stone. On the stone floor were a number of wooden boxes containing grave-goods; one had flanged axes, another forty fine flint arrowheads and a bronze dagger, and near by were three daggers, decorated with gold nails, and a few amber beads. Similarly at south Guingamp in the Côtes-du-Nord, an old excavation had produced bronze weapons with gold studs and an electrum diadem. However, in both cases there are nearby mounds with very few grave-goods, and in the case of the Finistère site, the nearby Plouzevède mound had no grave-goods at the centre apart from a few potsherds and flint scrapers (Briard, 1973).

A more precise appraisal of the relative richness of grave-goods has been attempted for Bronze Age Denmark. The majority of sites date from between 2200 and 1250 B.C., and lack skeletal remains completely. Only in about 100 spectacular instances were remains of bodies, in many cases with flesh still on the bones, and clothing, accidentally preserved because of the effects of tannic acid in the oak coffins in which they were buried (Glob, 1974). Thus Randsborg, who analysed the grave-goods from the Danish graves, was limited for the most part to the bronze and gold work deposited with them. He established which were female and which were male graves by assuming that weapon burials belonged to males, while jewellery burials belonged to females. The bronze artifacts deposited as grave goods, over 10,000 in all, were weighed. Histograms of the weights showed a tripartite distribution, with three main weight groups. The first were those near 0 g, next there was a group between 300 and 500 g in weight, and finally a group between 700 and 900 g. Contrary to some other European archaeologists, who believe that gold was used in the same way as bronze and was not specially important in the Bronze Age, Randsborg considers that it was a definite wealth indicator, because gold artifacts occurred most frequently in the graves with the greatest weight of bronze. The histograms of weight showed that male graves were more often rich than female graves (528 male to 236 female rich graves), but there is a possible increase in female social status towards the end of the period (Fig. 57).

Randsborg buttresses his study by indicating the agricultural potential of the different regions which he is discussing. This is done in terms of the quantity of hard corn recoverable per hectare, as determined by present-day Danish agriculture. In all but one case the quantity of bronze was greater in areas with good agricultural potential than in areas with less good agricultural potential. The three areas studied on the Danish peninsula were north-west Jutland, north-east Jutland and south Jutland, and the island of Bornholm and the Danish Baltic islands were the two other areas. In all these areas in the three time periods into which Randsborg divides the study there is a normal distribution of wealth deposited in burials, i.e. there are more poor than rich graves in each area and period. The only exception is in north-west Jutland where in period III there are more rich male graves than would be expected. It may reflect a change in the social structure in this area. It is interesting that western Denmark in general has a greater weight of bronzes in graves than in hoards while the eastern zones seem to emphasize 'destruction' of wealth in hoards rather than in graves (Randsborg, 1973, 1974).

The evidence from the graves, the rich variety of metallurgical products, and the rock art of southern Scandinavia suggest a well-established Bronze Age society in this area. The settlements of the people who created these artifacts and art are much harder to find, but traces of Bronze Age stone clearances around the edges of the fields and of houses have been found in recent rescue excavations near Gothenberg, Sweden (Sandberg, 1974).

The pattern of settlement in Sweden seems to be of small units, such as the settlements excavated in the vicinity of the cemeteries at Löderup and Valleberga in south Sweden (Strömberg, 1975). Welinder has recently reconsidered the evidence from these sites in the framework of an inquiry into the 'expansionist' nature of farming economy in Middle Bronze Age

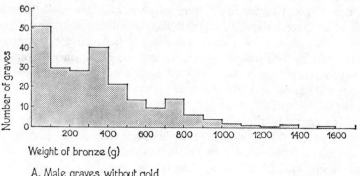

A. Male graves without gold

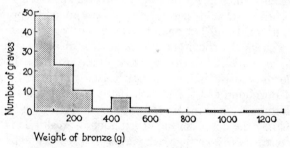

B. Female graves without gold

Fig. 57. Histograms of weights of bronze in Danish Early Bronze Age (period II) graves (after Randsborg 1974, figs. 1, 6 and 7)

Sweden (1977). He visualizes a continuity in subsistence practice (cattle breeding and fallow agriculture) from the Late Neolithic to the Bronze Age, but suggests that the organization of metal transport and manufacture altered the social structure to a chiefdom. Expansion of farming from the 'central' to the 'marginal' areas took place in the Middle Bronze Age because of population increase in a 'filled cultural landscape'. In this model, the chief and his bronzesmith would have been at Valleberga (the majority of bronze grave-goods were found in the Valleberga cemetery) and Löderup would have been one of the lesser settlements sending its surplus to the centre and getting back a small quantity of bronze in return (Welinder, 1977) (Fig. 58).

Traces of plough marks and of repeated ploughing have been located on different sites in South Norway and these traces, allied with the finds of ards such as the Hvorslev ard dated *c.* 2050 B.C., and the other wooden artifacts discovered in the Danish bogs, indicate the pursuit of agriculture

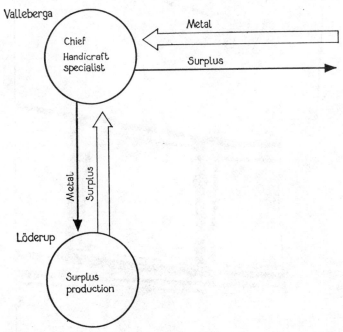

Fig. 58. Model of Early Bronze Age social and settlement hierarchy in southeast Sweden (after Welinder, 1977, fig. 30)

in south Scandinavia in the early second millennium B.C. Research in the northern two-thirds of Scandinavia has revealed a number of prosperous coastal settlements, including the settlements of the Varanger fjord over 1000 miles north of Oslo. At approximately 1250 B.C. the Grasbakken settlement consisted of oval and rectangular houses, with earth benches and elongated hearths built of stones on edge. The economy was based on fishing, as the fishing gear in bone and antler reveals. Eighty per cent of the bones found were of cod, and the hunters of the Grasbakken settlement also ate whalemeat and the meat of the Harp seal (Hagen, 1967).

Across the North Sea in Britain most of the Early and Middle Bronze

Age huts and farms which have been excavated are located along the coast or in upland areas (Burgess and Miket, 1976). Among the lowland sites discussed are the settlement at Gwithian in Cornwall, where there is evidence of field clearance and cultivation, and the site of Fengate in eastern England, where in the Middle Bronze Age a series of large

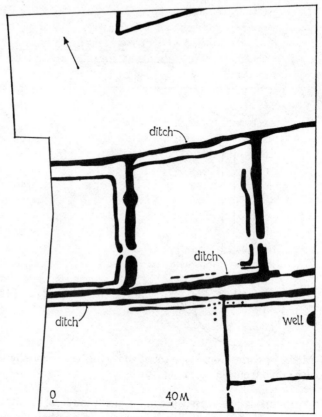

Fig. 59. Part of Middle Bronze Age field system defined by ditches at Fengate, eastern England (after Pryor, 1976, fig. 3.6)

enclosures for cattle herding were created by digging long, deep ditches (Fig. 59). The evidence for agriculture prior to about 1800 B.C. in areas denuded today has already been referred to. There are suggestions that a number of the systems of field enclosures and hut circles in upland areas as far apart as Yorkshire and Dartmoor may turn out to date from as early as the Middle Bronze Age. Three separate ditches enclosed the settlement at Thwing in Yorkshire which dates from about 1250 B.C. and at a similar period in Derbyshire settlers braved the exposed conditions at 1700 feet (518 m) above sea level on the crest of Mam Tor plateau. In these upland areas, burials in round barrows seem to have been placed just beyond the limit of the fields, on pastoral ground. A recent study by Glenn of the buried population in another part of the British Isles, eastern Scotland, has suggested that only a section of the population was given special treatment (in this case burial in stone cists) consisting, in the sample studied, of eighty-two males, thirty-eight females and seventeen sub-adults. The sub-adults qualified for more elaborate burial treatment at about thirteen years of age, when presumably they had the social status of adults. By using multivariate discriminant analysis Glenn has demonstrated some geographical variability in the physical characteristics, especially those of males (1976).

Lakeside settlements of Early and Middle Bronze Age date are known in eastern France, Switzerland and North Italy. The Swiss and French ones at Auvernier and Clairvaux respectively were occupied from the Late Neolithic into the Early Bronze Age, and consisted of rectangular houses. These were arranged in rows at Auvernier (Fig. 60), while four separate houses were constructed at Clairvaux (Fig. 61). Based on the sizes of the structures, populations of approximately fifty persons could be assumed (Boisaubert *et al.*, 1974). In southern France most of the settlements are cave sites including the inland cave of Peyroche II, Ardèche, which was occupied between 2140 and 1800 B.C. Hearths were lit in the cave, and bones of young sheep and goat, cattle and wild boar revealed some of the foodstuffs of the inhabitants; querns and net-weights suggest that plants and fish also played a part in the diet. The cave occupied an area of approximately 80 m², and could have accommodated about a dozen people. Some open sites have been located, and Courtin has recently excavated a defended spur settlement to the west of Marseilles (1976). A wall over 2 m wide, reinforced by bastions, cut off the end of the spur. Querns and sickle blades, and the bones of small cattle, sheep and goat, suggest a mixed economy. The Spanish data are very limited, but the fact that there were 200 burials within the defended hilltop settlement at El Oficio, with its rectangular, closely packed houses, suggests that a sizeable population was involved. At Bastida de Totana, Murcia, the settlement consisted of rectangular houses up to 40 m² in size, each of them capable of housing about nine people. Unfortunately, we do not know how many of the houses were standing at the same time.

In southern Italy excavations at Tufariello have only revealed four rectangular houses, but the maximum area available to the village was

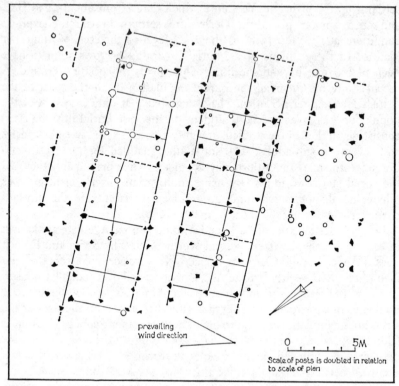

prevailing
wind direction

0   5M

Scale of posts is doubled in relation
to scale of plan

Fig. 60. Possible agglomerated house plans at Auvernier, Switzerland, of Early
Bronze Age date (after Boisaubert *et al.*, 1975, fig. 14)

over 15,000 m² on a plateau site, and the construction of a defensive wall
about 2700 B.C. suggests that a relatively large population was involved
(Holloway *et al.*, 1975). Oval houses, rather than rectangular ones, were
normal on Sicily, and a few of these have been revealed at the Early Bronze
Age defensive sites of the Lipari acropolis and Castelluccio on Sicily
itself. Not all the huts were excavated at these two sites, but in the Middle
Bronze Age a settlement at Milazzo, again on a defensive spur, consisted
of thirty-three huts, all but one oval, while on Salina island, the Portella
settlement contained ten huts. Bronze Age cemeteries associated with
Sicilian settlements contain anything from approximately fifty to over 100
tombs (Brea, 1957). Evans has recently discussed the evidence for settlement size in the Mediterranean in the Bronze Age, and concluded that
nearly all of the settlements were relatively small, except for Knossos and
Mallia, each of which seem to have extended over 50 ha in size (Evans,

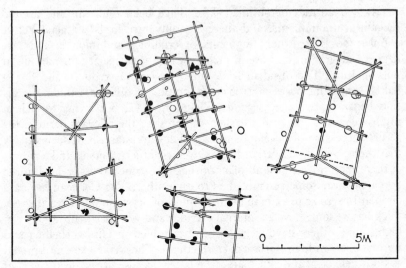

Fig. 61. Hypothetical Early Bronze Age house plans at Clairvaux, eastern France (after Boisaubert *et al.*, 1975, fig. 6)

1976). Unfortunately, fully excavated settlement sites are rare on the west Mediterranean islands of Corsica, Sardina and the Balearics, so the units of population are not known, although the large-stone architecture which typifies this period throughout the islands suggests local groups, if not population units, of several hundred persons.

On Corsica, as in nearby southern France, megalithic tomb building had begun about 3200 B.C. From small box-like cists the tombs expanded in size. The burial style was used throughout the island although the majority of tombs are to be found in the south-west. Lanfranchi and Weiss emphasize that the hillsides and buttes of this region have produced many signs of settlement, and they suggest that the grinding grooves found on granite outcrops are also connected with this Late Neolithic and Copper Age occupation (1973). At some sites, for instance Le Monti, there are the remains of huts and defences. The same authors suggest that apart from these agriculturally based populations, pastoralist groups would have been located in the highland areas. It is also possible that like other contemporary societies of Bronze Age Europe, the inhabitants of Corsica practised mixed farming, with an element of mobility in the economy, and transported their flocks to higher ground during the summer. In addition to using large stones to construct the cist tombs, the Corsicans erected standing stones, sometimes stood beside the tombs, sometimes in rows like the Palaggiu alignment near Sartène.

Large quantities of obsidian flakes have been found in and around megalithic monuments, and there are only rare finds of metal before about 1800 B.C., when fragments of crucibles and moulds and rare daggers suggest an increase in metal use and the capacity for melting, if not smelting. The obsidian trade into Corsica was reduced and finally halted some time between 2100 and 1500 B.C. A different building tradition began in the early second millennium B.C., but owing to lack of intensive excavation and of carbon-14 dates for the relevant periods, the actual succession of developments is difficult to establish. It seems likely that there were close relationships between southern Corsica and Sardinia at this time, and the ground plans of the giant stone towers erected in the two areas bear some resemblances to each other. The Corsican *torre* are circular towers 10 to 15 m in diameter built of drystone walling, with very thick bases; some have an internal corridor and were originally about 3 m high, while others have a main chamber roofed in false corbelling and were about 7 m high (Grosjean *et al.*, 1976). They have been interpreted as both defensive and ritual sites (the latter because of the deep layers of ash inside some of the chambers). There is a group of sixteen *torre* in south-west Corsica, the most famous being at Filitosa. The builders of Filitosa re-used anthropomorphic standing stones in the form of warriors with helmets, armour, swords and daggers, in much the same way that tomb builders at Sion in Switzerland had re-used stelae several hundred years earlier. The rest of the some 100 *torre* known are scattered over the rest of the island, and this distribution is attributed by local researchers to the expansion of the (foreign) Torrean population at the expense of the native groups of the island.

There are tantalizing similarities and differences between the cultural sequences in the neighbouring islands of Corsica and Sardinia. About the time that cist-grave usage was commencing in Corsica, rock-cut tombs were being used for the first time to bury the dead on Sardinia. These were the work of the Ozieri or San Michele people, who also made fine-walled, richly incised pottery and built the only square mound structure in Mediterranean architecture – the 'temple' at Monte d'Accodi in north-west Sardinia. San Michele pottery is found widespread from this good agricultural land of north-western Sardinia through the rich plains of the Campidano (Lilliu, 1972). This distribution suggests a basically agricultural subsistence, with some element of mobility, perhaps goat and sheep transhumance as today. Considerable amounts of ground-stone tools are found on these sites, including querns and rubbing stones, and mace heads and ordinary axes. In addition, sea shells are frequent on many Sardinian sites. When sieved samples of deposits have been analysed, it may be possible to see whether these shells were collected simply for decoration, or whether they formed part of a larger marine exploitation including the collection of fish and crustacea, still exploited today. Small amounts of metalwork are found both on the San Michele sites, and on sites dating from *c.* 2200 B.C. onwards containing both Bell Beaker sherds (possibly deriving from southern France or northern Spain) and Monte Claro pottery. In the second half of the third millennium B.C., the first megalithic tombs and standing stones were set up, although standing stones were less frequent than on Corsica. Also dating from this period may be some of the elaborate internal features of certain rock-cut tombs, for instance the carved beams and rafters illustrated by Ceruti (1967). At the Monte d'Accodi site rectangular rooms to the east of the temple contained tripod wares dating to approximately 2100 B.C., and there was evidence for agriculture in the shape of querns and grinding stones. The results of the excavations at Monte d'Accodi, with its sequence of occupation from the Copper to the Late Bronze Age, are awaited with much interest (Sassari Museum excavation). There is much local and regional development of pottery styles throughout the second millennium in Sardinia, and it is difficult to establish the relationship between the makers of Monte Claro pottery and those who made a different plainer ware, known as Bunnanaro, which is mostly located in the south-western mountainous zone (Lilliu, 1972). There must certainly have been some exchange relationships between the two groups, since rare examples of the Bunnanaro pottery are found in these northern and central parts of Sardinia. Bunnanaro ware is at least partly later than Monte Claro, commencing approximately 2000 B.C. and lasting to about 1500 B.C., and it is found in connection both with huge new megalithic graves called 'giants' tombs' and with the first nuraghic building.

Nuraghi are circular stone structures, of which about 7,000 are still known in Sardinia, 108 of which have been analysed by Lilliu (1967). Their construction is taken to represent defensive or warlike intent, but again, the lack of rigorous dating of the sequence of occupation at each *nuraghe* is a hindrance to the study of their development and their successive roles. Carbon-14 dates reveal that they began as early as 1800 B.C. and their early roles could have been as territorial markers for a local segment of the population, centres of technology (pottery-making, metallurgy), or as centres of redistribution for lowland and upland products. All these functions could be undertaken either instead of, or in addition to, the role of the centre of defence in case of incursions (at a period when piracy was probably a frequent occurrence in the Mediterranean sea). Recent excavations at the Ortu Comidu *nuraghe* near Sardara, located on a low knoll on the rich agricultural plain of the Campidano, have revealed that already by about 1400 B.C. *nuraghi* had grown from single tower units to complex structures with curtain walling and extra towers for technological activities (Balmuth, personal communication). It is assumed that villages grew up around certain *nuraghi* at about the same time. It is significant that Grosjean has also calculated that the first fortified villages in Corsica began around 1400 B.C. However, while fortified villages in Corsica only lasted for a few hundred years, the development of the *nuraghi* and their associated settlements lasts for another millennium. Meanwhile, comparable but again different developments take place on the Balearic Islands in the far western Mediterranean, where occupation of caves and open sites in the second half of the third millennium B.C. gives way to the building of massive stone towers, *talayots*, by about 1400 B.C. The *talayot* towers are rapidly surrounded by houses and presumably reflect the same sort of stratified, territorially based societies as on the other islands (Rossello-Bordoy, in: Pericot García, 1972).

From the second quarter of the second millennium B.C., the tendency towards centralization of multiple activities in certain settlements is widely visible in Europe: the Lusatian hill-forts of Poland and East Germany form one case in point. Similarly in Hungary, the recent excavations at the Otomani site of Spišský Štvrtok, north Carpathians, have revealed a settlement of economic, administrative and strategic importance (Vladar, 1972, 1974). The site has 170 metres of stone wall, plus an outer wall and ditch in places, and special protection is afforded the 'acropolis' area where the best houses lie in a U-shaped arrangement around a stone-plastered courtyard. Poorer architecture and artifacts typify the other rectangular houses found in the rest of the settlement. Bronze workshops were found on the site, one of them with twelve sandstone moulds, and over 100 bronzes and thirty gold artifacts. Other manufactures on the site included pottery, bone and stone, and the excavator feels strongly that artifact similarities demonstrate Greek influence and that the importance of the site relates to trade with the Mycenaean world.

THE AEGEAN

On Crete new palaces were constructed at the three previous sites of Knossos, Mallia and Phaistos and at Ayia Triadha and Zákros, from about 2050 B.C. onwards. (The old palaces may have been destroyed by earthquakes.) The new palaces consisted of ranges of rooms, many of them decorated with wall-plaster and friezes, and a number with furnishings like benches or 'thrones', set around wide courtyards. Massive oil and wine storage areas full of *pithoi* vases or stone-cist containers, and enormous circular pits for grain storage, testify to the bureaucratic and redistributive organization. At Zákros, in east Crete, well placed for trade with the east Mediterranean, recent excavations produced elephant tusks and copper ingots (Platon, 1971), and at many sites workshop areas for metallurgy, pottery and fine stone-working have been found. Trace elements in ingots from Zákros and elsewhere suggest they may be made of Cypriot ores (Wheeler *et al.*, 1975). Tablets with Linear A script, presumably detailing the organization of the different crafts, are found both in the palaces and in nearby Aegean islands, where the Cretans presumably penetrated for trade and exchange, while their fine vases with floral and marine designs are widespread in the Aegean, and are copied on mainland Greece. Optical-emission spectroscopy has revealed that the Minoan and mainland vases can easily be distinguished from each other by their trace elements (Catling *et al.*, 1963).

In addition to the palaces and their surrounding towns, there are a number of smaller Cretan towns (e.g. Gournia), and other settlements ranging from farms to country houses emulating the palace styles. Area surveys are beginning to fill in the details of the settlement pattern. Roads linked the different centres, and the use of wheeled transport seems likely. The increase of habitation centres indicates a greatly increased population, and the lack of defences suggests unified control.

On the mainland, recent discussions suggest that the palaces at Pylos, Mycenae, Tiryns etc. were only constructed *c.* 1700 B.C. (Warren, 1977), but a stratified and wealthy society is reflected by the beaten-gold face masks and other treasures discovered in the shaft-grave tombs of the first walled cemetery at Mycenae, possibly dating to as early as 1850 B.C. The grave slabs with their sculptured designs of drivers and horses and chariots seem to indicate a possible new method of hunting or warfare. At the same time, colonies of Mycenaeans were being established outside mainland Greece, for instance on Cyprus, and in the next century these spread even further into the Middle East and the west Mediterranean. Most of the palaces and great houses of Minoan Crete were destroyed in the Late Minoan Ib period, possibly due to an earthquake. Pumice from the volcano on the island of Thera destroyed Late Minoan houses on the island, and the event is recorded by a carbon-14 date on wood from one of the houses, which calibrates between 1730 and 1690 B.C. (Pichler and Friedrich, 1976). If earthquakes were a major factor in destroying Minoan settlements, Mycenaean sailors and warriors must have taken speedy advantage of the opportunities offered.

Characterization of Greek Late Bronze Age pottery (over 1000 samples had been tested by the optical-emission technique by 1970, and neutron activation analysis has also been used more recently) has demonstrated that various factories existed on mainland Greece, Crete, Rhodes, Cyprus etc. and that the products of these factories, and their distribution patterns, can be demonstrated (e.g. Harbottle, 1970). Mycenaean pottery was mainly distributed in the east Mediterranean, with a little penetrating as far west as southern Italy, and a very small amount into the Balkans (Harding 1975). This would suggest that the Mycenaeans were not interested in the products produced in the areas beyond those to which they traded, and throws doubt on the likelihood that they exchanged ores with the Balkans. Metal-work is also mutually exclusive between the two regions (Harding, 1975). Only one material can be proved to have come into the Aegean area from northern Europe, amber. Studies on amber by infra-red absorption techniques have revealed that a particular spectrum is typical for Baltic amber and that in fact the amber found in Late Bronze Age Greece is of Baltic origin (Renfrew, 1973c).

From Late Minoan II or III onwards the presence of Mycenaean artifacts and of tablets in the Linear B script (an ancient form of Greek) seems to indicate that the Mycenaeans had occupied Knossos, which survived the first earthquakes only to be destroyed in Late Minoan IIIA (Hallager, 1977). According to the tablets, they continued the Minoan economy. According to place-names on the tablets, the palace at Knossos was heavily involved with central and western Crete, and with the sanctuary at Dikte in central-eastern Crete for religious offerings. Wheat seems to have come from the Messara plain, saffron from western Crete and vines from the centre (Killen, 1977). The importance of sheep is demonstrated by tablets detailing the allocation of c. 700,000 sheep to different shepherds, the shearing of the sheep and the units of wool obtained, and finally the bolts of finished cloth woven up (Killen, 1964). Linear B signs also appear on stirrup jars, which were exported to the mainland. There is controversy over whether Linear B writing was first developed on the mainland, or on Crete; J. Chadwick regards the mainland and Cretan styles as distinct, possibly deriving from a lost common ancestor (1972). They deal with the same kind of economic data, however, and archaeologists have spent some time analysing the order in which place-names appear, to get a geography of Late Bronze Age Crete and Greece. The palace at Pylos provided a series of tablets from which the geography of Messenia (divided into 'near' and 'far' provinces) has been analysed both from internal evidence and by computer simulation (A. Chadwick, 1977; Cherry, 1977) (Fig. 62).

The tablets reveal a complex redistribution system, giving the names of

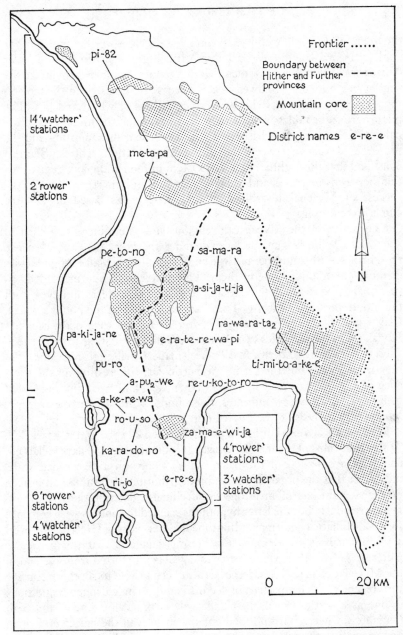

Fig. 62. Settlement network of Hither and Further provinces in Late Bronze Age Messenia, Greece, as derived from Linear B tablets (after Chadwick, 1972, figs. 7–1 and 9–6)

the towns and people who had to contribute certain weights of bronze or gold to the palace, and also detailing contributions of textiles and hides (Chadwick, 1972). Both raw materials and foodstuffs for craftsmen like the smiths and spinners employed in the palaces are indicated in the tablets; the women spinners at Pylos were given rations of wheat and figs. The picture from the tablets reveals tight organization of the hinterland of the palace, and organization based both on seaborne communication and the presence of roads between the different population centres. Sherratt considers that this tightly organized system of food and goods redistribution between the plains and upland areas was an important factor in the success of Mycenaean civilization and that it was based on suitable climatic conditions.

Knowledge of the Mycenaean religious subsystem increased when in 1968 Lord William Taylour located under the great baulk at Mycenae two shrines, with a number of large and small pottery figures of goddesses in the room adjoining one of them. The thirteen tall figurines stood approximately 24 ins high (60 cm) and had huge noses, ears and eyes, with the mouth outlined in white. They had been made on the potter's wheel. Clay snake figurines were also discovered. In the 1977 excavations at Phylakopi in the Cyclades two shrines were located, dating from c. 1680–1400 B.C. (Renfrew, 1978). A tall wheel-made female figurine came from the earlier levels, but the shrine was particularly interesting for the presence of a number of male figurines (five in clay, and two 'Smiting Gods' in bronze). As Renfrew indicates, these finds *in situ* will enable a proper 'contextual analysis' to be carried out.

Mycenaean civilization broke down between *c.* 1350 and *c.* 1250 B.C. At this time most of the mainland palace economies seem to have collapsed, and later occupation of the palace sites is only on a very small scale, indicating that the organization and redistribution patterning had broken down. Suggestions of invasions or of climatic deterioration have been made previously but the latter hypothesis seemed to contrast with evidence for good climatic conditions at this time in other parts of Greece. However, a useful analysis by Bryson *et al.* (1974) suggests that the particular patterning of weather which seems to have been reported from the end of the Mycenaean period in Greece has also been visible in southern Europe very recently. Such a pattern of vectors could include drought conditions in one area of the Greek mainland such as the Peloponnese, and high rainfall elsewhere. With no food coming in to feed the palace craftsmen and specialists the whole redistributive system would break down. It is interesting to see modern studies of the weather used in this way to suggest a reason for prehistoric culture change.

The collapse of Mycenaean civilization was paralleled by the fall of the Hittites in Anatolia, and general disorder in the East Mediterranean. The 'Peoples of the Sea' mentioned in Egyptian documents as causing havoc *c*. 1200 B.C. probably came from a number of areas, e.g. Cyprus and South Anatolia (Hopper, 1976), in one of the earliest historically attested population movements.

These movements and resultant conflict disrupted the patterns of trade and exchange previously established, and may have been another factor (or even the main factor) in the Mycenaean decline. One by-product was that iron metallurgy replaced bronze, probably because copper and tin had become difficult to acquire (Maddin *et al.*, 1977). The new technique was being practised in Greece and south-east Europe by *c*. 1300 B.C., and thereafter spread slowly westwards and northwards. The relationships of the Aegean and the Balkans were intensified about this time, with exchange of metal goods and pottery, as a recent study of Albanian material has shown (Kilian, 1972). This was just the beginning of a new set of European relationships which would develop in the final prehistoric period.

THE EARLY URN-FIELD PERIOD (1500 TO 1250 B.C.)

During the fifteenth and fourteenth centuries B.C. a new form of burial practice came into use in east and central Europe, that of cremating the dead and burying their remains in a pot; in certain areas cemeteries formed by these urn-fields contain over a thousand graves and are only 1 to 2 km apart (e.g. Gernlinden and Kelheim, south Bavaria – Müller-Karpe, 1959). The increased populations suggested by the large cemeteries are also indicated by the size of settlements and by increased quantities of artifacts, especially tools such as bronze sickles, axes and knives, found in graves and hoards. The first centres of the new burial rite were in Hungary, Austria and East Germany (the Lausitz culture group in this area will be discussed in the next chapter). The rite was rapidly disseminated through-out the area of Central and Eastern Europe, however, and was also practised in North Italy in the fifteenth century, and in Yugoslavia in the fourteenth. In later centuries it spread throughout Italy and the Low Countries, and to eastern and southern France, and Catalonia, only being practised around the west Mediterranean after about 1250 B.C. There is considerable regional variation, with enclosure ditches being a feature of some cemeteries, e.g. in the Netherlands, while others contain tumuli or a number of inhumation burials. A certain amount of population movement may have been associated with the spread of the cremation rite, but archaeologists have identified a continuity of tradition in other fields (such

as artifact typology, continuation of hoard burial and water offerings etc.)
and local populations must have persisted to a greater or lesser degree
(Gimbutas, 1965).

Higher populations either necessitated (or themselves resulted from)
the greater technological skill and more profitable subsistence techniques
of the Later Bronze Age. Deeper mines were exploited, e.g. in the Austrian
Tirol, and more metal smelted. The plough seems to have been generally
used in this period, and counts of metal tools from Swiss and south German
sites indicate a vast predominance of implements for agriculture, particularly sickles and axes. The same statistical study (Primas, 1977)
indicates that of the sixty sites, valley sites are the poorest in metal goods
or signs of metallurgy, while high sites have produced a number of
artifacts and smiths' tools. The majority of moulds, metallurgical tools
like anvils, hammers, tongs and chisels, and of agrarian tools, come from
lakeside sites, however. Recent excavations at Auvernier, in a site under
Lake Neuchâtel revealed by aerial photography, have produced evidence
of two separate blacksmiths' workshops, with numerous artifacts, slag and
moulds. The same site was also rich in preserved wood, bark and woven
materials (Egloff, 1972). Although the Auvernier site is probably of Late
Urnfield date, similar underwater sites around the French Jura lakes have
earlier carbon-14 dates (e.g. Aiguebelette, Savoy). It has been possible to
detect the plans of rectangular houses within such settlements, e.g. at
Grésine, Savoy.

Metal artifacts, often of baroque forms (massive ribbed bracelets and
pins, heavy swords and decorated spearheads), are found in high numbers
in graves and hoards. At the Yugoslav burial cave of Sv. Skocijan, the
1200 offerings included many sickles, knives and axes (Alexander, 1972).
At Achsolshausen, Bavaria, a grave group rescued after mechanical
digging, and dated c. 1250 B.C., contained thirty-eight pots with ribbed
bulbous bodies and small bases, and numerous bronzes (Pescheck, 1974).
A sword had vanished all but for its rivets, but a spearhead, knives, pins
and a bracelet survived, as well as beaten bronze vessels in the shape of a
cup, a bowl, and a cult wagon. The latter, a four-wheeled vehicle bearing
a bronze urn, and with a duck-figure at each corner, is one of a number of
similar vessels in bronze and pottery known from Scandinavia to eastern
Europe, and which performed a little-understood role in the religious subsystem. A number of burials, particularly in Hungary, are accompanied by
gold objects. The majority of graves, however, resemble those in the
cemetery at Aulnay-les-Planches, northern France, discovered by aerial
photography, and contain just a few pots and animal bones and odd
bronzes, such as a knife, razor or pin, accompanying the urn.

In the Late Bronze Age, fewer hoards are known in some areas than in the Middle Bronze Age, but they contain many pieces. At Villethierry, also in northern France, over 900 pins and other ornaments have been studied as a manufacturing series, using spectroscopic analyses and metallography, and the use of clay moulds and a lathe are suggested (Mordant and Mordant, 1976).

As far as agricultural economy is concerned, the use of the plough and of bronze reaping implements seems to have helped increase subsistence output. Grain, especially emmer wheat and barley, is found preserved as imprints on pottery or as carbonized material in underwater sites. Cattle and pig are frequently mentioned in site reports, and seem to have been the main animal resources north of the Mediterranean coastlands. The salt industry is obvious for the first time in the Late Bronze Age, and salt-workings in Brittany (Curnic II, Finistère) have been dated to the fifteenth century B.C.

THE IRON AGE
(*c.* 1250 B.C. TO A.D. 1)

When archaeologists approach the end of the prehistoric period they are often faced with much bigger sites than before, both settlements and cemeteries, and with a more complex material culture. Because the sites are larger, they are more easily located by aerial or ground survey. However, sites are rarely excavated totally, for lack of funds. Certain excavations on a large scale, such as at Manching, Bavaria and Danebury, southern England, reveal something of the complexity of successive occupations on high sites, while in the Netherlands, for instance, vast lowland areas with field systems and attached settlements are under study. Such huge excavations produce their own problems of interpretation and publication. Normally, however, total excavation of Iron Age sites is impractical and theoretically derived sampling procedures are beginning to be used in an attempt to bridge the gap. Central-place theory has been applied to explain the pattern of a few large defended settlements surrounded by a range of smaller sites, proposing that most functions and services took place at the head of the pyramid.

IRON AGE ECONOMIES

Subsistence was still on an agricultural and pastoral basis, with suggestions of long-distance transhumance of herds deriving from settled villages, and of much greater clearances of forest for fields (shown up by pollen analysis). Manuring is suggested by the occurrence of broken potsherds and other household rubbish on fields, while the use of iron tools, plus the heavier plough, would have allowed heavier soils to be brought into cultivation.

Aerial photography has been invaluable in revealing patterns of field systems over much of north-western Europe, both in heathland and in the areas of present-day agriculture, the rich plains and river valleys. Sophisticated interpretations of some field systems have included suggestions of in- and out-fields, estimates of the sizes of field units, and have related them to nearby settlements, and to social changes.

Climatic deterioration has been recognized in the late prehistoric period in many parts of Europe. The problems caused by increased rainfall, erosion and flooding must have affected settlement locations and the movement of foodstuffs and raw materials. Detailed studies in Scandinavia have shown that agriculture in marginal environments ceased with the deteriorating climate. Evans accounts for the different developments in highland and lowland Britain from the Iron Age onwards in terms of rainfall; so that while in about 1250 B.C. a highland area like North Wales was extensively settled, by the time of the Roman conquest settlements were much greater in size and complexity in the lowland regions (J. G. Evans, 1975).

TECHNOLOGY AND SOCIETY

Although, as mentioned in the previous chapter in the section on the Aegean, knowledge of iron metallurgy reached Greece around the end of the fourteenth century B.C., it is not documented in other parts of Europe until later – the eleventh century in Italy and the ninth century B.C. in east and central Europe. Later still it was generally practised in western Europe. The slowness in the spread of this technique may be due to the technological expertise in bronze manufacture already present in continental Europe, and the social and technological subsystems that would have been disturbed by a change in raw-material procurement and smelting techniques. Iron metallurgy requires much timber for charcoal, and smelting tends to be carried out where such timber is available. Rocks of high iron content such as haematite and limonite, as well as poorer ironstones, are very widespread, and hardpan in bogs provides a very pure source. Iron was acquired by both surface grubbing and deep mining. The relative ease of acquisition meant that iron objects were more numerous than bronze ones: iron in the form of sickles, scythes, ploughshares and spades aided farmers, iron tools were used in other crafts, such as leather- and wood-working, and iron was used to provide much household equipment. Unfortunately corrosion means that iron artifacts survive less well than bronze ones.

Most sites throughout Europe produce pottery, quern-stones and loom-weights, but wooden and iron implements are only preserved in favourable environments. The larger sites produce evidence of crafts ranging from metallurgy in bronze and iron, and less often in silver, gold, lead and tin, to pottery-making in kilns, leather-working, carpentry and bone-working (the bone 'weaving combs' and decorated horse-trappings), and glass manufacture. The organization of such crafts in centres tends to suggest a complex organization of society, with over-production of food to compensate for the non-involvement of specialists such as craftsmen or warriors in subsistence pursuits. A certain amount of elaboration and variability can be produced today by blacksmiths in African or other simple societies, working as part-time specialists, but the excessive elaboration of ornament and design found at the end of the first millennium B.C. among workers in both bronze and iron (La Tène) suggests a more permanently established work-force.

A considerable amount of work has been done in testing iron products by metallography, and determining the techniques of manufacture by carbon addition, hammering and so on. Smelting experiments in furnaces similar in design to Iron Age ones have revealed their efficiency. Thin-sectioning of pottery has been used to establish provenance, and distribution networks from pottery kilns have been studied.

One of the most difficult problems for Iron Age archaeologists is dating. The rapid corrosion of iron plus the lack of diagnostic pottery (or even of any pottery) in certain areas, makes typological dating impractical in some instances. Carbon-14 dates are often crucial, especially in more northern parts of Europe, and well-preserved wood can in some cases be linked to master dendrochronological sequences (e.g. that of the Trier bridge) to give very accurate dates. The carbon-14 dating of slag could be used to more effect where iron-smelting workshops are found. Further south, especially at certain time periods, metal and ceramic imports from the Mediterranean civilizations give historic dates for their contexts. Many of the absolute dates (B.C.) quoted in this chapter derive from such sources.

Frequently, excavations in flat cemeteries or huge barrow cemeteries near large settlements reveal differences in grave-goods and thus possibly in social position among those buried. A society with a few rich individuals (buried with their chariots) lived in Wetwang Slack, Yorkshire. Aerial photography of areas cleared for gravel-digging revealed a cemetery of square-ditched burials (Pl. 19), the majority of them less richly furnished, containing items of jewellery, weapons or joints of meat. The sixth-century B.C. Magdalenenberg barrow, in south Germany, began as a monument to a single important man, around whose central grave more than a hundred other members of the society were interred in their turn. Some of the most richly furnished graves in European prehistory are those built by the Dacians in Romania in the final centuries B.C., crammed with gold and silver treasures. However, near many single farmsteads or small villages, the dead were buried with relatively few grave-goods, so leaving little indication of their status in death (and by inference in life). The large numbers of skeletons from the newly excavated cemeteries will provide an important sample for physical anthropological studies.

The seventy-one Iron Age skeletal populations then available were used by Schwidetzky (1972) to make comparisons of various skull measurements and indices. This revealed an east–west difference in brachycephaly (especially skull breadth), the mid-point occurring east of the Black Sea. In the western area under discussion in this book, most populations were only relatively broad-headed, a trend persisting from earlier Neolithic and Bronze Age series examined by the same author. Data on a similarly wide scale for other parameters (age at death, pathology, female fertility, blood-groups) would be of great value.

One problem for archaeologists studying the late prehistoric period is to consider how far changes result from basically internal developments, and how far they are the reflection of contacts with the civilizations of the Mediterranean. Phoenician influence touches the central and west Mediterranean from at least the eighth century B.C., causing reactions in local societies in north Africa, the Mediterranean islands, and Southern Iberia in particular. By approximately the same time period, urban settlements and complex societies had evolved in Greece and in central Italy (the Etruscans). The Etruscans exported metalwork and other luxuries to the continental European groups to the north of them, while the dispatch of colonists by various Greek cities looking for trade outlets meant that two widely separated areas in particular, the coastlands of present-day Bulgaria, Romania and the Ukraine, and the coastlands of southern France, had to adjust to new ideas and trade links.

European archaeologists frequently refer to the influence that Mediterranean civilization may have exerted both on the tangibles of life, from imported coral and mud-brick architecture, both found in southern Germany, to the intangibles like social structure and religion. The influences were particularly strong at certain periods, such as the Late Hallstatt/Early La Tène (sixth to fifth centuries B.C.) and Late La Tène (first century B.C.).

Iron Age archaeologists are both aided and constrained by the availability of written sources, including coins, to explain some of their data. The classical authors have been searched for: geographical information;

historical information (identifying societies by name; mentioning movements of people, and conflicts); and anthropological information (on
society, religion, clothing, weapons etc.). In some cases, particularly with
geographical information, errors are easy to identify, but in others critical
analysis by scholars of ancient history, and archaeological contradictions,
are the only guides to ancient misinterpretation. Identification of the
Celtic and Germanic peoples mentioned in ancient texts is one of the
thorniest problems. Hachmann has indicated the influence on classical
writings caused by the fifth century B.C. Greek authors' conception of the
area to the north-east of them as being inhabited by Scythians, and that to
the north-west by Celts; and by Caesar's strategic-political identification
of the Rhine as the frontier between the Celtic and German worlds (1971).
Hachmann uses archaeological typology to demonstrate the unity of La
Tène material culture from central France to Bohemia and south Poland,
whereas the material culture identified as 'Germanic' could be found to
the north, in north Germany and Poland, and Scandinavia from the fifth
and fourth centuries B.C. onwards. The identification of particular
German tribes, especially the origins of migrating groups, is a difficult
matter, and archaeologists have tended to divide the material into geographical rather than tribal sub-units, such as the North Sea Coastal,
Holstein and Lower Elbe, Jutland and Danish islands, and South Swedish
groups (Todd, 1975).

Continuity of material culture in central Europe from the Late Bronze
Age urn-field groups onwards has led to the assumption that the origins of
later Celtic peoples lie here, if not in fact further back (Hatt, 1970). As has
been mentioned above, the Greeks identified all groups living to the
north-west of their territory as Celts, and the term was widely applied by
Roman writers. Particular tribes that continued to occupy the same area
after Roman subjection can be identified by name, but archaeologists
generally are loath to regard all populations with La Tène assemblages as
Celts, preferring to deal with the vast area covered by the finds in regional
subgroups (Collis, 1975).

NORTH-EAST EUROPE

The Lusatian populations of East Germany and Poland have been studied
intensively during the last decade. The similarities of pottery and bronze
vessels and artifacts over time have been taken as indicating stable populations, and the culture complex spans the Late Bronze Age and the Early
Iron Age periods (c. 1660 to c. 500 B.C.).

The Lusatians are represented by their settlements, cemeteries, cult-

places and quarries, and by features of the agricultural, pastoral, industrial
and trading environment in which they lived (Bukowski, 1974). Variations
can be seen in settlement distribution in different regions: in Silesia, for
instance, there were well-occupied regions separated by more empty ones.
Bukowski has represented this in an 'isorhythmic' map (Fig. 63), where
contour lines link settlement zones of equal density, from the most
sparsely to the most thickly inhabited. The high, defended sites tended to
start up either within, or on the edge of, thickly settled regions. In some
areas their building influenced the settlement pattern, which tended to
concentrate around these high sites. In Silesia the defended sites lay on
average 15 to 20 km apart, and measured 2 to 6 ha in area. The lowland
sites rarely exceeded 2 ha in area. It is suggested, from the rather limited

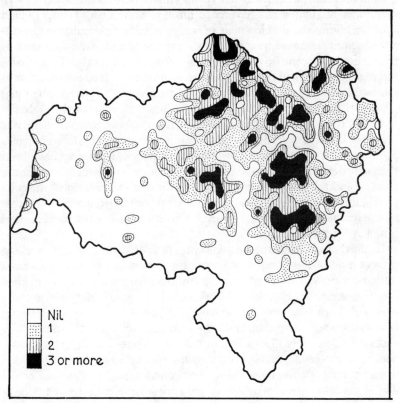

Fig. 63. 'Isorhythms' indicating Lusatian settlement patterns in Wrocław
district of western Poland (after Bukowski, 1974, fig. 7). Numbers of sites per
2 km² indicated in key

selection of artifacts found on the lowland sites, that they may have been used for short-lived occupations over 200–300 years, rather than being permanently occupied. The majority of sites are near or on soils of light or middle type, easy to work. Of the over 100 open settlements known in Silesia, only a few have been excavated, revealing houses 20–30 m² in area, and rare indications of crafts like metallurgy. The cemeteries associated with the lowland settlements were used over a long period. Bukowski visualizes a change over time from widely distributed settlement by small groups that changed their living sites relatively frequently, continuing to use the same cemetery, to a concentration of settlement in the defended sites in the Hallstatt period. The high sites have their own new cemeteries, and tend to acquire many political, social and economic functions. Their high point is during the Hallstatt B2/3 to final Hallstatt periods (Fig. 64). A number of suggestions have been made to account for the large high sites, including the development of trade, which would enhance the importance of permanent, protected sites, especially near passes or roads. It is interesting that in the western Lausitz zone, the largest defended sites (up to 18 ha) occur in the Late Bronze Age; they tend to develop first in the south, then the settlement pattern spreads north (Herrmann, 1969) (Fig. 64). In the east Lusation zone, the locations are sometimes due to trade, such as sites located in the Moravian Pforte passes. There was probably a strong feedback relationship between the different roles assumed by the permanent defended settlements. They may have been primarily defensive, or trade-linked, but smelting is indicated at a number of sites, and religious sanctuaries are known elsewhere. Most of the cult-places, however, were at sites like salt springs, or the iron-rich Holy Cross mountains (a very important source of iron ore, as recent metallurgical tests have demonstrated).

In northern Poland the best-known site is Biskupin, where excellent preservation of the wooden houses and walkways has revealed two main settlement periods, the earlier one with much larger areas for individual dwellings than the later. Special workshops had housed craftsmen working in bronze, horn and bone. An estimated population of c. 1000 people would have taken about a year to build the settlement (Bukowski, 1974). Only craftsmen are clearly identifiable in Lausitz cemeteries, which are mostly poor in grave-goods, and it is only by interpretation of the effort needed to construct both the large lowland sites and the great defences of the hilltop sites that ideas about a stratified society have been derived. One of the sources of wealth and thus status may have been amber, for rich graves are found on the Baltic island of Komorowo, a seat of the amber workshops (Malinowski, 1973). Indications of domesticated plants in impres-

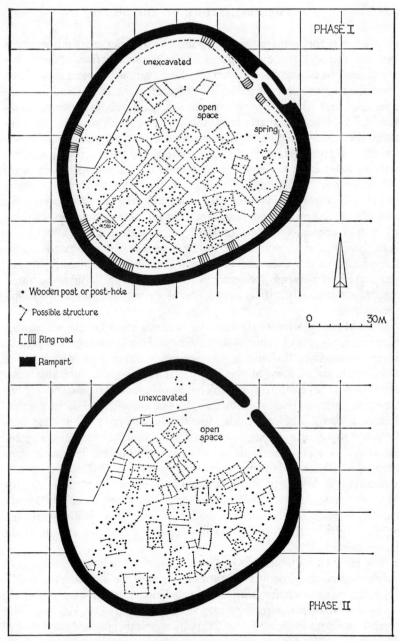

PHASE I

unexcavated

open
space

spring

• Wooden post or post-hole

⟩ Possible structure

[⫿⫿⫿ Ring road

▰ Rampart

0   30M

unexcavated

open
space

PHASE II

Fig. 64. Plans of settlement in Phases I and II at the defended site of Senft-
enberg, East Germany (Hallstatt C–D period) (after Herrmann, 1969, figs. 6
and 9)

sions on clay, or in pollen analyses, show that barley was important, as well as millet and oats, at the site of Kotlin, Jarocin district, while bread-wheat and flax were less important. However, differences have been demonstrated in the proportions of different crops at lowland and up-land sites, and wheats, barleys, rye, millet, flax, peas and beans are reported from other Lusatian sites (Coblenz, 1971). With regard to animals, as on other Lusatian settlements, cattle are the most frequently represented species at Kotlin, followed by pig, then sheep and goat, with a few horses and dogs, red and roe deer. It is suggested that the economy was pushed to its limits by the high populations built up during the Hallstatt period, and that the deterioration in climate about 500 B.C. may have been at the root of the decline of these large agglomerations of population. In some areas there are signs of flooding of the better pastures.

In La Tène A/B, settlement in the Silesian area reverts to smaller settlements, mostly open and short-lived according to artifact typologies, and served by new small cemeteries (Bukowski, 1974). Bukowski interprets this settlement shift as a reflection of a partly settled, partly mobile life-style.

The collapse of some of the Lusatian settlements in Greater Poland has been linked in part to incursions by the Scythians. Movements of peoples are indicated c. 500 B.C. in the historic record, and these may have helped to cause the breakdown of previously viable systems by breaking trade networks. However, the main problems, as seen for instance at the fortified village of Jankow (Bydgoszcz district) were economic and social (Ostoja-Zagorski, 1976). The best lands, near the Jezioro river, which had been fertilized by yearly floods, developed into marshes through climatic deterioration, so that agriculture had to be based on the less satisfactory terraces. In the Jankow micro-region, according to Ostoja-Zagorski, agricultural and other products declined first in quality, then in quantity, with the result that eventually the large settlement broke up, and people moved to more family-based economies. There was thus a social and political shift, and culturally the new developments are known as the Pomeranian culture.

The Holy Cross mountains of Poland, mentioned above, were particularly exploited from the final centuries B.C., until the fourth century A.D. (Pleiner, 1977). Together with Schleswig-Holstein, they were one of the most extensive iron-smelting regions. Several dozen workshops, with several thousand smelting furnaces, roasting hearths, piles of charcoal and deep mine shafts for the haematite iron have been discovered. In the older period the furnaces are in groups, possibly indicating different working seasons. Estimates of total production are possible from the slag remaining. To the north of the Holy Cross mountains, field and magnet-ometer surveys have located further hundreds of smelting-places.

In Britain the complexes of enclosures and homesteads visible in the mid second millennium B.C. persisted to the end of the millennium. Sites such as Itford Hill, with its huts and surrounding enclosures, have carbon-14 dates spanning the turn of the millennium. By *c.* 500 B.C. high defended sites, hill-forts, are visible in several areas of Britain. In north Wales, two carbon-14 dates (930–900 B.C. in absolute years) have been produced for the burning of timber-fronted defences at the Breidden site. The Breidden is one of several hill-forts in north-east Wales; as with the Polish Lusatian sites, these upland sites were not entirely defensive in purpose. Stake-built round-houses were erected in the fifth century B.C.; the site has produced carbonized grain and numerous saddle querns, and aerial photography has revealed field boundaries around the hilltop. It is suggested, therefore, that settlement was permanent and at least partly based on agriculture (Guilbert, 1977).

Similar stake-walls round houses, and four-post structures (granaries?) were aligned behind the curving rampart wall at the nearby Moel y Gaer site (Guilbert, 1975). The careful excavations at these sites are dependent on carbon-14 dates for their chronology, since pottery is rare on sites in north Wales. This situation is in contrast with that further south, where Peacock has used pottery thin-sectioning and heavy mineral analysis to identify pottery manufacturing centres in the Malvern Hills (1968).

Aerial photography has been crucial in revealing massive areas of Iron Age field systems, both in upland areas like Wales, where it was recently estimated that as many as 40 per cent of Iron Age sites now known were missing from the ordnance survey map of Montgomeryshire in the Iron Age (Spurgeon, 1972), and in lowland areas like the major river valleys. Organized field-walking in many areas has also revealed under-representa-tion of sites on earlier maps.

In the valley of the Tame, a tributary of the Trent in the English Midlands, Smith has used aerial photography to suggest that the whole zone was being exploited for pasture or arable purposes, with very little primary woodland surviving by the last few centuries B.C. (1977). Excavations in the valley at Fisherwick, a small settlement site surrounded by drove-ways and field boundaries, has been very rewarding in providing ecological data from waterlogged ditch deposits, and the presence of

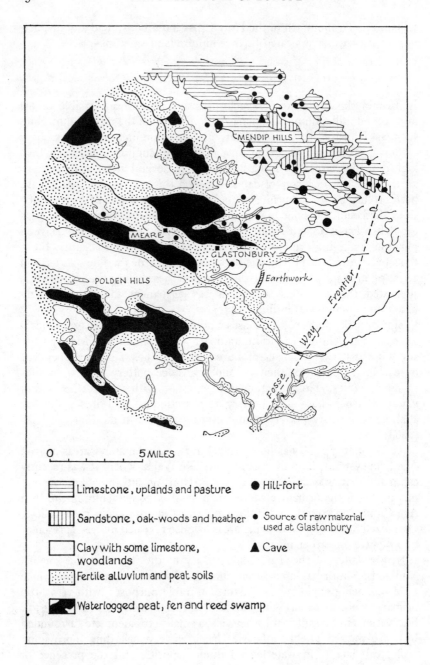

MENDIP HILLS

MEARE

GLASTONBURY

POLDEN HILLS

Earthwork

Fosse Way Frontier

0   5 MILES

▤ Limestone, uplands and pasture	● Hill-fort
▥ Sandstone, oak-woods and heather	• Source of raw material used at Glastonbury
▢ Clay with some limestone, woodlands	▲ Cave
▨ Fertile alluvium and peat soils	
◼ Waterlogged peat, fen and reed swamp	

hedges along the ditch-sides has been suggested on the basis of apparent hedge-trimmings in the ditches.

Aerial research has also been an important factor in the Thames valley, where recent excavations by the Oxfordshire Archaeological Research Unit have revealed a village settlement at Ashville with several penannular ditches surrounding probable post-built houses. The faunal results indicate a predominance of sheep (65 per cent) and smaller quantities of cattle and pig, plus a few horses. The fact that the sheep were slaughtered at earlier ages than in the Roman period suggested to the excavators that the exploitation was for meat rather than wool (Parrington, 1977). The sheep exploitation on this second Thames terrace was contrasted with the emphasis on cattle on the wetter ground of the first gravel terrace, at Farmoor. Here cattle, especially cows, are found more frequently than sheep, leading the excavators to suggest dairying as a prime occupation. Farmoor appears to have been a small open farmstead, with numerous Early Iron Age pits, and enclosure ditches (Lambrick, 1977). Occupation continued at Farmoor during the Middle Iron Age (c. 250/200 to 100/50 B.C.) but ceased both there and at Ashville in the Late Iron Age (c. 100/50 B.C. to A.D. 50). Extensive field systems were laid out at Ashville in this latter period, but no habitations; the Roman field system in the area follows the Late Iron Age alignment.

Clarke commenced an interesting study of a much older excavation, that of Glastonbury, Somerset, studying the resources available to this small enclosed settlement in a marshy environment. The site-exploitation territory (Fig. 65) was assumed to be ten miles in radius, which permitted acquisition of the various clay, wood, stone and metal resources used on the site (Clarke, 1972, fig. 21.7). Clarke suggested that the sources of many of the different clay, oak, antler and quernstone materials were in the neighbourhood of the Maesbury hill-fort, and in the Mendip hills immediately to the north of it. He proposed a social and economic model to account for the presence of these raw materials at Glastonbury and for the variety of settlement types in the exploitation territory. The fen-edge site, which was flooded every spring, could only have supported such a large population if the latter moved its sheep herds up to the Mendip hills, in cooperation with other groups, and used communally built hilltop enclosures during the annual droves. Like Glastonbury, the Tame and Thames valley sites discussed above can be visualized as units

Fig. 65. Exploitation territory of Glastonbury site, south-west England (after Clarke, 1972, p. 841)

in the networks of small sites which had varying relationships with each other and with larger, major settlements.

Cunliffe (1976) has followed the process of intensification of occupation at selected hill-forts: from several thousand in the fifth century B.C. these decline rapidly in number. At Danebury there are streets of four- and six-post buildings (with pits near by containing household rubbish), from the end of the fifth to the end of the second century. Although Danebury was only one of four major sites between the Test and Bowne rivers in the early fourth century, all the rest had been abandoned by the third century. This is just one example of the general reduction in numbers of sites and the increase in size, and presumably influence, of certain upland settlements over time. Cunliffe and others believe that a proto-urban stage had been reached in southern Britain by the time of Caesar's invasions. Hodder has looked at the same area in terms of distributions of coins, pottery and metal-work (1977), and tried to assess what the settlement distribution and the finds distribution reflect. Coins of the late pre-Roman period, with dynastic stamps, seem to reflect boundaries of such tribes as the Dobunni, Durotriges and Atrebates, and it is interesting that pottery-type distributions also seem to follow the same boundaries. It is very difficult to establish the contemporaneity of all sites, however, and to detect the trade or exchange links at work.

There are good data for the settlement and economy of the late prehistoric period in the Netherlands and Scandinavia. In the late second and early first millennium B.C. the type-site of settlement in the Netherlands is the Elp homestead, with its main farmhouse and subsidiary buildings (Waterbolk, 1975) (Fig. 66). Todd claims that this type of settlement is the norm for Northern Europe until the Middle Ages (1975). At the coastal settlement of Ezinge, settlement commenced in the sixth century B.C. during a period of drying and sand-drifting. The sand-drifting helped the formation of a 'terp' or small tell, on which successive occupations took place, each of a few houses. Remains of dung from Ezinge (used as fuel) were analysed for vegetal remains, indicating that oil-rich flax and carmeline had been cultivated, together with turnip, in the last two phases of the site (300–100 B.C.). Experiments have shown the feasibility of planting in the summer even in this brackish environment, and at another contemporary coastal settlement, Paddepoel, barley, oats, emmer and carrot seem to have been cultivated, in addition to the Ezinge crops (van Zeist, 1974).

Along the coasts of the western Netherlands, research in the polder Het Grootslag has revealed the patterns of Late Bronze Age and Iron Age settlement (Altena, 1977). In the Late Bronze Age settlements with

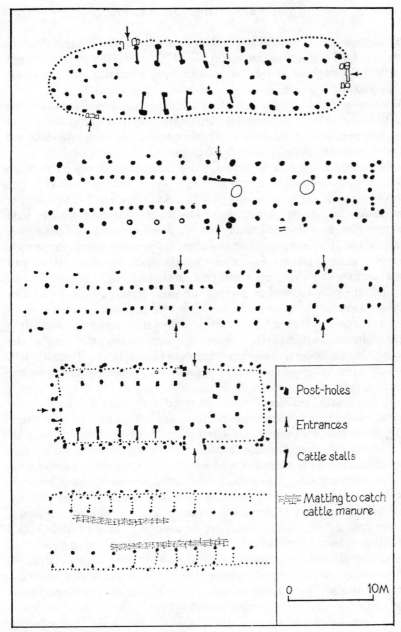

Post-holes

Entrances

Cattle stalls

Matting to catch
cattle manure

0   10M

Fig. 66. Bronze and Iron Age house plans (as indicated by post-holes) in the
Netherlands (after Waterbolk, 1975, fig. 1)

rectangular houses were established on the flanks of sandy ridges. Analysis of the animal bones from one site, Andijk II, has revealed over 85 per cent cattle, but no horses, and the analysts have suggested that cattle may have provided the traction for ploughing (van Mensch and Ijzereef, 1975). Marks of ard ploughing, and lines of field enclosures, have been revealed in the extensive research on Het Grootslag polder, and this work is of great importance for the study of economic systems over about a thousand years in lowland areas of northern Europe.

In Scandinavia the Early Iron Age is generally held to begin about 500 B.C., and to continue until the first century of the Christian era. The preceding period (1400/1300 to 500 or 400 B.C.) is referred to as the Late, or Middle and Late, Bronze Age. The main evidence from the Late Bronze Age, as from the Earlier, described in Chapter 6, is from graves and hoards. There is increasing use of cremation, and fewer grave-goods (razors, tweezers and needles) accompany the dead; by contrast there is an increase in hoards. Votive deposits continue to be made in bogs, and these include not only pairs of neck-rings and small female figurines, but also human sacrifices by the time of the Iron Age. It would be interesting to know what role male and female sacrifices (by garrotting or throat-cutting) played in the socio-religious subsystem. From the point of view of the economic subsystem the stomach contents of Graubølle and Tollund Men, indicating that they had consumed basically wild plant foods for their last meal, are also of interest.

In the Danish peninsula both field-systems revealed by aerial photography and excavations of village sites based completely on agriculture (e.g. in west Jutland) seem to indicate a primarily agrarian population with few status differences. The population of the fourth-century Grontoft settlement, which consisted of nine long-houses with stalls, four with no stalls and five smaller buildings, was buried in a cemetery near by, with no great variation between the graves and their offerings. The Löderup cemetery in south Sweden, having shown some degree of inegalitarianism in the Bronze Age, reverts to very egalitarian treatment of the dead in the pre-Roman Iron Age. Both at Löderup 15 and nearby Simris 2 cemeteries burials were predominantly by cremation with little differentiation of effort in their preparation. Forty-one per cent and 50 per cent respectively of the graves had bronze implements, in addition to the more usual pots, and stone and flint tools (Strömberg, 1975).

The main signs of possibly higher-status individuals (and possibly higher-status settlements) are in eastern and northern Jutland. At the Kraghede site in north Jutland, where a number of post- and wicker-work houses were excavated in addition to a cemetery, one outstanding grave,

No. A1, held the remains of a chariot and two horses, in addition to twenty-three pots, and spearheads, knives and a gold ring. In east central Jutland and on Bornholm hill-forts are known, and it is possible that these were the central places of territories fulfilling a number of economic as well as defensive roles.

Studies in a number of different areas have indicated the patterns of subsistence of the first millennium B.C. Welinder has studied the Väst-manland area in east central Sweden, to the north of Lake Mälaren (1975b). He suggests that there was a series of stages of farming expansion in the Lake Mälaren plain, starting with a Late Bronze Age exploitation c. 1200 to 500 B.C. He reconstructs the economy as being dependent on a central settlement lasting one or two centuries, with the area around the settlement being farmed in a cyclical movement, leaving fields for a long fallow period.

Using eight pollen profiles, Welinder has demonstrated a climatic deterioration with the worst effects occurring after 500 B.C. He adopts a technique suggested by East German pollen analysts (e.g. Lange, 1971) whereby the ratio between the quantities of cereal pollen and the pollen of a weed (Plantago lanceolata) is used as indicative of the relative import-ance of cereals and stock-raising at any given time. According to this pollen analysis, the importance of cereals drops from c. 75 per cent about 600–500 B.C. to about 50 per cent by the turn of the millennium. The pollen analyses, both in the Lake Mälaren plain and on the slightly higher 'forest lowland', reveal that the mixed oak forest declined during the first millennium B.C., to end c. 250 B.C. in the forest lowland, and c. 100 B.C. on the plain; as this climax forest declined, spruce moved in, c. 500 B.C., and continued to increase in volume. The farming system apparently failed to deal successfully with the changed environmental situation, and about 100 B.C. a completely new system was set up, with the use of in-fields and out-fields, and manuring. Welinder's view of societies nearing the ecological limits with one type of exploitation, and changing abruptly to another, bears some resemblance to the interpretation of Golson for exploitation of intermontane valleys in New Guinea (1976).

Further to the north, the Norrland project in north Sweden has produced pollen data relating to the exploitation of the area, revealing a sequence of development. Agriculture is first indicated in the late Sub-Boreal (c. 700 B.C.) when pollen of barley, wheat, oats, rye and of weeds of cultivation appear in the pollen record. At the same time spruce trees seem to have been discouraged at the expense of birch, which is useful for winter feeding to livestock. This situation seems to persist for about 300 years, when the climatic deterioration at the beginning of the Sub-

Atlantic seems to lead to the recolonization of arable and pasture land by spruce, and thus the abandonment of agriculture in Norrland (Engelmark Olsson *et al.*, 1976). There is still some population present (eight skis are datable by pollen analysis to the Early Iron Age), and in south Sweden at this time there is no comparable break in the pollen record, but Norrland's botanical history seems to be paralleled in southern Norway, where Hafsten showed that corn-growing ceased before *c.* 400 B.C. It is obvious from these examples that zones marginal for agriculture, and even for pastoralism, were in difficulties by the later part of the first millennium B.C., and that this may have had some effect on population numbers, and indirectly on migrations in the immediately pre-Christian centuries.

A ground survey, later supplemented by aerial photography, on the island of Gotland, off the east coast of Sweden, has produced different but equally valuable types of information. Here Lindquist (1974) realized that government land surveys had differentiated sandy baulks of ancient field boundaries from the mould surface of the fields, and that this provided an excellent method for establishing old field boundaries. Eventually he was able to detect field systems stretching over 130 ha (320 acres) at Rone, Gotland. Excavations under baulks (which revealed plough-marks under the edges, but not the middle of the baulks) and radiocarbon dates of a number of samples revealed that there had been Neolithic and Middle Bronze Age settlement on the site, prior to the establishment of the Late Bronze Age/Early Iron Age field-system. These fields were roughly rectangular, with the shorter sides three-quarters or two-thirds the length of the longer. A computer test of their areas revealed that there was an 'area module' of 195 m², and that this module fitted well into the differently shaped fields (Fig. 67). This might well have important bearing on the questions of land division and ownership in the late first millennium B.C.

Lindquist interprets the exploitation system as one of 'extensive farming' with long fallow (as Welinder proposed for Västmanland); about 100 B.C. the sandy baulks were replaced by a differently arranged stone-walled field system, of 'intensive' type, where each of the different activities – e.g. arable, meadow and grazing – was confined to particular areas. Thus the same sorts of changes seem to occur as further north on the Swedish mainland, and the pursuit of such studies, and of the pollen analyses and aerial surveys which are so crucial to their interpretation, is obviously a major goal in Scandinavian Late Bronze Age and Iron Age archaeology.

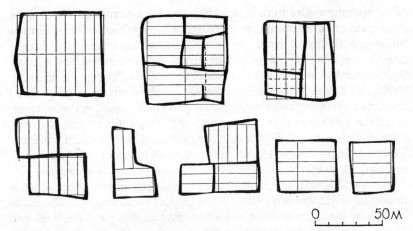

Fig. 67. 'Area module' of Late Iron Age fields on the island of Gotland, Sweden (after Lindquist, 1974, fig. 17)

CENTRAL EUROPE

Between the eighth and the fifth centuries B.C. similarities in pottery and metal types, burial practices and architecture, linked a wide area of central Europe between the rivers Saône, Po and Danube, and the central German mountains. This was the Hallstatt culture group or technocomplex, named after an Austrian type-site and deriving from the Late Bronze Age urn-field groups in the area. It is possible to divide this area into the Western Hallstatt zone, consisting of north Italy, Switzerland, eastern France, south Germany and Bohemia, and the Eastern Hallstatt zone, consisting of north-west Yugoslavia, west Hungary, Austria, west Slovakia and Moravia. Over this vast area there was obviously variability over time and space in local developments and in the amount of influence exerted by the civilizations of the Mediterranean world. At this time the Etruscan civilization was just developing and the Greeks were just beginning to send out colonies. Rome was founded in the mid eighth century B.C., and much of the early north–south trade was channelled over the alpine passes.

The main subsistence base among Hallstatt populations seems to have been mixed farming. At the Heuneburg hill-fort on the Upper Danube, excavation in the south-east corner of the interior revealed small farmsteads build in wood and separated by fences, occupied during the sixth and fifth centuries B.C. (Kimmig, 1975). The Heuneburg is located in what has been described as the Western Hallstatt area, but the type-site of the technocomplex itself is in Austria, in the eastern block. There have been recent publications (e.g. Häusler, 1968; RGZM, 1970) about the nineteenth century excavations at Hallstatt, which produced a total of 1045 graves and a few badly reported house structures, although no definite settlement area was found. The *raison-d'être* for the Hallstatt settlement was the salt-mines, and these have recently been investigated over vast areas (western mine areas 72,000 m², northern mine areas 30,000 m², eastern mine areas 54,000 m²). The salt was exploited over such wide areas probably because of repeated flooding or roof collapses. The salt-miners may have been specialists, and two groups of them may be represented by the differently shaped handles of the mallets used to pick off the salt. These were square-sectioned in the northern group and flatter in section in the eastern group. The excellent preservation of the mines has meant that caps in fur and leather and woven material in wool and flax have survived. Recent research on the wool materials obtained indicates that two types of sheep hair were being used, a natural brown wool which gave coppery red and black colours in dyeing and lighter wool types which gave a series of greens, coppery reds, blues and yellows.

The graves at Hallstatt have been the subject of controversy for many years, since the skeletal material was lost or discarded after its excavation in the last century. Although drawings are preserved showing that 55 per cent of the burials were by inhumation and 45 per cent by cremation, the latter being the most richly furnished with grave-goods, it is a matter of controversy whether the graves were always of males or whether there was a fairly even mix of males and females with some elderly people and children. Barth and Hodson have recently published a discussion of the records of Ramsauer, who excavated the majority of the cemetery finds in the mid nineteenth century (1976). In testing the recurring association of different categories of artifact in the grave-goods listed by Ramsauer, they were able to establish two main groupings of functional types, one of them consisting of mostly tools and weapons, and the other consisting of the majority of the ornaments (except multi-headed pins which belong to the first group) and metal belt fittings. The two broad categories of functional types seemed to confirm that both male and female burials were represented in the cemetery. Further study suggested that child burials could be identified by the presence of small bracelets with a maximum internal measurement of 50 mm diameter. This produced a possible 103 child burials. Females as well as males were cremated and inhumed, and Hodson's further studies are trying to separate the higher-status male and female graves from the lower ones and to redefine these categories more closely (Hodson, 1977). Recognizable weapons in the graves include swords and spearheads and daggers, while the male graves also contained metal vessels. Grave no. 994, dating to the fifth or fourth century B.C., contained a bronze sieve, two spearheads, a sword and a knife, and a helmet. Bronze sieves are relatively rare, despite the fact that bronze drinking sets had been well known in the area since urn-field times, and the idea may have been borrowed from the Etruscans. Other evidence of wealth, presumably obtained in exchange for the salt mined at Hallstatt, is the giant bronze platter from the north Adriatic area found in grave no. 696 and the sword handle from grave 573 which consisted of ivory inlaid with amber.

The Hallstatt type-site itself therefore reflects an exploitation zone whose products would be in considerable demand and which could command in exchange exotic artifacts in materials such as amber, ivory and bronze. The mining settlement probably developed over time; it has been estimated that during the eighth and seventh centuries B.C. there were at least 150 people living at Hallstatt and that this number would have doubled in size in the sixth century B.C.

In the later part of the Hallstatt period the importance of industry seems to increase. On the Heuneburg, in the level overlying the sixth-century B.C. farmsteads, a workshop quarter with smelting furnaces was established in the south-west corner of the hill-fort, in which were found the remains of bronze metallurgy. Lanes and drainage ditches divided up the workshop area. Presumably the dwelling area was separated from the industrial part in this period, an idea which may have emanated from the southern civilizations. Workshops are also known from the Molpir hill-fort in Czechoslovakia, which lay on an important communication route from the Danube via the Jablonica pass to Moravia. Here the workshop area revealed remains of iron and bronze metallurgy; there were six ovens for the drying of grain and fruit, and it was possible when excavating the houses to locate the areas used for weaving and pot-making (Dusek, 1974). The houses, probably sixty of them, were laid out in long rows, some of them using the rampart wall as their back wall, others standing away from the rampart. Their average dimensions were 30 to 35 m², so that a population of several hundred people can be hypothesized. Molpir was important because of its strategic placement, and apart from the aspects of the technology which have been briefly described, the religious sub-system is reflected by a partly rock-cut cult-place with a clay floor and an inner room. The precise cult is not clear, although there is a suggestion of a moon idol; burials of children up to two years old were found in the internal area.

One of the features of the location of Hallstatt oppida is the presence of impressive princely graves in their neighbourhood (Kimmig, 1975). Around the Heuneburg, there are nine enormous burial mounds including the sixth-century B.C. Hohmichele, still preserved up to 13 m in height. The Hohenasperg oppidum is associated with rich burials like Kleinaspergle, and the oppidum of Mont Lassois in eastern France has the princely Vix grave associated with it. Zürn has recently discussed these large oppida, regarding them as town-like in character because they were neither simple refuges nor simple industrial centres but had political importance (1974). In the sixth century (Hallstatt D) the Heuneburg site was importing Mediterranean goods like Greek and Marseilles-made amphorae, Greek black-figure pottery and coral. By the early fifth century Etruscan gold jewellery and bronze flagons and drinking vessels were coming into the site. The most extraordinary import, however, is the architectural style which resulted in the building in Hallstatt D1 of a sun-dried brick wall as part of the defences. This Mediterranean technique, totally unsuitable for the European temperate zone, shows the importance of Mediterranean influences at the time.

Technological advances at the Heuneburg by the end of the sixth century B.C. included the use of the fast wheel and new firing techniques for the pottery, the manufacture of fibulae including the snake fibula, the production of bronze arm and neck rings, and lignite bracelets, and the use of Baltic amber and Mediterranean coral in jewellery. There is some question as to whether drills and lathes were used to produce the tiny perforations made on horn spacer beads. The faunal remains of the Heuneburg consisted of mainly small cattle, plus pig, which presumably could be turned into the nearby forests, a few other domesticated animals, and rare wild deer, boar and fur-bearing mammals.

In the Black Forest, the defended site of Kapf was occupied in Hallstatt D1. Multidisciplinary studies at the nearby tumulus of Magdalenenberg have suggested that the central grave, robbed in the last century, probably dated to Hallstatt C-D, but the majority of the other burials in the same burial mound were contemporary with the Kapf occupation. Tests of mosses and grasses from the original ground surface indicated that it had not been wooded (Wilmann, 1972). Pollen analysis indicated that the area was generally open, though there were woods of fir trees near by at about 600 B.C., and, since there were few weed types and no grain pollens in the sample, that agriculture had presumably not been practised in the immediate vicinity. Dendrochronology on the planks which made up the central great chamber (Pl. 13) revealed that these were of oak cut on the spot and used without being dried out, so that the death of the occupant of this grave was contemporary with the final year of growth of the trees

(Spindler, 1972*a*). Dendrochronology was also used for the relative dating of two wooden structures which went radially into the mound. It seems possible that spades had been used in the construction of the turf mound and that large baskets of woven reeds were used to carry the earth. The presence of cow excrement and remains of insects and piles of twigs might indicate the use of animal power in the construction, although this is not certain. Total excavation of the barrow (Spindler, 1976) revealed 127 graves, although the excavators believe that some central ones had probably been lost because of ground erosion. The majority of the graves were single extended inhumations. Nearly all of them circle the grave in a tangential position to the central burial except for no. 123 which is in a radial position with its feet towards the centre of the mound, at a point where the burials change from a clockwise to an anti-clockwise direction, suggesting that perhaps this was the first inhumation after the main central burial (Spindler, 1976).

The women's graves seem to be the richest, containing numerous arm bands of bronze or lignite and also hairpins and rings of all types (e.g. grave 60, which has lots of iron rings, and grave 78). The men's graves contained mostly razors and the majority of the large fibulae. An iron antenna dagger was taken from grave 67, a male grave, and X-ray photography revealed clearly its original structure (Spindler, 1973). In several cases the graves were furnished with wood coffins, in other cases the bodies were laid on stone packings; in all cases the skeletal remains were very fragmentary indeed. The excavation and prompt publication of this barrow is of considerable importance for Hallstatt studies in northern Europe.

Interpretation, rather than straight description, of Late Hallstatt burials in north Württemberg has concentrated on the very small differences visible between grave-goods, particularly in the Mühlacker barrow cemetery to the north-west of Stuttgart (Pauli, 1972). Pauli was looking for within-society differences, and felt that it was possible to detect within the burials three main groups, one being of male burials (group 3) another female burials (group 1, where the typical grave-goods were a pair of fibulae of the same type, although not always of the same casting), and a third group (group 2) which consisted of mostly juvenile but also some female graves. Group 1 females have larger girdle-buckles than group 2. Pauli feels that the group 2 graves consist (where they are of women) of those women still treated as children, i.e. perhaps not yet married; the fact that burials of infants are only found with group 1 type of graves suggests to him that a change of status came with marriage. Pauli emphasizes that these suggestions are based on poorly excavated data and supports the excavation and publication of sites such as the Magdalenenberg before a better understanding can be achieved of the burial systems and the social systems behind them in the Hallstatt period.

Fischer has recently looked at the interpretations made to account for the rich grave horizon of the Hallstatt D period (1973). Graves such as the Magdalenenberg barrow, or the Vix burial, which contained a human-size vase of Greco-Etruscan workmanship, a gold diadem and an exquisite realistic bronze statuette (perhaps the 'princess' for whom the grave was made) demand some sort of explanation as to the social structure which produced them. The presence of exotic burial items has been interpreted in a number of ways, as political or diplomatic marriage gifts to local rulers (Zürn); as evidence of trade, with the settlements near the rich barrows acting as 'central places'; and in connection with the practice of transhumance. Dehn has suggested that the dominant men at the central places of south Germany were shepherd-kings, who travelled with their flocks via the passes of eastern France down to the region of Marseilles to barter with the merchants for fine bronzes, cloth and wine (1972). Fischer agrees with Zürn on the interpretation of the very varied rich artifacts (those buried near the Hohenasperg were of varying dates, reflecting acquisition over several generations) as political or marriage gifts, perhaps individually commissioned. In support of this argument he uses the works of Homer and other classical authors where they describe the giving of political gifts, and the importance of these gifts in binding the donor and recipient and their descendants in friendship.

Frankenstein and Rowlands have explained the richness of the south-west German Hallstatt in terms of a prestige-good economy model: some of the prestige goods were imported, some were manufactured in local centres. They transfer the explanation into social terms by visualizing the finest burials as those of paramount chiefs and lesser chiefs, with a sliding scale of grave-goods dependent on the position of the chief in the chain of power (Frankenstein, 1977).

The short period of very rich Hallstatt graves was soon over, however, and the evidence from graves and settlements seems to reflect a less stratified society.

The changes of the later fifth century B.C. in central Europe are reflected in a change of nomenclature, from the Hallstatt to the La Tène culture complex. Joachim has published a description of the (mainly burial) sites of the Middle Rhine of the first millennium B.C., indicating considerable continuity in this area, permeated with slow changes following introductions such as the potter's wheel, but with no great population changes (1968). The local Hunsrück-Eifel culture is divided into two phases, however, with the break occurring in the fifth century. The changeover to La Tène is not always easy to detect, particularly in this period where much dating is achieved by typology rather than independent means. Zürn has suggested that in south Germany during the Hallstatt D3 phase there were a number of burial 'schemes', so that the dead might be buried with (a) snake fibulae or drum-decorated-foot fibulae (so-called Hallstatt) or (b) yellow-glass beads and various rings and bracelets (so-called La Tène) or (c) a mixture of both groups of artifacts. New goods were infiltrating in a rather erratic manner into the area, and the presence of glass, a technological process linked with the southern civilizations, suggests that Mediterranean elements may have been important in the formation of the new culture complex. In a material-culture sense the La Tène period is differentiated from the Hallstatt by different styles of ornaments, new manufactures such as glass, and a generally greater dependence for weapons, wine-drinking sets and ornament design on the Mediterranean civilizations.

Collis has divided the La Tène culture complex, lasting from c. 475/450 B.C. to the first century B.C., into a temperate and western, and a north-European–Scandinavian zone (1975). There are many variations in settlement distribution and organization over the 500 years and over the European area. However, similar metal types and pottery types demonstrate cultural links, and there are widespread similarities in burial rites (inhumation in the early centuries (e.g. Pl. 17), cremation from the third century onwards). Collis is interested in the widespread prevalence of fortified settlements in the Late La Tène, and charts their origins in different regions via six 'settlement systems'. Different areas of Europe practise different systems and follow different 'trajectories'. System 3, for instance, where a region has many small cemeteries, some very rich, but no hill-forts, is fairly common in the Early and Middle La Tène periods, and indicates the abandonment of the large Hallstatt defensive centres in many parts of Europe. By Late La Tène the trajectories have led to large nucleated units of population with lots of trade and industrial production, either situated on trade routes and undefended (System 5) or in defensive positions (System 6).

During the last half of the first millennium B.C. there was an accelerated progress in all forms of economic life, in the manufacture of pottery on the wheel, in metallurgy of all types including elaborate body armour, and in the extensive trade and exchange and working of other raw materials. Filip has claimed that master craftsmen were at work in the fourth century B.C. in Bohemia as well as further west (1971). Kruta has studied the relationships between the different classes of settlement in the same area (1975). The rural settlements were not just agricultural, but included some workshop areas for pottery and metal manufacture. Here the ordinary kitchen wares were continued from the Late Hallstatt into the Early La Tène period, although the finer wares were replaced by new ones, wheel-thrown in type. Although only a limited number survive, Kruta estimates that the rural settlements of the La Tène period were as dense as the flat inhumation cemeteries (average 2–5 km apart) on the fertile plains of central, north-eastern and north-western Bohemia (Czechoslovakia). Open-area excavation over 150 ha has recently been carried out at the cemetery of Vikletice, north-west Bohemia. Similar open-area excavations of a number of settlements have clarified the types of houses used, with up to ten post-built houses or semi-subterranean huts in each settlement. In the densely occupied region of Bohemia Late La Tène oppida were commonly located on important trade routes and near important resources such as iron ores (Stradonice), graphite (Třisov) and silver sand (Nevřzice) (Kruta, 1975). Both the structure of the oppida or hill refuges in the Late La Tène and the unequal provision of grave-goods in the cemeteries in the earlier phases (for instance graves with only a few pots as compared with richly armoured warriors with swords and jewelled armour) indicate much greater stratification than before, with, in particular, important roles for craftsmen.

Interaction of the increased activity in iron and stone tools (including the rotary quern) and of the development of such farming improvements as manuring and crop rotation must have led to greater agricultural output. Was this a response to, or a cause of, increased population size?

The Neustupnys, discussing the iron manufactures of the late La Tène period in Czechoslovakia, point to ploughshares, spades, sickles, scythes and many other tools, all except the axe persisting until today in the same shapes that were established in the early centuries preceding the Christian era. They conclude that this mass employment of iron tools must have had a revolutionary effect on the economy and society (Neustupny and Neustupny, 1961).

The type-site of the La Tène culture in northern Switzerland was interpreted in 1923 as a 'fortified warehouse' and later as a place of sacrifice (Sauter, 1976). The site consisted of the remains of a double bridge, over the Zihl river, numerous finds, especially iron weapons (over 3,000 finds were recently catalogued by de Navarro, 1972), and several bodies found in disarray. The finds date from the second to the first century B.C. Schwab has recently excavated a similar site two miles downstream at Cornaux (1972). At Cornaux excavation revealed a broken bridge of oak planks which had collapsed apparently due to an unexpected flood, and trapped a number of people under water (Schwab, 1972). Iron fibulae of La Tène C–D periods on the skeletons dated the event to the final centuries B.C. and other finds at the location included swords in sheaths, spearheads and angular pots. The La Tène site itself was reinterpreted by Schwab as being an ideal centre for trade since it was centrally located near three lakes and consisted of a series of house remains beside the Aare river, with a palisade enclosing those houses on the north bank. There seem to have been boat moorings on the old river channel at La Tène and the wooden remains from the site can now be reinterpreted as coming from a similar bridge to that at Cornaux. It is interesting that many of the finds made at La Tène were grouped together as though in packets, which might support the hypothesis of goods for trade. La Tène may also have been an important industrial site, as the site of 'Prefargier', 'near the forges', lies near by and it is at least a possibility that metallurgical activity was carried out at the site.

Hodson's recent new publication on the Münsingen cemetery near Berne rounds out the picture of Middle and Late La Tène Switzerland by listing the grave-goods of the 140 burials (out of 226) provided with them, and defining twenty-three time horizons on the basis of combinations of ornament types. Hodson has used a variety of statistical techniques to demonstrate the clustering of these types, and has been able to demonstrate a north-to-south spread of the cemetery over its approximately 300 years of use (1968).

Factor analysis has been used in the north French area to detect possible subregional boundaries within the Marnian variant of the La Tène culture (Pollnac and Rowlett, 1977). These authors interpreted areas with the greatest stylistic similarity in artifacts and burial treatment as areas of greater social integration. The boundaries between these areas contained many of the warrior graves with chariots, while the graves of craftsmen were usually located within the zones of greater social stability, where there was greater likelihood of their being supported by the local population unit.

The site of Manching, the largest La Tène settlement in Europe, dating to the second and first centuries B.C., is located on a gravel terrace of the Danube, in an excellent position for controlling communications both east–west along the Danube and also to the south along the Paar valley (Fig. 68). There have been changes in the position of the Paar and of the Danube (the latter flowed to within 1 km of the oppidum until 1827), but the surrounding landscape must always have included bogs and marshes, and have been poor in agricultural potential. Today the main fields lie within the oppidum, over the area of maximum occupation in the Late La Tène period. It is assumed that the importance of the site lay in its communications and in the rich local iron-ore resources.

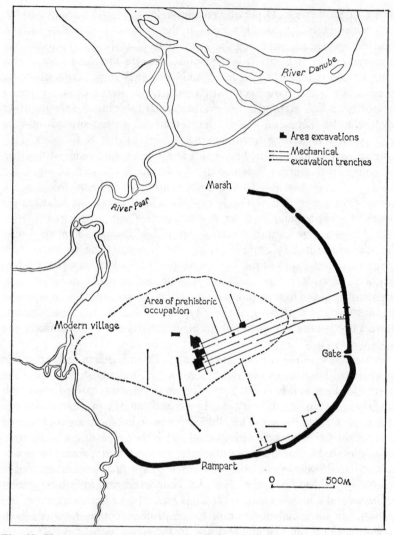

Fig. 68. Site and outline of excavations, Manching, southern Germany (after Selkirk, 1969, p. 41, and Krämer and Schübert, 1970, Beilage 3)

The Manching ramparts enclose an area of 380 hectares, and excavations have been correspondingly huge (Krämer and Schübert, 1970). Trenches have been dug by mechanical excavators, revealing the sleeper-beam trenches and post-holes of metal workshop quarters, together with some houses, and lots of daub from the walling. The workshops run broadly east–west, with apparent paths between them, and are identified by the presence of slag and smelting equipment. The iron finds listed include smithing hammers, anvils and tongs, wood- and leather-working equipment including saws and needles, ploughshares, hoes and sickles, and a range of braziers, tripods and fire-dogs (Jacobi, 1974). Pieces of horse-trappings and fragments of wagons were also found, a reminder of the more efficient transportation available in the final millennium B.C.

The three main pottery types at the site were graphite clay ware (three sources of the clay, examined by thin-sectioning, lie on the Middle Danube, but the ware was widely distributed throughout Europe); painted wares; and more localized burnished wares (Collis, 1973).

Reports on the coarse pottery, and the imported Mediterranean fine-wares, have not yet been published. Some pottery was made on the site (there are potter's tools). Other crafts included minting (there are coins and moulds for them); glass-making; weaving; and the working of amber, sapropelite (a type of slate favoured for bracelets) and bone (Krämer and Schübert, 1970).

With regard to the subsistence base the evidence seems to suggest that about half of the meat eaten was beef, with approximately 25 per cent pork, and rather less sheep and goat meat. Horse and dog were also represented (Boessneck et al., 1971). Cattle and sheep lived to over two and three years old respectively, which seems to indicate that they were of importance for milk/traction and wool rather than for meat. Collis (1973) comments on the wide range of measurements obtained from this faunal sample, which seem to indicate that a large number of species and breeds were being brought into Manching. This would fit with the general picture of the site being the central place for a very large region and exploiting animal and plant populations from many different micro-environments in the area.

An important feature of the La Tène period is the development of art into more complex forms, reflecting influences from the Mediterranean and the Near East. Sandars (1971) has recently discussed the presence of a Persian expeditionary force and of Scythian groups in south-east Europe in the sixth to mid fifth century B.C., and the Persian practice of offering state presents, which might have disseminated their art styles. The phases of development of La Tène art, first defined by Jacobsthal

(1944) are still followed: his Early style, which includes plant and animal motifs, and which spread from the Rhineland to much of central and western Europe in the fifth century B.C., is illustrated, for instance, by two gold horns and the Greek drinking cup found in the Kleinaspergle barrow near the Hohenasperg oppidum. Other Late Hallstatt burials such as the rich graves at Bad Canstatt with their gold diadems and bowls, and the Erstfeld torcs and bracelets found on the St Gotthard pass, bear similar animal and plant motifs (Megaw, 1970). There is evidence of Etruscan influence in the large drinking vessels, in that there are scenes of men wrestling and of military parades. Another style emerged in the fourth century, also in the Rhineland, named after the rich female grave at Waldalgesheim, North Germany. Here the bronze torc and bracelets deposited in the tomb were decorated in a less representational style, with motifs derived from the classical palmette and tendril. Two contrasting styles are found in the third century B.C., in particular the Plastic style, with high-relief ornament in sweeping swags and whorls, and the crisper, more asymmetrical ornament of the Sword style, found particularly on sword scabbards of the Rhineland and Hungary, possibly due to migrations of the Rhenish tribes (Szabo, 1971).

Dacian art in Romania drew on the same external influences, but produced less effective and controlled styles (Sandars, 1971). After about 100 B.C. these art styles ceased except in Britain and Ireland where some of the most famous pieces, such as the bronze mirrors, are dated to the early first century A.D. Most of the Celtic artwork known is found in metal form, in designs on metal vessels, swords, scabbards, armour and jewellery. Inlays of precious ornaments such as imported Mediterranean coral were in favour and gold and silver were widely used. The electrum and gold neck-rings from Snettisham, Norfolk, were manufactured by a series of different techniques including twisting the wire strands and punching and engraving the terminals (the electrum torc), and core casting and repoussé relief ornament (on the gold torc). The most outstanding example of European metalwork is the Gundestrop cauldron. The cauldron was found in its component parts of bowl, iron rim, and decorative plates, in what had been a Danish pond, and was obviously deliberately deposited. Made in silver-gilt, it bears mythical animal and human figures and is an elaborate *tour de force* by craftsmen working in both Celtic and Oriental traditions. The use of silver-gilt, and the presence of animals such as lion and elephant in the design, has led to suggestions that it was manufactured on the border of the two artistic areas, perhaps in southern Slovakia.

Much more rarely, Celtic sculpture in wood and stone is found. At

Hirschlanden, Germany, a massive figure in local Stuben sandstone, found in a barrow excavation, has been dated to the end of the sixth century B.C. It is suggested that it originally stood on the top of the barrow mound. The figure is of a naked warrior wearing a pointed helmet, a belt with a dagger in it, and a neck-ring. Experts regard the style of the sculpture as resembling that of the Etruscans and similar 'schools' to the south of the Alps (Arts Council of Great Britain, 1970). A number of other large stone sculptures have been found, particularly in southern France in the period immediately prior to Roman invasion, and it is suggested that Gallic craftsmen were also competent in wooden sculpture, since numerous wooden figures from the middle of the first century A.D. have been found in sanctuaries at the source of the Seine and in central France (Martin, 1965; Vatin, 1972).

By the final centuries before Christ, the Celtic world to the north of the Mediterranean civilized world had an established stratified social struc-ture, in which both craftsmen and also religious specialists had a place, and it has been suggested that the infiltration of Mediterranean and especially Roman ideas, as well as artifacts, helped the development of a ruling aristocracy. Crumley has recently discussed this problem, suggesting that lower orders of society were in a client relationship towards the aristo-cracy and that there may have been some degree of land tenure from the top echelon of society. Crumley sees the effect of long-distance trade from the Mediterranean as increasing social stratification along the trade routes and in areas of valuable natural resources, and feels that statehood had already been reached in certain locations, for instance around the oppida of Bibracte and Alesia. She sees Celtic society as moving from inherited to achieved status, this change being activated by the wealth of the classical world, and being effective most particularly in the patron/client relationship, and in the increase of markets. The effect of this in western Europe was that Gallic political organization became party-based rather than kin-based by La Tène II and III (Crumley, 1974). That this may have been the case in eastern Europe also is suggested by a statistical analysis of Boii coins which indicated that they bore mainly single-stemmed or abbreviated names, not the compound names of the old aristocracy (Szabo, 1971).

SOUTH-WEST EUROPE

During the course of the first millennium B.C., local societies in the west Mediterranean coast lands were exposed to a variety of different civil-izations. The central part of Italy saw the rise of the Etruscan civilization from the local Villanovan culture in about the eighth century B.C. The Etruscans expanded northwards into the Po valley, where some of their largest cemeteries are found near Bologna, and southwards along the Tyrrhenian coast. Their exports over the Alps, and into the west Mediterranean (particularly into Sardinia, Corsica and southern France), represent some of the earliest influences of the new Mediterranean civilizations on the hinterland. At the same time, however, Greeks and Phoenicians were exploring and trading throughout the Mediterranean basin; the Phoenicians established colonies in north Africa, western Sicily, Sardinia and Spain, building cities and temples and setting up elaborate trading networks in ores and other raw materials. The Greeks established their trading colonies principally in southern Italy and Sicily and southern France, founding the city of Marseilles on a defended spur, probably already occupied by potential customers, in 600 B.C. Chronology in settlements along the west Mediterranean seaboard still depends to a large extent on the presence of imports from such trading cities. There were conflicts between the Greeks on the one hand, and the Carthaginians (the Phoenician settlers of north Africa) and Etruscans on the other, and battles took place at sea and on land. By the fourth century B.C., however, the city of Rome and its allies also commenced a programme of expansion and by the second century Rome had absorbed the territories and colonies of the three warring groups under its own control.

The native cultures in the Mediterranean coast lands and islands settled by the Greeks or Carthaginians, or visited by Etruscan traders, continued their own cultural paths until dominated militarily by the intruders, as the continuity of nuraghic culture in Sardinia (Pl. 18) until the mid sixth century shows. In Corsica, the Greek town founded in 540 B.C. on the east coast at Alalia expanded its interests inland along the lines of transhumance routes (Jehasse, 1976). In Iberia, a recent study by Frankenstein suggests that the Phoenicians, in their search for ores, reorganized the patterns of trade within the peninsula, linking the metalworking zones of the north-west and south, and encouraged mining and smelting on a large scale (1977).

In south-west France a variety of facies are grouped under the umbrella of the Mailhac culture; excavations by the Taffanels at Mailhac, north of Narbonne, have revealed a sequence of settlements and cemeteries from about the eighth century B.C. onwards (the dating of the early phase is uncertain owing to lack of carbon-14 dates). The first phase consisted of a settlement of family groups on a fortified hilltop, working bronze and making pottery, with an emphasis on sheep-herding, and probably agriculture. The over 1000 graves discovered contain inurned cremations, apparently again in family groups. In the second phase, at the beginning of the seventh century, burials were more varied, with large pits and cairns in some cases, and the grave goods of bronze and iron also suggested some inequality. From the sixth century onwards Etruscan amphorae and black ware (*bucchero nero*) were found on both the defended settlement and in the cemetery. In the same century buildings in the Greek style were erected at Agde, probably an important trade post. Barruol has listed the types of site occupied during these three phases in Languedoc: apart from some high sites like Mailhac, occupation occurs in valleys and along the seaside lagoons (1976).

On the Provençal coast to the west of Marseilles, sherds of seventh-century Etruscan ware, Italo-Corinthian and Rhodian pottery date the beginnings of the trading city of St-Blaise (Hatt, 1970). From *c*. 600 B.C. onwards, with the founding of Marseilles, the Rhône valley became an important trade route, and was the source of many of the exotic items found in Hallstatt contexts. Native settlements in the Rhône basin were established on high points, while much smaller and more ephemeral hilltop sites were occupied further east (Arcelin, 1976).

Pots for grain storage are known from the sixth century, and are often grouped in granaries: at Le Pègue, in the Rhône valley, thirty-five 100-litre jars contained three types of wheat, barley and acorns. The vine was definitely grown from the sixth century onwards. Apart from the usual domesticated animals, there is evidence for hunting and marine fishing. Research on Provençal pottery indicates that village-to-village trading systems were broken around the turn of the fifth century, to be replaced by a regional distribution of local and imported wares (Arcelin, 1976).

The Rhône-valley trade route broke down *c*. 500 B.C. Hatt claims that the cause of the breakdown was population movements, particularly the incursions of Celts into southern France. The Marseilles merchants turned their attention more to the littoral, founding colonies from Nice westwards, and there is evidence for the trade expansion in numerous wrecks off the south French coast, e.g. the first-century B.C. wreck off Giens (Pl. 16). Hatt feels that local princedoms, strongly influenced by the Greek colonies, developed along the Languedoc coastline. The period from *c*. 500 to 100 B.C. saw the rise of defended oppida in Langue-doc, 1 to 20 ha in extent, along the coastal lagoons, beside the numerous valleys and dominating routes (e.g. the Mont-Cavalier site at Nîmes). Barruol regards these sites as permanent and acting as central places for agricultural goods, but with varying political, religious or commercial roles (1976). The sites grew, and were further fortified, during the period of Roman expansion during the first century B.C. Defensive walls were also built in Provence, both at the colonial emporia of Saint-Blaise and Saint-Rémy, and at Entremont. Entremont, a native site and capital of the Saluvii, was built on a steep-sided plateau, and the square-bastioned rampart was added in the mid third century. It was among a number of sites near to Marseilles, which was influenced by the techniques of urbanization (massive architecture, sculpture, the potter's wheel and kiln, coinage and literacy). None the less, the domestic buildings and religious sanctuaries remained Saluvian (Benoit, 1975). The sanctuaries held square pillars with severed heads engraved on them, or contained hollows to hold human skulls. Entremont represents the complex mixture of native and exotic elements which was typical of societies in the immediate vicinity of the cities and trading posts of the Mediterranean civilizations.

SOUTH-EAST EUROPE

In Bulgaria and Romania the Hallstatt A period began c. 1200 B.C. with the import of iron objects into the area, followed by the manufacture of iron in Hallstatt B (Lazlo, 1976). Bronze-working remained important, especially for ornaments, vessels, horse trappings and armour, and was used in conjunction with iron. Some Romanian archaeologists stress the continuity in bronze metallurgy and other cultural features from the rich Middle and Late Bronze Ages of the Carpathians to the first Iron Age (Berciu, 1967). Berciu sees a tendency towards stock-breeding, and towards larger, defended settlements, as continuing from the Late Bronze Age. Other archaeologists feel that towards the end of the Late Bronze Age nomadic groups invaded the Carpathian basin (Horedt, 1974), possibly as part of population movements ultimately originating in western Siberia (Mongait, 1961; Sulimirski, 1975). According to this view, the Andronovo people of western Siberia gradually moved westwards, causing displacement of other groups both in north-east and in south-east Russia. So-called Cimmerian settlements (small fortified centres with semi-subterranean houses and a flourishing bronze industry) are found in the early first millennium B.C. in south-west Russia. Assyrian texts refer to raids by both Cimmerians and Scythians in the eighth century B.C., and the relationship between the two groups is not clear. However, the 'ethno-cultural and socio-economic processes' leading to the emergence and evolution of the historic Scyths are presently being studied (Shelov, 1975). There is a need for information about possible population pressures or environmental changes at this time in southern Russia which may have provoked either population movements or changes in economic or cultural activity. There seems to have been some population movement, and considerable trading, between the east Balkans and south Russia. Scythian bronzes and pottery are known in the sixth century B.C., and appear in contemporary burials as grave-goods (e.g. Ferigile cemetery, Histria Greek city). At the southern Carpathian cemetery of Ferigile, the earliest cremation burials under the 150 tumuli excavated (in the north of the cemetery) were accompanied by some of the finest grave-goods, including fine pottery, glass beads, bronze open-work belts and iron weapons. The warriors' graves in particular held, in addition to the few fragmentary burnt bones transported from the cremation area, bent fighting knives and spearheads, and in a few cases 'Scythian' daggers or *akinakes* (Vulpe, 1967). These are regarded by the excavator as exchange items coming into an essentially local society.

Recent rescue excavations of barrow cemeteries and of a number of settlements in the path of canals and irrigation schemes in the lower reaches of the Dnieper, Dniester and Don, and in the Crimea, have produced both artifacts and information about Scythian economy and society. Many Scythian barrows were plundered in the nineteenth century, with the result that the general typology of burials, weapons and pottery is already well known. Recent excavations have confirmed that the dead were buried in a shaft- or pit-grave, lying extended on the back, and accompanied by a varying number of other human and horse burials. Although the central grave had been robbed, even the secondary burial at the fifth-century barrow of Arkhangelskaya Sloboda contained grave-goods consisting of quivers, wooden cups and a cloak, all covered in decorated gold plates (Shelov, 1975). Shelov indicates that there is variability between different regions controlled by the Scyths, and that these people demonstrate a shift over time from the clan-tribe level of organization to the class society and the state. By the fourth century B.C. a Scythian king, Atei, ruled from the Kamenskoe hill-fort on the Dnieper, a central place with 12 km^2 of fortified area, and great zones of metallurgical workshops. Unfortified villages, also with metalwork-shops, formed the lower part of the settlement hierarchy.

Šramko has recently described the development of both iron and non-ferrous metallurgy in south-east Europe (including south-west Russia), suggesting that the concentration of people of the steppe and forest steppe into defended settlements provoked the development of crafts (1974). At the largest European Iron Age site, Belsk, on the Vorskla river, a tributary of the Dnieper, an area of over 4000 ha was enclosed by a 34-km long wall. The wall joined three strongholds together, of which the two main forts, the eastern and the western, were respectively 7500 m^2 and 1000 m^2 in area (Fig. 69). Excavations since 1958 at Belsk have revealed well-organized settlements dating from the seventh to the third centuries B.C. The houses were of either earth or wood, with cellars or stalls in some of them, as well as pits for grain storage. Amphorae and red- and black-figure wares were imported from the Greek Black Sea coast cities. Six metalwork-shops contained two clay furnaces and many smiths' tools. Bronze was mostly used for ornaments, horse trappings and mirror handles, and Šramko has identified the quantities of tin and other impurities used as hardeners. Lead, for instance, was the usual hardener for copper 'kettles' made by the lost-wax method.

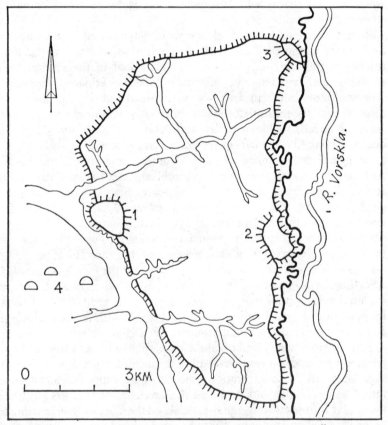

Fig. 69. Plan of forts and perimeter wall at Belsk, Ukraine (after Šramko, 1974, fig. 4)

1 West fort, 2 East fort, 3 North-east fort, 4 Barrow cemetery

There was variability between the eastern and western settlements at Belsk at any given time. The two settlements are interpreted by Šramko as the homes of two kin groups ('Stämme'), possibly the Helonos and Budinen mentioned by Herodotus (1974). Publication of full reports of the excavations, and quantification of the activities in the two settlements, will provide fascinating data about the functioning o these complex societies.

The Greek cities founded on the Black Sea coast from the seventh century onwards exchanged their fine pottery, metalwork and textiles with the Scythians for grain, honey, cattle, wax, salt fish and slaves.

Excavations at Olbia, on the north shore of the Bosphorus, have revealed the usual Greek buildings and amenities; in addition, the wharves of the town, now flooded, are being excavated by underwater researchers. Investigations have also traced the estate zone belonging to the town, where the workers lived in simple semi-subterranean huts. A similar broad pattern of research is being followed at Chersonesus in the north-west Crimea, where apart from fifth-century B.C. fish-salting cisterns, wine presses, glass shops and public buildings, the boundaries of the fields belonging to the settlement have been traced. The nearby hill-fo꞉t of Chaika was a trade factory for Chersonesus, but was sacked and taken over by the Scythians in the second century B.C. (Shelov, 1975).

Greek cities elsewhere on the Black Sea coast and along the Adriatic coast also influenced their hinterland by trading activities. Recent work in Bulgaria has included the survey and partial excavation of an area due to be flooded behind the Batak dam (Concev and Milcev, 1970). The investigators located thirty-five cemeteries and five settlements in the area, and excavation of some of the barrows revealed two phases of settlement, in the final Hallstatt/beginning La Tène, and in the late Roman period. Concev and Milcev describe the fifth-century B.C. graves as consisting of cremations covered with a small stone tumulus, or defined by a ring of stones, and then covered with earth. Hearth areas near by indicated that cremation had been on the spot. Grave-goods included both Thracian pots and Greek imports, and local copies of the Greek vessels. Concev and Milcev interpret the contemporary society as passing from primitive tribalism to a stage of military democracy, to be followed by class society. How far the trade goods and art styles of the Greek cities were influential in this evolution is difficult to estimate. Homer mentions a king of the Thracians, Rhesus, whose territory covered present-day Bulgaria, as owning magnificent horses and armour and chariot trappings in gold and silver, and certainly recent archaeological discoveries in Bulgaria (e.g. the Vratsa treasure of the mid fourth century B.C.) suggest that there were some extremely rich members of the society. The Vratsa treasure includes armour (Pl. 14) and horse-trappings in gold and silver, and huge amounts of silver and gold are also used for great dishes and bowls. The vast numbers of burial mounds, containing multiple burials, suggest a populous and economically self-sufficient society with widespread trade links. However, the fourth and early third centuries B.C. seem to have been a time of population movement and conflict in the Balkans, according to the classical authors. The Scythians apparently made a massive incursion, but were beaten back. Greek expeditions such as that of Alexander the Great in 335 B.C. reached beyond the Danube, and c. 300 B.C. there were movements of 'Celts' from central Europe into the south-east.

One of the fortified sites of Romania, Racatau, on the Siret river, may have been a centre for exchange of Mediterranean products with more distant tribes, as excavations have revealed quantities of imported Greek and Roman vases (Capitanu, 1976). Greek and Roman styles also influenced local metallurgy, with changes taking place from the fourth to the mid second century, followed by an explosion of metal products, specialized tools in particular, by the time of the Roman takeover of the Dacians in A.D. 106. Glodiaru correlates the presence of important metallurgical centres with regions of high population density and political integration (1976).

By the first century B.C. the Dacians, a Thracian subgroup, centred on the metal-rich Carpathians, had grown into a state, perhaps because of pressure from the Roman world as well as the Greek, perhaps because of internal increase in complexity. In the first century B.C. the Dacian king Burebista apparently abandoned a defended site at Popesti near Bucharest, with its corridored main house, its temple, workshops and houses, for the more remote settlement of Costesti in the southern Carpathians (Mac-Kendrick, 1975). Here a substantial fortification enclosed 30 acres (12 ha), with houses and workshops, and a 'column sanctuary', containing short squat columns arranged in groups of six. It is suggested that the arrangements of columns or drums here and at other late Dacian sites are connected with their calendar. Romanian archaeologists regard the Dacians as having definitely reached statehood prior to Roman takeover, with their strongholds acting as economic, political, military and religious centres (Berciu, 1967).

POSTFACE

A number of points emerge from this brief survey of recent developments in European prehistory. One is the crucial importance of being able to date events in the past: greater precision in the dating of the earliest European prehistory is still badly needed, though the new carbon-14 dating process should ease the problem. As far as later periods are concerned, given sufficient funds and laboratory availability, there are few sites that cannot be reasonably well dated. The possibilities of independent dating (and the climate of research advocating study of past social systems and past environments) has meant that archaeologists working in the last two decades have been able to dig horizontally and to research single-period behaviour – whether of a cave frequented by Mousterian hunters or a small town boasting planned streets, a rampart wall and adjacent fields.

This development, plus the participation of specialists from other fields in research projects, has permitted the interlocking nature of many modern studies, which seek to identify the role of the artifact in the assemblage and the role of the assemblage in its environmental and geomorphological setting. The back-up for this approach is provided by twentieth-century technology and laboratory techniques, while the data thus derived is woven into an explanation of the past situation by the use of theoretical concepts and models. It is certain that not all the explanations derived will stand the test of time and future research, but they are vital and challenging in their attempt to account for what is left of the past.

A specific trend touched upon in this book has been the study of raw materials, and their exploitation, manufacture and distribution as finished tools. In early time periods these studies are linked to questions of group territories, and of primitive exchange relationships. In later millennia the distribution of artifact types in a variety of raw materials, and the technology involved in their production, are studied in the frameworks of trade or exchange between mainly settled societies, and the social structures of those societies.

An archaeological idealist, looking forward to the next decade of European archaeology, could hope for more basic data from certain areas, particularly the Mediterranean basin, and for further studies on the skeletal remains of prehistoric Europeans. In many areas the pace of building and transportation developments will demand large-scale funding for both straight rescue projects (which may well reveal unsuspected past activities), and for well-thought-out sampling of particular areas and periods. Both extensive funds and improved processing methods will be necessary for the resultant flood of data. The proliferation of models, theories and questions is also to be encouraged, both as a guide to specific lines of research and, in a more general sense, to improve the yet imperfect vision of the prehistoric past of Europe.

BIBLIOGRAPHY AND INDEX

BIBLIOGRAPHY

Aigner, J. S. 1976. Chinese Pleistocene
cultural and hominid remains: a consideration of their significance in
reconstructing the pattern of human
biocultural development. *IXe Congr.
UISPP, Nice*, Coll. VII, pp. 65–90.
Paris, CNRS.

Albrethsen, S. E. & Brinch Petersen,
E. 1975. *Gravene pa Bøgebakken Vedbæk.*

Alexander, J. 1972. *Jugoslavia.* London,
Thames & Hudson.

Altena, J. F. van Regteren. 1977. Living
east of the North Sea – some aspects of
the settlement history of the Western
Netherlands in the Bronze and Iron
Age. *Conf. Lowland Iron Age Communities, Oxf., 1977.*

Ammerman, A. J. & Cavalli-Sforza, L. L.
1971. Measuring the rate of spread of
early farming in Europe. *Man*, 6, pp.
674–88.

Ammerman, A. J. & Feldman, M. W.
1974. On the 'making' of an assemblage of stone tools. *Am. Antiq.*, 39, pp.
610–16.

Angel, J. L. 1969. Basis of paleodemo-
graphy. *Am. J. Phys. Anthrop.*, n.s.,
30, pp. 427–37.

Angel, J. Lawrence. 1972. Ecology and
population in the eastern Mediterranean. *Wld Archaeol.*, 4, 1, pp. 88–
105.

Angel J. 1973. Early Neolithic people of
Nea Nikomedeia. In: F. Schwabedissen
(gen. ed.), *Anfänge des Neolithikums
vom Orient bis Europa*, VIII, *Anthropology* (ed. I. Schwidetzky), pp. 103–12.

Arcelin, P. 1976. Les civilisations de
l'Âge du Fer en Provence. In: J.
Guilaine (ed.), *La Préhistoire Française*,
vol. III, pp. 657–75. Paris, CNRS.

Arts Council of Great Britain. 1970. *Early
Celtic Art.* Edinburgh Univ. Press.

Asmus, G. 1973. Mesolithische Men-
schenfunde aus Mittel-, Nord- u.
Osteuropa. In: F. Schwabedissen (gen.
ed.), *Anfänge des Neolithikums vom
Orient bis Europa*, VIII, *Anthropology*
(ed. I. Schwidetsky), pp. 28–86.

Atkinson, R. J. 1975. Megalithic astron-
omy – a prehistorian's comments. *J.
Hist. Astr.*, 6, pp. 42–52.

Bailloud, G. 1972. Datations C14 pour
le site de Basi (Serra-di-Ferro, Corse).
Bull. Soc. Préhist. Fr., 69, C.R.s.m. 3,
pp. 71–2.

Bakels, C. & Arps, C. 1977. Stone implements from Linear Pottery sites.
(Paper presented at) *Conf. Neolithic
and Bronze Age Stone Implements*,
Nottingham.

Balcer, B. 1971a. The state and the needs
of research on flint industry in the Neolithic and the Early Bronze Age. *Wiad.
Archeol.*, 36, pp. 51–70.

Balcer, B. 1971*b*. The flint mine at Świeciechówo-Lasek, Krasvik district, in the light of the 1967 excavation. *Wiad. Archeol.*, 36, pp. 72–132.

Balmuth, M. S. & Tylecote, R. F. 1976. Ancient copper and bronze in Sardinia: excavation and analysis. *J. Fld Archaeol.*, 3, pp. 195–201.

Bandi, H.-G. 1976. Eiszeitkunst, Zoologie und Verhaltensforschung. *IXe Congr. UISPP, Nice*, Coll. XIV, pp. 146–52. Paris, CNRS.

Bandi, H.-G. & Mariner, J. 1955. *Kunst der Eiszeit*. Basel, Holbein.

Banesz, L. 1968. *Barca bei Košice: Paleolithische Fundstelle*. (Archaeol. Slovaca – Fontes, VIII.)

Banesz, L. 1976*a*. Les structures d'habitat au Paléolithique supérieur en Europe centrale. *IXe Congr. UISPP, Nice*, Coll. XIII, pp. 8–53. Paris, CNRS.

Banesz, L. 1976*b*. Quelques considérations sur l'Aurignacien en Europe et au Proche-Orient. *IXe Congr. UISPP, Nice*, Coll. XVI, pp. 178–200. Paris, CNRS.

Banesz, L. 1976*c*. L'Aurignacien en Slovaquie. *IXe Congr. UISPP, Nice*, Coll. XVI, pp. 30–50. Paris CNRS.

Barfield, L. 1971. *Northern Italy before Rome*. Thames & Hudson.

Barker, G. 1975*a*. Early Neolithic land use in Yugoslavia. *Proc. Prohist. Soc.*, 41, pp. 85–104.

Barker, G. W. W. 1975*b*. Prehistoric territories and economies in central Italy. In: E. S. Higgs (ed.), *Palaeoeconomy*, pp. 111–76. Cambridge Univ. Press.

Barker, G. & Slater, E. 1971. The first metallurgy in Italy in the light of the metal analyses from the Pigorini Museum. *Boll. Paletnol. Ital.*, n.s., 80, pp. 183–210.

Barruol, G. 1976. Civilisations de l'Âge du Fer en Languedoc. In: J. Guilaine, *La Préhistoire Française*, vol. III, pp. 676–86. Paris, CNRS.

Barta, J. & Banesz, L. 1971. Erforschung der älteren und mittleren Steinzeit in der Slowakei. *Slov. Archeol.*, 19, 2, pp. 291–317.

Barth, F. E. & Hodson, F. R. 1976. The Hallstatt Cemetery and its documentation: some new evidence. *Antiquar. J.*, 56, pp. 159–76.

Bass, G. F. 1972. The earliest seafarers in the Mediterranean and the Near East. In: G. F. Bass (ed.), *A History of Seafaring Based on Underwater Archaeology*. London, Thames & Hudson.

Bath-Bilkova, B. 1973. Zur Herkunftsfrage der Halsenringbarren. *Pam. Archeol.*, 44, pp. 38–9. (Germ. summ.)

Baumann, W. & Quietzsch, H. 1969. Zur ur- und frühgeschichtlichen Besiedlung der Lommatzscher Pflege. *Ausgrab. u. Funde*, 14, 2, pp. 64–9.

Beck, C. W. & Liu, T. 1976. Origine de l'ambre des grottes du Hasard et du Prével. *Gallia Préhist.*, 19, 1, pp. 201–8.

Behrens, H. 1972. Die Rössener, Gaterslebener und Jordansmühler Gruppe im mitteldeutschen Raum. In: F. Schwabedissen (gen. ed.), *Anfänge des Neolithikums vom Orient bis Europa*, Va, *W. Central Europe* (ed. J. Lüning), pp. 270–82.

Behrens, L. 1975. Gab es in der Entwicklung des Neolithikums im Mittelelbe-Saale-Gebiet Unterschiede in der Haustierhaltung. In: A. T. Clason (ed.), *Archaeological Studies*, pp. 395–6. Amsterdam.

Benac, A., Garasanin, M. & Tasic, N. (eds.). 1971. *Époque Préhistorique et Protohistorique en Yougoslavie. Recherches et Résultats*. Belgrade.

Bender, B. 1975. *Farming in Prehistory. From Hunter-Gatherer to Food-Producer*. John Baker.

Benoit, F. 1975. The Celtic oppidum of Entremont, Provence. In: R. Bruce-Mitford (ed.), *Recent Archaeological Investigations in Europe*, pp. 227–59. London, Routledge & Kegan Paul.

Berciu, D. 1967. *Rumania*. Thames & Hudson.

Bergmann, J. 1968. Ethnosoziologische Untersuchungen an Grab- und Hortfundgruppen der älteren Bronzezeit in Nordwestdeutschland. *Germania*, **46**, pp. 224–40.

Bergmann, J. 1970. *Die ältere Bronzezeit Nordwestdeutschlands*. Marburg.

Bernabó Brea, L. 1957. *Sicily Before the Greeks*. London, Thames & Hudson.

Bibikov, S. N. 1969. Un essai de modeler le paléolithique au point de vue paléoéconomique. *Sov. Archeol.*, **3–4**, pp. 5–22. (French summary.)

Bibikov, S. 1971. La densité de la population et l'importance des territoires de la chasse en Crimée à l'époque du paléolithique. *Sov. Archeol.*, **4**, pp. 11–22.

Bietti, A. & Mussi, M. 1976. Considerazioni sul Mesolitico in Italia sulla base dei più recenti dati. *IXe Congr. UISPP, Nice*, Coll. XIX, p. 134. Paris, CNRS.

Billy, G. 1972. L'Évolution humaine au paléolithique supérieur. *Homo*, **28**, pp. 2–12.

Binford, L. R. 1972a. *An Archaeological Perspective*. Seminar Press.

Binford, L. [R.]. 1972b. Contemporary model building: paradigms and the current state of Palaeolithic research. In: D. Clarke (ed.), *Models in Archaeology*, pp. 109–66. London, Methuen.

Binford, L. 1973. Interassemblage variability – the Mousterian and the 'functional' argument. In: C. Renfrew (ed.), *The Explanation of Culture Change*, pp. 227–54. London, Duckworth.

Binford, L. R. & Binford, S. R. (eds.). 1968. *New Perspectives in Archeology*. Aldine.

Binford, S. 1968. A structural comparison of disposal of the dead in the Mousterian and the Upper Palaeolithic. *Sthwest. J. Anthrop.*, **24**, pp. 139–54.

Bintliff, J. 1977. The history of archaeogeographic studies of prehistoric Greece, and recent fieldwork. In: J. Bintliff (ed.), *Mycenaean Geography: Proc. Cambridge Colloquium, September 1976*, pp. 3–16. Cambridge Univ. Library Press.

Bintliff, J. (ed.). 1977. *Mycenaean Geography: Proc. Cambridge Colloquium, September 1976*. Cambridge, Univ. Library Press.

Birdsell, J. B. 1972. *Human Evolution*. Chicago, Rand McNally.

Bishop, W. W. & Miller, J. A. (eds.). 1972. *Calibration of Hominoid Evolution*. Wenner-Gren Foundation.

Bitiri, M. 1976. La culture aurignacienne dans le Nord de la Roumanie. *IXe Congr. UISPP, Nice*, Coll. XVI, pp. 51–74. Paris, CNRS.

Blance, B. 1971. *Die Anfänge der Metallurgie auf der Iberischen Halbinsel*. Römisch-Germanisches Zentralmuseum. (Stud. Anfängen Metall. Bd. 4.)

Bocquet, A. 1974. Les poignards néolithiquos de Charavines (Isère) dans le cadre de la civilisation Saône-Rhône. *Étud. Préhist.*, **9**, pp. 7–17.

Boessneck, J. et al. 1933. *Seeberg Burgäschisee-Süd: Die Tierreste*. Bern. (*Acta Bernensia*, II, Tl 3.)

Boessneck, J. et al. 1971. *Die Tierknochenfunde aus dem Oppidum von Manching*. Wiesbaden, Franz Steiner Verl.

Bognar-Kutzian, I. 1972. *The Early Copper Age Tiszapolgar Culture in the Carpathian Basin*. Budapest, Akadémiai Kiado.

Bognar-Kutzian, I. 1976. The Carpathian Basin and the development of early European metallurgy. *IXe Congr. UISPP, Nice*, Résumés des Commun., p. 421. Paris, CNRS.

Boisaubert, J.-L., Schifferdecker, F. & Pétrequin, P. 1974. Les villages néolithiques de Clairvaux (Jura, France) et d'Auvernier (Neuchâtel, Suisse). Problèmes d'interprétations des plans. *Bull. Soc. Préhist. Fr.*, **71**, pp. 355–82.

Bökönyi, S. 1969. The vertebrate fauna of the prehistoric settlement at Lepenski Vir. *Archaeol. Ért.*, **96**, p. 157–60.

Bolomey, A. 1973. An outline of the late Epipalaeolithic economy at the 'Iron Gates': the evidence on bones. *Dacia*, **17**, pp. 41–52.

Bonifay, E. 1975. Stratigraphie du quaternaire et âge des gisements préhistoriques de la zone littorale des Alpes-Maritimes. *Bull. Soc. Préhist. Fr.*, 72, C.R.s.m., 7, pp. 197-208.

Bordes, F. 1968a. *Old Stone Age*. London, Weidenfeld & Nicolson.

Bordes, F. 1968b. Emplacements de tentes du Périgordien supérieur évolué à Corbiac (près Bergerac), Dordogne. *Quatär*, 18/19, pp. 251-62.

Bordes, F. 1970a. *A Tale of Two Caves*. New York, Harper & Row.

Bordes, F. 1970b. Rapport de la direction de la circonscription des antiquités préhistoriques–Dordogne. *Gallia Préhist.*, 13, pp. 502-4.

Bordes, F. 1974. Notes de typologie paléolithique. *Zephyrus*, 25, pp. 53-64.

Bosinski, G. 1969. Der Magdalénien-Fundplatz Feldkirchen-Gönnersdorf, Kr. Neuwied. *Germania*, 47, pp. 1-38.

Bosinski, G. 1976a. Middle Paleolithic structural remains from western central Europe. *IXe Congr. UISPP, Nice*, Coll. XI, pp. 64-77. Paris, CNRS.

Bosinski, G. 1976b. L'art mobilier paléolithique dans l'Ouest de l'Europe centrale et ses rapports possibles avec le monde franco-cantabrique et méditerranéen. *IXe Congr. UISPP, Nice*, Coll. XIV, pp. 97-117. Paris, CNRS.

Bouchud, J. 1966. *Essai sur le renne et la climatologie du paléolithique moyen et supérieur*. Périgueux.

Bouzek, J., Jäger, K. D. & Lozek, V. 1976. Climatic and settlement changes in the Central European Bronze Age. *IXe Congr. UISPP, Nice*, sect. VII, p. 2. Paris, CNRS.

Briard, J. 1973. Bronze Age Cultures 1800-600 B.C. In: S. Piggott, G. Daniel & C. McBurney (eds.), *France Before the Romans*, pp. 131-56. Thames & Hudson.

Brinch Petersen, E. 1970. Ølby Lyng. An Ertebølle coastal settlement in eastern Sjaelland. In: *Aarb. Nord. Oldkyndig Hist.*, pp. 5-42. (Engl. summ. pp. 38-42.)

Brinch Petersen, E. 1971. Svaerdborg II. A Maglemose hut from Svaerdborg bog, Zealand, Denmark. *Acta Archaeol.*, 42, pp. 43-77.

Brinch Petersen, E. 1973. A survey of the Late Palaeolithic and the Mesolithic of Denmark. In: S. K. Kozlowski (ed.), *The Mesolithic in Europe*, pp. 77-127.

Brinch Petersen, E. 1976. Maglemose art and culture in Denmark. In: P. Mellars (ed.), *Conf. Early Post-Glacial Settlement of North-West Europe: Economic and Social Perspectives*. (In press.)

Briuer, F. 1976. New clues to stone tool function: plant and animal residues. *Am. Antiq.*, 41, pp. 478-83.

Broglio, A. 1976. L'epipaléolithique de la Vallée du Po. *IXe Congr. UISPP, Nice*, Coll. XIX, pp. 9-31. Paris, CNRS.

Bruce-Mitford, R. (ed.). 1975. *Recent Archaeological Investigations in Europe*. London, Routledge & Kegan Paul.

Brunnacker, K. 1975. The Mid-Pleistocene of the Rhine Basin. In: K. W. Butzer & G. Isaac (eds.), *After the Australopithecines*, pp. 189-224. The Hague, Mouton.

Bryson, R. A., Lamb, H. H. & Donley, D. L. 1974. Drought and the decline of Mycenae. *Antiquity*, 48, pp. 46-50.

Bukowski, Z. 1974. Besiedlungscharakter der Lausitzer Kultur in der Hallstattzeit am Beispiel Schlesiens und Grosspolens. In: B. Chropovský (ed.), *Symp. Problemen der jüngeren Hallstattzeit in Mitteleuropa*, pp. 15-40. Bratislava.

Bulgarian Committee for Art and Culture and Trustees of the British Museum. 1976. *Thracian Treasures from Bulgaria*. London, British Museum Publs.

Burchard, B. 1973. The investigation of a Neolithic trapezoid-shaped building at Niedzwiedz, District of Miechow (Site 1). *Spraw. Archaeol.*, 25, pp. 39-48.

Burgess, C. & Miket, R. (eds.). 1976. *Settlement and Economy in the Third and Second Millennia B.C.* Oxford. (Br. Archaeol. Rep. 33.)

Burleigh, R., Longworth, I. H. & Wainwright, G. J. 1972. Relative and absolute dating of four Late Neolithic enclosures: an exercise in the interpretation of radiocarbon determinations. *Proc. Prehist. Soc.*, 38, pp. 389–407.

Burow, G. M. 1973. Die Mesolithischen Kulturen im äussersten Europäischen Nordosten. In: S. K. Kozlowski (ed.), *The Mesolithic in Europe*, pp. 129–49.

Butler, J. & van der Waals, J. 1964. Metal analysis, SAM 1, and European prehistory. *Helinium*, 4, pp. 3–39.

Butzer, K. W. & Isaac, G. (eds.). 1975. *After the Australopithecines*. The Hague, Mouton. (World Anthropology ser.)

Cadogan, G. 1976. *Palaces of Minoan Crete*. London, Barrie & Jenkins.

Camps, G. 1976. Navigations et relations interméditerranéennes préhistoriques. *IXe Congr. UISPP, Nice*, Coll. II, pp. 168–79. Paris, CNRS.

Camps-Fabrer, H. 1974. *Premier Colloque International sur l'Industrie de l'Os dans la Préhistoire*. Univ. de Provence.

Capitanu, V. 1976. L'établissement fortifié dacique de Racatau. *IXe Congr. UISPP*, Commun. p. 581. Paris, CNRS.

Carciumaru, M. 1973. Analyse pollinique des coprolithes livrés par quelques stations archéologiques des deux bords du Danube dans la zone des 'Portes de Fer'. *Dacia*, 17, pp. 53–60.

Cardini, L. 1946. Gli strati mesolitici e paleolitici della Caverna delle Arene Candide. *Riv. Stud. Liguri*, 12, pp. 29–37.

Carlisle, R. C. & Siegel, M. I. 1974. Some problems in the interpretation of Neanderthal speech capabilities: a reply to Lieberman. *Am. Anthrop.*, 19, pp. 319–22.

Carraro, F. *et al.* 1976. Studio interdisciplinare del 'rilievo isolato' di Trino (bassa pianura vercellese, Piemonte). *Gruppo Stud. Quat. Padano*, 3, pp. 161–253.

Case, H. 1969. Neolithic explanations. *Antiquity*, XLIII, 171, pp. 176–86.

Casino, E. S. 1976. Peuplement ancien d'Extrême-Orient. *IXe Congr. UISPP, Nice*, Coll. VI, pp. 409–24. Paris, CNRS.

Catling, H. W., Richards, E. E. & Blin-Stoyle, A.C. 1963. Correlations between composition and provenance of Mycenaean pottery. *Br. Sch. Athens J.*, 58, pp. 94–115.

Centre de Recherche Protohistorique de l'Université de Paris (CRPUP). 1976. *Les Fouilles Protohistoriques dars la Vallée de l'Aisne*. CNRS. (Rapport d'activité 4.)

Cerda, F. J. 1974. Formas de vida económica en el arte rupestre levantino. *Zephyrus*, 25, pp. 209–23.

Cerda, F. J. & Fortea Perez, J. 1976. El Paleolítico superior y Epipaleolítico mediterráneo español en el cuadro del Mediterráneo occidental. *IXe Congr. UISPP, Nice*, Coll. II, pp. 99–127. Paris, CNRS.

Cernych, E. N. 1976. Metallurgische Bereiche des 4–2. Jahrt. v. Chr. in der Udssr. *IXe Congr. UISPP, Nice*, Coll. XXIII, pp. 177–208. Paris, CNRS.

Ceruti, M. 1967. Domus de jana in località Monumentos (Benetutti, Sassari). *Boll. Paletnol. Ital.*, 18, pp. 69–136.

Chadwick, A. 1977. Computer simulation of settlement development in Bronze Age Messenia. In: J. Bintliff (ed.), *Mycenaean Geography: Proc. Cambridge Colloquium, September 1976*, pp. 88–93. Cambridge, Univ. Library Press.

Chadwick, J. 1972. The Mycenaean documents. In: W. A. McDonald & G. R. Rapp Jr (eds.), *The Minnesota Messenia Expedition*, pp. 100–16. Univ. of Minnesota.

Chaline, J. 1975. Le Quaternaire raconté par les rongeurs. *Sci. Avenir*, 335, pp. 76–81.

Chaplin, R. E. 1975. The ecology and behaviour of deer in relation to their impact on the environment of prehistoric Britain. In: J. G. Evans, S. Limbrey & H. Cleere (eds.), *The Effect of Man on the Landscape: the Highland Zone*, pp. 40–42.

Charles, J. A. 1967. Early arsenical bronzes: a metallurgical view. *Am. J. Archaeol.*, 71, 1, pp. 21–6.

Charles, J. A. 1973. Heterogeneity in metals. *Archaeometry*, 15, 1, pp. 105–14.

Cherry, J. 1977. Investigating the political geography of the early state by multidimensional scaling of Linear B tablet data. In: J. Bintliff (ed.), *Mycenaean Geography: Proc. Cambridge Colloquium, September 1976*, pp. 76–83. Cambridge, Univ. Library Press.

Childe, V. Gordon 1925, rev. ed. 1955. *Dawn of European Civilisation*. London, Routledge & Kegan Paul.

Childe, V. G. 1958. *The Prehistory of European Society*. Harmondsworth, Middx, Penguin.

Chmielewski, W. 1971. The continuity and discontinuity of the evolution of archaeological cultures in Central and East Europe between LV and XXV millenaries B.C. *Archaeol. Pol.*, 16, pp. 61–74. (Engl. summ.)

Chronicle (BBC 2). 16 January 1976. *The Gold of the Thracian Horsemen.*

Chropovský, B., Dusek, M. & Podborsky, V. 1974. *Symp. Problemen der jüngeren Hallstattzeit in Mitteleuropa.* Bratislava.

Clark, J. G. D. 1965. Radiocarbon dating and the expansion of farming culture from the Near East over Europe. *Proc. Prehist. Soc.*, 31, pp. 58–73.

Clark, J. G. D. 1969, 1977. *World Prehistory.* Cambridge Univ. Press.

Clark, J. G. D. 1970. *Aspects of Prehistory.* Univ. of California Press.

Clark, J. G. D. 1974. Star Carr: a case study in bioarchaeology. *McCaleb Module*, No. 10, pp. 1–42.

Clark, J. G. D. 1975. *The earlier Stone Age settlement of Scandinavia.* Cambridge Univ. Press.

Clark, J. G. D. & Piggott, S. 1965. *Prehistoric Societies.* Harmondsworth, Middx, Penguin.

Clark, R. J. 1976. New cranium of *Homo*

erectus from Lake Ndutu, Tanzania. *Nature*, 262, pp. 485–7.

Clarke, D. L. 1968. *Analytical Archaeology.* Methuen.

Clarke, D. L. 1972. A provisional paradigm of an Iron Age society. In: D. L. Clarke (ed.), *Models in Archaeology*, pp. 801–69.

Clarke, D. L. (ed.). 1972. *Models in Archaeology.* London, Methuen.

Clarke, D. L. 1973. Archaeology: the loss of innocence. *Antiquity*, 57, pp. 6–18.

Clarke, D. L. 1976a. Mesolithic Europe: the economic basis. In: G. de G. Sieveking, I. H. Longworth & K. E. Wilson (eds.), *Problems in Economic and Social Archaeology*, pp. 449–81. London, Duckworth.

Clarke, D. L. 1976b. The Beaker network – social and economic models. In: N. Lanting & J. D. van der Waals (eds.), *Glockenbecher Symp., Oberried, 1974*, pp. 459–77.

Clason, A. T. 1971. Die Jagd- und Haustiere der mitteldeutschen Schnurkeramik. *Jschr. Mitteldt. Vorgesch.*, 55, pp. 105–12.

Clason, A. T. (ed.) 1975. *Archaeological Studies.* Amsterdam.

Clottes, J. 1973. Informations archéologiques. Circonscription des antiquités préhistoriques Midi-Pyrénées. *Gallia Préhist.*, 16, 2, pp. 489–92.

Coblenz, W. 1971. Die Lausitzer Kultur der Bronze- und frühen Eisenzeit Ostmitteleuropas als Forschungsproblem. *Ethnogr.-Archäol. Z.*, 12, pp. 425–38.

Coblenz, W. 1974a. Internationales Kolloquium über den Beginn der Bronzezeit in Zentral- und Osteuropa, Igolomia bei Krakow 1973. *Ethnogr.-Archäol. Z.*, 15, pp. 332–5.

Coblenz, W. 1974b. Die Burgwälle und das Ausklingen der westlichen Lausitzer Kultur. In: B. Chropovský, M. Dusek & V. Podborsky (eds.), *Symp. Problemen der jüngeren Hallstattzeit in Mitteleuropa*, pp. 85–100. Bratislava.

Coles, J. 1969. Metal analyses and the

Scottish Early Bronze Age. *Proc. Prehist. Soc.*, 35, pp. 330–44.

Coles, J. 1973. *Archaeology by Experiment.* Hutchinson.

Coles, J. M. 1976a. Forest farmers: some archaeological, historic and experimental evidence relating to the prehistory of Europe. In: S. J. De Laet (ed.), *Acculturation and Continuity in Atlantic Europe*, pp. 59–66. (Diss. Archaeol. Gandenses XVI.)

Coles, J. M. 1976b. The origins of metallurgy in the British Isles. *IXe Congr. UISPP, Nice*, Coll. XXIII, pp. 15–17. Paris, CNRS.

Coles, J. & Taylor, J. 1971. The Wessex culture: a minimal view. *Antiquity*, XLV, 177, pp. 6–14.

Coles, J., Orme, B., Bishop, A. C. & Woolley, A. R. 1974. A jade axe from the Somerset Levels. *Antiquity*, 48, pp. 216–20.

Collins, D. 1976. The geography of the European Lower Palaeolithic. *IXe Congr. UISPP, Nice*, Coll. X, pp. 156–65. Paris, CNRS.

Collins, M. B. 1975. Lithic technology as a means of processual inference. In: E. Swanson (ed.), *Lithic Technology: Making and Using Stone Tools*, pp. 15–33. Mouton.

Collis, J. 1973. Manching reviewed. *Antiquity*, XLVII, 188, pp. 280–83.

Collis, J. 1975. *Defended Sites of the Late La Tène.* (Br. Archaeol. Rep., Oxf. Suppl. Ser. 2.)

Collis, J. 1977a. An approach to the Iron Age. In: J. Collis (ed.), *The Iron Age in Britain – a Review*, pp. 1–7. Sheffield Univ. Press.

Collis, J. (ed.). 1977b. *The Iron Age in Britain – a Review.* Sheffield Univ. Press.

Collison, D. & Hooper, A. 1976. Nouvelles informations sur la Grotte des Eglises à Ussat (Ariège). *Préhist. Ariég.*, 31, pp. 13–20.

Combier, J. 1976. Stades évolutifs et faciès du Paléolithique inférieur dans le bassin du Rhône et l'Est du Massif Central. *IXe Congr. UISPP, Nice*, Coll. X, pp. 134–5. Paris, CNRS.

Comsa, E. 1976. Les quatre agglomérations néolithiques superposées de Radovanu. *Préhist. Ariég.*, 31, pp. 63–70.

Concev, D. & Milcev, A. 1970. Fouilles et recherches dans le bassin de retenue du barrage de Batak. *Izv. Arkheol. Inst.*, 32, pp. 149–205. (French summary.)

Contu, E. 1964. *La tomba dei vasi tetrapodi in località Santu Pedru (Alghero-Sassari).* Accademia Nazionale de Lincei, Rome. (Monum. Antichi XLVII.)

Coombs, D. 1975. The Dover Harbour bronze find – a Bronze Age wreck? *Archaeol. Atlant.*, 7, 2, pp. 193–5.

Coombs, D. 1976. Callis Wold round barrow, Humberside. *Antiquity*, 198, 130–31.

Coppens, Y. et al. (eds.). 1976. *Earliest Man and Environments in the Lake Rudolf Basin.* Chicago, Univ. of Chicago.

Courtin, J. 1974. *Le Néolithique de la Provence.* Paris, Klinksieck.

Courtin, J. 1976. Le Camp de Laure, Le Rove (Bouches-du-Rhône). In: M. Escalon de Fonton (ed.), Rapport de la Direction des Antiquités Préhistoriques de Provence-Côte d'Azur, *Gallia Préhist.*, 19, pp 589–93.

Courtin, J., Gagnière, S., Granier, J., Ledoux, J. C. & Onoratini, G. 1970–72. La Grotte du Cap Ragnon, commune du Rove (Bouches-du-Rhône). *Bull. Soc. d'Etud. Sci. Nat. Vaucluse*, pp. 113–70.

Crelin, E. S. 1973. The Steinheim skull: a linguistic link. *Yale Sci. Mag.*, 48, pp. 10–14.

CRPUP. See Centre de Recherche Protohistorique de l'Université de Paris.

Crumley, C. 1974. *Celtic Social Structure: the Generation of Archaeologically Testable Hypotheses from Literary Evidence.* Museum of Anthropology, Univ. of Michigan. (Anthropological Papers 54.)

Cubuk, G. A. 1976. Erste Altpaläolithische Funde in Griechenland bei Nea Skala,

Kephallinia (Ionische Inseln). *IXe Congr. UISPP, Nice*, Coll. VIII, pp. 152-77. Paris, CNRS.

Cullberg, C. 1972. Hasslingehult Göteberg, settlement area, Late Stone Age. *Fynd Rapp.*, 1972, pp. 375-448.

Cullberg, K. 1972. Distribution of Late Bronze Age settlements. *Fynd Rapp.*, 1972, pp. 3-64.

Cummins, W. A. 1974. The neolithic stone axe trade in Britain. *Antiquity*, XLVIII, 191, pp. 201-5.

Cunliffe, B. 1974. *Iron Age Communities in Britain*. London, Routledge & Kegan Paul.

Cunliffe, B. 1976. Hill forts and oppida in Britain. In: G. de G. Sieveking, I. H. Longworth & K. E. Wilson (eds.), *Problems in Economic and Social Archaeology*, pp. 343-58. London, Duckworth.

Dagnan-Ginter, A. 1976. L'outillage sur éclat dans le paléolithique supérieur d'Europe Centrale. *IXe Congr. UISPP, Nice*, Résumés des Commun., pp. 173-6. Paris, CNRS.

Daniel, G. 1970. Megalithic answers. *Antiquity*, **43**, pp. 260-9.

Daniels, S. 1972. Research design models. In: D. L. Clarke (ed.), *Models in Archaeology*, pp. 201-29.

Dastugue, J. 1973. Les crânes trépanés de la Vallée du Petit-Mason. *Bull. Mém. Soc. d'Anthropol. Paris*, **10**, pp. 249-63.

Dastugue, J., Torre, S. & Buchet, L. 1973. Néolithiques de Basse-Normandie. Le deuxième tumulus de Fontenay-le-Marmion. *L'Anthropologie*, **77**, 5-6, pp. 579-620.

Davidson, I. 1976. Las Mallaetes and Monduver: the economy of a human group in prehistoric Spain. In: G. de G. Sieveking, I. H. Longworth & K. E. Wilson (eds.), *Problems in Economic and Social Archaeology*, pp. 483-99. London, Duckworth.

Dehn, W. 1972. 'Transhumance' in der westlichen Späthallstattkultur? *Archäol. KorrespBl.*, **2**, pp. 125-7.

Dehn, W. 1974. Einige Bemerkungen zum eisenzeitlichen Befestigungswesen in Mitteleuropa. In: B. Chropovský, M. Dusek & V. Podborsky (eds.), *Symp. Problemen der jüngeren Hallstattzeit in Mitteleuropa*, pp. 125-36. Bratislava.

De Laet, S. J. (ed.). 1976. *Acculturation and Continuity in Atlantic Europe*. (Diss. Archaeol. Gandenses XVI.)

Delibrias, G. & Le Roux, C.-T. 1975. Un exemple d'application des datations radiocarbone à l'interprétation d'une stratigraphie complexe: la fouille des ateliers de Plussulien (Côtes-du-Nord). *Bull. Soc. Prehist. Fr.*, **72**, pp. 78-83.

Delpech, F. & Prat, F. 1976. Évolution des faunes au cours du paléolithique dans le Sud-Ouest de la France. *IXe Congr. UISPP, Nice*, Livret-guide A4, pp. 192-7. Paris, CNRS.

Delporte, H. 1976. Typologie et technologie de l'art paléolithique mobilier. *IXe Congr. UISPP, Nice*, Coll. XIV, pp. 37-53. Paris, CNRS.

de Lumley, H. 1969a. A Paleolithic camp at Nice. *Sci. Am.*, **220**, pp. 42-50.

de Lumley, H. (ed.). 1969b. Une cabane acheuléenne dans la grotte du Lazaret. *Mém. Soc. Préhist. Fr.*, **7**.

de Lumley, H. 1971. L'homme de Tautavel. *Courrier (Centre National de la Recherche Scientifique, Paris)*, **2**, pp. 16-20.

de Lumley, H. (ed.). 1972. *La Grotte de L'Hortus (Valflaunès, Hérault)*. (Et. Quat., Mém. no. 1.)

de Lumley, H. (ed.). 1976a. *La Préhistoire Moderne*, vols. I, II.

de Lumley. 1976b. *IXe Congr. UISPP, Nice*, Livret-Guide B1. Paris, CNRS.

Dembińska, M. 1971. O metodach badań paleobotanicznych. *Archaeol. Pol.*, **16**, pp. 45-60.

de Navarro, J. M. 1972. *The Finds from the Site of La Tène 1. Scabbards and the Swords Found in Them*. British Academy.

Dennell, R. & Legge, A. J. 1973. Plant remains. In: Recent excavations at Nahal Oren, Israel (by T. Noy, A. J.

Legge & E. S. Higgs), *Proc. Prehist. Soc.*, **39**, pp. 91–3.

Dennell, R. W. 1976. The economic importance of plant resources represented on archaeological sites. *J. Archaeol. Sci.*, **3**, pp. 229–47.

Dennell, R. W. & Webley, D. 1975. Prehistoric settlement and land use in southern Bulgaria. In: E. S. Higgs (ed.), *Palaeoeconomy*, pp. 97–110. Cambridge Univ. Press.

Dent, J. 1978. Wetwang slack. *Curr. Archaeol.*, **61**, pp. 46–50.

Diamond, J. A. 1977. Colonization cycles in man and beast. *Wld Archaeol.*, **8**, pp. 249–61.

Dickinson, O. 1977. Mycenaean geography: an Archaeological viewpoint. In: J. Bintliff (ed.), *Mycenaean Geography: Proc. Cambridge Colloquium, September 1976*, pp. 18–21. Cambridge, Univ. Library Press.

Dinu, M. 1974. Le problème des tombes à ocre dans la région orientale de la Roumanie. *Preist. Alp.*, **10**, pp. 261–75.

Dixon, J. E., Cann, J. R. & Renfrew, C. 1968. Obsidian and the origins of trade. *Sci. Am.*, **218**, pp. 38–46.

Dobosi, V. T. 1975. Register of Palaeolithic and Mesolithic sites in Hungary. *Archaeol. Ért.*, **102**, 1, pp. 64–76.

Doluchanov, P. M. 1971. Zur absoluten Chronologie und Paläogeographie des Neolithikums im europäischen Teil der USSR. *Ethnogr.-Archäol. Z.*, **12**, pp. 381–2.

Doran, J. E. & Hodson, F. R. 1975. *Mathematics and Computers in Archaeology*. Edinburgh Univ. Press.

Doumas, C. 1974. The Minoan eruption of the Santorini volcano. *Antiquity*, **XLVIII**, pp. 110–15.

Driehaus, J. 1970. Urgeschichtliche Opferfunde aus dem Mittel- und Niederrhein. *Abh. Akad. Wiss. Göttingen*, **24**, pp. 40–54.

Dumitrescu, V. 1974. La cronologia dell'Eneolitico rumeno alla luce degli esami C14. *Preist. Alp.*, **10**, pp. 99–105.

Dusek, M. 1974. Der junghallstattzeitliche

Fürstensitz auf dem Molpir bei Smolenice. In: B. Chropovský, M. Dusek & V. Podborsky (eds.), *Symp. Problemen der jüngeren Hallstattzeit in Mitteleuropa*, pp. 137–50. Bratislava.

Duval, P.-M. & Kruta, V. (eds.). 1975. *L'Habitat et la Nécropole à l'Âge du Fer en Europe Occidentale et Centrale*. Paris

Dzambazov, N. 1969. Trouvailles du Paléolithique Ancien près de Nikopol. *Arkheol. (Sofia)*, **11**, pp. 55–67.

Dzieduszycka Machnik, A. & Machnik, J. 1974. Frühbronzezeitlicher Siedlungskomplex in Iwanowice (Kleinpolen) und seine Verhinderungen mit dem Karpatenbecken. *Preist. Alp.*, **10**, pp. 57–66.

Egloff, M. 1972. *Archéologie et Routes Nationales*. Neuchâtel. (Catalogue d'exposition.)

Elster, E. S. 1976. The chipped stone industry. In: M. Gimbutas, *Neolithic Macedonia*, pp. 257–78. UCLA.

Engelmark Olsson, I. U., Renberg, I. & Zackrisson, O. 1976. Palaeoecological investigations in coastal Västerbotten, N. Sweden. *Early Norrland*, **9**.

Eogan, G. 1969. Excavations at Knowth, Co. Meath, 1968. *Antiquity*, **169**, pp. 8–14.

Escalon de Fonton, M. 1976. La constitution de l'Épipaléolithique et du Mésolithique dans le Midi de la France. *IXe Congr. UISPP, Nice*, Coll. XIX, pp. 53–70. Paris, CNRS.

Esin, U. 1976. Die Anfänge der Metallverwendung und Bearbeitung in Anatolien (7500–2000 v. Chr). *IXe Congr. UISPP, Nice*, Coll. XXIII, pp. 209–45. Paris, CNRS.

Evans, J. D. 1971a. Neolithic Knossos. The growth of a settlement. *Proc. Prehist. Soc.*, **37**, pp. 95–117.

Evans, J. D. 1971b. *The Prehistoric Antiquities of the Maltese Islands: a Survey*. London, Athlone.

Evans, J. D. 1976. Village, town and city: some thoughts on the prehistoric background to urban civilization in the

Aegean and Italy. In: G. de G. Sieveking, I. H. Longworth & K. E. Wilson (eds.), *Problems in Economic and Social Archaeology*, pp. 501–12. London, Duckworth.

Evans, J. D. & Renfrew, C. 1968. *Excavations at Saliagos, near Antiparos.* Cambridge Univ. Press.

Evans, J. G. 1975. *The Environment of Early Man in the British Isles.* London, Elek.

Evans, J. G., Limbrey, S. & Cleere, H. (eds.). 1975. *The Effect of Man on the Landscape: the Highland Zone.* Council for British Archaeology. (Res. Rep. no. 11.)

Farrugia, J. P., Kuper R., Lüning J. & Stehli, P. 1973. Untersuchungen zur neolitischen Besiedlung der Aldenhovener Platte III. *Bonn. Jb.*, **173**, pp. 226–56.

Fedele, F. 1974. Scoperte paletnologiche a Trino Vercellese. Notizia preliminare. *Stud. Trentine Sci. Nat.*, **51**, pp. 175–83.

Fejfar, O. 1969. Human remains from the Early Pleistocene in Czechoslovakia. *Curr. Anthrop.*, **10**, 2–3, pp. 170–73.

Ferembach, D. 1972. L'ancêtre de l'homme du paléolithique supérieur, était-il néanderthalien? In: Unesco, *The Origin of Homo Sapiens: Proc. Paris Symposium, 1969*, pp. 73–9. Paris, Unesco.

Ferembach, D. 1973. Les hommes du bassin méditerranéen à l'Épipaléolithique. In: F. Schwabedissen (gen. ed.), *Anfänge des Neolithikums vom Orient bis Europa*, VIII, Anthropologie (ed. I. Schwidetzky), pp. 1–27.

Ferguson, C. W., Gimbutas, M. & Suess, H. E. 1976. Historical dates for Neolithic sites of southeast Europe. *Science*, **191**, pp. 1170–2.

Fernándes-Miranda, M. & Moure, A. 1974. Verdelpino (Cuenca): nuevas fechas de C-14 para el neolítico peninsular. *Trab. Prehist.*, **31**, pp. 311–16.

Feustel, R. 1974. *Die Kniegrotte. Eine Magdalénien-station in Thüringen.* Weimar.

Filip, J. 1971. Die Keltische Besiedlung Mittel- und Südosteuropas und das problem der zugehörigen Oppida. *Archeol. Rozhl.*, **23**, pp. 263–72.

Fischer, F. von. 1973. Keimhaia: Bemerkungen zur kulturgeschichtlichen Interpretation des sogenannten Südimports in der späten Hallstatt- und frühen Latene-Kultur des westlichen Mitteleuropa. *Germania*, **51**, pp. 436–9.

Fitzhugh, W. (ed.). 1975. *Prehistoric Maritime Adaptations of the Circumpolar Zone.* The Hague, Mouton.

Fleming, A. 1972. Vision and design: approaches to ceremonial monument typology. *Man*, **7**, pp. 57–73.

Fleming, A. 1973. Models for the development of the Wessex culture. In: C. Renfrew (ed.), *The Explanation of Culture Change*, pp. 571–85. Duckworth.

Fleming, A. 1976. Early settlement and the landscape in west Yorkshire. In: G. de G. Sieveking, I. H. Longworth & K. E. Wilson (eds.), *Problems in Economic and Social Archaeology*, pp. 359–73. London, Duckworth.

Fleming, S. J., Keisch, B. & Callahan, R. C. 1976. Bronze provenance and chronology: a new approach using mass spectroscopy and thermoluminescence. (Paper presented at) *Int. Symp. Archaeometry and Archaeological Prospection, Edinburgh (1976)*.

Fornaca-Rinaldi, G. & Radmilli, A. M. 1968. Datazione con il metodo $Th^{2\cdot 0}/U^{238}$ di stalagmiti contenute in depositi Mousteriani. *Atti Soc. Toscana Sci. Nat. (Pisa)*, Ser. A, **75**, 2, pp. 639–46.

Fortea Perez, F. J. 1975. Algunas aportaciones a los problemes del arte levantino. *Zephyrus*, **24**, pp. 225–57.

Fortea Perez, F. J. 1976. El arte parietal epipaleolítico del 6° al 5° milenio y su sustitución por el arte levantino. *IXe Congr. UISPP*, Nice, Coll. XIX, pp. 121–33. Paris, CNRS.

Frankenstein, S. M. 1977. *The Impact of Phoenician and Greek Expansion on the Early Iron Age Societies of southern Iberia and southwestern Germany.* Institute of Archaeology, Univ. of London. (Ph.D thesis.)

Freeman, L. G. 1973. The significance of mammalian faunas from Paleolithic occupations in Cantabrian Spain. *Am. Antiq.*, 38, pp. 3–44.

Freeman, L. G. 1975. Acheulian sites and stratigraphies in Iberia and the Maghreb. In: K. W. Butzer & G. Isaac (eds.), *After the Australopithecines*, pp. 661–743. The Hague, Mouton.

Freeman, L. G. 1976. Middle Paleolithic dwelling remnants from Spain. *IXe Congr. UISPP, Nice*, Coll. XI, pp. 35–48. Paris, CNRS.

Freund, G. 1974/5. Ein jüngpaläolithischer Depotfund aus der Sesselfelsgrotte in Unteren Altmühltal. *Jb. Fränk. LdForsch.*, Bd 34/35, pp. 17–36.

Freund, G. 1975. Zum Stand der Ausgrabungen in der Sesselfelsgrotte im Unteren Altmühltal. *Ausgrabungen in Deutschland*, I, pp. 25–41. Monogr. Römisch-Germ. Zentralmuseum 1.

Fridrich, G. 1972. Altpaläolitische Industrie aus dem Altpleistozän in Prezletice, Kr. Prague-Ost. *Archeol. Rozhl.*, 24, 3, pp. 241–8.

Fridrich, J. 1976. The first industries from eastern and south eastern Central Europe. *IXe Congr. UISPP, Nice*, Coll. VIII, pp. 8–23. Paris, CNRS.

Furmánek, V. 1973. Zu einiger sozialökonomischen Problemen der Bronzezeit. *Slov. Archeol.*, 21, 2, pp. 401–8.

Furumark, A. 1941a. *The Mycenaean Pottery, Analysis and Classification.* Stockholm.

Furumark, A. 1941b. *The Chronology of Mycenaean Pottery.* Stockholm.

Gábori, M. 1976a. *Les Civilisations du Paléolithique Moyen entre les Alpes et l'Oural.* Budapest, Akadémiai Kiado.

Gábori, M. 1976b. Le rôle du Paléolithique de Transcaucasie dans le peuplement de l'Europe Orientale. *IXe Congr.*

UISPP, Nice, Coll. VII, pp. 180–99. Paris, CNRS.

Gábori-Csánk, V. 1968. *La Station du Paléolithique Moyen d'Erd, Hongrie.* Budapest. (Monum. Hist. Budapest. III.)

Gábori-Csánk, V. 1970. C-14 dates of the Hungarian Palaeolithic. *Acta Archaeol. Acad. Sci. Hung.*, 22, pp. 3–11.

Gábori-Csánk, V. 1976. Le mode de vie et l'habitat au Paléolithique moyen en Europe centrale. *IXe Congr. UISPP, Nice*, Coll. XI, pp. 78–104. Paris, CNRS.

Gale, N. H. 1978. *Lead Isotopes and Aegean Metallurgy.* (Paper delivered at Science and Archaeology Symposium, Bradford.)

Gallay, A. 1972. Recherches préhistoriques au Petit-Chasseur à Sion. *Helv. archaeol.*, 10/11, pp. 35–61.

Gallay, A. 1976. Origine et expansion de la civilisation du Rhône. *IXe Congr. UISPP, Nice*, Coll. XXVI, pp. 5–26. Paris, CNRS.

Gallay, G. & Spindler, K. 1972. Le Petit-Chasseur – chronologische und kulturelle Probleme. *Helv. archaeol.*, 10/11, pp. 62–87.

Garrido Roiz, J. P. 1973. Las nuevas campañas de excavaciones arqueológicas en la necrópolis orientalizante de la Joya en Huelva. *XIIo Congr. Arqueol. Nac. de Arqueol., Jaén*, pp. 395–400.

Georgiev, G. I. & Merpert, N. J. 1966. The Ezero mound in south-eastern Bulgaria. *Antiquity*, XL, 157, pp. 33–7.

Gersbach, E. 1974. Vorläufige Ergebnisse der Ausgrabungen 1959–1969 auf der Heuneburg (die Siedlungsstadien der Periode IV). In: B. Chropovský, M. Dusek & V. Podborsky (eds.), *Symp. Problemen der jüngeren Hallstattzeit in Mitteleuropa*, pp. 189–204. Bratislava.

Gimbutas, M. 1965. *Bronze Age Cultures in Central and Eastern Europe.* Mouton.

Gimbutas, M. 1973. The beginning of the Bronze Age in Europe and the Indo-Europeans 3500–2500 B.C. *J. Indo-eur. Stud.*, 1, 2, pp. 163–214.

Gimbutas, M. 1974a. Achilleion: a neolithic mound in Thessaly. *J. Fld Archaeol.*, 1, pp. 277–302.

Gimbutas, M. 1974b. Anza, ca. 6500–5000 B.C.: a cultural yardstick for the Study of Neolithic southeast Europe. *J. Fld Archaeol.*, 1, pp. 26–66.

Gimbutas, M. 1974c. *The Gods and Goddesses of Old Europe 7000–3500 B.C. Myths, Legends and Cult Images.* London, Thames & Hudson.

Gimbutas, M. 1974d. The mask in old Europe from 6500 to 3500 B.C., *Archaeology*, 27, 4, pp. 262–9.

Gimbutas, M. 1976. *Neolithic Macedonia*, UCLA. (Monum. Archaeol. 1.)

Ginter, B. 1973. Remarks on the origins of some Mesolithic cultures in Poland. In: S. K. Kozlowski (ed.), *The Mesolithic in Europe*, pp. 177–86.

Glenn, E. J. 1976. Early Bronze Age populations in Scotland. *IXe Congr. UISPP, Nice*, Sect. VI. Paris, CNRS. (Paper.)

Glob, P. 1974. *The Mound People.* London, Faber.

Glodiaru, I. 1976. La metallurgie du fer en Dacie (époque La Tène). *IXe Congr. UISPP, Nice*, Commun. p. 561. Paris, CNRS.

Golson, J. & Hughes, P. J. 1976. The appearance of plant and animal domestication in New Guinea. *IXe Congr. UISPP, Nice*, Coll. XXII, pp. 88–100. Paris, CNRS.

González Echegaray, J., Freeman, L. G. et al. 1971. *Cueva Morín: Excavaciones 1966–8.* (Publs del Patronato de las Cuevas Prehistóricas de la Provincia de Santander VI.)

González Echegaray, J., Freeman, I. G. et al. 1973. *Cueva Morín: Excavaciones 1969.* (Publs del Patronato de las Cuevas Prehistóricas de la Provincia de Santander X.)

Gramsch, B. 1973. *Das Mesolithikum im Flachland zwischen Elbe und Oder.* Berlin.

Gramsch, B. 1976. Bemerkungen zur Palökologie und zur Besiedlung während des jüngeren Boreals und des älteren Atlantikums im nordlichen Mitteleuropa. *IXe Congr. UISPP, Nice*, Coll. XIX, pp. 114–19. Paris, CNRS.

Graziosi, P. 1975. Nuove manifestazioni d'arte mesolitica e neolitica nel riparo Gaban presso Trento. *Riv. Sci. Preist.*, 30, pp. 237–78.

Grosjean, R. et al. 1976. Les civilisations de l'âge du bronze en Corse. In: J. Guilaine (ed.), *La Préhistoire Française.* vol. III, pp. 644–53. Paris, CNRS.

Guerreschi, G. 1971. La problematica dell'ambra nella protoistoria italiana. *Mem. Mus. Civ. St. Nat. Verona*, 18, pp. 319–36.

Guichard, G. 1976. Laugerie-Haute. *IXe Congr. UISPP, Nice*, Livret-Guide A4, pp. 91–6. Paris, CNRS.

Guilaine, J. 1976. *Les Premiers Bergers et Paysans de l'Occident Mediterranéen.* Paris/The Hague, Mouton. (École des Hautes Études en Sciences Sociales, Civilisations et Sociétés 58.)

Guilaine, J. (ed.). 1976. *La Préhistoire Française*, vol. III. Paris CNRS.

Guilbert, G. 1975. Moel y Gaer: defences and settlement plans. *Conf. on Beginnings of Hill-Forts, Newcastle upon Tyne, 1975.*

Guilbert, G. 1977. The northern Welsh Marches: some recent developments. In: J. Collis (ed.), *The Iron Age in Britain – a Review*, pp. 41–50. Sheffield Univ. Press.

Gunn, J. 1975. Idiosyncratic behaviour in chipping style: some hypotheses and preliminary analysis. In: E. Swanson (ed.), *Lithic Technology: Making and Using Stone Tools*, pp. 35–61. Mouton.

Guth, C. 1974. Découverte dans le Villafranchien d'Auvergne de galets aménagés. *C.R. Acad. Sci. Paris.*, t. 279, ser. D, pp. 1071–2.

Hachmann, R. 1971. *The Germanic Peoples.* London, Barrie & Jenkins.

Hagen, A. 1967. *Norway.* London, Thames & Hudson.

Hahn, J. 1972. Das Aurignacien in Mittel-

und Osteuropa. *Acta praehist. archaeol.*, 3, pp. 77–107.

Hahn, J. 1976a. Les industries aurignaciennes dans le Bassin du Haut-Danube. *IXe Congr. UISPP, Nice*, Coll. XVI, pp. 10–29. Paris CNRS.

Hahn, J. 1976b. Das Gravettien im westlichen Mitteleuropa. *IXe Congr. UISPP, Nice*, Coll. XV, pp. 100–20. Paris, CNRS.

Hajnalova, E. 1973. Beitrag zu Studium, Analyse, und Interpretierung der Funde von Kulturpflanzen in der Slowakei. *Slov. Archeol.*, 21, 1, pp. 211–20.

Hallager, E. 1977. *The Mycenaean Palace at Knossos. Evidence for Final Destruction in the III B Period.* Stockholm.

Hallam, B., Warren, S. & Renfrew, C. 1976. West Mediterranean obsidian. *Proc. Prehist. Soc.*, 42, pp. 85–110.

Hansel, B. 1968. *Beiträge zur Chronologie der mittleren Bronzezeit in Karpathenbecken.* Bonn, Habelt.

Harbottle, G. 1970. Neutron activation analysis of potsherds from Knossos and Mycenae. *Archaeometry*, 12, 1, pp. 23–34.

Harding, A. 1975. Mycenaean Greece and Europe: the evidence of bronze tools and implements. *Proc. Prehist. Soc.*, 41, pp. 183–202.

Harding, A. 1976. Bronze agricultural implements in Bronze Age Europe. In: G. de G. Sieveking, I. H. Longworth & K. E. Wilson (eds.), *Problems in Economic and Social Archaeology*, pp. 513–22. London, Duckworth.

Harris, D. R. 1976. A theoretical approach to early Post-Pleistocene changes in subsistence. (Paper given at) *Conf. Early Post-Glacial Settlement of North-West Europe: Economic and Social Perspectives* (ed. P. Mellars). (In press.)

Harris, E. C. 1975. The stratigraphic sequence: a question of time. *Wld Archaeol.*, 7, 1, pp. 109–21.

Harris, J. W. K. & Isaac, G. 1976. The Karari industry: early Pleistocene archaeological evidence from the terrain

east of Lake Turkana, Kenya. *Nature*, 262, pp. 102–7.

Harrison, R., Quero, S. & Priego, M. C. 1975. Beaker metallurgy in Spain. *Antiquity*, 49, pp. 273–8.

Harrison, T. 1976. The Upper Palaeolithic in Malaysia (Malaya and Borneo) and adjacent areas: gateways to the Pacific? *IXe Congr. UISPP, Nice*, Coll. XVIII, pp. 12–27. Paris, CNRS.

Hassan, F. A. 1973. On mechanisms of population growth during the Neolithic. *Curr. Anthrop.*, 14, 5, pp. 535–40.

Hatt, J.-J. 1970. *Celts and Gallo-Romans.* Geneva, Nagel.

Häusler, A. 1968. Kritische Bemerkungen zum Versuch soziologischer Deutungen ur- und frühgeschichtlicher Gräberfelder – erläutert am Beispiel des Gräberfeldes von Hallstatt. *Ethnogr. Archäol. Z.*, 9

Häusler, A. 1976. *Die Gräber der älteren Ockergrabkultur zwischen Dnepr und Karpaten.* Berlin, Akademie-Verlag.

Hawkins, G. 1966. *Stonehenge Decoded.* London, Souvenir Press.

Hays, J. D., Imbrie, J. & Shackleton, N. J. 1976. Variations in the earth's orbit: pacemaker of the Ice Ages. *Science*, 194, 4270, pp. 1121–32.

Herrmann, J. 1969. Burgen und befestigte Siedlungen der jüngeren Bronze- und frühen Eisenzeit in Mitteleuropa. In: K.-H. Otto & J. Hermann (eds.), *Siedlung, Burg und Stadt*, pp. 56–94. Berlin.

Higgs, E. S. 1966. The climate, environment and industries of Stone Age Greece, pt II. *Proc. Prehist. Soc.*, 32, pp. 1–29.

Higgs, E. S. 1970. Greek Mousterian sites. *Prehistoric Society Conf. Aegean Prehistory, London.* (Paper).

Higgs, E. S. (ed.). 1972. *Papers in Economic Prehistory.* Cambridge Univ. Press.

Higgs, E. S. (ed.). 1975a. *Palaeoeconomy.* Cambridge Univ. Press.

Higgs, E. S. 1975b. Agriculture in prehistoric Europe: the uplands. In: *The*

Early History of Agriculture. (British Academy/Royal Society meeting.)

Higgs, E. S. & Jarman, M. R. 1975. Palaeoeconomy. In: E. S. Higgs (ed.), *Palaeoeconomy*, pp. 1–8. Cambridge Univ. Press.

Hinout, J. 1975. Gravures et peintures mésolithiques du bassin parisien. *Bull. Soc. Préhist. Fr.*, **72**. C.R.s.m. 5, pp. 130–1.

Hodder, I. 1977. How are we to study distributions of Iron Age material? In: J. Collis (ed.), *The Iron Age in Britain – a Review*, pp. 8–16. Sheffield Univ. Press.

Hodder, I. & Orton, C. 1976. *Spatial Analysis in Archaeology.* Cambridge Univ. Press.

Hodson, F. R. 1968. *The La Tène Cemetery at Münsingen-Rain: Catalogue and Relative Chronology.* (Acta Bernesia, Bd V.)

Hodson, F. R. 1969. Searching for structure within multivariate archaeological data. *Wld Archaeol.*, **1**, pp. 90–105.

Hodson, F. R. 1977. Quantifying Hallstatt: some initial results. *Am. Antiq.*, **42**, pp. 394–413.

Holloway, R. *et al.*, 1975. Buccino: the Early Bronze Age village of Tufariello. *J. Fld Archaeol.*, **2**, pp. 12–81.

Honea, K. 1976. Mesolithic settlement of the Greek Cyclades islands. *IXe Congr. UISPP, Nice*, Summ., p. 259. Paris, CNRS.

Hopper, R. J. 1976. *The Early Greeks.* Weidenfeld & Nicolson.

Horedt, K. 1974. Befestigte Siedlungen der Spätbronze- und der Hallstattzeit im innerkarpatischen Rumänien. In: B. Chropovský, M. Dusek & V. Podborsky (eds.), *Symp. Problemen der jüngeren Hallstattzeit in Mitteleuropa*, pp. 205–28. Bratislava.

Howell, F. Clark. 1966. Observations on the earlier phase of the European Lower Paleolithic. *Am. Anthrop.*, pp. 86–201.

Howell, F. Clark. 1972. Pliocene/Pleistocene Hominidae in Eastern Africa: absolute and relative ages. In: W. W. Bishop & J. A. Miller (eds.), *Calibration of Hominoid Evolution*, pp. 331–68. Wenner-Gren Foundation.

Hundt, H. J. 1966. Bronzezeitliche Siedlungsfunde von Nonn. *Bayer. VorgeschBl.* (*Münch.*), **31**, pp. 34–48.

Hundt, H. J. 1974. Donaulandische Einflüsse in den älteren Bronzezeit Oberitaliens. *Preist. Alp.*, **10**, pp. 143–78.

Hutchinson, R. 1962. *Prehistoric Crete.* Harmondsworth, Middx, Penguin.

Isaac, G. 1972a. Early phases of human behaviour: models in Lower Palaeolithic archaeology. In: D. L. Clarke (ed.), *Models in Archaeology*, pp. 167–99. London, Methuen.

Isaac, G. 1972b. Chronology and the tempo of cultural change during the Pleistocene. In: W. W. Bishop & J. A. Miller (eds.), *Calibration of Hominoid Evolution*, pp. 381–430. Wenner-Gren Foundation.

Isaac, G. 1975. Conclusions. In: K. W. Butzer & G. Isaac (eds.), *After the Australopithecines*, pp. 875–87. The Hague, Mouton.

Isaac, G. & Curtis, G. H. 1974. Age of early Acheulian industries from the Peninj Group, Tanzania. *Nature*, **249**, pp. 624–7.

Jacobi, G. 1974. *Werkzeug und Gerät aus dem Oppidum von Manching (Manching 5).* Wiesbaden, Franz Steiner Verl.

Jacobsen, T. W. 1973. Excavations in the Franchthi Cave 1969–1971. *Hesperia*, **42**, pp. 45–88, 253–83.

Jacobsthal, P. 1944 (1969). *Early Celtic Art.* Oxford.

Jalmain, D. 1970. *Archéologie Aérienne en Île-de-France.* Paris, Technip.

Jalut, G. 1975. Données chronologiques, paléosylvatiques et paléoclimatiques sur le Tardiglaciaire et le Postglaciaire de l'extrémité orientale des Pyrénées, *Inqua, Montpellier*, pp. 10–12.

Jankuhn, H. 1969. Dorf, Weiler und Einzelhof in der Germania Magna. In: K. H. Otto & J. Hermann (eds.),

Siedlung, Burg und Stadt, pp. 114–28. Berlin.

Janossy, D. 1975. Mid-Pleistocene microfaunas of continental Europe and adjoining areas. In: K. W. Butzer and G. Isaac (eds.), *After the Australopithecines*, pp. 375–97. The Hague, Mouton.

Jarman, H. N. 1972. The origins of wheat and barley cultivation. In: E. S. Higgs (ed.), *Papers in Economic Prehistory*, pp. 15–26. Cambridge Univ. Press.

Jarman, H. N. 1975. Agriculture in prehistoric Europe: the lowlands. In: *The Early History of Agriculture*. (British Academy/Royal Society meeting.)

Jarman, M. 1972. European deer economies and the advent of the Neolithic. In: E. S. Higgs (ed.), *Papers in Economic Prehistory*, pp. 125–47. Cambridge Univ. Press.

Jarman, M. 1976. Prehistoric economic development in sub-alpine Italy. In: G. de G. Sieveking, I. H. Longworth & K. E. Wilson (eds.), *Problems in Economic and Social Archaeology*, pp. 523–48. London, Duckworth.

Jarman, M. & Webley, D. 1975. Settlement and land use in Capitanata, Italy. In: E. S. Higgs (ed.), *Palaeoeconomy*, pp. 177–221. Cambridge Univ. Press.

Jarman, M. & Wilkinson, P. 1972. Criteria of animal domestication. In: E. S. Higgs (ed.), *Papers in Economic Prehistory*, pp. 83–96. Cambridge Univ. Press.

Jehasse, J. 1976. Les civilisations de l'âge du fer en Corse. In: J. Guilaine (ed.), *La Préhistoire Française*, vol. III, pp. 847–55. Paris, CNRS.

Jelinek, J. 1969. Neanderthal man and Homo sapiens in central and eastern Europe. *Curr. Anthrop.*, **10**, pp. 475–503.

Jelinek, J. 1976. Praeneanderthal man in Europe, east from Elbe river. *IXe Congr. UISPP, Nice*, Coll. IX, pp. 33–4. Paris, CNRS.

Joachim, H. E. 1968. *Die Hunsrück-Eifel-Kultur am Mittelrhein*. (Bonn. Jb., Beih. 29.)

Jockenhövel, A. 1971. Die Rasiermesser in Mitteleuropa. *Prähistorische Bronzefunde*, Abt. VIII, 1 Bd.

Joffroy, R. 1972. Vix: habitats et nécropoles. In: P.-M. Duval & V. Kruta (eds.), *L'Habitat et la Nécropole a l'Âge du Fer en Europe Occidentale et Centrale*, pp. 71–4. Paris.

Johanson, D. C. & Taieb, M. 1976. Plio-Pleistocene hominid discoveries in Hadar, Ethiopia. *Nature*, **260**, pp. 293–7.

Johnstone, P. 1972. Bronze Age sea trial. *Antiquity*, XLVI, 184, pp. 269–74.

Jordan, T. G. 1973. *The European Culture Area. A Systemic Geography*. New York, Harper & Row.

Jovanovic, B. 1972. Early Neolithic mining in the Central Balkans. *Starinar*, **23**, pp. 1–14.

Jovanovic, B. & Ottoway, B. 1976. Copper mining and metallurgy in the Vinča culture. *Antiquity*, **50**, pp. 104–13.

Junghans, S., Sangmeister, E. & Schröder, M. 1960. *Kupfer und Bronze in der frühen Metallzeit Europas*. Römisch-Germanisches Zentralmuseum. (Stud. Anfängen Metall. Bd 1.)

Junghans, S., Sangmeister, E. & Schröder, M. 1968. *Kupfer und Bronze in der frühen Metallzeit Europas*. Römisch-Germanisches Zentralmuseum. (Stud. Anfängen Metall. Bd 2.)

Kaelas, L. 1976. Pitted Ware culture – the acculturation of a food-gathering group? In: S. J. de Laet (ed.), *Acculturation and Continuity in Atlantic Europe*, pp. 130–41. (Diss. Archaeol. Gandenses XVI.)

Kalicz, N. 1968. *Die Frühbronzezeit in Nordost-Ungarn (C19–C16)*. Budapest. (Archaeol. Hung. XLV.)

Kalicz, N. 1970. *Clay Gods: The Neolithic Period and Copper Age in Hungary*. Corvina Press.

Kalicz, N. 1972. Cemetery of Aszod. *Mitt. Archäol. Inst. Ung. Akad. Wiss.*, **3**, pp. 65–71.

Keeley, L. 1974. Technique and methodology in microwear studies: a critical review. *Wld Archaeol.*, 5, pp. 323–6.

Kilian, K. 1972. Zur Bemalten Keramik der Ausgehenden Bronzezeit und der Früheisenzeit aus Albanien, *Archäol. KorrespBl.*, 2, pp. 115–23.

Killen, J. 1964. The wool industry of Crete in the Late Bronze Age. *A. Br. Sch. Athens*, 59, pp. 1–15.

Killen, J. 1977. The Knossos texts and the geography of Mycenaean Crete. In: J. Bintliff (ed.), *Mycenaean Geography: Proc. Cambridge Colloquium, September 1976*, pp. 40–46. Cambridge, Univ. Library Press.

Killian-Dirlmeier, I. 1972. Die hallstattzeitlichen Gürtelbleche und Blechgürtel Mitteleuropas. *Prähistorische Bronzefunde*, Abt. XII, I Bd.

Kimmig, W. 1975. Early Celts on the Upper Danube: the excavations at the Heuneburg. In: R. Bruce-Mitford (ed.), *Recent Archaeological Investigations in Europe*, pp. 32–64. London, Routledge & Kegan Paul.

Kivikoski, E. 1967. *Finland*. Thames & Hudson.

Klein, R. G. 1969a. Mousterian cultures in European Russia. *Science*, 165, pp. 257–65.

Klein, R. G. 1969b. *Man and Culture in the Late Pleistocene*. San Francisco, Chandler Publishing.

Klein, R. G. 1973. *Ice-Age Hunters of the Ukraine*. Univ. of Chicago.

Klima, B. 1963. *Dolni Vestonice. Erforschung eine Lagenplatzes der Mammutjäger an der Jahren 1947–52*. (Monum. Archaeol., XI.)

Klima, B. 1968. Das Pavlovien in den Weinberghohlen von Mauern. *Quatär*, 18/19, pp. 263–73.

Klima, B. 1974. Dolni Vestonice. *Přehl. Výzkumů (Brno)*, 1973, pp. 14–15.

Klima, B. 1976. Le Pavlovien. *IXe Congr. UISPP, Nice*, Coll. XV, pp. 128–41. Paris, CNRS.

Kobusiewicz, M. 1969. On the distribution of Late Paleolithic and Mesolithic sites in [the] western part of [the] Great Poland Plain. *Archeol. pol.*, 14, 2, pp. 295–307.

Kobusiewicz, M. & Kozlowski, S. K. 1975. Outline of the development of Polish research work on the Palaeolithic and the Mesolithic, the period 1945–73. *Archeol. pol.*, 20, 1, pp. 23–56.

Kooijmans, L. P. Louwe, 1974. The Rhine/Meuse delta, four studies on its prehistoric occupation and holocene geology. *Oudh. Meded. (Leiden)*, 53/54.

Kooijmans, L. P. Louwe. 1976a. The Neolithic at the Lower Rhine. In: S. J. De Laet (ed.), *Acculturation and Continuity in Atlantic Europe*, pp. 150–73. (Diss. Archaeol. Gand. XVI.)

Kooijmans, L. P. Louwe. 1976b. Prähistorische Besiedlung im Rhein-Maas-Deltagebiet und die Bestimmung ehemaliger Wasserhöhen. *Probl. Küstenforsch. südl. Nordseegeb.*, 11, pp. 119–43.

Korkuti, M. & Zhaneta, A. 1972. Fouilles 1969–1970 dans l'agglomération Néolithique de Cakran (Fieri). *Stud. Alban.*, 9, 1, pp. 15–30.

Kowalezyk, J. 1969. The origins of the Neolithic age in Polish territories. *Wiad. Archeol.*, 34, pp. 3–69.

Kozlowski, J. K. 1965. Études sur la différentiation de la culture dans le paléolithique supérieur de l'Europe centrale. *Pr. Archaeol.*, 7, pp. 1–147. (French summ., pp. 145–7.)

Kozlowski, J. K. 1972–3. The origin of lithic raw materials used in the Paleolithic of the Carpathian countries. *Acta Archaeol. Carpath.*, 13, pp. 5–19.

Kozlowski, J. K. 1976a. Les industries à pointes à cran en Europe Centre-Est. *IXe Congr. UISPP, Nice*, Coll. XV, pp. 121–7. Paris, CNRS.

Kozlowski. J. K. 1976b. L'Aurignacien dans les Balkans. *IXe Congr. UISPP, Nice*, Coll. XVI, pp. 124–42. Paris, CNRS.

Kozlowski, J. K. & Kubiak, H. 1972. Late Palaeolithic dwellings made of mammoth bones in South Poland. *Nature*, 237 (June), pp. 463–4.

Kozlowski, S. K. (ed.). 1973*a*. *The Meso-lithic in Europe.*

Kozlowski, S. [K.] 1973*b*. Introduction to the history of Europe in the Early Holocene. In: S. K. Kozlowski (ed.), *The Mesolithic in Europe*, pp. 331–66.

Kozlowski, S. K. 1976*a*. Les courants interculturels dans le mésolithique de l'Europe occidentale. *IXe Congr. UISPP, Nice*, Coll. XIX, pp. 135–60. Paris, CNRS.

Kozlowski, S. K. 1976*b*. The system of providing flint raw materials in the Late Palaeolithic in Poland. *2nd Int. Symp. on Flint, Maastricht, 1975*, pp. 66–9. Sittard, Ned. Geol. Veren.

Krämer, W. & Schübert. F. 1970. *Die Ausgrabungen in Manching 1955–1961 (Manching 1)*. Wiesbaden, Franz Steiner Verl.

Kretzoi, M. 1975. New ramapithecines and *Pliopithecus* from Lower Pleisto-cene of Rudabanya in north-eastern Hungary. *Nature*, 257, pp. 578–81.

Kretzoi, M. & Vértes, L. 1965. Upper Biharian (Intermindel) Pebble-industry occupation site in western Hungary. *Curr. Anthrop.* 6, pp. 74–87.

Kroitzsch, K. & Simon, L. 1972. Zum Siedlungsbild der Lausitzer Kultur im Gebiet um Radeberg. *Ausgrab. u. Funde*, 17, pp. 75–81.

Kruk, J. 1973. *Studies on the Neolithic Settlement of the Loess Uplands*. Polska Akademia Nauk, Inst. Hist. Kultury Materialnej. (In Polish.)

Kruk, J. 1975. Studies on the settlement of the Loess uplands. *Pol. Archaeol. Abstr.*, 5, pp. 94/75.

Kruta, V. 1975. Les habitats et nécropoles Lateniens en Bohème. In: P. M. Duval & V. Kruta (eds.), *L'Habitat et la Nécropole à l'Âge du Fer en Europe Occidentale et Centrale*, pp. 95–102. Paris.

Kukla, G. J. 1975. Loess stratigraphy of Central Europe. In: K. W. Butzer & G. Isaac (eds.), *After the Australopi-thecines*, pp. 99–188. The Hague, Mouton.

Kuper, R. 1976. Recherches sur le peuple-ment néolithique de 'Plateau d'Alden-hoven' (Rhénanie). *IXe Congr. UISPP, Nice*, Sect. VI. Paris, CNRS. (Paper.)

Kuper, R. & Piepers, W. 1966. Eine Siedlung der Rössener Kultur in Inden (Kr. Jülich) und Lamersdorf (Kr. Düren), Vorbericht. *Bonn. Jb.*, 166, p. 370.

Kurten, B. 1968. *Pleistocene Mammals of Europe*. London, Weidenfield & Nicol-son.

Lambrick, G. 1977. Farmoor. *C.B.A. Grp 9 Newsl.*, 7, p. 69.

Lanfranchi, F. de & Weiss, M. C. 1973. *La Civilisation des Corses: les Origines*. Ed. Cyrnos et Méditerranée.

Lange, E. 1971. Botanische Beiträge zur Mitteleuropäische Siedlungsgeschichte. *Schr. Ur- u. Frühgesch.*, 27, pp. 47–50.

Lanting, J. N. & van der Waals, J. D. (eds.). 1976. *Glockenbecher Symp., Oberried, 1974.*

Lanting, J. N. & van der Waals, J. D. 1976. Neolithic beakers from the Netherlands: the potter's point of view. In: J. N. Lanting & J. D. van der Waals (eds.), *Glockenbecher Symp., Oberried, 1974*, pp. 81–139.

Laville, H. 1973. The relative position of Mousterian industries in the climatic chronology of the Early Würm in the Périgord. *Wld Archaeol.*, 4, 3, pp. 323–9.

Lazlo, A. 1976. Les débuts de la métallur-gie du fer dans l'espace Carpatho-Danu-bien. *IXe Congr. UISPP, Nice*, Summ., p. 509.

Leakey, L. 1972. *Homo sapiens* in the Middle Pleistocene and the evidence of *Homo sapiens*' evolution. In: Unesco, *The Origin of Homo Sapiens: Proc. Paris Symposium, 1969*, pp. 25–30. Paris, Unesco.

Leakey, M. 1976. The early hominids of Olduvai Gorge and the Laetolil beds. *IXe Congr. UISPP, Nice*, Coll. VI, pp. 296–313. Paris, CNRS.

Leakey, R. 1974. Further evidence of

Lower Pleistocene hominids from East Rudolf, North Kenya, 1973. *Nature*, 248, pp. 653–6.

Leakey, R. E. & Lewin, R. 1977. *Origins*. London, Macdonald & Jane's.

Leroi-Gourhan, A. 1968. *The Art of Prehistoric Man in Western Europe*. London, Thames & Hudson.

Leroi-Gourhan, A. 1976a. L'art mobilier au Paléolithique supérieur et les liaisons européennes. *IXe Congr. UISPP, Nice*, Coll. XIV, pp. 25–35. Paris, CNRS.

Leroi-Gourhan, A. 1976b. L'habitat au Paléolithique supérieur. *IXe Congr. UISPP, Nice*, Coll. XIII, pp. 85–92. Paris, CNRS.

Leroi-Gourhan, A. & Brezillon, M. 1972. Fouilles de Pincevent. Essai d'analyse ethnographique d'un habitat magdalénien. *Gallia Préhist.*, VIIth suppl.

Le Roux, C.-T. 1975. Fabrication et commerce des haches en pierre polie. *Doss. Archéol.*, 11, pp. 43–59.

Lieberman, P. & Crelin, E. S. 1971. On the speech of Neanderthal man. *Ling. Inq.*, 2, 2, pp. 203–22.

Lies, H. 1974. Zur neolithischen Siedlungsintensität im Magdeburger Raum. *Jschr. Mitteldt. Vorgesch.*, 58, pp. 57–111.

Lilliu, G. 1967. *I Nuraghi: Torri Prehistoriche di Sardegna*. Cagliari, La Zattera.

Lilliu, G. 1972 (2nd ed.). *La Civiltà dei Sardi dal Neolitico all'Eta dei Nuraghi*. Italy, ERI.

Lindquist, S. O. 1974. The development of the agrarian landscape on Gotland during the Early Iron Age. *Norw. Archaeol. Rev.*, 7, 1, pp. 6–32.

Lorblanchet, M. 1976. Quelques considérations sur l'art rupestre australien et paléolithique. *IXe Congr. UISPP, Nice*, Coll. XXII, pp. 152–77. Paris, CNRS.

Lose, I. 1969. Un nouveau centre du travail de l'ambre a l'Époque Néolithique dans le pays baltique est. *Sov. Archeol.*, 3–4, pp. 124–34.

Lüning, J. 1976. Un nouveau modèle de l'habitat du Néolithique ancien. *IXe*

Congr. *UISPP, Nice*, Sect. VI. Paris, CNRS. (Paper.)

McBurney, C. B. M. 1976. *Early Man in the Soviet Union*. British Academy.

McDonald, W. A. & Rapp, G. R. Jr (eds.). 1972. *The Minnesota Messenia Expedition. Reconstructing a Bronze Age Regional Environment*. Univ. of Minnesota.

McHenry, H. M. 1975. Fossils and the mosaic nature of human evolution. *Science*, 190, 4213, pp. 425–31.

MacKendrick, P. 1975. *The Dacian Stones Speak*. Univ. of North Carolina Press.

Maddin, R., Muhly J. D. & Wheeler, T. S. 1977. How the Iron Age began. *Sci. Am.*, 237, 4, pp. 122–31.

Malez, M. 1976. Excavation of the Villefranchian site Sandalja 1 near Pula (Yugoslavia). *IXe Congr. UISPP, Nice*, Coll. VIII, pp. 104–23. Paris, CNRS.

Malinowski, T. 1973. Investigations of an earthwork of the Lusatian culture at Komorowo, District of Szatnotuly, in 1970 and 1971. *Spraw. Archeol.*, 25, pp. 83–100.

Malinowski, T. 1974. An amber trading-post in Early Iron Age Poland. *Archaeology*, 27, 3, pp. 195–200.

Mania, D. 1970. Stratigraphische Gliederung und Ablauf der Weichselkaltzeit im mittleren Elb-Saale-Gebiet. *Ausgrab. u. Funde*, 15, pp. 1–9.

Mania, D. L. 1976. Altpaläolithischer Rastplatz mit Hominidenresten aus dem Mittelpleistozänen Travertinkomplex von Bilzingsleben (DDR). *IXe Congr. UISPP, Nice*, Coll. IX, pp. 35–47. Paris, CNRS.

Mania, D. &. Toepfer, V. 1971. Zur Jungquartären Landschaftsgeschichte und Mesolitischen Besiedlung des Geiseltales. *Jschr. Mitteldt. Vorgesch.*, 55, pp. 11–34.

Mania, D. & Toepfer, V. 1973. *Gliederung, Ökologie und Mittelpaläolitische Funde der letzten Eiszeit*. (Veröff. Landesmus. Vorgesch. Halle Bd 26.)

Maringer, J. 1973. Das Wasser in Kult und Glauben der vorgeschichtlichen Menschen. *Anthropos*, **68**, pp. 705–76.

Marks, A. E. 1976. Terminology and chronology of the Levantine Upper Paleolithic as seen from the central Negev, Israel. *IXe Congr. UISPP, Nice*, Coll. III, pp. 49–76. Paris, CNRS.

Marshack, A. 1970. *Notation dans les Gravures du Paléolithique Supérieur*. Bordeaux, Delmas.

Marshack, A. 1972. Upper Palaeolithic notation and symbolism. *Science*, **178**, 4063, pp. 817–28.

Marshack, A. 1975. Exploring the mind of Ice Age man. *Natn. Geogr.*, **147**, 1, pp. 62–89.

Marshack, A. 1976a. Use versus style in the analysis and interpretation of Upper Paleolithic image and symbol. *IXe Congr. UISPP, Nice*, Coll. XIV, pp. 118–46. Paris, CNRS.

Marshack. A. 1976b. Some implications of the Paleolithic symbolic evidence for the origin of language. *Curr. Anthrop.*, **17**, 2, pp. 274–81.

Martin, R. 1965. Wooden figures from the source of the Seine. *Antiquity*, **39**, pp. 247–52.

Masset, C. 1972. The megalithic tomb of La Chaussée-Tirancourt. *Antiquity*, **XLVI**, 184, pp. 297–300.

Mateescu, C. N. 1975. Remarks on cattle breeding and agriculture in the Middle and Late Neolithic on the Lower Danube. *Dacia*, **19**, pp. 13–19.

Matthias, W. & Schultze-Motel, J. 1971. Kulturpflanzen-Abdrücke an Gefässen der Schnurkeramik und der Aunjetitzer Kultur aus Mitteldeutschland. *Jschr. Mitteldt. Vorgesch.*, **55**, pp. 113–34.

Megaw, V. 1970. *Art of the European Iron Age*. Bath, Adams & Dent.

Meier-Arendt, W. 1972. Die ältere und mittlere Linienbandkeramik im westlichen Mitteleuropa, ein Überblick. In: F. Schwabedissen (gen. ed.), *Anfänge des Neolithikums vom Orient bis Europa,* Va, W. *Central Europe* (ed. J. Lüning), pp. 66–76.

Meiklejohn, C. 1976. Taille du grotte, taille du site, et vestiges concernant les populations Mésolithiques en Europe. *IXe Congr. UISPP, Nice*, Résumés des Commun., p. 253. Paris, CNRS.

Mellars, P. 1969. The chronology of Mousterian industries in the Périgord region of southwest France. *Proc. Prehist. Soc.*, **35**, pp. 134–71.

Mellars, P. 1973. The character of the middle-upper palaeolithic transition in south-west France. In: C. Renfrew (ed.), *The Explanation of Culture Change*, pp. 255–76. Duckworth.

Mellars, P. 1975. Ungulate populations, economic patterns, and the Mesolithic landscape. In: J. G. Evans, S. Limbrey & H. Cleere (eds.), *The Effect of Man on the Landscape: the Highland Zone*, pp. 49–56. Council for British Archaeology.

Mellars, P. 1976. Settlement patterns and industrial variability in the British Mesolithic. In: G. de G. Sieveking, I. H. Longworth & K. E. Wilson (eds.), *Problems in Economic and Social Archaeology*, pp. 375–99. London, Duckworth.

Mellars, P. (ed.). *The Early Postglacial Settlement of Northern Europe: an Ecological Perspective*. London, Duckworth. (In press.)

Mercer, J. 1976. The occupation sequence on the Isle of Jura, Argyll. (Paper given at) *Conf. on Early Post-Glacial Settlement of North-West Europe: Economic and Social Perspectives* (ed. P. Mellars). (In press.)

Mercer, R. J. 1976. Grime's Graves, Norfolk. In: C. Burgess & R. Miket (eds.), *Settlement and Economy in the Third and Second Millennia B.C.*, pp. 101–11. Oxford. (Br. Archaeol. Rep. 33.)

Meszaros, G. & Vértes, L. 1955. A paint mine from the Early Upper Palaeolithic age near Lovas (Hungary, County Veszprém). *Acta Archaeol. Hung.*, **5**, pp. 1–34.

Milisauskas, S. 1973. Investigation of an Early Neolithic community in Poland. *Curr. Anthrop.*, **14**, 3, pp. 287–90.

Milisauskas, S. 1976. Olszanica – an early farming village in Poland. *Archaeology*, **29**, pp. 31–41.

Milojcic V. *et al.* 1962–76. *Die deutsche Ausgrabungen auf der Argissa-Magula in Thessalien*. Bonn. 3 vols.

Miskovsky, J.-C. 1976. Les changements climatiques durant le Pléistocène et l'Holocène autour de la Méditerranée. *IXe Congr. UISPP, Nice*, Coll. II, pp. pp. 20–49. Paris, CNRS.

Miszkiewicz, B. von. 1972. Die Aunjetitzer Bovölkerung aus Tomice, Kr. Dzierzoniow. *Homo*, **23**, pp. 145–54.

Moberg, C. A. 1966. Spread of agriculture in the north European periphery. *Science*, **152**, 3720, pp. 315–19.

Moberg, C. A. 1975. Circumpolar adaptation zones east–west and cross-economy contacts north–south: an outsider's query, especially on Ust'-Poluj. In: W. Fitzhugh (ed.), *Prehistoric Maritime Adaptation of the Circumpolar Zone*. The Hague, Mouton.

Modderman, P. J. 1972. Hausbauten und Siedlungen der Linienbandkeramik. In: F. Schwabedissen (gen. ed.), *Anfänge des Neolithikums vom Orient bis Europa*, Va, *W. Central Europe* (ed. J. Lüning), pp. 77–84.

Møhl, U. 1970. Animal bones from Ølby Lyng. In: E. Brinch Petersen, *Ølby Lyng. An Ertebølle coastal settlement in eastern Sjaelland*, *Aarb. Nord. Oldkyndig Hist.*, pp. 43–77.

Mongait, A. L. 1961. *Archaeology in the U.S.S.R.* Harmondsworth, Middx, Penguin.

Montet-White, A. 1973. *Le Malpas Rockshelter*. Univ. of Kansas.

Mordant, C. &. Mordant, D. 1976. Le dépôt de bronze de Villethierry. *Gallia Préhist.*, IXth suppl.

Morrison, A. 1976. The coastal environment as a habitat of Mesolithic man, with particular reference to northern Britain. *IXe Congr. UISPP, Nice*, Résumés des Commun., p. 275. Paris, CNRS.

Mozsolics, A. 1967. *Bronzefunde des Karpatenbeckens*. Budapest.

Mozsolics, A. 1968. *Goldfunde des Depotfundhorizontes von Hajdú-Sámson*. Berlin, De Gruyter.

Mozsolics, A. 1973. *Bronze- und Goldfunde des Karpathenbeckens*. . . . Budapest, Akadémiai Kiado.

Mozsolics, A. 1974. Domestication of the horse in the Danube basin. *Preist. Alp.* **10**, pp. 107–11.

Muhly, J. D. 1970. *Copper and Tin: the Distribution of Mineral Resources and the Nature of the Metals Trade in the Bronze Age*. Ann Arbor, Mich., Univ. Microfilms. (Yale Univ. Ph.D. 1969.)

Müller-Beck, H. 1965. *Seeberg Burgäschisee-Süd. Holzgeräte und Holzbearbeitung*. *Acta Bernensia*, II, Tl 5.

Müller-Beck, H. 1976. Sur les industries à bifaces en Allemagne du sud. *IXe Congr. UISPP, Nice*, Coll. X, p. 65. Paris, CNRS.

Müller-Karpe, H. 1959. *Beiträge zur Chronologie der Urnenfelderzeit nordlich und südlich der Alpen*. Berlin, De Gruyter.

Musson, C. 1975. The Breiddin, Montgomeryshire. *Conf. on Beginnings of Hill-Forts, 1975, Newcastle upon Tyne*.

Nandris, J. 1970. The development and relationships of the earlier Greek Neolithic. *Man*, **5**, pp. 192–213.

Nemeskeri, J. 1976. La structure Paléodémographique de la population epi-paléolithique-prénéolithique de Vlasac (Yougoslavie). *IXe Congr. UISPP. Nice*, Sect. V. Paris, CNRS.

Neustupny, E. & Neustupny, J. 1961. *Czechoslovakia*. London, Thames & Hudson.

Newcomer, M. 1976. 'Punch technique' and Upper Palaeolithic blades. In: E. Swanson (ed.), *Lithic Technology: Making and Using Stone Tools*, pp. 97–102. Mouton.

Newell, R. 1973. The post-glacial adaptations of the indigenous population of the northwest European plain. In: S. Kozlowski (ed.), *The Mesolithic in Europe*, pp. 399–440.

Nobis, G. 1978. Problems of the early husbandry of domestic animals in northern Germany and Denmark. (Paper delivered at) *Symp. Archaeometry, Bonn, 1978*.

Noe-Nygaard, N. 1975. Bone injuries caused by human weapons in Mesolithic Denmark. In: A. T. Clason (ed.), *Archaeological Studies*, pp. 151–9. Amsterdam.

Northover, P. 1978. The application of metallurgical studies to Late Bronze Age material. (Paper presented at) *Symp. Archaeometry, Bonn, 1978*.

Novotna, M. 1970. Die Äxte und Beile in der Slowakei. In: H. Müller-Karpe (ed.), *Prähistorische Bronzefunde*, IX, Bd 3. Munich.

Nowinski, K. 1970. Remarks on the settlement of the Bzura basin in the final La Tène and Roman periods. *Wiad. Archeol.*, **35**, 1, pp. 5–13.

Ostoja-Zagorski, J. 1974a. Siedlungskomplex der Lausitzer Kultur in Smolno Wielkie, Kreis Sulechów 33–47. *Fontes, Archaeol. Posnan.*, **24**, (1973). Poznan, 1974. (Engl. summ. 46.)

Ostoja-Zagorski, J. 1974b. From studies on the economic structure and the decline of the Bronze Age and the Hallstatt period in the north and western zone of the Odra and Vistula basins. *Przegl. Archeol.*, **22**, pp. 123–50.

Ostoja-Zagorski, J. 1976. Research on problems of decline of Castra of Lusatian culture. *Slav. Antiq.*, **23**, pp. 39–73.

Ottaway, B. 1973. An analysis of cultural relations in neolithic north-central Europe based on copper ornaments. In: C. Renfrew (ed.), *The Explanation of Culture Change*, pp. 609–16. Duckworth.

Ottaway, B. 1974. Cluster analysis of impurity patterns in Armorico-British daggers. *Archaeometry*, **16**, 2, pp. 221–32.

Ottaway, B. & Strahm, C. 1975. Swiss Neolithic copper beads: currency,

ornament or prestige items? *Wld Archaeol.*, **6**, 3, pp. 307–21.

Otto, K.-H. & Hermann, J. (Eds.). 1969. *Siedlung, Burg und Stadt*. Berlin.

Palma di Cesnola, A. 1974. Su alcune recenti scoperte nei Livelli gravettiani della Grotta Paglicci (promontorio del Gargano). *Zephrus*, **25**, pp. 65–79.

Palma di Cesnola, A. 1976. Le Leptolithique archaïque en Italie. *IXe Congr. UISPP, Nice*, Coll. XV, pp. 66–99. Paris, CNRS.

Palmer, S. 1976. A Mesolithic site with structures on the Isle of Portland. *IXe Congr. UISPP, Nice*, Résumés des Commun., p. 255. Paris, CNRS.

Palmer, S. 1977. *Mesolithic Cultures of Britain*. Dolphin Press.

Parrington M. 1977. Abingdon, Ashville Trading Estate 1974–6. *C.B.A. Grp 9 Newsl.*, **7**, pp. 60–65.

Pauli, L. 1972. Untersuchungen zur Späthallstattkultur in Nordwürttemberg. *Hamb. Beitr. Archäol.*, **2**, 1.

Payne, S. 1975. Faunal change at the Franchthi cave. In: A. T. Clason (ed.), *Archaeological Studies*, pp. 120–31. Amsterdam.

Peacock, D. 1968. A petrological study of certain Iron Age pottery from western England. *Proc. Prehist. Soc.*, **34**, pp. 414–27.

Peacock, D. 1969. Neolithic pottery production in Cornwall. *Antiquity*, **43**, pp. 145–9.

Pequart, M. L. N., Pequart, S. J., Boule, M. & Vallois, H. V. 1937. *Téviec – Station-Nécropole Mésolithique du Morbihan*. (Arch. Inst. Paléont. hum., mém. 18.)

Pericot García, L. 1972. *The Balearic Islands*. London, Thames & Hudson.

Perlès, C. 1971. Review of 'Milieu et Développement de la Société Préhistorique dans la Partie Européenne de l'URSS'. *L'Anthropologie*, **75**, pp. 665–8.

Pesce, V. D., Giove, C. & Scattarella, V. 1975. Il 'Micromusteriano Meridionale'. Valutazioni comparative e paleoecologiche. *Atti III Simp. naz. Cons. Nat.*, *Bari*, II, pp. 299–308.

Pescheck, C. 1974. Fürstengrab der späten Bronzezeit aus Nordbayern. *Antike Welt*, 5, pp. 15–20.

Peschel, K. 1972. La Steinsburg près de Romhild: un centre du peuplement de la Thuringe a l'âge du fer. In: P.-M. Duval & V. Kruta (eds.), *L'Habitat et la Nécropole à l'Âge du Fer en Europe Occidentale et Centrale*, pp. 107–14. Paris.

Phillips, P. 1975. *Early Farmers of West Mediterranean Europe*. London, Hutchinson.

Piaskowski, J. 1968–70. Problems of beginnings of iron metallurgy on Polish territory. *Przegl. Archeol.*, 19–20, pp. 48–9.

Pichler, H. & Friedrich, W. 1976. Radiocarbon dates of Santorini volcanics. *Nature*, 262, pp. 373–4.

Piggott, S. 1965. *Ancient Europe*. Edinburgh.

Piggott, S., Daniel, G. & McBurney, C. (eds.). 1973. *France Before the Romans*. Thames & Hudson.

Pilbeam, D. 1975. Middle Pleistocene hominids. In: K. W. Butzer & G. Isaac (eds.), *After the Australopithecines*, pp. 809–56. The Hague, Mouton.

Piningre, J. F. 1974. Un aspect de l'économie néolithique: le problème de l'Aphanite en Franche-Comté et dans les régions limitrophes. *Ann. Litt. Univ. Besançon*.

Pittioni, R. 1957. Urzeitlicher Bergbau auf Kupfererz und Spuranalyse. *Archaeol. Austriaca*, Beih. 1.

Planchais, N., Renault-Miskovsky, J. L. & Vernet, J. L. 1975. Les facteurs d'évolution de la végétation dans le sud-est de la France – côte à moyenne montagne – depuis le Tardiglaciaire d'après les résultats de l'analyse pollinique et de celle des charbons de bois. *Inqua*, *Montpellier*, pp. 13–16.

Platon, N. 1971. *Zákros*. London.

Pleiner, R. 1977. Eisenverhüttungsgebiete im freien Germanien. In: B. Chropov-

ský (ed.), *Symp. Ausklang der La Tène-Zivilisation und Anfänge der Germanischen Besiedlung im mittleren Donaugebiet*. Bratislava, Verl. der Slovakischen Akademie der Wissenschaften.

Pleinerova, I. 1972. Die vorgeschichtliche Fundstelle in Brezno. *Archeol. Rozhl.*, 24, pp. 371–2. (Germ. summ.)

Pleslová-Štiková, E. 1971. Die Äneolitische Grundlage der Frühbronzezeitlichen Kulturen in Mitteleuropa. *Ser. Archeol.*, 18, pp. 7–34.

Pollnac, R. B. & Rowlett, R. M. 1977. Community and supracommunity within the Marne culture: a stylistic analysis. In: D. Ingersoll, J. E. Yellen & W. MacDonald (eds.), *Experimental Archaeology*, pp. 167–90.

Pradel, L. & Pradel, J. H. 1970. La station paléolithique de Fontmaure, commune de Vellèches (Vienne). *L'Anthropologie*, 74, 7–8, pp. 481–526.

Price, T. D. 1973. A proposed model for procurement systems in the Mesolithic of northwestern Europe. In: S. Kozlowski (ed.), *The Mesolithic in Europe*, pp. 455–76.

Price, T. D. 1976. Mesolithic subsistence-settlement systems in the Netherlands. (Paper given at) *Conf. on Early Post-Glacial Settlement of North-West Europe: Economic and Social Perspectives* (ed. P. Mellars). (In press.)

Primas, M. 1977. Beobachtungen zu den Spätbronzezeitlichen Siedlungs- und Depotfunden der Schweiz. In: *Festschrift Walter Drack*, pp. 44–55. Zürich.

Protsch, R. & Berger, R. 1973. Earliest radiocarbon dates for domesticated animals. *Science*, 179, 4070, pp. 235–9.

Pryor, F. 1976. Fen-edge land management in the Bronze Age. In: C. Burgess & R. Miket (eds.), *Settlement and Economy in the Third and Second Millenia B.C.* Oxford.

Quitta, H. 1967. The C14 chronology of the Central and SE European Neolithic. *Antiquity*, XLI, 164, pp. 263–70.

Quitta, H. 1970. Zur Lage und Verbreitung der bandkeramischen Siedlungen im Leipziger Land. *Z. Archäol.*, **4**, 2, pp. 155–76.

Radmilli, A. M. 1976. The first industries of Italy. *IXe Congr. UISPP, Nice,* Coll. VIII, pp. 35–74, Paris, CNRS.

Raikes, R. L. 1976. Climate of the Mediterranean and Middle East semi-arid zones from the Mesolithic to Chalcolithic (VIII–III millennia B.C.). *IXe Congr. UISPP, Nice,* Summ., p. 81. Paris, CNRS.

Ralph, E. K., Michael, H. N. & Han, M. C. 1976. Tree rings and carbon 14 scale. *IXe Congr. UISPP, Nice,* Coll. I, pp. 101–28. Paris, CNRS.

Randsborg, K. 1973. Wealth and social structure as reflected in bronze age burials – a quantitative approach. In: C. Renfrew (ed.), *The Explanation of Culture Change,* pp. 565–70. Duckworth.

Randsborg, K. 1974. Social stratification in Early Bronze Age Denmark: a study in the regulation of cultural systems. *Prähist. Z.*, **49**, pp. 38–61.

Randsborg, K. 1975. Social dimensions of Early Neolithic Denmark. *Proc. Prehist. Soc.*, **41**, pp. 105–18.

Renault-Miskovsky, J. 1972. Situation des gisements étudies dans leur cadre géographique, géologique, botanique et stratigraphique. *Bull. Mus. Anthrop. préhist. Monaco,* **18**, pp. 147–83.

Renault-Miskovsky, J. 1976. Les flores quaternaires dans le bassin occidental de la Méditerranée. *IXe Congr. UISPP, Nice,* Coll. II, pp. 50–76. Paris, CNRS.

Renfrew, C. 1967. Colonialism and Megalithismus. *Antiquity,* **XLI**, 164, pp. 276–88.

Renfrew, C. 1969. The development and chronology of the Early Cycladic figurines. *Am. J. Archaeol.*, **73**, 1, pp. 1–32.

Renfrew, C. 1970. The tree-ring calibration of radiocarbon: an archaeological evaluation. *Proc. Prehist. Soc.*, **36**, pp. 280–311.

Renfrew, C. (ed.). 1973a. *The Explanation of Culture Change.* Duckworth.

Renfrew, C. 1973b. *Before Civilization.* London. Jonathan Cape and Penguin.

Renfrew, C. 1973c. *The Emergence of Civilisation.* Methuen.

Renfrew, C. 1978. The Mycenaean sanctuary at Phylakopi. *Antiquity,* **52**, pp. 7–15.

Renfrew, C. & Dixon, J. 1976. Obsidian in western Asia: a review. In: G. de G. Sieveking, I. H. Longworth & K. E. Wilson (eds.), *Problems in Economic and Social Archaeology,* pp. 137–49. London, Duckworth.

Renfrew, J. M. 1973. *Palaeoethnobotany. The Prehistoric Food Plants of the Near East and Europe.* Methuen.

RGZM (Römisch-Germanisches Zentralmuseum). 1970. *Krieger und Salzherren. Hallstattkultur im Ostalpenraum.* Mainz. (Ausstellungskat.)

Richter, I. 1970. Der Arm- und Beilschmuck der Bronze- und Urnenfelderzeit in Hessen und Rhein-Hessen. *Prähistorische Bronzefunde,* Abt. X, 1. Bd.

Rigaud, J.-P. 1976a. Les structures d'habitat d'un niveau de Périgordien supérieur de Flageolet I (Bézenac, Dordogne). *IXe Congr. UISPP, Nice,* Coll. XIII, pp. 93–102. Paris, CNRS.

Rigaud, J.-P. 1976b. Données nouvelles sur le Périgordien supérieur en Périgord. *IXe Congr. UISPP, Nice,* Coll. XV, pp. 53–65. Paris, CNRS.

Riquet, R. 1970. *Anthropologie du Néolithique et du Bronze Ancien.* Poitiers, 1970.

Rittatore Vonwiller, F. 1974. Il problema del passaggio tra l'eneolitico et l'antica eta del Bronzo nell' Italia centrale tirrenica. *Preist. Alp.*, **10**, pp. 253–9.

Roche, J. 1972. Les amas coquilliers (*concheiros*) mésolithiques de Muge (Portugal). In: F. Schwabedissen (gen. ed.), *Anfänge des Neolithikums vom Orient bis Europa,* VII, *W. Mediterranean and British Isles* (ed. J. Lüning), pp. 72–107.

Roche, J. 1974. État actuel de nos connaissances sur le Solutréen portugais. *Zephyrus,* **25**, pp. 82–94.

Roche, J. 1976. Les origines de l'industrie de l'amas coquillier de Moita do Sebastião (Muge, Portugal). *IXe Congr. UISPP, Nice,* Coll. XIX, pp. 161–5. Paris, CNRS.

Roe, D. A. 1976a. The earliest industries in Britain. *IXe Congr. UISPP, Nice,* Coll. VIII, pp. 76–95. Paris, CNRS.

Roe, D. A. 1976b. The evolution of the Acheulian in Britain. *IXe Congr. UISPP, Nice,* Coll. X, pp. 31–46. Paris, CNRS.

Roper, M. K. 1969. A survey of the evidence for intrahuman killing in the Pleistocene. *Curr. Anthrop.,* 10, 4, pp. 427–59.

Roudil, J.-L. & Soulier, M. 1976. La salle sépulcrale IG (de la grotte du Hasard, Gard) et le commerce de l'ambre en Languedoc-oriental. *Gallia Préhist.,* 19, 1, pp. 173–200.

Rowlands, M. 1971. The archaeological interpretation of prehistoric metalworking. *Wld Archaeol.,* 3, 2, pp. 210–34.

Rozoy, J. G. 1976. Évolution des groupes humains en France et en Belgique de 6500 à 500 avant J. C. *IXe Congr. UISPP, Nice,* Coll. XIX, pp. 32–51. Paris, CNRS.

Sachse-Kozlowska, E. 1976. The Aurignacian in Poland, *IXe Congr. UISPP, Nice,* Coll. XVI, pp. 98–111. Paris, CNRS.

Sackett, J. 1966. Quantitative analysis of Upper Palaeolithic stone tools, *Am. Anthrop.,* 68, 2, pp. 356–94.

Sackett, J. & Gaussen, J. 1976. Upper Paleolithic habitation structures in the south-west of France. *IXe Congr. UISPP, Nice,* Coll. XIII, pp. 55–83. Paris, CNRS.

Sandars, N. 1971. Orient and orientalizing in early Celtic art. *Antiquity,* 45, pp. 103–12.

Sandberg, B. 1974. Lilleby Björlanda 242, 268. Settlement site Bronze Age, Early Iron Age. *Fynd Rapp.,* 1974, pp. 95–142.

Sangmeister, E. 1971. Die Kupferperlen im Chalcolithikum Sudfrankreichs. In:

Mélanges de Préhistoire . . . offerts à André Varagnac, pp. 641–79. Paris, École des Hautes Études, VIe Sect.

Sangmeister, E. 1973. Aufkommen der Arsenbronze in SO-Europa. *VIIIe Congr. UISPP, Prague,* pp. 109–29.

Sangmeister, E. & Schubart, H. 1972. Zambujal. *Antiquity,* 46, pp. 191–7.

Sarnowska, W. 1973. (Plant food of the Unetician culture population in Poland.) *Silesia Antiq.,* 15, pp. 93–115. (In Polish; Engl. summ.)

Sartono, S. 1976. The Javanese Pleistocene Hominids, a re-appraisal. *IXe Congr. UISPP, Nice,* Coll. VI, pp. 456–64. Paris, CNRS.

Sauter, M. R. 1976. *Switzerland.* Thames & Hudson.

Savory, H. N. 1968. *Spain and Portugal.* Thames & Hudson.

Schlette, F. 1970. Ursprung, Zielsetzung und Ergebnisse des Forschungsunternehmens Wahlitz. *Jschr. Mitteldt. Vorgesch.,* 5, pp. 7–26.

Schmid, E. 1972. A Mousterian silex mine and dwelling place in the Swiss Jura. In: Unesco, *The Origin of Homo Sapiens: Proc. Paris Symposium, 1969,* pp. 128–31. Paris, Unesco.

Schwab, H. 1969–70. Moosbühl Rettingsgrabung 1960. *Jb. Bern. Historisch. Mus.,* pp. 189–97.

Schwab, H. 1972. Entdeckung einer Keltischen Brücke an der Zihl und ihre Bedeutung für La Tène. *Archäol. KorrespBl.,* 2, pp. 289–94.

Schwabedissen, F. (gen. ed.). 1971–6. *Die Anfänge des Neolithikums vom Orient bis Europa:* Va (1972) *W. Central Europe* (ed. J. Lüning). Vb (1976) *W. Central Europe* (ed. J. Lüning). VI (1971) *France* (ed. J. Lüning). VII (1972) *W. Mediterranean and British Isles* (ed. J. Lüning). VIII (1973) *Anthropology* (ed. I. Schwidetzky).

Schwidetzky, I. von. 1972. Vergleichend-statistische Untersuchungen zur Anthropologie der Eisenzeit (letztes Jahrtausend v.d.z.). *Homo,* 23, 3, pp. 245–72.

Selkirk, A. 1969. Manching. *Curr. Archaeol.*, 13, pp. 41-2.

Semenov, S. A. 1964. *Prehistoric Technology.* London, Adams & Dart.

Shackleton, N. J. 1975. The stratigraphic record of deep-sea cores. In: K. W. Butzer & G. Isaac (eds.), *After the Australopithecines,* pp. 1-24. The Hague, Mouton.

Shackleton, N. & Renfrew, C. 1970. Neolithic trade routes re-aligned by oxygen isotope analyses. *Nature,* 228, pp. 1062-5.

Shelov, D. B. 1975. Scythians, Sarmatians and Greeks. In: R. Bruce-Mitford (ed.), *Recent Archaeological Investigations in Europe,* p. 188. London, Routledge & Kegan Paul.

Shennan, Susan. 1975. The social organization at Branč. *Antiquity,* 59, pp. 279-88.

Shennan, S. J. 1976. Bell beakers and their context in Central Europe. In: J. N. Lanting & J. D. van der Waals (eds.), *Glockenbecher Symp., Oberried, 1974,* pp. 231-9.

Sherratt, A. 1972. Socio-economic and demographic models for Europe. In: D. Clarke (ed.), *Models in Archaeology,* pp. 477-542.

Sherratt, A. 1973. The interpretation of change in European prehistory. In: C. Renfrew (ed.), *The Explanation of Culture Change,* pp. 419-28. Duckworth.

Sherratt, A. 1976. Resources, technology and trade in early European metallurgy. In. G. de G. Sieveking, I. H. Longworth & K. E. Wilson (eds.), *Problems in Economic and Social Archaeology.* London, Duckworth.

Sielmann, B. 1971. Zur Interpretationsmöglichkeit ökologischer Befunde im Neolithikum Mitteleuropas. *Germania,* 49, pp. 231-8.

Sieveking, G. de G., Craddock, P., Hughes, M. J., Bush, P. & Ferguson, J. 1970. Characterization of flint mine products. *Nature,* 228, pp. 251-4.

Sieveking, G. de G., Longworth, I. H. & Wilson, K. E. (eds.). 1976. *Problems in Economic and Social Archaeology.* London, Duckworth.

Simmons, E. G. 1975. The ecological setting of Mesolithic man in the Highland zone. In: J. G. Evans, S. Limbrey & H. Cleere (eds.), *The Effect of Man on the Landscape: the Highland Zone,* pp. 57-63. Council for British Archaeology.

Simonsen, P. 1975. When and why did occupational specialization begin at the Scandinavian north coast? In: W. Fitzhugh (ed.), *Prehistoric Maritime Adaptations of the Circumpolar Zone,* pp. 75-85. The Hague, Mouton.

Slater, E. & Charles, J. A. 1970. Archaeological classification by metal analysis. *Antiquity,* 44, pp. 207-13.

Smith, C. 1977. The valleys of the Tame and middle Trent – their populations and ecology during the late first millennium B.C. In: J. Collis (ed.), *The Iron Age in Britain – a Review,* pp. 51-61. Sheffield Univ. Press.

Smith, I. F. 1977. The chronology of British stone implements. In: T. Clough & W. Cummins (eds.), *Stone Axe Studies,* CBA report.

Sonneville-Bordes, D. de. 1973. The Upper Palaeolithic, c. 33,000-10,000 B.C. In: S. Piggott, G. Daniel & C. McBurney (eds.), *France Before the Romans,* pp. 30-60. Thames & Hudson.

Soudsky, B. (ed.). 1974, 1975. *Les Fouilles Protohistoriques dans la Vallée de l'Aisne, Rapports d'Activité 2 (1974), 3 (1975).* Centre de Recherche Protohistorique de l'Université de Paris 1. (Cent. Rech. Archéol. (CNRS), URA No. 12.)

Spencer, P. J. 1975. Habitat change in coastal sand-dune areas: the molluscan evidence. In: J. G. Evans, S. Limbrey & H. Cleere (eds.), *The Effect of Man on the Landscape: the Highland Zone,* pp. 96-103. Council for British Archaeology.

Spindler, K. 1971, 1972a, 1973, 1976. *Magdalenenberg I* (1971). *Magdalenenberg II* (1972a). *Magdalenenberg III* (1973). *Magdalenenberg IV* (1976). Neckar-Verl., Villengen.

Spindler, 1972a. *See* Spindler, K., 1971 . . . *above*.

Spindler, K. 1972b. Funde und Befunde organischer Materialien vom Magdalenenberg bei Villingen (Baden-Württemberg). *Archäol. KorrespBl.*, 2, pp. 133–41.

Spindler, K. 1972c. Vorbericht über die Grabungscampagne 1970 am hallstattzeitlichen Fürstengrabhügel Magdalenenberg bei Villingen im Schwarzwald. *Germania*, 50, pp. 56–65.

Spindler, 1973. *See* Spindler, K., 1971 . . . *above*.

Spindler, 1976. *See* Spindler, K., 1971 . . . *above*.

Spurgeon, C. J. 1972. Enclosures of Iron Age type in the upper Severn basin. In: F. Lynch & C. Burgess (eds.), *Prehistoric Man in Wales and the West*, pp. 321–44. Bath, Adams & Dent.

Šramko, B. A. 1968–71. Der Hakenpflug der Bronzezeit in der Ukraine. *Tools & Tillage*, 1, pp. 223–4.

Šramko, B. 1974. Zur Frage über die Technik und die Bearbeitungszentren von Buntmetallen in der Früheisenzeit. In: B. Chropovský, M. Dusek & V. Podborsky (eds.), *Symp. zu Problemen der jüngeren Hallstattzeit in Mitteleuropa*, pp. 469–85. Bratislava.

Srejovic, D. 1967. *Lepenski Vir*. Beograd, Narodni Muzej.

Stead, I. M. 1976. La Tène burials between Burton Fleming and Rudston, North Humberside. *Antiquar. J.*, LVI, II, pp. 217–26.

Steensberg, A. 1973. 6000 year old ploughing implements from Satrup Moor. *Tools & Tillage*, 2, 2, pp. 105–18.

Stickel, E. 1976. *A Temporal and Spatial Analysis of Underwater Neolithic Settlements in the Alpine Foreland of Switzerland*. Ann Arbor, Mich., Univ. Microfilms Int.

Stjernquist, B. 1972. Technical analysis as a factor in archaeological documentation. *Reg. Soc. Hum. Litt. Lund. Scr. Min.*, 3, 1971–2.

Strahm, C. 1974. Der Übergang vom Spätneolithikum zur Frühbronzezeit in der Schweiz. *Preist. Alp.*, 10, 21–42.

Straus, L. G. 1976. A new interpretation of the Cantabrian Solutrean. *Curr. Anthrop.*, 17, 2, pp. 342–3.

Strömberg, M. 1975. *Studien zu einem Gräberfeld in Löderup*. (Acta Archaeol. Lund. No. 10.)

Sturdy, D. A. 1972. The exploitation patterns of a modern reindeer economy in west Germany. In: E. S. Higgs (ed.), *Papers in Economic Prehistory*, pp. 161–8. Cambridge Univ. Press.

Sturdy, D. A. 1975. Some reindeer economies in prehistoric Europe. In: E. S. Higgs (ed.), *Palaeoeconomy*, pp. 55–95. Cambridge Univ. Press.

Sulimirski, T. 1970. *Prehistoric Russia, an Outline*. London, John Baker.

Swanson, E. (ed.). 1975. *Lithic Technology: Making and Using Stone Tools*. Mouton.

Szabo, M. 1971. *The Celtic Heritage in Hungary*. Budapest, Athenaeum Printing House.

Taffanel, O. & Taffanel J. 1972. Les habitats et les nécropoles de Mailhac (Aude). *Actes du Premier Colloque Archéologique de la 4e Section de l'École Pratique des Hautes Études (Paris, 1972)*, pp. 23–32.

Taschini, M. 1968. Il livello mesolitico del Riparo Blanc al Monte Circeo. *Boll. Paletnol. Ital.*, 73, pp. 65–88.

Taschini, M. 1976. Considérations sur le Mésolithique en Italie sur la base des données récentes. *IXe Congr. UISPP, Nice*, Coll. XIX. Paris, CNRS.

Tauber, H. 1972. Radiocarbon chronology of the Danish Mesolithic and Neolithic. *Antiquity*, 46, pp. 106–10.

Tavoso, A. 1976. L'Acheuléen dans le bassin du Tarn. *IXe Congr. UISPP, Nice*, Coll. X, pp. 114–33. Paris, CNRS.

Taylor, J. A. 1975. The role of climatic factors in environmental and cultural changes in prehistoric times. In: J. G. Evans, S. Limbrey & H. Cleere (eds.), *The Effect of Man on the Landscape: the*

Highland Zone, pp. 6–19. Council for British Archaeology.

Taylour, Lord W. 1969. Mycenae, 1968. *Antiquity*, XLIII, 170, pp. 91–7.

Teichert, L. 1975. Ergebnisse zu Haus- und Wildtierknochenfunde aus Siedlungen und Gräberfeldern der Schönfelder Gruppe im Raum der DDR. In: A. T. Clason (ed.), *Archaeological Studies*, pp. 206–12. Amsterdam.

Teichert, M. 1969. Zur Bedeutung der Schweinehaltung in ur- und frühgeschichtlicher Zeit. *Ethnogr.-Archäol. Z.*, 10, 4, pp. 543–6.

Ters, M. 1975. Le déplacement de la ligne de rivage, au cours de l'Holocène, le long de la côte atlantique française. *Inqua, Montpellier*, pp. 39–40.

Thibault, C. 1975. Gisement paléolithique très ancien d'El Alculadero, baie de Cádiz (Espagne). *Bull. Soc. Préhist. Fr.*, 72, C.R.s.m. 5, p. 130.

Thom, A. 1967. *Megalithic Sites in Britain*. Oxford, Clarendon.

Thoma, A. 1976. Le peuplement anté-néandertalien d'Europe dans le contexte paléoanthropologique de l'Ancien Monde. *IXe Congr. UISPP, Nice*, Coll. IX, pp. 7–16. Paris, CNRS.

Todd, M. 1975. *The Northern Barbarians 100 B.C.–A.D. 300*. London, Hutchinson.

Topál, S. 1973. A Bronze Age jewel find at Osca. *Archaeol. Ért.*, 100, 1, pp. 3–18.

Torma, I. 1972. Befestigte Siedlung in Tokod. *Mitt. Archäol. Inst. (Budapest)*, 3, pp. 73–7.

Tringham, R. 1971. *Hunters, Fishers and Farmers of Eastern Europe 6000–3000 B.C.* London, Hutchinson.

Tringham, R. 1973. The mesolithic of south-east Europe. In: S. Kozlowski (ed.), *The Mesolithic in Europe*, pp. 551–72.

Tringham, R., Cooper, G., Odell, G., Voytek, B. & Whitman, A. 1974. Experimentation in the formation of edge damage: a new approach to lithic analysis. *J. Fld Archaeol.*, 1, pp. 171–96.

Trump, D. 1980. *The Prehistory of the Mediterranean*. London, Allen Lane.

Tsitsishvili, A. L. 1975. Tierknochenreste aus Kurganbestattungen der mittleren Bronzezeit von Vardzia (Ostgeorgien). In: A. T. Clason (ed.), *Archaeological Studies*, pp. 431–7. Amsterdam.

Turner, C. 1975. The correlation and duration of Middle Pleistocene interglacial periods in north-west Europe. In: K. W. Butzer & G. Isaac (eds.), *After the Australopithecines*, pp. 259–308. The Hague, Mouton.

Tylecote, R. F. 1970. The composition of metal artifacts: a guide to provenance? *Antiquity*, XLVI, pp. 19–25.

Ucko, P. & Rosenfeld, A. 1967. *Palaeolithic Cave Art*. London, Weidenfeld & Nicolson.

UISPP (IXe Congr.). 1976. *Conf. Publs Ninth Int. Congr. Pre- & Protohist. Sci., Nice, 1976*. Paris, CNRS.

Unesco. 1972. *The Origin of Homo Sapiens: Proc. Paris Symposium, 1969*. Paris, Unesco.

Uzarowiczowa, A. 1970. Cemetery of Funnel Beaker culture at Klementowice. *Wiad. Archeol.*, 35, pp. 492–513.

Valoch, K. 1972. Rapports entre le Paléolithique moyen et le Paléolithique supérieur en Europe central. *Origine de l'Homme Moderne*, pp. 161–71. Paris, Unesco. (Écologie et Conservation 3.)

Valoch, K. 1976a. L'Aurignacien en Moravie. *IXe Congr. UISPP, Nice*, Coll. XVI, pp. 112–23. Paris, CNRS.

Valoch, K. 1976b. Aperçu des premières industries en Europe. *IXe Congr. UISPP, Nice*, Coll. VIII, pp. 178–83. Paris, CNRS.

Valoch, K. 1976c. Un groupe spécifique de Paléolithique ancien et moyen d'Europe Centrale. *IXe Congr. UISPP, Nice*, Coll. X, pp. 86–91. Paris, CNRS.

van der Leeuw, S. E. 1976. Neolithic beakers from the Netherlands: the potter's point of view. In: J. N. Lanting & J. D. van der Waals (eds.), *Glockenbecher Symp., Oberried, 1974*, pp. 81–139.

van der Velde, P. 1973. A note on the provisional factor analysis of Linear Pottery ware. *Anlcta Praehist. Leiden.*, VI, pp. 66-8.

van der Waals, J. D. 1967. Die durchlochten Rössener Keile und das frühe Neolithikum in Belgien und in den Niederlanden. In: F. Schwabedissen (gen. ed.), *Anfänge des Neolithikums vom Orient bis Europa*, Va, *W. Central Europe* (ed. J. Lüning, pp. 153-84.

van Mensch, P. J. A. & Ijzereef, G. F. 1975. Animal remains from a Bronze Age settlement near Andijk, Province of N. Holland. *Berichten van de Rijksdienst voor het Oudheidkundig Bodemonderseok*, 25, pp. 55-68.

van Zeist, W. 1974. Palaeobotanical studies of settlement sites in the coastal area of the Netherlands. *Palaeohistoria*, 16, pp. 223-371.

Vatin, C. 1972. Wooden sculpture from Gallo-Roman Auvergne. *Antiquity*, XLVI, 181, pp. 39-42.

Velitchko, A. A. 1972. Dynamiques des modifications naturelles dans le Pléistocène supérieur et problème du passage des néanderthaliens à l'*Homo Sapiens*. In: Unesco, *The Origin of Homo Sapiens: Proc. Paris Symposium*, pp. 265-70. Paris, Unesco.

Vencl, S. L. 1970. Peuplement Mésolithique du Karst de Bohème. *Archeol. Rozhl.*, 22, 6, pp. 643-57.

Vencl, S. L. 1971. The topography of Mesolithic sites in Bohemia. *Archeol. Rozhl.*, 23, 2, pp. 169-87.

Vernet J.-L. 1976. La flore et la végétation méditerranéennes. A propos de leur mise en place en Europe de l'ouest. *IXe Congr. UISPP, Nice*, Coll. II, pp. 8-19. Paris, CNRS.

Villa, P. 1976. Sols et niveaux d'habitat du Paléolithique inférieur en Europe et au Proche-Orient. *IXe Congr. UISPP, Nice*, Coll. X, pp. 139-55, Paris, CNRS.

Vita-Finzi, C. 1969. *The Mediterranean Valleys*. Cambridge, Univ. Press.

Vladar, J. 1972. Vorbericht über die systematische Ausgrabung der befestigten Siedlung der Otomani-Kultur in Spišsky Štvrtok. *Archeol. Rozhl.*, XXIV, pp. 18-25.

Vladar, J. 1973. Osteuropäische und Mediterräne Einflüsse im Gebiet der Slovakei während der Bronzezeit. *Slov. Archeol.*, 21, 2, pp. 253-357.

Vladar, J. 1974. Mediterranean influences on the North Carpathian basin in the Early Bronze Age, *Preist. Alp.*, 10, pp. 219-36.

von Koenigswald, G. H. 1976. The oldest hominid remains of Asia. *IXe Congr. UISPP, Nice*, Coll. VI, pp. 425-9. Paris, CNRS.

Vulpe, A. 1967. *Necropola Hallstattiana de la Ferigile*. Bucharest, Monografie Arheologica.

Warren, P. 1977. The emergence of Mycenaean Palace civilisation. In: J. Bintliff (ed.), *Mycenaean Geography: Proc. Cambridge Colloquium, September 1976*, pp. 68-72. Cambridge, Univ. Library Press.

Waterbolk, H. T. 1972. Radiocarbon curves from Palaeolithic sites in western Europe, compared with the climatic curve of the Netherlands. In: Unesco, *The Origin of Homo Sapiens: Proc. Paris Symposium*, pp. 245-52. Paris, Unesco.

Waterbolk, H. T. 1975. Evidence of cattle stalling in excavated pre- and proto-historic houses. In: A. T. Clason (ed.), *Archaeological Studies*, pp. 383-94. Amsterdam.

Waterbolk, H. T. & Butler, J. 1965. Comments on the use of metallurgical analysis in prehistoric studies. *Helinium*, 5, pp. 227-51.

Watson, K. A. 1970. Neanderthal and Upper Palaeolithic burial patterns: a re-examination. *Mankind*, 7, 4, pp. 302-6.

Watson, P. J., Leblanc S. A. & Redman C. L. 1971. *Explanation in Archeology. An Explicitly Scientific Approach*. New York, Columbia Univ. Press.

Weertman, J. 1976. Milankovitch solar radiation variations and ice age ice sheet sizes. *Nature*, 261, pp. 17-20.

Welinder, S. 1973. Mesolithic sites with flint in eastern Middle Sweden. In: S. K. Kozlowski (ed.), *The Mesolithic in Europe*, pp. 583–91.

Welinder, S. 1975*a*. Agriculture, inland hunting and sea hunting in the western and northern region of the Baltic 6000–2000 B.C. In: W. Fitzhugh (ed.), *Prehistoric Maritime Adaptations of the Circumpolar Zone*. The Hague, Mouton.

Welinder, S. 1975*b*. *Prehistoric Agriculture in Eastern Middle Sweden*. (Acta Archaeol. Lund., 8° Min., No. 4.)

Welinder, S. 1977. *Prehistoric Economy During an Expansion Stage*. (Acta Archaeol. Lund., 8° Min., No. 7.)

Wertime, T. A. 1973. The beginnings of metallurgy: a new look. *Science*, 182, 4115, pp. 875–87.

Wheeler, T. S., Naddin, R. & Muhly, J. D. 1975. Ingots and the Bronze Age copper trade in the Mediterranean: a progress report. *Expedition*, 17, pp. 31–9.

Whitehouse, R. 1972. The rock-cut tombs of the central Mediterranean. *Antiquity*, XLVI, 184, pp. 275–81.

Whitehouse, D. & Whitehouse, R. 1975. *Archaeological Atlas of the World*. Thames & Hudson.

Wieckowska, H. 1971. Contribution to the discussion on the beginnings of the Polish Neolithic age. *Wiad. Archeol.*, 36, pp. 253–8. (Pol. Archaeol. Abstr. XVII, 4, 1632.) (Engl. summ.)

Wilmann, O. 1972. Untersuchungen an Pflanzenmaterial des Hallstattzeitlicher Grabhügels Magdalenenberg bei Villingen. *Germania*, 50, pp. 74–6.

Winn, M. 1974. The signs of the Vinca Culture: an internal analysis; their role, chronology and independence from Mesopotamia. *Diss. Abstr. Int.*, Sect. A (Ann Arbor, Mich.), 34, pp. 4130–31.

Wintle, A. G. & Aitken, M. J. 1977. Thermoluminescence dating of burnt flint: application to a Lower Palaeolithic site, Terra Amata. *Archaeometry*, 19, (2).

Wislanski, T. 1975. Studies on the origin of the Funnel Beaker Culture. *Pol. Archaeol. Abstr.*, 5, pp. 83/75.

Wobst, H. M. 1974. Boundary conditions for Palaeolithic social systems: a simulation approach. *Am. Antiq.*, 39, pp. 147–78.

Woodman, P. 1976. An insular Mesolithic economy: recent work on the Irish Mesolithic. In: P. Mellars (ed.), *The Early Post-Glacial Settlement of North-West Europe: Economic and Social Perspectives*. (In press.)

Wozniak, Z. 1974. La formation des zones de colonisation dans la partie ouest de la petite Pologne pendant les phases C-D de l'époque de la Tène. *Slav. Antiq.*, 21, pp. 59–60. (Summ.)

Wyss, R. 1972. Sépultures, sanctuaires, sacrifices, et leurs rélations avec l'habitat en Suisse a l'Époque Celtique. In: P.-M. Duval & V. Kruta (eds.), *L'habitat et la Nécropole à l'Âge du Fer en Europe Occidentale et Centrale*, pp. 75–86. Paris.

Wyss, R. 1976. L'évolution écologique et culturelle du Mésolithique en Europe centrale. *IXe Congr. UISPP, Nice*, Coll. XIX, pp. 93–112. Paris, CNRS.

Zagorski, F. 1973. Das Spätmesolithikum in Lettland. In: S. K. Kozlowski (ed.), *The Mesolithic in Europe*, pp. 651–69.

Zbyszewski, G. 1976. Rapport sur les plus anciennes industries paléolithiques de Portugal. *IXe Congr. UISPP, Nice*, Coll. VIII, pp. 96–102. Paris, CNRS.

Zeylandowa, M. 1974. Eine Hallstatt-Siedlung der Lausitzer Kultur in Kotlin, Kreis Jarocin. *Fontes Archaeol. Posnan.*, 24 (1973), pp. 50–131. Poznan, 1974.

Zürn, H. 1974. Zur Chronologie der sudwestdeutschen Späthallstattzeit und die Datierung der Fürstengräber. In: B. Chropovský, M. Dusek & V. Podborsky, *Symp. Problemen der jüngeren Hallstattzeit in Mitteleuropa*, pp. 487-500. Bratislava, Verl. der Slovakischen Akademie der Wissenschaften.

INDEX

Abri Blanchard, France, 108, Fig. 33
Ach valley, 70, 72, 87
Acheulian technocomplex, 41ff., 46f., 49
Achilleion, Greece, 159f.
Achsolshausen, W. Germany, 226
acorns, 130, 137, 150, 259
Africa: Acheulian industries, 42; East,
    early-man sites, Fig. 5; Ethiopia, 32,
    34f.; North, 17, 37, 46, 231; primate
    and hominid fossils, 29, 32; South, 35
agriculture, 114, 147, 149 170, 192, 211f.,
    214, 217f., 228, 233, 237, 242, 258;
    abandonment of, 244; see also cul-
    tivation; farming
Aibunar, Bulgaria, 207
Aiguebelette, France, 226
Alalia, France, 258
Albania, 225
Aldenhoven plateau, 116
Alexander the Great, 264
Alleröd climatic period, 94
Alps, 102, 113f.
Altamira, Spain, 104, 108
amber, 124, 178, 193, 222, 234, 247f., 255
Ambrona, Spain, 45-6
amino-acid racemization, 26, 40, 41
analytical techniques: calcium carbonate
    analysis, 23, Fig. 2; heavy metal
    analysis, 237; infra-red absorption
    spectroscopy, 222; laser-beam stu-
    dies, 20; lead-isotope analysis, 195;
    metallography, 193, 227, 230; neu-
    tron-activation analysis, 152, 193,

222; nitrate tests, 168; optical-emis-
    sion spectroscopy, 152, 193, 221f.;
    oxygen-isotope analysis, 23, Fig. 2;
    petrographic analysis, 102; spectro-
    scopic analysis, 108, 227; trace-
    element analysis, 194-5, 221; X-ray
    fluorescence testing, 193
Anatolia, 15, 17, 150, 162, 183, 192, 202,
    205, 225
Ancylus, lake, 116
Andijk, Netherlands, 242
animals: associated with man, 35f., 42,
    46, 60, 74, 79, 87, 115, 124, 126, 128,
    157, 169f., 180; domesticated, 169–
    70, 172, 191 (decreasing size of); see
    also domestication and under indivi-
    dual animals
annual territory, 118
antelope, 35, 66, 79, 94
antimony, 184; as trace element, 194
Anzabegovo, Greece, 161, 163, 180
Arene Candide, Italy, 125, 158
Argissa Magula, Greece, 150, 159, 161,
    Pl. 6
Arkhangelskaya Sloboda, U.S.S.R., 261
arsenic: as trace element, 194; as copper
    additive, 196, 202
art: Aurignacian, 74-6; Australian, 107;
    Bronze Age, 192; carvings, 189;
    Celtic, 256-7; development, 104-7;
    geometric and naturalistic, 145;
    Levantine, 145; Magdalenian, 93;
    Mesolithic, 137, 141-6; mobiliary,